THE
BELGIAN CONSTITUTION

COMMENTARY

by Robert SENELLE

Professor in Ordinary of the University of Ghent

PREFACE

by Renaat VAN ELSLANDE,
Minister of Foreign Affairs and
Co-operation in Development

One of the most important tasks incumbent on the Information Service of the Ministry of Foreign Affairs, External Trade and Co-operation in Development, is to promote a better objective knowledge of Belgium abroad.

This, among other things, is the purpose of the Ministry's information brochures which are designed to illustrate as clearly as possible the major trends and most important aspects of the economic, intellectual and artistic life of our country and the development of its institutions.

From this standpoint, it seems particularly useful to devote an issue of "Memo from Belgium" to a detailed commentary of our Constitution, article by article, as it now stands after the recent Revision. During the period lasting from 1967 to 1970, the structural organisation of the Belgian State was subjected to profound and far-reaching change for the first time since 1831. The constitutional reforms undertaken in 1892-1893 and in 1919-1921 did not, in fact, modify the fundamental aspects or the basic principles of the Belgian Constitution.

The following in-depth analysis, carried out by Professor Robert Senelle of the Faculty of Law at the University of Ghent, whose writings have already appeared in these "Memos from Belgium" on the subject especially of the problems raised by the latest Revision of the Constitution, is therefore most welcome. It enables the Ministry of Foreign Affairs, through its informational work abroad, to highlight one of the vital aspects of Belgium's evolution and the development and functioning of her institutions.

As Minister of Foreign Affairs and Co-operation in Development, I should like to express my sincere thanks to Professor Senelle for his invaluable contribution, which will be of inestimable service to my Department.

Renaat VAN ELSLANDE.

INTRODUCTORY COMMENTS

During the four-year period of 1967 to 1971, the Belgian Parliament undertook a Third Revision of the Constitution.

Without intending to disparage the work done by previous Constituent Assemblies, it is nevertheless permissible to state that this Third Revision is a fundamental one, for it has profoundly changed the face of Belgium. It is this new aspect that we shall attempt to show foreign readers by means of this survey.

The Constitution was first promulgated on 7 February 1831, barely seven months after the Belgians rose in revolt against what they regarded as the excessively selfish policy of the King of the Netherlands. The Constitution was the work of the National Congress which had been set up on 10 November 1830, and which terminated its work on 21 July 1831.

At the time when it was written, the Belgian Constitution was considered to be a revolutionary one, and in subsequent years it was taken as a point of reference by many other countries. The French Revolution had juridically sanctioned the philosophical concept of the sovereignty of the Nation, but its achievement was soon to be set aside: indeed, immediately following the Restoration, the King once again became the absolute master who alone held all power and authority. He alone could give the Nation a charter which he was fully empowered to retract at his own pleasure.

In complete contrast to this state of affairs, as soon as it was set up the independent State of Belgium took as its foundation stone the principle of national sovereignty. In lapidary, unambiguous words Article 25 of the Constitution sets the seal on this principle: "All powers stem from the Nation". There can be no restriction surrounding this principle and no derogation from it.

Thus, the Belgian Constitution stands out as the work of some exceptionally enlightened statesmen. Owing to the clear, concise and unequivocal wording of its articles, the essential principles they embody were revealed as being of permanent value despite all the historical developments which have taken place since 1831. Indeed, over sixty years elapsed before it became necessary to change it in any way, and there have only been two prior revisions in 1892-1893 and in 1919-1921. Even so, they were merely an extension of the basic tenets of the Constitution, for their purpose was to pursue its democratic principles to their logical conclusion through the progressive institution of universal suffrage pure and simple.

But the objectives of the Third Revision of 1967-1971 were quite different. The increasingly rapid evolution of philosophical, political, economic and social ideas, not on the national plane alone but throughout the world, represented a genuine challenge to a constitution conceived originally in a Napoleonic spirit of centralisation in keeping with the period when it was drafted. There were definite grounds, therefore, for apprehension lest a serious crisis should threaten the very foundations of the State and its institutions. The Belgian Parliament and Government courageously faced up to this danger when, from 1967 to 1971, they undertook to adapt the fundamental charter in keeping with the irreversible change of outlook. Their task was undoubtedly a difficult and complex one, but the passage of time will allow of a proper assessment of the reforms they have introduced.

In this way, the Third Revision of the Belgian Constitution has made some extremely important alterations to the organisational structure of the State while it has preserved the essential principles of political democracy.

This is what the following work attempts to explain. It might seem a rash undertaking at a time when the new institutions created by the Revision have only just gone into action, when our experience of the changes thus brought about has barely begun, and when eminent jurists are still writing monographs—some of which have caused considerable comment—in an attempt to analyse the particular problems raised by the Revision. It was not, however, expedient to delay informing foreign readers of the modifications which have taken place. It was felt that this should be done in as much detail as possible. This pragmatic intention will serve to explain the publication of the present survey.

It does not provide a systematic review of the subject matter; to help the reader it presents the Constitution article by article, each followed by a commentary restricted to the single clause under examination. Nor does this commentary claim to be an exhaustive one. Its purpose is rather to make the reader understand the reality concealed beneath the legal phraseology than to provide a purely theoretical glimpse of the concepts stated. That is also why, insofar as it was possible to do so, the commentary attempts to give a brief historical review to explain the genesis of the article under consideration. The same pragmatic intention will serve to explain the lengthy treatment of certain articles. We are referring here to Articles 59-B, 86-B and 107-D in particular, for these are effectively new clauses inserted for the purpose of bringing Belgium into step with the realities of our time, and accordingly they may be of greater interest to the reader than certain other articles which have remained virtually unchanged, and for which many erudite commentaries are already extant.

Robert SENELLE.
15 November 1974.

HEADING I

THE TERRITORY AND ITS DIVISIONS

ARTICLE 1

"Belgium is divided into provinces.

"These provinces are: Antwerp, Brabant, East Flanders, West Flanders, Hainaut, Liège, Limburg, Luxemburg, Namur.

"It is up to the law, if necessary, to divide the territory into a larger number of provinces.

"An act of Parliament may exempt certain territories, whose boundaries it shall determine, from being divided into provinces, place them directly under the executive authority, and subject them to an individual status.

"Such an act must be passed by a majority vote in each linguistic group of each of the Houses, on condition that the majority of the members of each group is present and that the total number of votes in favour in each of the two linguistic groups attains two-thirds of the votes cast."

This article, first drafted in 1831, was modified in 1893 and again in 1970.

Initially, the article consisted of the first three paragraphs of the present article with the addition, at the end of the second paragraph, of the words "except for the relations between Luxemburg and the Germanic Confederation". These words were struck out in 1893 and a fourth paragraph added which read as follows:

"The colonies, overseas possessions or protectorates that Belgium may acquire are subject to special laws. Belgian troops raised for their defence may only be recruited on the basis of voluntary enlistment."

Abrogated in 1970, this provision was replaced by paragraphs four and five as they now stand.

In 1831, the territory which was later to become the Grand Duchy of Luxemburg was an integral part of the provinces which had risen in revolt against King William I of the Netherlands, and were consequently part of the Kingdom of Belgium. The new State was therefore obliged cautiously to announce its intention of respecting the bonds which linked part of its territory to a foreign political body.

The boundaries of the Kingdom were only fixed definitively in 1839. By the Treaty of London signed on 19 April 1839, part of the Luxemburg province was separated from Belgium and raised to the status of a Duchy within the Germanic Confederation. In this way, the reservation made concerning the relations between the Luxemburg province and Germany became redundant: however, it was formally abrogated only during the revision of the Constitution in 1893.

During that same revision, the clause relating to overseas territories was inserted in the Constitution to provide for the contemplated annexation of the Independent Congo State, of which the then King of the Belgians, Leopold II, was the Head of State. This annexation took place in 1908.

In 1960, however, the Congo's accession to independence (1) made this clause redundant. As Belgium no longer has any colonialist aims, the abrogation of paragraph 4 brings this article into line with contemporary realities.

The abrogation went hand in hand with the approval of a new Paragraph 4, the purpose of which was totally different, namely: it was designed to settle the fate of six boroughs known as the Fourons, located in the eastern region of the country between the Dutch and German frontiers. These six boroughs, which until 1963 were part of the Liège province and were solely Dutch-speaking, were detached from that province by a law passed on 8 November 1963 at the time when the linguistic boundary was drawn, and re-attached to the Limburg province; they then came under the Dutch language regime which included the provision of administrative and educational facilities for French-speaking citizens (2).

Since that time, there has been some controversy as to which province these six boroughs should belong to. As a gesture of appeasement, the government proposed in 1968 that the six Fouron boroughs should be grouped together to form an autonomous canton coming directly under the Minister of the Interior, and to set up within it an administrative and educational system allowing the inhabitants of the canton a free choice as to which language should be used.

As the Minister of the Interior is not solely competent in such matters, the Constituent Assembly decided to draft a text in very general terms, stating that a law may exempt certain territories, whose boundaries it

---

(1) Now known as Zaïre.
(2) These were the boroughs of Mouland, Fouron-le-Comte, Fouron-Saint-Martin, Fouron-Saint-Pierre, Remersdaal, and Teuven.

shall determine, from being divided into provinces, place them directly under the Executive authority (i.e. the Central Government) and subject them to an individual status.

Thus it is the Legislative which is entrusted with the task of designating the competent Ministers.

The extraprovincialisation of certain territories, in the case of the Fourons and in any other similar case which may arise in the future, will constitute a compromise solution between the two great cultural communities formed by the Dutch and French speaking populations; acts of Parliament voted on such subjects must secure a majority vote in each language group in both of the Houses on condition that the majority of the members of each group are present at the sitting (see the new Article 32-B); furthermore, the total of the votes in favour secured in both of the language groups must amount to at least two-thirds of the total votes cast.

Even before this, Belgian parliamentary law had laid down two kinds of majority required for the approval of bills tabled for voting in the Houses:

a) the   ordinary majority (in ordinary cases);

b) the two-thirds qualified majority which is required in certain cases, such as: the law granting voting rights to women (passed in 1948); permission granted to the King to become the Head of another State; any revision of the Constitution; the creation of new categories of candidates eligible for the Senate; permission granted to the King to nominate his heir.

The Constituent Assembly of 1967-1971 added a third kind of majority to the above two, namely: a special qualified majority, or cumulative majority, comprising an ordinary majority vote in each of the language groups and a two-thirds majority of the votes cast in each House as a whole. Consequently, each language group holds very real powers of veto on the fundamental issues enumerated below.

This special qualified majority is required in six cases :

— the extraprovincialisation of territories;

— any modification of the boundaries of the four language regions;

— the definition of the way in which the cultural councils are to function;

— the definition of cultural matters, i.e. the sphere and content of cultural autonomy;

— the forms which cultural co-operation shall take;

— the organization of the various regions (on a basis other than a linguistic and cultural one).

To understand what is meant by linguistic or language group in each House, readers should refer to the new Article 32-B.

It should be pointed out that in the case of the special qualified majority, the quorum is raised: the majority of the members of each group must be present at the sitting.

As already stated, the new clause was inserted for the purpose of solving the problem of the Fourons. Now, the question might arise as to whether this clause might also become applicable to other territories. The rejection of any amendments tending to prohibit this, coupled with the fact that the clause in question has been drafted in the most general terms, incline to the view that the answer to this question would be in the affirmative.

The special qualified majority required in all cases of this kind precludes any danger of arbitrary action and abuse by the effective majority of the cultural community with the larger population figure.

As for the first three paragraphs of Article 1, it should be noted that, the Executive being totally excluded, only the Legislative may increase the number of provinces. Furthermore, the Legislative may not reduce the number of provinces, even by merging one with another: only a Constituent Assembly is competent to do so. The preservation of the provinces as separate entities is therefore a constitutional principle. In terms of Article 3 of the Constitution, an act of Parliament is invariably necessary to make any modification affecting the boundaries of the provinces, districts, cantons and boroughs. Finally, it should be emphasized that all the provinces are equal: that is why the Constituent Assembly has classified them in alphabetical order.

Article 1, which we have just analysed, only deals with territories on land.

However, the Belgian State also exercises sovereign rights over a stretch of sea which comprises:

— the territorial waters, extending outwards for a distance of three sea miles (5.556 metres) from the tideline established at low tide. The territorial waters come under the sovereignty of the Belgian State subject to the right of peaceful passage extended to foreign ships;

— the contiguous zone, extending outwards for ten kilometers from the base line used as the point of departure in calculating the stretch of territorial waters; in terms of a law of 1832, the Belgian State is here empowered to exercise a certain measure of authority in the sphere of customs and excise inspection of vessels with a draught of less than 50 tons;

— the continental shelf, the extent of which is defined by the median line, all points of which are equidistant from the nearest points of the basic lines from which the width of the territorial waters belonging respectively to Belgium and Great Britain is measured; over the Belgian sector of the continental shelf the Belgian State exercises sovereign rights in regard to the exploration and development of its natural resources. The term "continental shelf" designates the sea-bed and subsoil of the underwater regions adjacent to the coastline but located outside the territorial waters themselves. The continental shelf is not part of the territory of the Belgian State, and the latter only exercises divided rights of sovereignty in this area, in terms of a law of 1969.

Belgium also exercises sovereign rights in the air space above her territory. This is known as the territorial air space, and it is governed by the Chicago Convention of 7 December 1944, duly ratified by Belgium.

On the other hand, Belgian sovereignty does not extend to the upper atmosphere. This sphere is governed by three international agreements:

— Treaty covering the principles governing the activities of States in the matter of the exploration and utilisation of the upper atmosphere and outer space, including the moon and other celestial bodies (27 January 1967).

— Agreement on the rescue of astronauts, the return to earth of astronauts, and the recovery and restitution of objects launched into the upper atmosphere (22 April 1968);

— Convention on international responsibility for damage caused by spatial objects (29 March 1972).

The first treaty has been ratified by Belgium; the other two agreements are in course of ratification.

These three instruments which together constitute the basis of international space law, will shortly be rounded off by another convention on which Belgium is also working, covering the registration of objects launched into space.

At the present time, within the framework of the United Nations Organisation, Belgium is working on an international project establishing the principles governing direct radio and television transmissions by means of satellites.

ARTICLE 2

"The sub-divisions of the provinces can only be established by law."

This article dates from 1831 and has never been modified.

An act of Parliament is necessary for any alteration to the sub-divisions of the provinces which, at the present time, consist of districts (constituencies) and cantons.

The article is a logical one: indeed, any modification of the limits of districts and cantons would have a direct effect on the electoral system, the establishment of which, within the framework of the principles laid down by the Constitution, has been entrusted to the Legislative in terms of Articles 47 to 56-B. It is therefore normal that the Legislative alone should be competent to make such decisions, and not the Executive.

ARTICLE 3

"The boundaries of the State, the provinces and the boroughs may only be changed or rectified by virtue of a law."

This article dates from 1831 and has never been modified.

The boundaries of the State are, in practice, only changed by an international treaty, and this must receive the assent of both Houses. Such assent is given in the form of an Act of Parliament.

Furthermore, the respect of provincial and municipal autonomy to which the first Constituent Assembly was greatly attached (see Articles 31 and 108) requires that the boundaries of these entities be protected from any interference by the Executive unless the latter secures the authorization of the Legislative. This may take the form of a ratification by both Houses of royal decrees implementing such modifications of the provincial and municipal boundaries.

"Belgium comprises four linguistic regions: the French language region, the Dutch language region, the bilingual region of Brussels-Capital, and the German language region.

"Every borough in the Kingdom belongs to one of these linguistic regions.

"The boundaries of the four regions may only be altered or amended by an Act of Parliament passed on a majority vote in each linguistic group of each of the Houses, on condition that the majority of the members of each group are present and that the total votes in favour within the two linguistic groups attain two-thirds of the votes cast."

This article dating from 1970 is an entirely new one.

Belgium's division into three linguistic and one bilingual region was accepted with very little debate during the charting of the Constitutional Reform (1967-1971).

But the work of defining the boundaries of these regions aroused a great deal of criticism, most of it levelled at one target: the boundaries of the bilingual region of Brussels-Capital; some representatives wished them to be greatly enlarged by including in this area a certain number of peripheral boroughs which would then form part of Greater Brussels. As the boroughs in question belonged to the Dutch language region, no balanced system could be worked out to satisfy the demands put forward by some Brussels members, these demands being based on the growing number of people in the city itself who were moving out to take up residence on the outskirts of Brussels.

In order to fix the boundaries of the four regions covered by Article 3-B, the Constituent Assembly took as its frame of reference the situation as defined by the law of 2 August 1963 governing the use of languages for administrative purposes, which had been further clarified by the law of 23 December 1970.

Apart from the bilingual region of Brussels-Capital, these two Acts of Parliament officially sanction the existence of homogenous language regions in which all civil servants and Government employees must in principle use only the language of the region in the conduct of their business and in their contacts with other bodies and private persons. The road leading to this linguistic homogeneity had been charted by the law of 8 November 1962 which laid down the linguistic boundary between the French-speaking and Dutch-speaking areas on the basis of the research done by the Harmel Centre; it also modified provincial, district and borough boundaries so as to attach every inch of Belgian territory to an administrative entity using a single language. Similarly, with a view to ensuring that the linguistic frontier should be a stable one, the said law of 1962 did away with any changes in the ruling language that a borough might find itself obliged to make as a result of the latest ten-yearly census, when either 50% or 30% of its inhabitants state that they customarily speak the other national language rather than the one used by the linguistic group to which the borough belongs.

Consequently, no further difficulties arose when the law of 2 August 1963 brought the linguistic regions into being, except insofar as the boundaries of the bilingual district of Brussels-Capital were concerned, as already mentioned above.

As no full political agreement could be secured by the 1963 Parliament, six boroughs on the outskirts of Brussels were grouped together to form a separate and distinct administrative district under the Vice-Governor of the Brabant Province and were given a special status (1).

By the law of 23 December 1970, these boroughs, while still retaining their special status, were attached to the Hal-Vilvorde administrative district which is part of the Dutch language region.

This concluded the work of defining homogenous linguistic regions which became the territorial platform of the Cultural communities referred to in Article 3-B of the Constitution.

As the territorial integrity of the cultural communities was at stake, the two Houses decided that the boundaries of the four linguistic regions, as defined at the time when Article 3-B was adopted, could no longer be changed or modified except by an Act of Parliament passed on the basis of a special qualified majority vote, so that in future the legislator will be unable to amputate any portion of the territory comprised in one language region and transfer it to another without the approval of a majority of Deputies and Senators specifically representing the linguistic region in question.

It should be pointed out that:

1. The Dutch language region comprises the provinces of East and West Flanders, Antwerp and Limburg, as also the districts of Louvain

---

(1) These were the boroughs of Drogenbos, Kraainem, Linkebeek, Rhode-Saint-Genèse, Wemmel, and Wezembeek-Oppem.

and Hal-Vilvorde which are both part of the Brabant Province; this covers the northern part of the country.

2. The French language region comprises the provinces of Hainaut, Namur, Luxemburg and Liège (except for the eastern part) and the district of Nivelles which is part of the Brabant Province. This covers the southern part of the country.

3. The German language region comprises the eastern part of the Liège Province.

4. The bilingual region of Brussels-Capital comprises the 19 boroughs of Greater Brussels, including the city of Brussels itself, the capital of Belgium.

On the following page is a map showing the language regions and a map of the Greater Brussels Urban Area.

The genesis of Article 3-B is further reviewed in the commentary on Article 59-B.

Brussels ——————

—————— and surroundings

xxxx Linguistic

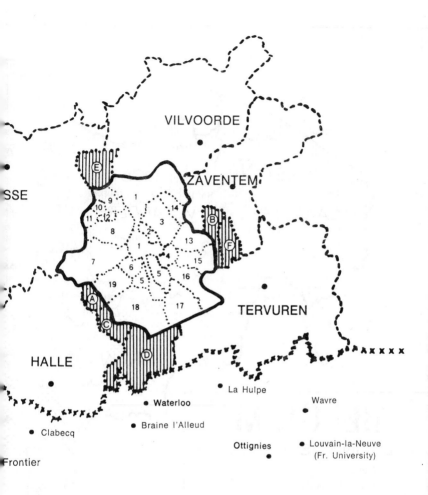

VILVOORDE

ZAVENTEM

SSE

TERVUREN

HALLE

La Hulpe

Waterloo

Wavre

Clabecq

Braine l'Alleud

Ottignies

Louvain-la-Neuve
(Fr. University)

Frontier

THE FIVE PERIPHERAL URBAN FEDERATIONS

(in the Dutch-language region)

Asse
Vilvoorde
Zaventem
Tervuren
Halle

HEADING 1-B

THE CULTURAL COMMUNITIES

ARTICLE 3-C

"Belgium comprises three cultural communities: French, Dutch and German.

"Each community enjoys the powers vested in it by the Constitution or such legislation as shall be enacted by virtue thereof."

This is an entirely new article, adopted during the third revision (1967-1971).

The first clause of the new article records the official existence of the three cultural communities co-existing on the territory of the Belgian State.

The second clause refers back to Article 59-B defining the powers and prerogatives of the institutions belonging to those communities.

Taken as a whole, Article 3-C is a statement of principle, the actual implementation of which must be done on the basis of Articles 32-B and 59-B.

The importance of this article lies in the fact that it introduces an entirely new concept in Belgian public law: that of a "cultural community".

Until then, the Belgian State only recognised the existence of Belgian citizens taken as individuals, and beyond them, the official organs of State. However great the importance of municipal and provincial autonomy may have been initially, the fact remains that the provinces and the boroughs were merely subdivisions of the national territory (see the first three articles of the Constitution, and the wording of the first heading in particular). Even the concept of freedom of association was laid down in 1831 as being a right conferred on individuals. The sole exception whereby the first Constituent Assembly acknowledged the existence of a collectivity which, as such, enjoyed certain rights, was that of various religions (see Article 16).

In Belgium, therefore, the cultural communities now exist legally from the standpoint of public law.

In the Dutch text of the Constitution, the Dutch cultural Community is mentioned first, while in the French text, the French cultural community takes precedence in the wording. In both texts, the German cultural community, which is by far the smallest (about 63.500 inhabitants) is mentioned last.

HEADING II

THE BELGIANS AND THEIR RIGHTS

ARTICLE 4

"Belgian nationality is acquired, retained and withdrawn in accordance with the rules laid down by civil law.

"The present Constitution and the other laws governing political rights determine what conditions, apart from nationality, are necessary for the exercise of those rights."

This article dates from 1831 and has never been modified.

The Constituent Assembly was at pains to remove the national status of citizens from any arbitrary decisions on the part of the Executive by stating that the law alone, in laying down a set of general and impersonal rules, decides who shall possess (or not possess) Belgian citizenship. The 1831 Constituent Assembly was respectful of the law which is both the supreme guarantee surrounding the rights of the individual and the collective work of the duly authorised representatives of the Nation (see Article 25).

Article 4 embodies another important principle, which is: that it is necessary to enjoy Belgian citizenship before one is allowed to exercise political rights in Belgium. While Belgian nationality automatically entitles one to exercise and enjoy civil rights, the same is not true of political rights the exercise of which may be subordinated to the fulfilment of certain conditions of age and status (see Articles 92 and 93).

ARTICLE 5

"Naturalisation is granted by the Legislative power.

"Only full naturalisation places the foreigner on an equal footing with the Belgian citizen where the exercise of political rights is concerned."

This article dates from 1831 and has never been modified.

Neither the Executive nor the Judiciary may grant naturalization. Only the Legislative may do this: in this field, the legislator not only lays down the general rules governing the acquisition or loss of Belgian nationality, but he also decides in each individual case whether naturalization should be granted or not. Here is one matter in which the Legislative is empowered to perform an executive function.

The Constituent Assembly provided for two kinds of naturalization: ordinary naturalization, which is not described in any other terms and which does not bestow full political rights on the individual concerned (it is sometimes known as "minor" naturalization), and full or major naturalization.

A foreigner who has obtained ordinary or minor naturalization becomes an elector and an eligible candidate at the level of municipal elections; but only full or major naturalization entitles him to become an elector and an eligible candidate at the level of provincial and national elections, and to be a member of the government.

Article 5 is of vital importance since it has always been in the Belgian tradition to welcome immigrants.

It should be noted that apart from Belgian citizens by birth and Belgian citizens by naturalization, there is a third category known as Belgian citizens by preferential option (such as, for instance, children born in Belgium of foreign parents) and Belgians by marriage (foreign women who have married Belgian citizens).

The acquisition, loss and recovery of Belgian nationality are regulated by the coordinated laws of 14 December 1932.

ARTICLE 6

"There is no distinction between orders in the State.

"All Belgians are equal in the eyes of the law; they alone are acceptable for civil and military posts, with some exceptions which may be established by law in special cases."

This article dates from 1831 and has never been modified.

The first sentence abolishes the orders that existed under the previous regime. The second sentence establishes the legal equality of all citizens. From this principle of total equality in the eyes of the law, it is clear that no privilege attaches to birth, except insofar as members of the Royal Family are concerned. The only distinctions that may be made by the public authorities are those which are justified by the public interest.

Such distinctions must rest on objective and generalized criteria. They must also be adequate, meaning that there must be some logical connexion between the criterion governing such a distinction and the purpose for which it is made.

The principle that all Belgians are equally suitable for employment does not prevent the authorities from subordinating certain appointments to conditions of aptitude. It is recognized that the authorities may reserve some forms of employment solely to male candidates, or to female candidates as the case may be, for special reasons connected either with the requirements of the post to be filled or with measures designed to protect women from the dangers inherent in certain jobs. It should be stressed that distinctions of this kind tend to disappear as women become integrated to a growing extent in the economic and social life of the nation.

The principle of equality is restated or implied in other articles of the Constitution:

— the absence of privilege in jurisdictional matters (Articles 7 and 8);
— the absence of privilege in fiscal matters (Article 112).

The second paragraph of this Article excludes foreigners from taking up civil and military employment, while leaving it up to the Legislative (and not the Executive) to provide for exceptions to this rule. But here again, it should be pointed out that the legislator may not establish such exceptions save in very special cases: Parliament may not, for instance, issue a general authorization to the government to admit foreigners to all posts.

It should be noted that Belgians by ordinary (or minor) naturalization may become civil servants, but they may not be appointed Cabinet Ministers nor Secretaries of State (see Articles 86 and 91-B).

ARTICLE 6-B

"Enjoyment of the rights and liberties to which Belgians are entitled must be ensured without discrimination. To this end, laws and decrees shall guarantee amongst other things the rights and liberties of ideological and philosophical minorities."

This article was inserted during the Third Revision (1967-1971).

Article 6 already provided for the legal equality of all Belgians, with the result that the rights and liberties set out under Heading II of the Constitution were to be granted to all citizens identically. Yet the 1970 Constituent Assembly deemed it necessary to define the scope of Article 6 by adding a new Article 6-B stating the general principle that any form of discrimination was prohibited; this arose out of the creation of Cultural Councils endowed with normative powers (see Article 59-B). Indeed, the guarantees afforded to minorities would seem superfluous in regard to those matters which are still incumbent on the national Parliament, where a *de facto* balance has been struck between the various ideological and philosophical trends. But from the moment when a share of the normative power has been vested in regional bodies within which one particular ideology may be paramount, then such a balance can no longer exist, and special protective measures accordingly become necessary. In other words, the Constituent Assembly has not formally ordered a law and a decree containing such measures of guarantee to be voted; but it has imposed on the national Legislature and on the Cultural Councils an obligation to take all steps that may be necessary to guarantee the rights and liberties of all ideological and philosophical minorities.

It should also be stated that the words "amongst other things" must be regarded as defining the scope of this article on the basis of examples, and not in any restrictive fashion.

Furthermore, it is difficult to arrive at a precise definition of a minority. On the other hand, what seems certain when one reads the preparatory work, is that the Constituent Assembly wished to exclude linguistic minorities from the sphere of application of its new Article 6-B so as to avoid any infringement of the principle surrounding the territorial nature of linguistic legislation.

Finally, this same preparatory work also makes it clear that the term "philosophical and ideological minorities" is in fact equivalent to "religious and agnostic minorities".

In order to guarantee the rights and liberties of those minorities, Parliament voted the law of 16 July 1973 guaranteeing the protection of all ideological and philosophical tendencies, in implementation of Articles 6-B and 59-B, para. 7, of the Constitution.

This law, which was published in the *Moniteur belge* (official gazette) of 16 October 1973, states in its first clause that the decrees enacted by each of the Cultural Councils may not contain any form of discrimination on ideological or philosophical grounds, nor may they infringe any of the rights and liberties vested in ideological and philosophical minorities.

The cultural measures implemented by all the public authorities and State-controlled organisations answerable thereto are subject to this law. In accordance with democratic principles, people who hold ideological and philosophical opinions that differ from the general trends must also be associated with the charting of cultural policy.

The legislator has been at pains to point out that the representation of such tendencies is based on their presence in the representative assembly of the public authority in question. It also insists on the fact that the number of members or supporters of any organisation may not be regarded as a criterion warranting a refusal to acknowledge it. Similarly, no given ideological or philosophical tendency may be ascribed to any persons, organisations or institutions save with their formal agreement.

Equality of treatment as between the various tendencies must therefore be strictly observed.

As for participation in the management and administration of cultural bodies set up by the public authorities or answerable to them, this is subject to the equitable, democratic representation of those groups which use it and of all the ideological or philosophical tendencies involved.

The legislator's scrupulous attention has extended to embrace details of the way in which subsidies are to be granted and the purposes for which they are to be used.

Article 13 of the law makes for objectivity when encouraging the public authorities to support citizens who are artists, scientists or sportsmen. The equality of rights enjoyed by all citizens, whatever their opinions may be, must be ensured when awarding prizes, scholarships, loans, etc. The latter are moreover the subject of a publication issued annually, giving names and full details (Article 14). Chapter VII of the law provides for guarantees surrounding the use of cultural infrastructures.

As the public authorities are particularly involved in the radio and television broadcasting establishments, it was logical that a special chapter of the law should deal with this question. Articles 18 and 19 do indeed rule on the access of the various ideological and philosophical tendencies represented within each Cultural Council and on the means of expression answerable to the public authorities, namely: radio and television.

Proportional representation of political groups within the Cultural Councils must be ensured where the bodies set up for administration and management are concerned, and these bodies must be assisted by a permanent advisory committee representing all known users of the facilities provided by the Council and of all ideological and philosophical tendencies. This committee, says the law, is entitled to be kept fully informed of all acts performed by the administrative and management bodies.

As for guarantees afforded to personnel performing cultural duties within the cultural bodies and organisations, these are covered by Article 20 aimed at upholding the principle of equal rights for all persons without any attempt at ideological or philosophical discrimination.

Observance of all these rulings must be supervised by a National Commission for the Cultural Compact, to which any complaints may be submitted.

This Commission consists of twenty-six effective members (13 French-speaking and 13 Dutch-speaking) and twenty-six substitute members (13 French-speaking and 13 Dutch-speaking). They are elected for a term of four years by the Cultural Council of their respective language community, on the basis of the proportional representation of the political groups which make up the councils. Furthermore, two effective and two substitute members are appointed by the Council of the German-language cultural community to deal with complaints involving their region.

ARTICLE 7

"Individual liberty is guaranteed.

"No person may be prosecuted except in cases laid down by the law and in the form it prescribes.

"Apart from the case of *flagrante delicto*, no person may be arrested save on a motivated order by a judge, which must be signified at the time of the arrest or within twenty-four hours at latest."

This article dates from 1831 and has never been modified.

The individual liberty referred to in para. 1 is the right to personal security: the right not to be placed under arbitrary arrest or detention. As individual freedom is the very foundation of political democracy, it was essential for the Constitution to ensure that it is respected.

The second paragraph guarantees the liberty of every citizen from any prosecution for reasons other than those laid down by the law; the latter must be in force at the time of the prosecution, and this provision guarantees that the penal code of laws shall not be retroactive. The principle of the non-retroactivity of the penal code has a corollary: that of restrictive interpretation of the laws by the judge. The latter may neither extend the scope of the penal code nor apply it by analogy. Furthermore, he may not base his judgment on a moral standard, even when this is generally recognised, nor on custom or tradition.

The third paragraph protects citizens from unwarranted arrest by providing that a judge must order it; all judges enjoy fixity of tenure in their office and, as such, are independent of the nation's rulers (see Article 100).

Even the judge's order is surrounded by further guarantees, since in sanctioning the arrest he must issue a *motivated* order, so that the person arrested is immediately apprised of the reason for his arrest; in other words, he is aware of the charge made against him.

Consequently, for a person to be arrested on whatever charge except for the case of *flagrante delicto*, there must be either a warrant for his arrest delivered by an examining magistrate, or a warrant issued by a court of enquiry, or again a sentence or judgment pronounced by a court or tribunal.

The principle of a legal warrant does not apply in the case of *flagrante delicto*. In this case, the presumptive author of an offence or a crime may be arrested and brought to justice on condition that, within 24 hours, an order for his arrest is notified to the person concerned. Even in the case of *flagrante delicto,* the person charged therefore benefits from the dual protection of, firstly, a judge's order and, secondly, the right to be informed of the charge laid against him.

ARTICLE 8

"No person may be withdrawn from the judge assigned to him by the law, save with his consent."

This article dates from 1831 and has never been modified.

While Article 7 protects citizens from abusive arrest and prosecution, Article 8 guarantees the right of all Belgians to be judged according to the rules of competence and the legal procedures laid down along general, impersonal and objective lines by the Legislative.

This article should be read in conjunction with Article 94 which constitutes its logical implementation: the latter prohibits the setting up of extraordinary commissions or courts.

ARTICLE 9

"No penalty may be decreed nor applied save in accordance with the law."

This article dates from 1831 and has never been modified.

It establishes the principle that the legislator alone is competent to determine the felonious nature of certain deeds. As the Constituent Assembly has used the words "in accordance with" and not the word "by", it follows that the legislator may entrust the King, the Cultural Councils, the provincial and municipal authorities with the task of establishing the penalties.

Here we should emphasize the parallel character of Article 7 which establishes the legality of crimes and misdemeanours, Article 8 which establishes the legality of judicial procedure, and Article 9 which establishes the legality of penalties. Legality is the very opposite of arbitrary or discretionary powers: it implies the existence of general, impersonal, objective rules in force prior to the perpetration of an act liable to provoke the arrest, prosecution or condemnation of the perpetrator. These rules are known to all, and were laid down by the representatives of the people.

ARTICLE 10

"The home is inviolable; no entrance into a private house may be made save in those cases laid down by the law and in the manner it prescribes."

This article dates from 1831 and has never been modified.

It enshrines the principle of ancient law according to which any man, be he never so poor, is master in his own house.

The Constituent Assembly was at pains to guarantee the effective implementation of this principle by providing that the legislator alone, exclusive of the Executive authority, is empowered to determine the conditions in which certain restrictions may be placed upon this ruling.

The inviolability of the home is not a corollary of the right of ownership but rather the natural complement of personal liberty provided for under Article 7. Indeed, the purpose of such protection in terms of the Constitution is not the building itself but the tranquillity of the persons living under its roof who are on their own ground; the constitutional principle corresponds to the fundamental, biological need of every living creature.

Protection of the home extends to all rented accommodations and to cabins, caravans, boats with living quarters, and motor vehicle trailers designed with living and sleeping facilities.

It goes without saying that premises open to all such as bars, restaurants, theatres, churches and shops, are outside the sphere of application of Article 10.

It should also be pointed out that the legislator has, in principle, forbidden house searches to be made at night.

In terms of Article 1 of the law dated 7 June 1969, no search or inspection on premises which are not open to the public may be made before the hour of 5 a.m. and after the hour of 9 p.m. (i.e., from 21 00 hours to 05 00 hours).

House searches conducted during the day can only be made by an examining magistrate, a public prosecutor, one of his deputies, or by his auxiliary judicial police officials.

Furthermore, the Penal Code punishes all violations of the home by representatives of the authorities as well as those committed by private persons.

ARTICLE 11

"No person may be deprived of his property save in the public interest, in cases laid down by the law and in the manner it prescribes, and on condition that just and prior compensation is made."

This article dates from 1831 and has never been modified.

In the mind of the first Constituent Assembly, the ownership of property was an absolute and inalienable right. Indeed, no exception has been provided for: the sole restriction placed on this strict principle by the Constituent Assembly does no more than allow the authorities to alter the form of ownership, since expropriations may only be carried out on the basis of due compensation, so that the overall fortune of the owner remains unchanged in terms of value. The word "just" used by the Constituent Assembly indicates that the compensation must be fully equal to the loss suffered by the person whose property has been expropriated. It is calculated on the basis of the market value of the property concerned and not on that of its replacement cost.

The expropriated person may not, therefore, claim the value of his property when new, nor the cost of rebuilding it. The compensation award is increased by a sum destined to cover the expenses that the expropriated person would incur should he decide to purchase another property of equal value, such as the transfer and legal fees in particular. It may also be increased by a sum to be agreed on should the expropriated person suffer other damages, for instance the loss of his customers, the depreciation in value of his property owing to partial expropriation, etc.

The expropriating authority is not required to compensate for the effects of currency devaluation.

It should be added that the mandatory intervention of the legislator is a further guarantee afforded property owners as a protection against any arbitrary action by the Executive authority.

Furthermore, the right to receive a just compensation awarded *before* expropriation takes place constitutes a civil right in terms of Article 92, so that any disputes arising out of this right come within the exclusive competence of the courts and tribunals.

It follows therefore that, in the event of a dispute between the person expropriated and the expropriating authority, the amount of the sum to be awarded as compensation is definitively fixed by the Judiciary.

Only those bodies set up under public law (the State, the provinces, the boroughs, the borough federations and urban areas, the intermunicipal organisations, etc.) are entitled to expropriate on the grounds of public utility.

*
* *

Procedure.

The procedure to be used in expropriations for the public weal is governed, depending on the degree of urgency in taking over the buildings, by the law of 17 April 1835 (ordinary procedure) and that of 27 May 1870 (which lays down the prior administrative formalities to be observed), and by the law of 10 May 1926 (procedure in cases of urgency) and the law of 26 July 1962 (emergency procedure).

Expropriation is undertaken in terms of a law or a royal decree authorising the work which makes such measures necessary.

If the question is one of a royal decree, as is usually the case, a prior enquiry is necessary : a project comprising the survey and programme of work, plus the ground plan, is deposited at the municipal offices where it is open to inspection; its deposit is notified individually and in writing to all the property owners concerned. It is also announced by means of posters and in the manner laid down for official publications. A warrant signed by the Mayor and Corporation attests that these formalities have been complied with. Complaints and queries are received by the Mayor and Corporation who draw up an official report on them. They are then submitted for the examination of the Town Council if the work is in the municipal interest, or that of the Permanent Deputation if the work is in the provincial interest. If an agreement is reached between the expropriating authority and the property owner regarding the amicable cession of the property, then the procedure is virtually at an end. The instruments of cession by private contract are then registered cost-free.

In the absence of such an agreement, legal proceedings are instituted along the following lines: the documents in support of the Administration's case are deposited with the Clerk of the Court. The property owners and usufructuaries are summoned to appear within the fortnight. The court rules on whether the formalities laid down by the law for purposes of expropriation have been complied with. If the ruling is a negative one, the Court orders the termination of the procedure. If it is an affirmative one, three experts and a Judge-Auditor are appointed to proceed with the inspection and valuation of the property under notice of expropriation. An opportunity is afforded all parties to deposit any documents and statements in support of their case, with the option of reply and rebuttal, each time within a fifteen-day period.

The experts are required to table their report within the forty-day period following the end of the time granted to the parties concerned for replying to the last comments of their opponent. At the hearing, after the defendants and the authorities have stated their case, the Court then decides the amount of compensation and this sum is paid into the Deposit and Consignment Office. Finally, a Court order from the presiding judge places the expropriating authority in possession of the property.

It should be noted in this connection that while, in terms of jurisprudence, the property due to be expropriated is already transferred to the expropriating authority when the Court rules that the formalities laid down by the law been complied with, actual possession of the property is withheld until the amount of compensation has been deposited. If this were not the case, there would be a derogation of the constitutional requirement that *prior* compensation must be made.

The procedure outlined above, as will be realised, affords the property owner under sentence of expropriation all the requisite constitutional guarantees regarding the equitable as well as the prior nature of the compensation. The procedure is often an arduous one, the stays of execution are numerous and for lengthy periods, especially where the expropriating authority is concerned for the latter may only take possession of the property when the whole procedure is completely terminated, even when there is an urgent need to proceed with the work that gave rise to it.

According to the urgency procedure instituted by the law of 10 May 1926, the state of urgency must be proclaimed by a separate, motivated royal decree. No alterations are made to the administrative proceedings as laid down by the law of 27 May 1870. But the legal proceedings are simplified from the point where the Court rules that all the preliminary legal formalities have been complied with. The ordinary procedure provides that the Court shall decide the amount of compensation to be paid to the parties concerned on the basis of the report submitted by the experts and after hearing statements by the plaintiff and the defendants—which in turn may call for a further valuation by the experts, and so on. But according to the procedure laid down by the law of 10 May 1926 the stays of execution are considerably shortened and it is the Judge-Auditor who, on the basis of the report submitted by the experts and the statements made by both parties, rules on the compensation to be awarded and authorises the expropriating authority to take possession on condition that the compensation money is deposited first. The parties concerned may, if they wish, have their case reopened according to the ordinary procedure, but, be it noted, the expropriating authority will already be in possession of the property involved.

The procedure established by the law of 10 May 1926 was revealed as still being too slow in certain cases, for instance when the authorities needed to take over the property almost immediately. So for these cases, a so-called emergency procedure was instituted by the decree-law of 3 February 1947. This was, however, rescinded by the law of 26 July 1962 which substituted the new procedure described hereunder.

After a royal decree has established that the immediate acquisition of one or several buildings is essential in the public interest, the procedure is put in hand straight away. With a minimum of delay—involving a summons to appear on the spot, the appointment of an expert to prepare an inventory of the buildings and their valuation, and a hearing before the judge— it leads to a Court ruling as to whether the legal formalities have been complied with. If so, the same ruling determines, by means of a summary valuation, the amount of the provisional compensation. This amount cannot be less than ninety per cent of the sum offered by the expropriating authority. As soon as a copy of the ruling has been handed to the defendants and to the applicants, along with the inventory compiled by the expert and a certificate attesting that the provisional compensation has been deposited with the Deposit and Consignment Office, the expropriating authority is empowered by a Judge's Order to take possession of the property.

As a general rule, possession may thus be gained after a period of forty days from the opening of the procedure. This is a very short time indeed when it is remembered that the ordinary procedure may, in the normal course of events, take anything up to 180 days, while the urgency procedure established by the law of 10 May 1926 requires a period of about 120 days before the expropriating authority can take over the property. At the end of a second, less hectic phase that now begins, a Court order based on the expert's report will decide the amount awarded as provisional compensation. This amount becomes final if, within two months of the notification of the order, neither of the parties has demanded its reassessment.

ARTICLE 12

"The penalty consisting of confiscation of property may not be decreed."

This article dates from 1831 and has never been modified.

Article 12, prohibiting the legislator from decreeing confiscation of property as a penalty, is the logical complement of Article 11.

Article 12 only prohibits general confiscation, and does therefore permit the confiscation of specific property. For instance, the penal laws provide for the confiscation of objects that have been used to commit a crime, or which are the fruit of it.

By prohibiting the general confiscation of property belonging to any citizen, the Constituent Assembly was at pains to prevent the State from seizing family estates and legacies.

ARTICLE 13

"The civil death penalty is abolished and may not be reinstated."

This article dates from 1831 and has never been modified.

The civil death penalty was a punishment which consisted in striking out the person condemned to it from the number of persons in society, and in prohibiting him from exercising any of his civil and political rights. While the man thus condemned was still biologically alive, he was dead to the world since he was no longer a member of society.

Such a person lost the ownership of his property and his estate was declared open. He could no longer institute proceedings in the law courts and tribunals, either as plaintiff or defendant. He could no longer testify in any court of law. His marriage was automatically dissolved; his children were declared orphans.

It was this terrible penalty that the Constituent Assembly was determined to abolish for ever and it expressly forbade even the legislator to reinstate it.

ARTICLE 14

"Freedom of worship and its public exercise, together with freedom to manifest personal opinions in every way, are guaranteed save for the punishment of offences perpetrated in exercising those liberties."

This article dates from 1831 and has never been modified.

Freedom of thought normally includes freedom of opinion on religious subjects and, as a result, freedom of worship. The reason why the Constituent Assembly deemed it necessary to mention this separately, and even to state this principle before going on to speak in wider terms of freedom of opinion in general, was because in former times religious conflicts had caused untold bloodshed and suffering.

It was necessary to recognise the fact that, within a single body politic, all citizens do not necessarily share the same philosophical ideas. In the early days, freedom of worship was regarded by many people as being a measure of tolerance, or even merely a compromise solution offering an alternative to the oppression and persecution exercised by the majority religion, or to civil wars.

Progressively, freedom of opinion has become a fundamental right vested in each individual citizen until, today, it is acknowledged as forming the basis of genuine intellectual wealth. At the present time, the diversity of ideological concepts is regarded as being essential to the development both of society and its culture.

It should be stressed that the Constituent Assembly established not only freedom of conscience, but also that of public expression of opinion.

Among the misdemeanours that may be perpetrated during the exercise of this freedom of expression, we may mention the direct provocation to commit certain crimes, even in cases when no crime is actually committed.

The freedom of opinion enjoyed by every citizen is coupled with his obligation to respect that of his fellow-citizens.

Accordingly, the following are punishable offences: firstly, any attacks made publicly by ministers of religion, in the performance of their ministry, on the Government, the laws, the royal decrees or any other acts by the public authorities; and secondly, the desecration of any objects destined for religious use, as well as libels, slanders, calumny

35

or other injuries directed at the reputation and well-being of any persons.

Such measures are not restrictions placed on liberty: on the contrary, they are so many guarantees surrounding the freedom of all.

Briefly, one may say that freedom of thought consists of the right freely to manifest one's philosophical, religious, political, personal or ideological convictions in speech, in writing and in one's personal conduct.

As for freedom of worship, this entails the right freely to organise religious ceremonies. Such freedom may be subject to certain restrictions when it is exercised on the public highway and when it is likely to cause breaches of law and order. Thus any ceremony, for instance a procession, may be prohibited, but the ban may only relate to one specific case and may never be a general and permanent one.

The religions officially recognised in Belgium are : Roman Catholicism, Evangelical Protestantism, Anglicanism, Judaism, and since quite recently (July 1974), the Islamic religion. This means that facilities for religious instruction in all five creeds are provided in all State educational establishments.

ARTICLE 15

"No person may be constrained to assist in any way in the acts and ceremonies of any form of worship, nor to observe its days of rest."

This article dates from 1831 and has never been modified.

It rounds off Article 14 by granting freedom of thought to agnostics also.

Whereas Article 14 establishes freedom of worship and, as a result, that of the various religious communities which are social groups, Article 15 on the contrary is concerned with protecting the rights of the individual.

The fact that Sunday—the traditional day of rest in the Catholic religion —is the day of rest observed by the vast majority of Belgians, by no means constitutes a form of religious constraint. Moreover, in many branches of industry and in the public administration, Saturday is also a day of rest. The «weekend», an Anglo-Saxon custom, has become general, and the usual working week lasts from Monday to Friday (8-hour working days = a total of 40 hours). But in some sectors (the food industry, public transportation, health services, factory maintenance, etc.) neither Saturday nor Sunday is an off-day. The laws governing working hours ensure that the statutory number of hours per week is not exceeded, irrespective of which particular day is chosen as a day of rest.

ARTICLE 16

"The State has no right to intervene either in the appointment or the induction of ministers of any form of worship, nor to forbid them to correspond with their superiors and to publish their acts save, in the latter case, for the ordinary responsibility bound up with the press and publishing.

"The civil wedding must always precede the nuptial benediction, save in exceptional cases to be established, where necessary, by law."

This article dates from 1831 and has never been modified.

In Belgium, as in many Catholic countries, the Roman Catholic Church enjoyed certain privileges; conversely, the State wielded some influence over the internal life of the Church and often held the right of appointment to certain high-ranking ecclesiastical posts.

The freedom of worship instituted by the Constituent Assembly ensured from that time on both liberty of conscience for the people, and independence for the Church. The separation of Church and State was instituted, except insofar as a few points were concerned (see Article 117).

The last sentence of the Article might be regarded as interference by the political authorities in the affairs of the Church, but in point of fact it was inserted at the request of the Catholic members of the 1831 National Congress who feared that, in default of such a ruling, certain Catholic citizens might think that the authority of a priest was sufficient to bestow official and legal validity on the marriage celebrated before him, and might therefore neglect to perform the civil wedding, a failure liable to give rise to various administrative difficulties.

The exception provided for in the last paragraph was established by the legislator in cases where the persons wishing to contract a marriage are in danger of death: in that case, the nuptial benediction may be given without performing the civil wedding. Such a union is still invalid from the standpoint of civil law, but the celebrant is immune from prosecution. Similarly, he will not be prosecuted if, in the same circumstances, he performs the religious wedding prior to the civil ceremony. In this latter case, however, the union will be valid in law since the civil wedding also takes place.

ARTICLE 17

"Education is free; any preventive measure is forbidden; the punishment of misdemeanours is regulated only by law.

" Public education provided at the expense of the State is also regulated by law."

This article dates from 1831 and has never been modified.

The 1831 Constituent Assembly wished to prevent any form of monopoly where education was concerned and to allow for free competition in this sphere. Furthermore, it provided for the creation of a network of State schools by means of legislation.

Article 17 therefore embodies the following principles:

1. the absolute freedom acknowledged in respect of any Belgian to organise any form of education;

2. the absence of any State monopoly on education;

3. the sole competence of Parliament in defining the criteria governing the provision of grants and subsidies to schools which are not organised and run by the public authorities.

In fact, there are official schools, namely those organised and run by the public authorities (the State, the provinces, boroughs, and associations of boroughs) and free schools, set up and managed by private persons. The latter benefit from substantial grants if they fulfil the conditions laid down by the State with regard to the structural specifications of school premises, the curriculum, the control and inspection provided by the State, the minimum number of pupils, the requirements surrounding health, hygiene, etc.

Freedom of education involves the parents' right to choose which school their children are to attend; it goes hand in hand with compulsory schooling which the legislator has laid down for all children aged from 6 to 14 years. Compulsory school attendance is a restriction placed on the freedom of parents, but it does uphold the genuine right of every future citizen to receive an education.

The problem of schooling gave rise to a long controversy which lasted over a century and was popularly known as the "schools war" even though no Belgian ever lost his life in that bitter but bloodless struggle in which the only weapons used were polemics and demontions.

Generally speaking, the Social Christian Party considered that schooling could or should be philosophically "involved"; this party was mainly bent on defending the interests of private schools run by Catholic organisations.

On the other hand, the Liberal and Socialist parties inclined to the view that schools should be kept apart from philosophical controversy: in other words, they upheld the official, neutral schools set up by the State, the provincial or municipal authorities.

In 1958 these three parties entered into the "Schools Covenant" which thus finally established the schools truce. This covenant represents such an outstanding event in Belgian history, and has become such an important factor of stability in the political life of the country, that the 1971 Constituent Assembly, in an indirect allusion to the concept of a "schools truce " (Article 59-B, Section 2, para. 2) has, so to speak, constitutionalised it. Consequently, it is important here to make a brief summary of its content.

The Schools Covenant, or Schools Pact, applies to pre-school, primary, intermediate, normalian, technical and artistic education.

It begins by announcing a bold and generous policy of educational expansion, in particular by raising the school-leaving age, by supporting all forms of education recognised as valid, by appropriating a portion of the national revenue for education, by the rational use and effective control of public funds, by a development programme bearing in mind future requirements, by providing that kindergarten, primary and secondary schooling in State and State-subsidised establishments shall be free of charge, and by the democratisation of advanced education through the progressive widening of the scholarship and grant system.

Under its heading of "Problems common to both schools networks" the Covenant institutes prior concertation on fundamental reforms to provincial and municipal schools and to private schools. It lays down a minimal syllabus and timetable to be fixed by law, allowing each school the possibility of improving on it and for latitude in teaching methods. Official sanction of studies shall be based on identical rules in official and private education alike. Any political activity or propaganda in scholastic establishments is prohibited, along with any unfair competition between schools.

The chapter entitled "Freedom of choice upheld" regulates, among other matters, the question of lessons on religion and ethics. It defines the concepts of official and neutral as applied to schools (respect for all philosophical ideas; two-thirds of the teaching staff to hold a diploma of official and neutral education). The State organises kindergarten, primary, intermediate, normalian and technical schooling and, as dictated by need, sets up the schools or extra facilities in existing schools that may be necessary. It grants subsidies to all schools that fulfil the legal standards and which are set up by the provincial and municipal authorities and by private persons. Parents must be able to send their children to a school of their choice within a reasonable distance. Criteria based on the number of children attending school shall be fixed jointly for the State, provincial, municipal and private schools.

In the chapter dealing with State education, the Covenant provides that the financing of State school buildings shall continue and increase in line with requirements until such time as the free choice of school is effectively guaranteed in all parts of the country. Apart from an annual endowment of 600 million francs, an annual credit of 600 million for the setting up of 20 secondary schools, 400 million for the setting up of 16 boarding schools, and 100 million for the setting up of 30 pre-primary and primary schools each year shall be included in the Budget under this heading. The posts of kindergarten mistress, primary school teacher and form-master in State schools shall be given on a priority basis to persons holding a non-confessional education diploma. As for teachers who are university graduates, priority shall be given to those who have graduated from a non-confessional university, on condition that care is taken to appoint a percentage of graduates from confessional establishments equal to the average percentage of the two previous legislatures.

As for provincial and municipal schooling, the Pact announces the creation of a Provincial and Municipal School Buildings Fund with an annual endowment of 600 million francs. It sets the subsidy rate at a uniform level of 60 per cent. For those members of the teaching staff eligible for the subsidy and who have the necessary qualifications to occupy the same post in State schools, the salary subsidy will be equal to the remuneration (salary plus other benefits) which the person concerned would be entitled to receive from the State in the event that the whole of his teaching career had been spent in a State school. An annual inclusive subsidy is allocated per pupil to the province or the borough in order to cover all operating expenses such as : heating, lighting, power, water, gas, supplies, basic materials, administrative expenses, prize-giving, and the hire, renewal, maintenance and cleaning of the premises, furnishings, equipment, fittings, library and laboratories, the transportation and insurance of the pupils, and school outings.

Where private schools are concerned, the Covenant provides under the heading of operating subsidies and salary subsidies for a system identical to that applicable to provincial and municipal schools. The operating subsidies must be allocated to the school for which they are destined and to which they are paid. The King organises the supervision of these appropriations. The granting of subsidies for school buildings is excluded. For the religious, secular and regular members of the kindergarten and primary teaching staff, the salary subsidies are equal to 60 per cent of the emoluments of a lay member. At the other levels of education, the salary subsidies are equal to the minimum salary, increased by 15 per cent after 15 years of service in education. The principle of a pension chargeable to the State Treasury is extended to all members of the teaching personnel who are eligible for the subsidies. Parity committees will be set up at every level of education for the purpose especially of framing, within a period of two years, a statute of permanent employment and a disciplinary statute. The financial contribution of the provinces and boroughs towards private schools is restricted to the supervision of health and hygiene and to the social advantages granted to pupils, care being taken to ensure that no distinction is made between the children depending on what category of schools they attend.

In its final resolutions, the Schools Covenant provides that the National Commission shall set up a permanent committee responsible for supervising the proper implementation of the Covenant, and that all measures contained therein must go into effect on 1 September 1958 or, in the case of a few special provisions, on 1 January 1959. The duration of the pact is set at 12 years, and its revision is to be undertaken on the basis of the same procedure.

In order to get the resolutions of the Schools Covenant sanctioned by our judicial system, it was necessary to translate them into the proper legal and statutory instruments. This was essentially accomplished by means of the law of 29 May 1959 modifying the previous legislation covering pre-school, primary, intermediate, normalian, technical and artistic education.

It should be emphasized that everything connected with the "schools truce" comes within the exclusive competence of the national parliament and is withheld from that of the cultural councils. The reason why all matters affecting the schools truce have been placed under the sole authority of Parliament must be sought in the fact that a balance has been struck in the Legislative Chambers between believers and agnostics, whereas this is not so within each of the Cultural Councils (1). The national Parliament is therefore an impartial arbiter, to a far greater extent than the Cultural Councils, when it comes to controversial educational matters (see Article 59-B).

---

(1) See table showing distribution of Members of Parliament, page 86.

After this compact had functioned for fourteen years, the signatory parties asked the Government to take adequate measures to ensure the implementation of a certain number of resolutions embodied in the Compact which had not been entirely complied with. Their recommendations were aimed particularly at questions pertaining to the School Building Fund and the status of teaching staff in the subsidised schools. This protocol of agreement between the parties, signed on 4 April 1973, stated in particular:

The Parties consider that the situation which led to the 1958 Compact has greatly changed since that time, and that it is important to examine the new problems which have arisen. They agree to undertake the negotiations designed to lead to the updating of the 1958 Compact so as to adapt it to the requirements of present-day education and that of the future.

In doing so, they will largely allow themselves to be guided by the following main objectives, and will be at pains to provide for the means and structuration of a progressive educational policy:

1. the charting of ways and means for the rationalisation and programming of all forms of education;

2. the pursuit of educational democratisation and improvements in the quality of education;

3. bearing in mind the characteristics special to each network of schools, the placing of pupils, parents, teachers and schools on a footing of equality, especially where school buildings are concerned;

4. the promotion and encouragement of concerted discussions, co-operation and closer relations between the school networks, particularly by means of the pluralist school.

On 11 July 1973, a law was passed modifying that of 29 May 1959. In particular, it increased from two-thirds to three-quarters the number of teachers holding neutral education diplomas working in neutral schools. It defined the exact meaning of fundamental reform of education: "a modification of the general orientation or the duration of studies, and of the conditions governing the entrance and graduation of pupils". Furthermore, it guaranteed the protection, outside the school, of the private life of teaching staff in the subsidised schools against arbitrary decisions made by the organising authority. The qualifications required for teaching staff at every level of education were defined on a uniform basis for all networks of schools. Similarly, insofar as it was possible to do so on the basis of the ruling laid down by the State, the following were officially and uniformly established:

a) the basic rules governing recruiting, appointment, selection and promotion;

b) administrative posts and the rules governing reclassification of personnel members released from their appointments;

c) the statutory leave system;

d) essential incompatibilities common to all networks;

e) fundamental duties common to all networks.

As for competence in regard to school buildings, this was transferred from the Ministry of Public Works to the Ministry of National Education. Four funds were set up:

1. The General School Buildings Fund;

2. The State School Buildings Fund;

3. The Provincial and Municipal School Buildings Fund;

4. The National School Buildings Guarantee Fund.

In order to receive aid from these Funds, it is necessary that the school which requests it meets the criteria set by a rationalisation and programming plan and also the standards set by royal decree.

1. The general School Buildings Fund is a legally constituted body operating under State guarantee. Its purpose is—at the request of an organising body, and for those educational establishments set up after 1 January 1973, as also for State boarding schools set up after that date—to carry out the definitive infrastructural work and provide for later accommodation. It is managed by the two Ministers of National Education, each acting for the language network which concerns him, assisted by a Management Committee comprising representatives of the two State education language systems, representatives of the provincial and municipal education authorities and of the free educational network. Numerical equality as between representatives of the neutral and "involved" schools is ensured. Five hundred million francs were appropriated for the General School Buildings Fund during the 1974 fiscal year.

2. The State School Buildings Fund is entrusted with providing premises for the day and boarding schools set up prior to 1 January 1973; it may also provide temporary premises for schools set up after that date.

It is managed by the two Ministers of National Education, each for his own language network, aided by an advisory committee the composition and work of which are defined by the Ministers.

3. The Provincial and Municipal School Buildings Fund has the task of subsidising, at a maximum rate of 60%, the work of building,

modernising, enlarging and improving all constructions intended for subsidised provincial and municipal schools.

It is managed by the two Ministers of National Education who decide, each for his own network, whether subsidies should be granted and to what extent, and supervise the use to which the money is put and the way in which the work is performed.

4. The National School Buildings Guarantee Fund has a twofold task:

a) to guarantee the reimbursement, in capital, interest and extras, of loans contracted for the purpose of financing the work of improving, modernising and enlarging existing buildings intended for subsidised schools, or for the resiting of an existing school.

b) to grant, in respect of those loans, an interest subsidy as determined by the law.

It should be noted that loans are repayable at set rates per annum, and that their duration may not exceed forty years. The Guarantee Fund is administered by a Board of Directors composed of twenty-four members appointed by the King for a term of six years which is renewable. These members represent the Ministers of National Education; the Ministers of Culture, Finance, and the Budget; the free subsidised schools; and subsidised provincial and municipal schools.

The law of 11 July 1973 has extended the system of subsidised salaries paid to the management, teaching and auxiliary educational personnel to include members of the administrative staff whose grades are fixed by royal decree debated in the Cabinet, and to include personnel employed in boarding schools attached to homes for children whose parents have no fixed abode. In the network of special schools, subsidised salaries are also paid to members of the medical, paramedical, psychiatric and social personnel. The principle of these salary subsidies is to bring the total earnings of these people up to the same level as those employed in the State schools. However, the salary subsidies granted to those members of schools personnel who are priests or religious living in communities are smaller, and the percentage basis differs according to the level of education. The law stipulates that "a member of the staff who is a priest or a religious is regarded as living in a community when, as of 1 January 1973, he resided in the same building with at least five other members of the staff who were also priests or religious subsidised by the Ministry of National Education and Culture, and that he normally took his meals with them".

As for the annual, inclusive operating subsidies granted to provincial, municipal and private schools, the law of 11 July 1973 has increased the amount per pupil from 750 to 1.670 francs for kindergartens and pre-school education; from 1.000 to 2.230 francs for primary schools; from 3.250 to 6.040 francs for intermediate and secondary schools, and from 3.750 to 6.960 francs for normal and advanced educational establishments. These amounts which, in terms of the law of 29 May 1959, were tied to the retail price index, now fluctuate either way, half in ratio to the consumer price index and half in ratio to the evolution of gross hourly earnings. The operating subsidies must be allocated, on the basis of at least 33 per cent in kindergartens and primary schools and at least 20 per cent in secondary and advanced schools, to the salaries of maintenance and service personnel and workmen.

One central parity committee and several other parity committees have been set up for official subsidised schools on the one hand, and for free subsidised schools on the other. Their main task is to look into general working conditions, to prevent or reconcile disputes between the organising authorities and members of the teaching staff, and to establish a statutory disciplinary system for subsidised personnel.

Finally, it should be noted that as long as the plan for rationalisation and programming has not been published, the law provides that the law of 8 July 1966, aimed at placing a temporary brake on the development of the school networks, remains in force except in regard to university education; it also stipulates that no new loan may be guaranteed under the responsibility of the National School Buildings Guarantee Fund.

ARTICLE 18

"The press is free; no form of censorship may ever be instituted; no cautionary deposit may be demanded from writers, publishers or printers.

"When the author is known and is resident in Belgium, the publisher, printer or distributor may not be prosecuted."

This article dates from 1831 and has never been modified.

It should first be pointed out that the word "press" refers not only to the daily and periodical press, but also to the printing and distribution of books, booklets, pamphlets, circulars, etc.

As for the penal sanctions applicable to authors of press misdemeanours, the article under review deviates from common law in that it prohibits any prosecution of the accomplices. This derogatory measure is justified: indeed, the Constituent Assembly wished to abolish all forms of censorship for all time, but if the publisher, printer or distributor ran the risk of being regarded as accomplices of the author of a felonious piece of writing, then they would be forced to exercise some form of censorship in respect of the authors whose writings they print and distribute. That is why the publisher is only liable to prosecution if the author cannot be found; the printer is only so liable when the publisher is not available to answer for it; and finally, the distributor is only liable when all three—author, publisher and printer—have defaulted. This is known as "serial responsibility". In other words, where press misdemeanours are concerned, only one person may be prosecuted: as only one person is held to be responsible, the Constituent Assembly has abolished private and reciprocal censorship.

As for the punishment of press misdemeanours, it should be underlined that in terms of Article 98, a jury is empanelled to try such cases (in the Assize Courts).

Freedom of the press therefore entails the absence of any prior censorship. It does, however, raise certain problems, such as the enormous cost of founding a new paper, and the vast capital sums required to print and publish a daily newspaper. These economic factors have led to a situation where persons without a private fortune and social groups which do not have substantial financial backing find it materially impossible actively to exercise their freedom to publish. On the other hand, most newspapers—even those of divergent tendencies—have certain special interests in common. This situation is responsible for the fact that the pluralism of the daily press is to some extent more apparent than real. Furthermore, we are witnessing a progressive reduction in the number of newspapers issued.

The importance of this question has not escaped political and parliamentary circles in which the possibility of granting some form of government aid to the press is currently being studied. The wide range of political and philosophical options is itself such as to guarantee the neutrality of any government intervention. The law of 16 July 1973 ensuring the protection of ideological and philosophical opinions is clearly applicable in this instance.

Furthermore, the large number of periodicals, coupled with journals imported from other countries, allow the Belgian reader to benefit from a very real freedom of the press, a freedom that is indeed far from negligible.

It is therefore necessary to stress the distinction between the *passive* freedom of the press: that of all citizens to obtain and read all publications; and the *active* freedom of the press: that of writing, printing and publishing all manner of information and opinions.

By proclaiming the active freedom of the press, the 1830-1831 Constituent Assembly believed that a certain rivalry would be instituted between writers, publicists, journalists, printers and publishers, thus automatically accomplishing the passive freedom of the press, namely: the right of all citizens to be kept informed. This objective has largely been attained.

But Article 18 does not solve the problem—which, of course, had not arisen in 1830—of those information media which do not lend themselves to institutional plurality, namely: broadcasting by means of radio and television. In Belgium, the right of all citizens to information has been met in this case by a certain degree of plurality within the national radio and television network, because it would obviously be too difficult, in fact impossible, to provide for a number of different broadcasting stations.

ARTICLE 19

"Belgians have the right to hold peaceful, unarmed meetings; they must comply with the laws which may regulate the exercise of this right without, however, subjecting it to prior authorisation.

"This clause does not apply to open-air meetings which remain entirely subject to the police laws."

This article dates from 1831 and has never been modified.

Freedom to meet is the natural counterpart of the liberty of association laid down in Article 20.

The restriction placed upon this freedom to meet, which consists of the prohibition of coming armed to meetings, is merely a guarantee of the liberty of those who do not attend the meeting: the right of assembly carries with it the right not to attend a meeting. The word "peacefully" is a reminder that private meetings may not entail the use of force, the latter remaining the sole prerogative of the public authorities.

As for the second paragraph, it constitutes a reminder that the legislator and those authorities he has designated may, in the event of meetings held on the public highway or in some open-air place which is not closed to the public, decree all measures necessary to preserve law and order, including preventive measures.

In principle, it is the task of the municipal authorities to enact measures designed to ensure the tranquillity of the inhabitants. The constitutional ruling does not prevent town councils from establishing regulations calling for permission to be solicited prior to the organisation of public balls and other such functions.

ARTICLE 20

"Belgians have the right to associate; this right may not be subjected to any preventive measure."

This article dates from 1831 and has never been modified.

The question here is one of a basic right: indeed, a man does not only aspire to be free as an individual, he also wishes to associate with others for specific purposes.

The right of association comprises:

— freedom to set up an association;
— freedom to belong to an association of one's choice;
— freedom not to belong to an association;
— freedom to withdraw from an association.

It goes without saying that the ban on private militia troops (law of 29 July 1934) and the fact that the legislator has established that the setting up of associations for the purpose of attempts on private persons and property is a criminal act (Art. 322 of the Penal Code) do not run counter to the constitutional ruling.

The two kinds of association which are most important in the economic and social life of the country are unquestionably the commercial companies and the professional associations (such as the workers and employees unions). In politics, there are the political parties which, thanks to the freedom of association, are able to ensure the democratic functioning of State institutions at the municipal, provincial and national levels.

It is also obvious that the right of association may be exercised outside the political, economic and social spheres, and that Belgians may freely set up literary, artistic, philosophical, religious, philanthropic, sporting, fashionable and other associations.

ARTICLE 21

"Every person has the right to address petitions signed by one or several people to the public authorities.

"The constituted authorities alone have the right to send in collective petitions."

This article dates from 1831 and has never been modified.

The right of petition was far more important in the 19th century than it is today. Indeed, in those days there were certain categories of citizens who were not entitled to vote, and the possibility thus afforded them of addressing petitions to the public authorities was the only way in which these second-class citizens could make their views known to the authorities (the mayor and corporation, the permanent deputation or the government) or to the representative bodies (town council, provincial council, Houses of Parliament). Today, however, as electors the citizens may approach any and all elected representatives with the certainty of being heard.

Nevertheless, the right of petition has by no means fallen into abeyance, and the Belgians continue to send in petitions frequently to the various constituted authorities.

The House of Representatives, the Senate and the Cultural Councils have set up parliamentary commissions whose special task it is to examine the petitions received.

ARTICLE 22

"The secrecy of correspondence is inviolable.

"The law shall determine what agents are responsible for the violation of secrecy in the case of letters sent by post."

This article dates from 1831 and has never been modified.

It should be noted that the inviolable secrecy of correspondence is a defence against attempts perpetrated either by private persons or by agents and employees of the public authorities.

In fact, the constitutional principle of the secrecy of all correspondence sent in envelopes is equally applicable to cables, telegrams, and telephonic communications.

While the Constituent Assembly did not provide that the Legislative should place any restrictions on the freedom of correspondence, the latter has been brought to decree some exceptions: for instance, an examining magistrate may order the seizure of letters sent by, or addressed to, a person accused of a crime; similarly, the Official Receiver in a case of bankruptcy may open letters addressed to the bankrupt person.

It is an established custom that fathers and legal guardians are entitled to open and to withhold letters addressed to minor children entrusted to their care.

On the other hand, a husband has no right to read his wife's correspondence without her permission, and conversely.

ARTICLE 23

"The use of the languages spoken in Belgium is optional: it may only be regulated by law, and only in respect of acts by the public authorities and for legal matters."

This article dates from 1831 and has never been modified.

It sets the seal on linguistic freedom, since all private persons are free to choose the language they use, whereas the legislator's intervention is restricted to acts by the public authorities and to legal matters.

In 1970, however, the Constituent Assembly added a third sphere in which the Legislative may regulate the use of languages: that of social relations between employers and their personnel, and the acts and documents of business and industrial enterprises required by the laws and regulations. This normative competence has been vested in each of the Cultural Councils (see article 59-B).

The problem regarding the use of languages is one of capital importance in a country where French, Dutch and German are all spoken. It gave rise to numerous laws by means of which the Government and Parliament have attempted to put an end to the interminable linguistic controversies that were further complicated by philosophical, economic and social factors.

This process of evolution ended in the country being divided into linguistic regions, a division which was officially sanctioned by the Constituent Assembly in 1970 (see article 3-B).

As for the laws governing the use of languages, the first dates back to 1873 and pertained to legal matters. Others followed with respect to education at various levels, the public administration, and the armed forces.

Briefly, this range of linguistic legislation was inspired by the following principles:

a) the Dutch language is the only language to be used in the Dutch-speaking region by the judiciary, the municipal and provincial administrations, and in all official and free educational establishments;

b) the French language is the only language to be used in the French-speaking region by the judiciary, the municipal and provincial administrations, and in all official and free educational establishments;

c) the German language and, accessorily, the French language, are to be used in the German-speaking region by the judiciary, the municipal administrations, and in all official and free educational establishments;

53

d) the French and Dutch languages are both to be used on an equal footing in the bilingual region of Brussels-Capital by the judiciary, the municipal administrations, and in all official and free educational establishments;

e) the French and Dutch languages are both to be used on an equal footing in all the central public administrations;

f) the Belgian armed forces are to be bilingual so as to preserve their unity and cohesion.

It is doubtless useful to examine the machinery regulating the use of languages in the various spheres mentioned above:

A. THE USE OF LANGUAGES IN LEGAL MATTERS

The law of 15 June 1935 provided for the regulation of the use of languages in legal matters, and placed the use of Dutch and French on a footing of complete equality.

This law is based on some general principles which may be summed up as follows:

1) The unilingual nature of legal acts and procedure. The legislator wanted the entire procedure, from the writ of summons right up to the implementation of rulings and sentences, to be carried out in the same language. Bilingual or multilingual acts are null and void.

2) In Wallonia and in Flanders, in obedience to the principle of their territorial status, it is the language of the region concerned which is the determining factor.

3) As the Brussels urban district is bilingual, it is the language of the interested party (the accused or the defendant) which is chosen in this area.

4) The individual liberty of each citizen regarding the use of language is preserved. Linguistic regulations apply only to magistrates, judiciary officials, the Bar, and official deeds and documents.

5) Any infringement of these regulations usually renders such acts null and void.

Any commentary on the law of 15 June 1935 regarding the use of languages in legal matters must operate a distinction between civil and criminal procedures.

1) *Civil procedure:*

Clauses 1 and 2 of the law stipulate that jurisdictions the seat of which is established in the Hainaut, Liège, Luxemburg and Namur provinces and in the French-speaking district of Nivelles, shall use the French language; while those jurisdictions the seat of which is established in the Antwerp, East Flanders, West Flanders and Limburg provinces and in the district of Louvain, shall use the Dutch language.

In the Brussels region, the language used is that spoken by the defendant.

In the German-speaking regions of Eupen and Saint-Vith, the procedural language is German, but the defendant may request that the procedure be undertaken in French. For Malmédy, the inverse is true.

When both parties in agreement request that procedure be undertaken in the other national language, the affair is referred to the nearest court of the same order in the other language region, or to that designated by the unanimous choice of the parties concerned (clause 7).

If papers or documents prepared in a language other than the procedural language are presented in court, the judge may, at the request of the party against whom such papers or documents are being offered as testimony, order them to be translated (Clause 8).

2) *Criminal procedure:*

With particular reference to criminal proceedings, it should be pointed out that the reports concerning the investigation and establishment of misdemeanours and felonies by the police and the gendarmerie must be written in French or in Dutch in the abovementioned unilingual regions, as dictated by the language of the region concerned. In the Brussels region, the choice of language is determined by the person who is the subject of the report. In the German-speaking municipalities, the language to be used is German except in certain bilingual regions where the person concerned may if he wishes opt for French. (Clause 11).

The procedural language to be used in courts and tribunals in the unilingual regions is dictated by the place in which they are sitting (Clause 14). In courts and tribunals established in Brussels, the procedural language is determined by the place of residence of the accused should he live outside the Brussels urban area (Clause 15). Should he live within this area, the defendant's choice is the decisive factor (Clause 16).

In police courts at Eupen and Saint-Vith, the procedure is conducted in German; in the German-French bilingual regions, the defendant may choose either of these two languages (Clause 17).

The law regulates the use of languages not only with regard to police courts and courts of summary jurisdiction, but also with regard to the commercial and labour courts, military tribunals, the assize courts, appeal courts, and the Court of Cassation.

A defendant who is only able to speak Dutch, or French, may request that a translation be added to his file of any document prepared in another language, i.e. reports, summonses, statements by witnesses, reports by experts (Clause 22). The accused may also request to be judged by a court in which the procedural language is his own national language. In such cases, the affair is referred to that court (Clause 23).

3) *Provisions common to both (1) and (2) above:*

When the judges, judicial agents or magistrates in charge of the investigation or hearing of a case do not understand the language spoken by the defendant, then they call on the services of a sworn translator. Translating expenses are borne by the State (Clause 30).

Every procedural act and every judgment which must be made known in another language region, with the exception of the Brussels urban area, must have a translation appended in the language of the region concerned (Clause 38).

4) *Other provisions:*

After thus regulating the procedural use of languages, the law goes on to lay down the conditions which must be met by the judiciary organisation and the knowledge of languages which magistrates, registrars and jurymen must possess. Similar regulations are also laid down for notaries-public and lawyers.

B. THE USE OF LANGUAGES BY THE PUBLIC ADMINISTRATION

The authority to regulate the use of languages in acts by the public authorities, vested in the Legislative by Article 23 of the 1831 Constitution, was only exercised in the administrative sphere for the first time by the law of 22 May 1878. Subsequently, legislative intervention was broadened and clarified in step with the development of contemporary thinking on the subject of the equality of the national languages and the unilingual character of the two regions.

Today, the use of languages in administrative matters is regulated meticulously and in great detail by the coordinated laws of 18 July 1966 (*Moniteur belge* of 2 August 1966).

The sphere of application of the latter is vast indeed: it embraces not only all the centralised and decentralised public offices of the State, the provinces, the urban areas, the federations of boroughs and the municipalities, but also the concessionaries and licence-holders of public services, the administrative acts accomplished by the judiciary, the

Council of State, the Audit Office, the educational authorities, and even private enterprise to the extent that the laws apply to the acts and documents required by law or intended for the use of personnel.

The laws governing the use of languages in administrative matters are public and mandatory. Any administrative acts and regulations the form or content of which is at variance with those laws are automatically regarded as null and void.

As a principle, these laws impose the exclusive use, in each language region, of the language of that region, subject to the special cases outlined hereunder.

1. *French-language region and Dutch-language region:*

The public offices, both local and regional, established there must exclusively use the language of the region in their internal operations, their relations with the administrations on which they depend or with other services in the same region and in the area of Brussels-Capital; in the notices, communications and forms intended for the public, their dealings with individual citizens, the drafting of documents pertaining to individual citizens, the transcription of birth, marriage and death certificates, and in all other certificates, statements, warrants and authorisations granted to private citizens.

However, some boroughs in these two regions—the so-called "linguistic frontier boroughs" (1) enumerated in Clause 8, paras. 3 to 10 of the coordinated laws, together with the Malmédy boroughs (2) where the inhabitants speak German—have been given a special regime for the purpose of protecting their minority groups. The facilities granted to those minorities pertain solely to relations between public offices and private citizens; thus, the notices and communications intended for the general public are drafted in the language of the region and in that of the protected minority; certificates from the public records are established in the language requested by the person concerned; and the public authorities address private citizens in the language used by the latter, or for which they express a preference; furthermore, the persons concerned may obtain a translation of any documents affecting them.

---

(1) In the district of Ypres: the borough of Lessines; in the district of Courtrai: the boroughs of Espierres and Helchin; in the district of Mouscron: the boroughs of Bas-Warneton, Comines, Dottignies, Herseaux, Houthem, Luigne, Mouscron, Ploegsteert and Warneton; in the district of Audenarde: the borough of Renaix; in the district of Ath: the borough of Flobecq; in the district of Hal-Vilvorde: the borough of Biévène; in the district of Soignies: the boroughs of Enghien, Marcq and Petit-Enghien; in the district of Tongres: the boroughs of Fouron-le-Comte, Fouron-Saint-Martin, Fouron-Saint-Pierre, Herstappe, Mouland, Remersdaal and Teuven.

(2) See page 214.

Finally, six so-called "peripheral" boroughs bordering on the urban area of Brussels-Capital (1) have also been endowed with a special linguistic status. The public authorities use the Dutch language, but facilities are granted to the French-speaking minority.

2. German-language region:

The public authorities use the German language, but the entire region has been given a special regime to protect the French-speaking minority. Such facilities relate solely to private citizens and are identical to those granted in the "linguistic frontier boroughs" and the Malmédy boroughs.

3. Brussels-Capital bilingual region:

Local and regional public offices established in the administrative district of Brussels-Capital use either French or Dutch depending on where the case is located, what language is chosen by the private citizen concerned or, failing this, the language of the official dealing with the matter. Deeds and documents relating to private persons and the certificates, statements, warrants and authorisations delivered to them, are drawn up in French or in Dutch at the choice of the person concerned. As for the notices, communications and forms intended for the general public, these are prepared in both French and Dutch.

4. Central administrative offices:

The central offices, i.e. those whose affairs cover the entire country, use the language of the region concerned in their dealings with local and regional offices in the French, Dutch or German language regions.

In their dealings with private persons and the drafting of documents, certificates, statements and warrants, they use whichever of the three languages is used or requested by the persons concerned.

Notices and communications issued directly to the general public are drafted in French and in Dutch; those issued through the medium of local offices are subject to the regulations imposed on those offices.

In their internal operations and their dealings with public offices in Brussels-Capital, the central administrative offices use the language dictated by the location of the affair, that spoken by the private citizen who initiated it, or again the language of the official called upon to deal with the matter.

---

(1) See page 15.

C. THE USE OF LANGUAGES IN THE EDUCATIONAL SPHERE

The freedom of education enshrined in Article 17 of the Constitution is exercised subject to certain conditions when the State assumes the expense of education or subsidises it. The State enacts regulations governing compulsory school attendance, implementation of the curriculum, the verification and homologation of marks and results, and the establishment, approval and organisation of schools and colleges. From this standpoint, the regulation of education and schooling within the context of one or the other of the national languages was a necessary corollary that developed progressively in line with the evolving policy on the general use of languages.

Whereas the law of 14 July 1932 laid down that the language of the region was compulsory in primary and secondary schools, the law of 30 July 1963 extended this principle to embrace kindergartens, teachers' training colleges and all technical colleges, art schools or special educational establishments.

The territorial limits are those laid down by the law of 2 August 1963. As for Brussels, legislation provides that the mother-tongue decides the language in which the child is to be taught, and it has also instituted the obligatory teaching of the second national language.

As for the 25 boroughs of the linguistic frontier which are now part of either the French or the Dutch region, schooling in a language other than that of the region concerned may no longer be provided in terms of the law of 30 July 1963 save on condition that a certain number of heads of families specifically request it, and that they adduce proof of the distance between their place of residence and a school which teaches in their language.

In the German-speaking region, a few exceptions are made to the general principle of upholding the language of the region as the educational language. Part of the curriculum may be taught in French by German-speaking schools, and in German by French-speaking schools, starting from the third grade of primary school. In terms of Clause 6 of the law of 30 July 1963, there can however be no derogation of the general principle in kindergartens and primary schools except for those children for whom German is not their mother-tongue or usual language. French-language secondary schools have no legal existence in boroughs of the German-speaking region. However, the Royal Decree of 30 November 1966 has defined how teaching is to be organised in German-language secondary schools, in which half the lessons may be taught in French in the three lowest classes, and two-thirds may be so taught in the upper classes.

The European Schools at Uccle in Brussels and at Mol in Limburg are, for their part, governed by a protocol of agreement signed on 13 April 1962, by the six Member States of the European Community on the basis of the statutes dated 12 April 1957 governing the European School in Luxemburg. These schools are open to children of the staff of the European Communities and to other children of foreign nationalities. Such schools do not come under the provisions of the language laws because they are the subject of international treaties. As for Belgian pupils, they remain subject to Belgian law.

As for university education, the law of 15 April 1930 made the State University of Ghent entirely Flemish, thus placing it on the same footing as the State University of Liège which, located as it is in the Walloon region, is entirely French-speaking. The free universities (Louvain Catholic and Brussels Free) have followed the same course of evolution designed to uphold the right of members of both the language communities to be educated at all levels in their own languages, especially since the State's financial aid in the form of subsidies to both these universities has grown to substantial dimensions. The siting of the French-language Catholic University of Louvain is governed by Article 132 of the Constitution, since the city of Louvain itself is located in the Dutch-language region. So the *Katholieke Universiteit Leuven* (K.U.L.) will stay in the city of Louvain, while the *Université Catholique de Louvain* (U.C.L.) is being progressively installed in the Walloon region on a site called "New Louvain" within the territory of Ottignies, and also in the bilingual territory of Brussels, at *Woluwe-Saint-Lambert,* where the Faculty of Medicine will have its permanent abode.

Brussels Free University instituted a Flemish-language Faculty of Law as far back as 1935. But the whole university was entirely duplicated in 1969 when the *Université Libre de Bruxelles* (U.L.B.) was rounded off by the *Vrije Universiteit Brussel* (V.U.B.) A law of 25 May 1970 sets the seal on this development.

D. THE USE OF LANGUAGES IN THE ARMED FORCES

For the language system set up in respect of the armed forces by the law of 7 November 1928, some ten years later the legislator substituted a new set of rules intended to consecrate the complete equality of the two national languages.

These rules are embodied in the law of 30 July 1938 governing the use of languages in the armed forces (published in the *Moniteur belge* of 22-23 August 1938) which, in turn, has been the subject of four subsequent amendments (the laws of 30 July 1955 and 27 December 1961, the Royal Decree of 15 October 1963, and the law of 10 June 1970).

This law provides for the grouping of soldiers into units according to language : French, Dutch or German, so that their complete training can be given in the soldiers' mother-tongue. Furthermore, all ranks of commissioned and non-commissioned officers must, in terms of this law, be conversant with the second national language and, if they are called upon to take command of a German-speaking unit, they must know German as well.

In this way, the programme covering the knowledge of languages required at the preliminary examination for promotion to officer rank (entrance examination to the Royal Military Academy, or preparatory examination for promotion from the ranks to Sub-Lieutenant) calls for a thorough knowledge of one of the two national languages and a working knowledge of the other.

Promotion to the rank of Sub-Lieutenant is subordinated to a knowledge of the second national language in order that the candidate for promotion is capable of being appointed to serve with a unit belonging to either of the national languages.

A thorough knowledge of both languages is required for promotion to all field-officers' ranks above that of captain.

Furthermore, the law has made all the necessary arrangements to ensure that training, orders, communications, commands, internal and inter-service relations, and general administration work are carried out in the language of the unit concerned.

This goes for internal operations, while relations with civil authorities and the general public are governed by the integral implementation of the laws regulating the use of languages in administrative matters, coordinated by the Royal Decree of 18 July 1966 published in the *Moniteur belge* of 2 August 1966.

An extension and expression of the Nation, the armed forces must of necessity be the privileged meeting-place of all classes of society, who are represented there as a result of the military service imposed on all male citizens.

Briefly, the law of 30 July 1938 does more than aim at consolidating the unity of the armed forces by guaranteeing the equality of all citizens who serve in them : it ensures that the armed forces identify with the social body of the nation in all its linguistic variety.

To make sure that the law was duly implemented, a clause 31-B was added in 1955 to institute an ad hoc commission of control. The use of the right to appeal to that commission, which has become the regulating body that ensures implementation of the law, became less and less frequent as time went by until recourse to it has been virtually unknown over the last three years.

Which leads one to conclude that the objectives of the law have been achieved.

ARTICLE 24

"No prior authorization is necessary to bring an action against civil servants with regard to their administrative acts, except as elsewhere specified for Ministers."

This article dates from 1831 and has never been modified.

If it were necessary to secure prior authorization in order to bring a legal action against a civil servant, it might be feared that such an official could, with impunity, jeopardize the rights and liberties of other citizens.

Furthermore, such impunity would be a privilege in complete contradiction to the principle of equality stated in Article 6. This kind of exception to the rule whereby all citizens are equal would only be acceptable if it were justified by the public interest. Such is not the case, however, for the impunity thus conferred would not only cover the acts regularly performed by a civil servant in the line of duty, but also any abuses of which he may be guilty.

As for the penal responsibility of Cabinet Ministers, this is dealt with in Articles 90 and 134.

Heading II of the Constitution (Articles 4 to 24) dealing with the rights vested in Belgian citizens, is today regarded as being incomplete.

For instance, the following are not mentioned:

— the right to work;
— the right to leisure and recreation;
— the right to participate in cultural activities;
— the right to security of existence in the event of sickness, disability and old age.

Other rights which are not expressly acknowledged by the Constitution but which are today part and parcel of the political rights enjoyed by all Belgians, must be seen in conjunction with certain rights already acknowledged by the 1831 Constituent Assembly:

— the freedom to form or join a trades union (which stems from the right of meeting and of association);
— the right of information (which is connected with the freedom of the press);

— the right to education (closely akin to the *freedom* of education);

— the right of privacy (which embraces the inviolability of the home and the secrecy of correspondence).

During the Third Revision of the Constitution (1967-1971) there were many proposals that these rights and liberties should be formally written into the Constitution. The reason why this was not done is that the Legislative, in the course of ordinary business, had already acknowledged them implicitly by passing a whole series of laws designed to uphold and implement them.

HEADING III

THE AUTHORITIES

FOREWORD

Before embarking on the chapter dealing with the exercise of authority, it seems useful to open a parenthesis in order to prevent any confusion, by drawing the reader's attention to a very important aspect: the way in which the exercise of political authority in Belgium has evolved since the second half of the 20th century.

Articles 63, 64 and 89 of the Constitution provide that the King may only exercise his powers under cover of the countersignature of his Ministers who alone are responsible to the Legislative Houses.

At the present time, whenever the Constitution mentions the King as head of the Executive, it actually refers to the Executive authority as a whole, i.e. the King who is constitutionally irresponsible, and the Government which is responsible to Parliament. It goes without saying that in this kind of political set-up, that of the Monarchy in a modern parliamentary democracy, political initiative and the day-to-day management of State business is the task of the Government. From the standpoint of the present-day concept of monarchy, and to use a term hallowed by custom, every reference to the King actually means "the King and his Cabinet", i.e. the King and the members of his Government, any political act of the King's accomplished without the consent of his Ministers being absolutely out of the question.

The Cabinet government system, whereby the team of Ministers in office reflects the parliamentary majority, necessarily implies that the Government is the active factor. Such a system inevitably sets the seal on the Government's fundamental role as the essential directing and coordinating body in charge of State affairs.

This modern variant of the parliamentary system cannot be construed purely and simply as a restriction of the part played by a hereditary Head of State in a active democracy. Quite the opposite: the psychological influence of the King as the national arbiter is of crucial importance. Indeed, the political irresponsibility of the Head of State in a parliamentary democracy places him above and beyond any suspicion of partiality. It is a striking fact that all the monarchies which have managed to survive into the second half of the 20th century are parliamentary monarchies. In this connection one may possibly draw the conclusion that the monarchy and the parliamentary system have exercised in the past what might be described as a mutual, reciprocal protective influence and, what is more, that they still do so today.

ARTICLE 25

"All powers stem from the Nation.

"They are exercised in the manner laid down by the Constitution."

This article dates from 1831 and has never been modified.

In Belgium, this article is the very foundation-stone of democracy. It arises out of fundamental concepts which it is important to define or summarise.

A nation is a number of people living together in a specific territory. It is the Belgian nation itself which the Constituent Assembly has established as the basis of the State. The State, therefore, is the Nation as it is organised on the judicial and political planes.

Thus, in Belgium, democracy is founded on national sovereignty. This sovereignty is inalienable, in the sense that the nation as such fundamentally possesses it. In this way, the competence which the nation confers on this or that body is always revocable, and indeed it is revoked through the medium of constitutional reform on the basis of Article 131.

Such sovereignty is not, however, absolute for it is subject to certain legal limits, in particular those laid down by the Constitution itself.

These limits consist first of all in the individual liberties enumerated in Chapter II which, so to speak, constitutes a preserve. This preserve is not placed above the law, but if its freedoms have to be regulated, this can only be done by the Legislative.

Another restriction placed on the absolute nature of national sovereignty is provided for in the Constitution by means of procedural organisation : the two-chamber parliamentary system, the separation of powers, etc.

The national sovereignty intended by the Constituent Assembly is not the same as the sovereignty of the people.

Where the sovereignty of the people is the rule, it is the assembled people who are in charge of the direct government of the country, in such a way that democracy is totalitarian in character and that each citizen personally wields a part of the collective power.

On the contrary, where the question is one of national sovereignty, the nation delegates its powers to some extent to a representative government, and the democratic system thus set up is endowed with a counter-weight, notably inherent in the separation of powers.

Article 25 also raises the question of what power is. The definition of "powers" in this context refers not only to the functions themselves, but also to the bodies that exercise them.

In the tradition originally represented by Montesquieu and his disciples, a tradition resumed and continued early in the 19th century, the Belgian Constituent Assembly has in fact based the institutions of the State on the theory of the separation of powers without, however, formally enshrining this principle in the fundamental charter. In fact, this theory has been tempered somewhat, for while the powers are indeed separate and while each theoretically is independent of the others in its own sphere, this is not to say that they form three distinct blocs in juxtaposition to each other but that they co-operate closely in the genuine protection of the rights of all citizens.

The separation of power involves the separation of bodies which, again in theory, are themselves sovereign ones, meaning that each is independent of the other two in its own sphere.

Immediately the separate powers begin to co-operate with each other, we shall see that the driving force is provided chiefly by the government.

These principles of national sovereignty and the separation of powers virtually allow of no derogation. Any delegation of the powers granted by the Constitution would end in a violation of the Constitution itself.

We shall see, however, that such delegations of authority have been admitted in practice when special and serious circumstances have, for instance, justified the granting of special powers to the Executive.

Similarly, as each power is in principle separate, it may not control either of the others save in accordance with the constitutional rules. In this way, the Belgian Constitution does not provide for any verification of constitutionality, and even less for any form of judicial censure of laws.

As worded, Article 25 precludes for instance the practice of referendums as it exists in some countries. This applies equally to a decision-making referendum and to a consultative referendum. We shall, however, see that owing to serious circumstances, Parliament did authorise a national consultation in 1950 although such a procedure is not constitutional; but it did so in terms of its residual competence.

The second sentence of Article 25 therefore indicates clearly that the Constituent Assembly wished to prevent the setting-up of a "policy state", i.e. a state wherein decisions are made on the basis of circumstances and individual cases. Its purpose even went beyond that of setting up a "state of law". The latter is already sufficient to guarantee the equality of all citizens in legal matters (cfr. Art. 6) but it does not necessarily rely on any hierarchy in the rules themselves.

In actual fact, the Belgian Constituent Assembly has set up a "state of legality", meaning that not only the equality of all citizens is guaranteed in terms of the regulations, but that the latter themselves must be based on law. The best implementation of this concept is Article 78 which lays down that the King may only act within the limits granted to him either by the Constitution itself, or by the laws enacted on the basis of that same Constitution.

*
* *

It goes without saying that while the three powers are theoretically separate and independent each in its own sphere, there are nevertheless certain relationships between them.

In the first place, the Constitution is the supreme rule to which all powers are subject, including the Legislative power. The Constitution is anterior to the separate existence of each of the powers. Yet we already know that the pre-eminence of the Constitution is a theoretical one, since there is no verification of constitutionality and the legislator, in the laws he enacts, is deemed in all cases to respect the formal provisions of the fundamental charter. Furthermore, where the Constitution is concerned, the Legislative power occupies a privileged position :

— firstly, the constituent function is vested in the same bodies as the legislative function. The only changes occur in regard to procedures and the requisite majorities;

— the legislator wields residual powers whereas the two other powers only wield such authority as is formally vested in them by the Constitution; in law, the term "residual powers" means that the legislator is vested with all powers of whatever kind, save only those which are formally denied him by the Constitution itself.

— the Judiciary power is not competent to pronounce on the constitutionality of any law;

— Article 28 of the Constitution confers on the Legislative alone the power to interpret laws authoritatively, and this includes the fundamental law — the Constitution itself.

The pride of place thus granted to the Legislative goes a long way to explaining the judicial pre-eminence it has acquired over the other two powers.

The pre-eminence of the Legislative has, however, itself altered as time went by, to such an extent that it even seems to have dwindled as the Executive branch grew in importance, particularly the government.

Alongside the powers that exist by right, there have in fact come to the fore an increasing number of *de facto* authorities. The latter consist chiefly of the political parties, which are often regarded today as the real powers in the State because they are the spokesmen or voice of the electorate. The political parties in Belgium are permanent citizens' organisations representing all the various trends of public opinion, whose purpose is the conquest and exercise of public authority with a view to implementing a given programme. Political democracy is in fact founded on a multiplicity of political parties, which enables the elector to make his choice when he is called upon to vote in a free and democratically organised election. Even though they are the real holders of political power, the parties are de facto organisations without any definitive legal status. They have, however, received official recognition in the Rules of the Belgian Houses of Parliament, where they are referred to as political groups. (1)

Yet, vast as they are, these powers are subject to limitations Furthermore, they vary from one party to another since some of them, on the basis of their composition, seniority and representative character, have come to be regarded as national parties with a vocation for government. Hence they have greater scope for participation in political affairs even though they may temporarily find themselves on the opposition benches.

The powers of the parties are subject to other limitations, in the sense that they themselves are subjected to the action of a growing number of pressure groups. The first of these are what is known as the "social partners", meaning the great associations of employers and the trades unions. These organisations exert an overwhelming influence on the life of the nation. Other, more specialised, pressure groups include such bodies as the mutual societies, professional associations such as those of the dispensing chemists or the medical profession, the farmers' unions, the women's movements, war veterans, old-age pensioners,

---

(1) Each political group must comprise at least three members. They meet once a week at least in order to designate their official spokesmen, chart their political strategy, or make political options.

The Steering Committee of the Lower House recently made a decision regarding increased subsidies to the political groups, a decision that was ratified by the House when it examined the Endowment Budget. This decision comprises the four following points : (1) the granting of an annual subsidy on the basis of 200.000 francs (tied to the C.O.L. index) per member, to be paid to the political groups with effect from 1 September 1974; (2) the subsidy is to be used in order to facilitate the work of Members of Parliament, the group, the party offices, exclusive of any expenditure on election campaigning; (3) the use to which the subsidy is put will be supervised by the House Steering Committee which, for this purpose, delegates its authority to the Accountancy Committee; (4) the decision as to which groups will receive the subsidy shall be made by the Steering Committee. In actual fact, all the groups already recognised in terms of the Rules will benefit.

The Senate has made a similar decision.

youth movements, language groups, religious bodies, and so forth. Nor should the vital part played by the press be forgotten in considering all the factors influencing the political life of the country.

The coexistence of *de jure* and *de facto* powers had to find some meeting-point, and this turned out to be the Government. That is why, with a few exceptions, governments have to an increasing extent become coalitions, or what is sometimes called "Cabinet administrations".

In fact, since 1919, Belgium has experienced only one single legislature between 1950 and 1954 in which there was an outright one-party majority. And even that majority can be explained as being the result of the troubles arising out of the royal question (King Leopold's abdication). On the other hand, except for two brief exceptions in 1925 and in 1946, every other government since 1919 was a coalition government. This phenomenon has inevitably affected the way in which statutory powers are exercised, even though constitutional rules have always been formally respected.

Coalition or Cabinet governments arise out of a prior agreement reached between the majority parties; the agreement is sealed by a "government pact" submitted for the approval of Parliament.

In this way, as will be indicated also when discussing Article 65, the King has seen his authority to appoint and dismiss his Ministers greatly modified, and a new institution has appeared on the political scene, known as the Council of Ministers (or Cabinet). The growing importance of the Council has moreover just been acknowledged by the Constitution which, apart from recognising its existence in exceptional circumstances outlined in Article 79, has now confirmed its permanent existence under Article 86-B.

Consequently, the question is no longer one of Ministers as separate and individual persons forming a government, but of a group of Ministers regarded as an entity.

Similarly, another result has been that early dissolutions of Parliament are generally no longer due to a vote of no-confidence by the Legislative in respect of the Executive, but to the rifts and breakdowns occurring in the Cabinet itself.

So today it happens that conflicts no longer oppose the Legislative and the Executive powers in Parliament so much as in former days; they have shifted to new ground as between the majority and the opposition, the Government as such reflecting the majority.

The Executive, and the Government in particular, has thus come to occupy a very important place since it is, so to speak, the executive arm of the political parties forming the majority. It is the government which is today the real stake in the contest between the parties, and it is the medium whereby the parties forming the majority try to implement their programme.

The Government has thus acquired an additional measure of prestige from the moment it is honoured by the confidence of Parliament, or in other words that of the majority which supports it. Parliament's role, therefore, has necessarily evolved, since the parliamentary work is first prepared by the Government which must ensure the proper conduct of parliamentary business in order to carry out its programme. Generally speaking, it is the Government which tables the bills and proposals that end up as laws, the budgets which it knows in advance will be approved insofar as it enjoys the confidence of its parliamentary majority; the government no longer runs the risk of encountering orders of the day that indict its policies, votes of no-confidence, etc. This situation is all the more real because the parties which have won the largest number of seats in Parliament, and which therefore form the majority, feel that they can rely on the support of the electorate which gave them their majority. In this way, the growing preponderance of the government is not at variance with the exigencies of democracy.

The reason why the first Constituent Assembly of 1831 was distrustful of the Executive branch was that the latter was then under the strong personal influence of the King. But when the government represents powerful political parties who have been voted into power by the people, then it feels that its legitimacy is in keeping with true democracy.

From this standpoint, and as long as the parliamentary majority holds together, the opposition parties must restrict themselves to supervising and criticising the Government's work.

It will be apparent from the foregoing that the separation of powers, as between the Legislative and the Executive, has become extremely blurred since, on the one hand, Parliament does in fact remain all-powerful through the Government which was formed from its majority, while on the other hand the Government itself, backed by that majority, is no longer afraid of being disowned by Parliament.

To get an exact picture of the relationship between the Legislative Houses and the Government in Belgium, it will be necessary to bear in mind that the activities of the Executive cannot be dissociated from the functions of the Legislative. Apart from its task of constant supervision of the use to which the State's money is put, Parliament—and the parliamentary majority in particular—has, as we have already seen, one essential function, and that is : to provide the country with a government that enjoys its confidence and which is thereby enabled to carry out its programme in stable conditions, and having done that, to keep such a government in office as long as possible. In turn the Government, relying as it does on Parliament, must ensure that parliamentary business is conducted smoothly and efficiently in accordance with its general policy. As the Government has developed into the prime mover of parliamentary work, it has come ipso facto to direct the work of legislation. Again, the stability of a government pre-supposes a loyal majority, and in important matters this is often reflected by a vote of discipline. Such discipline can only stem from strongly organised political parties desirous of avoiding too-frequent changes of Cabinet. Finally, the separation of authority—and particularly that of the Executive and the Legislative powers—has in fact been replaced by a degree of unity such that the power of decision belongs more and more to a coalition, the composition of which varies and in which the preponderant political forces of the moment and the powerful socio-economic bodies all exert maximum influence. It should also be noted that certain outstanding politicians who enjoy the confidence of several groups thereby occupy a very important position indeed where decision-making is concerned.

It should however be emphasized that this major evolution in practical terms of the way in which the three main authorities function, is nevertheless fully in keeping with constitutional rules, for these have been framed with such flexibility that the evolutionary process has been accomplished perfectly smoothly, with no sudden shocks that would be prejudicial to the vital interests of the nation.

Thus, in the eyes of nearly all Belgians, a parliamentary democracy remains, despite all its imperfections, the best and indeed the only acceptable form of government. To the vast majority of citizens, Parliament—the supreme expression of the sovereign will of the nation and also the supreme authority within the Parliamentary system—is the very corner-stone of democracy.

ARTICLE 25-B

"The exercise of given powers may be conferred by a treaty or law on institutions coming under international civil law."

This is an entirely new article voted in the House of Representatives on 28 May 1970, in the Senate on 7 July following, and promulgated on 20 July 1970. Apart from the urgent national problems awaiting its attention, the 1967-1971 Constituent Assembly also wished to bring the Constitution into line with the evolving prospects of Europe and the world at large, taking into account the existence of the European Economic Community.

Already in 1950 Belgium had participated in the foundation of the European Coal and Steel Community, set up under the Treaty of Paris of 18 April 1951 and ratified by a Belgian Act of Parliament on 15 June 1952.

Thereafter, Belgium helped to found the European Economic Community and the European Atomic Energy Community, both instituted by the Treaties of Rome signed on 15 March 1957 and ratified in Belgium by Act of Parliament on 2 December 1957.

Earlier though, in 1952, when Parliament was called upon to ratify the Treaty of Paris setting up the European Coal and Steel Community, the jurists were voicing their doubts concerning the compatibility of such treaties with Article 25 of the Constitution. It must be remembered indeed that Article 25 is a fundamental ruling and that it is the real basis of the whole political system in Belgium, since it states that the Nation itself is the seat of national sovereignty and that it is up to the people alone to provide themselves with the political institutions of their choice. In this regard, the original wording of the Constitution was a true reflection of the political thinking of the day at a time when international relations were more or less elementary in character. It is sufficient to recall that towards the end of the 18th century two German writers, Pütter and Ompteda, could only distinguish three kinds of treaties all dealing with the regulation of relations between States.

Yet how rapidly matters have evolved in this sphere, for not only have we witnessed a multiplication of treaties and the inclusion of their contents in the internal juridical systems of the signatory States, but we have also witnessed the appearance of numerous international and even supranational institutions. To the extent that these new bodies are empowered to enact measures that automatically become legally binding in each of the member States without any formal ratification being necessary; to the extent that such international authorities are qualified to make decisions against which there exists no form of legal and national appeal, a regime of supranationality has thus been created, and this opens a wide breach in the fundamental principle written into Article 25 of the Constitution. That will explain why Parliament was so hesitant when it was called upon to ratify the treaties instituting the European Communities. In the first place, it was inconceivable that Belgium should abstain from doing so, since she is situated geographically at the very heart of the new Communities. On the other hand, a revision of the Constitution in 1952 to settle this problem alone seemed inopportune.

Parliament nevertheless gave its approval to the treaties in question when it received assurances that the Constitution would be revised later in order to justify Belgium's membership of the new organisations. Thus, the decision to revise the Constitution which was made in 1954 arose partly from the need to make the first European treaties compatible with Articles 25 and 68 of the Fundamental Charter. For reasons connected with internal politics, this first attempt at revision did not go through, and neither did the next attempt which was to have been made during the following legislature from 1958 to 1961. Subsequently the Commission for Institutional Reform looked into the problem and gave its opinion that the Constitution should specifically provide for the possibility of conferring certain powers on the supranational organisations, and that this possibility should be sanctioned in precise terms in the form of a separate article 25-B.

While it gave due consideration to the conclusions reached by the Commission, the government of the day nevertheless thought that such an article was unnecessary; it proposed as an alternative that Article 68 should be revised in order to permit a more precise formulation of the rules pertaining to parliamentary approval of certain categories of international agreements, together with a more flexible approach to the ratification procedure. Furthermore, the Government proposed to insert under Chapter III of Heading III of the Constitution a new article 107-B designed to settle the question of the non-application of those provisions of internal law that might be at variance with international law or with the community law issuing from supranational institutions.

The Houses followed the government's lead where the revision of Article 68 and the introduction of Article 107-B were concerned, but considering those measures insufficient, they added a further proposal to the Government project calling for the insertion of an Article 25-B to rule on the juridical situation arising out of the setting up of international institutions. It was this Statement by the Houses, and the corresponding Statement by the King, which were published in the *Moniteur belge* (official gazette) on 17 April 1965.

On their side, the Prime Minister and the Minister of Foreign Affairs submitted to the Parliamentary Committees on 22 April 1967 a working paper containing a draft text for each of the three articles 25-B, 68 and 107-B. Thus, initially, Article 25-B was merely one of the panels in a triptych of clauses intended to settle the problem of any contradiction or conflict that might arise between the national sovereignty and the supranational institutions.

The dissolution of Parliament, which took place on 29 September 1971, put a full stop to Parliament's task as a Constituent Assembly, since the new Houses that convened as a result of the general election held on 7 November 1971 were not acknowledged as holding constituent powers. That explains why neither Article 68 nor Article 107-B were debated, and why the Constitution therefore remains unchanged on this point.

The Constituent Assembly was therefore obliged to abandon its task before it had accomplished all it set out to do, and this situation places the jurists in front of some undeniable difficulties. Indeed, while Article 25-B authorises the granting of certain powers to institutions set up under international law, the conditions governing the transfer of such authority have not been defined; Article 68 in particular, unchanged as it is, now reveals a number of lacunae and ambiguities. This question will be dealt with farther on, under the heading of Article 59-B, in connection with the Cultural Councils on the plane of international cultural co-operation.

The wording in the draft text of Article 25-B as proposed by the Government in 1967 differs only little from the wording finally adopted. In fact, the draft read as follows :

"The exercise of given competences may be conferred by a law or a treaty on persons coming under international civil law."

Concise though it was, this text nonetheless gave rise to lengthy debates, in such a way that every term used can be commented in detail.

1. Firstly, the term "exercise".

The use of this term shows that Parliament had no intention of allowing the relinquishment, pure and simple, of any forms of authority or powers.

In the first place, this term upholds the fundamental principle of Article 25, since the Nation remains the source of all the powers exercised in Belgium, but it will now be possible to delegate the exercise of one or another of these powers to a specific organisation. Parliament has thus reacted with caution, in the event that some institutions might vanish from the international scene, or that they might be set up for a limited period only. Should such institutions disappear, the Nation would automatically resume the exercise of a power which, in fact, it never ceded or relinquished.

2. The next question is that of "powers".

The Government proposal used the word "competences", thus embracing two spheres : that of the prerogatives, and that of the requisite authority to make use of them. Some members of the Senate Committee, however, considered that the term "competences" was not suitable for a text that was to take its place under Heading III of the Constitution, which is entitled "The Authorities" (Des Pouvoirs). Parliament thus opted for the word "powers" (which is also "pouvoirs") so as to preserve the homogeneity of the wording. However, there could be no question of any ambiguous interpretation of the term. Parliament emphasized in effect that when it is a question of "Pouvoirs" under Heading III of the Constitution, the meaning here is that of organs of the State who share authority between them. These powers must not be confused with either the normative or the jurisdictional authority. To avoid all possibility of misinterpretation, this expression must be taken as a whole and the Constitutional text must read "the exercise of powers", the term being taken in the sense of competences, which can be exercised, whereas powers are held.

3. The powers thus conferred are "given" ones. It was Parliament's intention to prevent any massive transfer of authority that might ultimately leave the State an empty word. The Houses may not, therefore, give blanket permission for the cession of all or part of Belgian sovereignty, even though it is not actually necessary to specify exactly which constitutional clauses are affected by the transfer of certain competences to international organisations.

Thus, it is the scope of the powers that must be defined, the State on the one hand aware of what it is granting, and the international institution on the other knowing what it is getting.

4. The exercise of these powers is "conferred".

The expression adopted by Parliament has intentionally been kept vague, as indeed the entire content of Article 25-B itself from the standpoint of who actually confers those powers.

5. Conferral can be done "by a treaty or by a law".

It should be noted in passing that the order of priority in the original Government proposal has been reversed in the final wording, because

Parliament considered that a treaty is the first instrument which calls for the conferral of competence on an international organisation—a treaty which must then be ratified by means of an Act of Parliament. However, the text has maintained the reference to a law because it might happen that national laws could, for instance, provide for the direct election in Belgium of members of the European Parliament without any need to modify existing treaties.

6. The exercise of powers is conferred "on institutions".

Some members of Parliament would have preferred the term "organisation", because in law, an institution does not necessarily lead to an organisation, whereas every organisation presupposes an institution.

The majority, however, rallied to the term "institutions" which was considered to be more in keeping with the terminology customarily used in Belgium.

7. They must be institutions "coming under international civil law".

These were the words that gave rise to the most heated discussions. Indeed, when the text was debated in the Senate, certain Parliamentarians would have preferred the terms "institutions coming under European civil law". They were, of course, defending the theory that there was no need to alter the Constitution in order to confer powers on institutions set up under international civil law, since for many years Belgium had been a member of many such : the League of Nations, the United Nations Organisation, the International Labour Office, the International Labour Organisation, the Atlantic Treaty, N.A.T.O., and so on. In their eyes, the new development was precisely the recent appearance on the scene of European institutions. At the same time they wished to forestall any possibility of alienating the sovereignty of the State for the benefit of any political entity or community other than Europe.

Most members of Parliament, however, deemed this formula to be too restrictive and indeed too ambiguous, because the first requirement here would be to define what Europe was. Moreover, should the possibility be excluded of transferring powers at some future date to organisations other than the European community? That is why, in a letter dated 14 April 1970 to the House of Representatives Committee, the Minister of Foreign Affairs pointed out that "the general terms of Article 25-B include transfers of power similar to those which have been sanctioned by the treaties instituting the European Communities." The majority of members also discovered that their partners in the European Community, in their revised Constitutions, were also using the expression "international institution or organisation" without specifically mentioning the supranational category; as examples they pointed to the revised constitutional texts of the German Federal Republic, Italy, France, Luxemburg and the Netherlands. It was therefore necessary to preserve some uniformity of terminology in the various Constitutions of those European nations directly involved in the problem.

To settle the difficulty, one member of Parliament proposed that the selected term should be rounded off by adding "and to institutions coming under European civil law". But the great majority of members considered that the terminology decided upon did in fact cover both the existing European supranational institutions and any European political institutions that might be set up in the future.

At all events, one thing that emerged from the debates, both in the Senate and in the House of Representatives, was the political determination to do nothing that might hinder, contradict or throw any doubt on the development of Europe as a community, and as it exists in its supranational form.

So it was in the wording which has just been analysed that the text was finally adopted, and so far Article 25-B remains the only clause in the Belgian Constitution governing relations between the State and the international institutions.

ARTICLE 26

"Legislative authority is exercised collectively by the King, the House of Representatives and the Senate."

This article dates from 1831 and has remained unchanged, in its wording at least. In connection with Article 25, we stressed that all powers are basically vested and grounded in the Nation. Of these three powers: the Legislative, the Executive and the Judiciary, the Constituent Assembly placed the Legislative power at the head of the list, thus according it priority over the Executive and the Judiciary.

According to Article 26, legislative authority is vested in three bodies or, as is more usually said, in three branches. These are: firstly, the King, and then Parliament established on the basis of a bicameral system.

Consequently, it is already clear that the King is associated in one way or another with the exercise of authority vested in all three powers (cfr. Articles 29 and 30).

Why has the King been associated with the exercise of the Legislative power? The reasons for such association are both political and practical ones.

On the political plane, the 1831 Constituent Assembly was inspired by the theories regarding constitutional law and political science set forth in the writings of the great English and French jurists of the 18th century; also it was historically inclined to react against the practices of the previous regime. Accordingly it was at pains to curtail what sovereignty still appertained to the King by upholding in contrast the principle of national sovereignty. It was therefore understandable that any action by the Head of the State should be counterbalanced by the existence of a Parliament representing public opinion.

From another standpoint, the Constituent Assembly was not, however, prepared to exclude the Executive's intervention entirely; on the contrary, it wished to associate this branch of authority with the work of the Legislative. In point of fact the King—or, more accurately, the Government—is well acquainted not only with general matters but also with the day-to-day problems confronting the nation, and is thus in the best position to appreciate whether it is opportune to modify, abrogate, amend or complete the arsenal of laws, since it is the Executive which is entrusted with the task of ensuring that the laws are implemented in individual cases, and it is thus best fitted to assess their effective worth and to appraise their practical efficiency or possibly their weaknesses and their eventual loopholes. Furthermore, the task of governing a country requires an overall view of the problems confronting the nation and in this respect, the organic entity formed by the Government is in a better position than a debating assembly to chart and implement a coordinated, well-balanced management programme.

But why should the Constituent Assembly have provided for a Parliament founded on the bicameral system? In recent times this system has often been set aside, and there are plenty of examples of countries which have done away with it.

However, we should remember that in 1831, the Constituent Assembly began with the concept of reacting against any abuse of authority from whatever source or body it might come. As a reaction against the divine right of kings, it would however have been equally dangerous to grant that same right to a single assembly. The reasons which inspired the two-chamber principle in Belgium are many and varied: it makes for a better preparation of the work of legislation; it reflects the desire to set up not a direct democracy but a representative democracy, and also the wish to ensure that all of the nation's interests were properly represented. As has already been stressed in connection with Article 25, the Belgian Constituent Assembly was, so to speak, bent on striking a perfect balance between the various powers by setting up a series of checks and balances to prevent any recurrence of the abuses under which Belgium so often had to suffer in the past.

How is the King associated with the exercise of the legislative power?

Apart from those instances in which he acts more in his capacity as Head of the Executive (Articles 70, 71, 72 and 80), two articles have formally provided for the intervention of the Head of the State in the exercise of the legislative authority:

— In the first place, Article 27 which acknowledges in his respect the same powers of initiative as those vested in the two other branches of authority;

— In the second place, Article 69 which gives him the right of sanctioning Acts of Parliament—a right, however, the scope of which has been curtailed to such an extent by the unwritten rules of public law that, today, it is to all intents and purposes purely a formal one.

In actual fact, every bill must receive the royal signature, but this must be countersigned by a Minister in office who, in doing so, renders himself responsible therefor on the political plane.

That is what is meant by the term "collectively" used in Article 26: the three branches of the Legislative, namely: the King, the Lower House and the Senate, must all join forces in performing the legislative act if this is to become a valid law binding on all citizens.

This was precisely the intention of the Constituent Assembly, as is shown by a report submitted on 23 December 1830 to the National Congress. One section of this report is indeed worded as follows: "The Legislative authority does not rest solely with the Houses. The Head of State is not restricted to exercising the Executive power alone: he participates in the exercise of the Legislative authority. It has therefore been deemed necessary to operate a less abstract division and to indicate the institutions themselves rather than their purpose."

*
**

In connection with Article 25, it has already been emphasized that the Constituent Assembly had rallied to the concept of the separation of powers—a concept that implies both the division of the State's authority and the legal predominance of the Legislative power. In doing so, it was merely following the general trend of development in contemporary ideas regarding public law.

It was also underlined that the Constituent Assembly did not apply this theory of the separation of powers in any rigid and dogmatic manner, so that while each power is theoretically independent of the other two, and while there is an organic separation between the three powers, this is compensated for by a process of functional co-operation between them so that a certain balance is achieved.

In this context, it is possible to pinpoint some important functions that are proper to the Legislative power.

The first of these is the budgetary function which, historically, constitutes the foundation-stone of democracy. This budgetary function, which involves the annual vote on the financial means placed at the disposal of the government, has as its necessary corollary the fiscal function, i.e. the authority to levy taxes. This is defined in particular under Heading IV of the Constitution entitled "Finances".

A second function that has grown up in the course of historical evolution is the jurisdictional function. Traces of this remain in the Belgian Constitution, particularly in Article 34 under which the Houses are instructed to verify the powers of their members and to settle disputes that may arise in this connection, and in Article 90 in which the House of Representatives—to the exclusion of the Senate—is empowered to impeach Ministers and to arraign them before the Court of Cassation.

The essential function on the political plane is that of government, which implies constant co-operation with the Executive authority, in particular by granting or withdrawing confidence in the Government.

Finally, the last function which, in the eyes of the public, often appears as the specific function of the Legislative power, is the normative function which implies the power to vote general and mandatory laws. To this must be coupled the constituent function since in terms of Heading VII of the Constitution, it is up to the Houses to decide whether this or that constitutional ruling, which is specifically designated, should be amended, and to undertake such amendment.

This latter function is the more important in that no constitutional court exists in Belgium. In full agreement with constitutional principles, both doctrine and jurisprudence almost unanimously agree that the Houses alone have the sovereign right to judge the constitutional character of their own enactments.

From these main functions vested in the Legislative power, certain essential competences arise.

First of these is the exclusive right to interpret the laws authoritatively (Article 28).

Then, the Legislative is competent to exercise political and financial control over the Executive. Political control is exercised by means of interpellations, or by parliamentary questions, or again by parliamentary investigations. Financial control is exercised by means of the same procedures, but chiefly by the annual vote on the budget, at which time the Legislative is able to debate the general policies being pursued by the Government.

Finally, the Legislative authority is also vested with residual competence, in the sense that while powers have been distributed with exactness between the three branches of sovereignty, the legislator alone holds all powers save only those which are formally withheld from him by the Constitution itself. Such residual competence has come to the fore on several occasions: for instance, in 1945 when the question was one of deciding that the King was no longer prevented from reigning (cfr. Article 82); again in 1950, when Parliament decided to hold a nation-wide referendum which was not provided for in terms of the Constitution (cfr. Article 82), and even in the very early days when, in 1832, Parliament created the Order of Leopold, which is both a civil and a military decoration, whereas Article 76 of the Constitution provided solely for the existence of military decorations. This residual competence has, moreover, given rise to debate: it is undoubtedly justified on the theoretical plane by the principle that the law may authorise anything not expressly prohibited by the Constitution.

*
**

The National Congress thus ensured that the Legislative power should take priority over the other two powers even though it preserved the foundations of harmonious co-operation between them, in such a way that the separation of powers is by no means a dogmatic and absolute rule.

In the first place, the Legislative is independent of the other two powers even though its independence is a relative one. Many precautions are embodied in the Constitution to ensure that this independence is preserved. A glance at Articles 34, 37, 44, 45 and 46 will be sufficient. Thus, the Constituent Assembly gave the primacy to the Legislative power.

While the Executive is in fact competent to frame regulations, it may only do so in implementation of a law (Article 67).

Similarly, the courts and tribunals may only implement decrees and regulations on condition that they are in accordance with the law (Article 107).

Finally, the subordinate institutions, both provincial and municipal and, recently, the urban centres and federations of boroughs as well, are also subject to and governed by laws.

Thus, the law is the supreme norm or standard of the nation, and it can only stem from the Legislative power itself, made up of the representative assemblies drawn from the nation.

That was the will of the Constituent Assembly in 1831. But here again we come up against a phenomenon frequently encountered in connection with the Belgian Constitution. Owing to its very concision, the wording of the Constitution can, according to one viewpoint, be adapted to fit all new developments or, from another viewpoint, it may on the contrary open the door to such developments. Indeed, while the constitutional structure of the regime remained unchanged for many years, it has happened that the relationship between the three powers has been profoundly modified, in particular owing to the increasing ascendancy of the Executive, and more specifically of the Government, over the Legislative.

The Judiciary itself has always declined to judge the constitutional character of the laws. Furthermore, in periods of difficulty it accepted that the Government should, to some extent, take the place of Parliament by issuing decrees having the force of law. Owing to circumstances, it has refused to discuss the validity of those decree-laws, so that the legal problem remains unsolved.

As for Parliament, this has undergone another process of evolution, largely owing to the increasingly important part played by the political parties. The result has been that the hierarchy of the essential functions acknowledged in respect of Parliament has been completely overturned.

Indeed, coalition governments usually rely on a parliamentary majority, and they remain in office as long as that majority holds together. While the principle of the separation of powers remains unassailable on the constitutional plane, the fact remains that, in actual practice, a dividing line has become established between the majority forming the Government and the parties forming the opposition.

Parliament has thus given increasing importance to the task of forming a government. Indeed, the main efforts of a newly elected Parliament are directed towards the formation of a new government, and once this has been formed, since it comprises members able to rely on the confidence of the majority, Parliament is then bisected into a majority which is supposed to accept the government's programme, once this has been charted after negotiations that are sometimes very arduous indeed, and an opposition which is practically the only body able to criticise that programme or exert some measure of supervision over it.

Similarly, in performing its legislative task, Parliament makes less use of its right of initiative since it is usually the Government, certain of the support of both Houses, which drafts the legislative texts and submits them for parliamentary approval. The latter is, of course, virtually a certainty since the Government is backed by a majority which it knows will support its initiatives, unless serious disagreements have arisen between the parties which constitute the majority. The fact remains, however, that the bills tabled by the Government are often amended, altered and improved as they go through the legislative procedure.

We see, therefore—and this has already been pointed out under Article 25 —that the political parties wield a growing measure of *de facto* powers. The appearance of the great political parties has moreover been promoted by the introduction of universal suffrage. It is the parties who dictate the choice of the Head of State when he appoints the Prime Minister and members of the Government. It is they who conduct the debates in Parliament and who decide the important options that arise in connection with political, social or economic problems.

Parliamentary control, when it is not reduced to a fight between the majority and the opposition, has thus been transposed into close contacts established between the Government and the majority supporting it.

It is therefore useful to take a brief look at the political parties existing at the present time.

Stemming from the traditional Catholic Party, the Social Christian Party first appeared on the scene in 1945 and, in 1968, split into two independent political formations based on the linguistic regions: the *Parti Social*

Chrétien (French-speaking) and the *Christelijke Volkspartij* (Dutch-speaking).

Then there is the Belgian Socialist Party stemming from the old Belgian Worker's Party (in French: *Parti Socialiste Belge;* in Dutch: *Belgische Socialistische Partij*) which has remained more unitary in structure even though, at the present time, it is steered by two presidents, one from each language group.

Thirdly, there is the Party of Liberty and Progress, set up in November 1961 as a successor to the former Belgian Liberal Party. This party is also split into two wings: the *Parti de la Liberté et du Progrès* for the French-language region, and the *Partij voor Vrijheid en Vooruitgang* for the Dutch-language region; plus a Brussels section going under the name of *Parti Libéral.*

Finally, we should also mention the Communist Party (French : P.C., Dutch: C.P.) which first came into being just after World War I but whose representation in Parliament has dwindled considerably since 1950.

Apart from these so-called traditional parties, the first three of which are moreover those which enjoy government-forming strength, there are a few so-called "community" parties which have sprung up in recent years owing to the language disagreements.

The first of these is the *Volksunie* (V.U.) which is regarded as a Flemish Nationalist Party.

Then there is the *Rassemblement Wallon* (R.W.), the youngest of the Belgian political parties, which in the Walloon region plays a part corresponding to that of the *Volksunie* in Flanders.

Finally, there is the *Front Démocratique des Francophones* or F.D.F. (French-speaking Democratic Front) which exists solely in the Brussels area, and which put up its first candidates for election in 1965.

A table showing the distribution of parliamentary seats among the political parties is given on Page 86.

Another important development has been given material form by the latest revision of the Constitution. This is, so to speak, a dismembering of the Legislative power by the creation of the Cultural Councils. As shown in Article 59-B, these Councils are in fact competent to regulate by means of decrees—and in certain cases even without reference to the Legislative—specific matters which were formerly handled by the Legislative. It should however be stressed that the law of 21 July 1971 which defines the competence and functioning of the Cultural Councils, has provided in its Article 13 that Cabinet Ministers have absolutely no political responsibility towards these Councils. In this regard, we refer our readers to the commentary under Article 59-B.

DISTRIBUTION OF MEMBERS OF PARLIAMENT ACCORDING TO POLITICAL PARTIES
(following the election on 10 March 1974)
HOUSE OF REPRESENTATIVES

Parties	French language region	Dutch language region	Brussels region	Total
P.S.C.–C.V.P.	18	45	9	72
P.S.B.-B.S.P.	27	25	7	59
P.L.P.-P.V.V.	9	19	2	30
P.L.D.P. (1)	—	—	3	3
F.D.F	—	—	9 }	
R.W.	13	—	— }	22
V.U.	—	19	3 }	22
P.C.-U.D.P. (2)	3	—	1	4
				212

SENATE

	French language region	Dutch language region	Brussels region	Total
P.S.C.-C.V.P. :				
directly elected	8	24	5	37
provincial	4	13	2	19
co-opted	3	5	2	10
Total	15	42	9	66
P.S.B.-B.S.P. :				
directly elected	14	13	2	29
provincial	7	6	1	14
co-opted	3	3	1	7
Total	24	22	4	50
P.L.P.-P.V.V. :				
directly elected	8	6	2	16
provincial	3	3	1	7
co-opted	2	1	1	4
Total	13	10	4	27
P.L.D.P. (1) :				
directly elected	—	—	2	2
provincial	—	—	1	1
co-opted	—	—	—	—
Total	—	—	3	3
F.D.F.-R.W. :				
directly elected	7	—	4	11
provincial	3	—	2	5
co-opted	1	—	1	2
Total	11		7	18
VOLKSUNIE :				
directly elected	—	8	2	10
provincial	—	4	—	4
co-opted	—	2	—	2
Total	—	14	2	16
P.C.-U.D.P. (2) :				
directly elected & total .	1	—	—	1

(1) P.L.D.P. : the Brussels P.L.P.
(2) P.C.-U.D.P. : Local progressive alliance in the Hainaut province.

ARTICLE 27

"The right of initiative is vested in each of the three branches of the Legislative authority."

This provision dates from 1831 but at that time it was completed by the following phrase : "Nevertheless, any law pertaining to State revenue or expenditure, or to the armed forces contingent, must first be voted on by the House of Representatives." This clause was abrogated during the Second Revision of the Constitution (1920-1921).

Legislative initiative comprises not only the right to table a bill or proposal but also the right of amendment, i.e. the right to table a proposed modification to a bill being debated, and that of modifying such a bill. Each of the three branches of the Legislative therefore has a full right to initiate legislation, and none of the three need restrict itself to a blanket expression of approval or disapproval.

It should be specified that the term "bill" refers either to a text initiated by the government, or to a text already approved by one of the two Houses; whereas the term "proposal" or "draft bill" is reserved for texts tabled by one or several members of Parliament and which have not yet been approved by either of the Houses.

The second paragraph, now abrogated, was justified in the 19th century : in those days, to be eligible for membership of the Senate, it was necessary to provide proof of personal means. Owing to this requirement, the Senate was a more conservative body than the House of Representatives. As the latter's members had been elected by more democratic procedures, it was felt necessary that the Lower House should give its prior approval to all measures pertaining to taxes and levies, in cash and in kind, to be imposed on the people.

The Revisions of 1893 and of 1920-1921 have placed both Houses on a completely democratic footing, so that the distinction made in the original wording of this article between the two Houses of Parliament was no longer justified.

ARTICLE 28

"The authoritative interpretation of laws is the sole prerogative of the Legislative authority."

This article dates from 1831 and has remained unchanged.

It is immediately obvious that however perfect the laws may be, it is virtually impossible to provide in all cases for the theoretical and practical difficulties that may arise with the passage of time and which make it essential to interpret the law with authority. Some pieces of legislation may be obscurely worded; others may lend themselves to varying interpretations.

It goes without saying that the Executive can never be entrusted with the task of interpreting the law authoritatively, as this would render democracy an empty word. The Executive is not an elected power.

Nor can the Judiciary be given this right. Indeed, the courts and tribunals may only pronounce judgment on the individual cases submitted to their examination. They are not allowed to issue general decisions, for the same reason as that given above. Furthermore, were this possibility to be conferred on them, it would give rise to an unacceptable subjection of the Magistrature to political influences, whereas this body must above all retain its independence. Judges are appointed on the basis of their legal knowledge, competence and experience. A magistrate who, by means of his judgments and rulings, sought to impose standards of a more general nature might be inspired by his own personal views and beliefs in such matters as ideology, philosophy, religion, politics and social or economic affairs.

Only the Houses who have voted the law and who may modify or abrogate it, have the equal right to impose an exact and definitive interpretation of its contents. Subjected to periodical re-election, the Houses embody the supreme power within the framework of the constitutional system, and they alone may decree the general rules of conduct governing life in society.

ARTICLE 29

"The Executive authority is vested in the King as laid down by the Constitution."

This article dates from 1831 and has never been modified.

Its contents are merely an implementation of the terms of Article 25 according to which, as we have seen, all powers stem from the Nation.

The scope of this article is twofold :

— firstly, it attributes the Executive authority to the King;

— secondly, the King may not exercise this power save in the manner laid down by the Constitution.

This article will, moreover, be further strengthened by Article 78.

Article 25 showed that the constitutional regime of Belgium was founded in principle on the separation of powers, but that such separation was not absolute: that it was framed primarily in the interest of the Belgian people and that it involved the separation of the instruments of government.

In terms of the Constitution, the King is therefore called upon to fulfil a dual role, since according to Article 26 he is one of the branches of the Legislative, whereas Article 29 simultaneously makes him the Head of the Executive. This dual attribution is an illustration of the collaboration which must exist between two theoretically separate powers.

As the wording indicates, the Executive power is above all the power of putting the laws into execution, and its content is further defined by Articles 59-B para. 5, and 67. The Executive therefore assumes the task of overseeing the practical implementation of laws and decrees.

In practice, the Executive power comprises the following functions in particular, according to the Constitution :

— the enforcement of rulings and judgments pronounced by the courts and tribunals (Article 30);

— appointments to ranks in the armed forces, to posts in the civil service and in the foreign service (Article 66);

— command of the armed forces, declarations of war, and the signing of treaties of peace, alliance and commerce (Article 68);

— exercise of the right of reprieve (Article 73);

— the granting of titles of nobility (Article 75);

— the award of military decorations (Article 76);

— the appointment of members of the Judiciary (Article 99);

— the appointment and dismissal of officials of the Public Prosecutor's Department in the courts and tribunals (Article 101);

— and, in more general terms, as previously stated, the enactment of measures necessary for the implementation of laws and decrees (Article 67 and 59-B, para. 5).

The Executive power is not, however, restricted to the mere implementation of decisions made by the other two powers. It is also of service to those powers since, in particular, it is the King who promulgates the laws, i.e. renders them executive. (Article 69).

Thus the King, surrounded by all the requisite constitutional precautions, is the sole wielder of the Executive power, but his competence is merely an attributory one since he may only exercise it in obedience to the rules laid down by the Constitution.

*
* *

It has been emphasized in connection with Article 25 that the formal rulings of the Constitution do not, in principle, authorise any derogation thereof.

It has also been pointed out that, in practice, such delegations of authority from one power to another have been known to occur, especially when special powers were granted to the Executive whenever serious and exceptional circumstances warranted it.

Should one conclude from Article 29 that any delegation of authority is prohibited even within the Executive itself, i.e. between the King and his Ministers ?

It should first be pointed out that by delegation of authority is meant rather a sharing out of powers of decision among several subordinate authorities.

In a ruling of 6 February 1891, the Court of Cassation laid down a strict, and thus negative, decision regarding the possible delegation of authority.

The Court of Cassation recalled that sovereignty was in fact vested in the Nation, and that the powers stemming from the Nation are already of themselves delegations of authority. Such delegated powers may not, in principle, be sub-delegated to others. All powers therefore have a common origin from which they stem directly, and from which they are inalienable and indefeasible. The court of Cassation added that these principles had inspired the Constituent Assembly to apply them to the royal power with the utmost stringency, especially as it had to react against real and systematic interference practised during the reign of King William of the Netherlands (1814-1830). It is, however, clear that the delegation of authority is an extremely practical legal way of relieving the higher authority of the detail work, and that is why the strictness of the constitutional principles has necessarily been tempered in order to deal with day-to-day requirements.

The Court of Cassation confirmed this by a ruling of 4 May 1920 stating that while authority was inalienable and indefeasible, the instrument of power delegated by the Nation was not forbidden to set up subordinate authorities empowered to act under its supervision when it came to implementing detailed measures. The Court of Cassation added that, subject to the expressed or tacit approval of the constitutionally competent authority, this precarious and always revocable task entrusted to subordinate authorities did not involve any alienation or transfer of authority.

Only practice may establish in each individual case whether a measure may be regarded as a secondary one, i.e. as a piece of detail work.

In this way, by a further ruling in 1921, the Court of Cassation again acknowledged that the King may authorise his Ministers to take certain measures to implement a regulation that he himself has established.

Furthermore, in some cases it is the Legislative itself which, in terms of its residual competence, confers executive powers directly on a Cabinet Minister. In this case, the question is one of a direct attribution of competence. But the Legislative may not do this when important matters are at stake without violating Article 67 of the Constitution. When it thus delegates a measure of statutory authority to a Minister, the Legislative must be at pains to avoid burdening the Head of the State with detail work, and in any event the King retains a residuum of competence in such matters. Similarly, the Legislative has sometimes expressly authorised the King to delegate statutory powers to his Ministers, but here again such legislative actions must remain exceptional ones.

In other cases, it is the King himself who delegates his powers to his Ministers in certain administrative matters, but in obedience to the Constitution — Article 66 in particular — he may only do so where measures of implementation are concerned. He may not instruct a Minister to issue decrees which create new rights or obligations in respect of persons under their jurisdiction, as for example by establishing statutes governing personnel in a public administrative office, and so on.

On the other hand, the King may very well delegate to his Ministers his powers of appointing persons to posts in the general administration, on condition that the appointments are to minor posts in the civil service. That is what was done, for instance, by means of the statute governing civil servants, in terms of which personnel at the 2nd echelon are appointed by the Minister, and personnel at the 3rd or 4th echelon are appointed either by the Minister or by the Head of the Department concerned, to whom the Minister in question has in turn delegated his authority.

When he delegates his powers, the King may moreover impose certain limitations and certain conditions on the exercise of the authority so delegated.

So once again we see that practice has to some extent made for greater flexibility in the apparent rigidity of constitutional principles, without in any way weakening those principles themselves, and without any infringement of the rights of persons affected by such decisions.

ARTICLE 30

"The Judiciary authority is exercised by the courts and tribunals. Their decisions and judgments are delivered in the name of the King."

This article dates from 1831 and has never been modified.

We have already seen that the first Constituent Assembly had introduced a certain measure of separation between the powers but that this separation, far from being a strict one, was very indeterminate indeed as between the Executive and the Legislative.

As for the Judiciary, in contrast this was clearly made separate and distinct from the other two powers, for the absolute independence of the courts of law was essential to ensure that the individual rights and liberties of all citizens were respected. Belgian judges are perfectly free since they owe no obedience save to the law itself; they need be afraid of no threat or coercion on the part of Ministers of the Crown, nor of any interference by a member of Parliament (see Article 100).

ARTICLE 31

"Interests which are exclusively municipal or provincial are regulated by the municipal or provincial councils in accordance with the principles laid down by the Constitution."

This article, which dates from 1831, has never been modified.

It establishes the principle of municipal and provincial autonomy. Initially, this autonomy was so great that it was described as the "fourth power" along with the Legislative, Executive and Judiciary powers.

In Belgium, the provinces, cities and boroughs constitute the elements of a certain concept of the State which might be described as the principle of decentralisation.

From the philosophical standpoint, decentralisation appears as a corrective to the Napoleonic state which allowed of no intermediary between the State and the individual citizen. In this way, the power stemming from the collective people was centralised during the 19th century in the hands of the central government.

From the social standpoint, decentralisation is a response to the diversity of the various regions within a strongly centralised state, and it tends to adapt the requirements of laws and regulations in keeping with the multifarious traditions, interests or needs of the people.

In this way, decentralisation therefore appears as one of the instruments of freedom.

THE PROVINCES

The nine provincial entities play a very important part in Belgium, especially by ensuring proper coordination between the central and local authorities (the latter being the boroughs).

The Provincial Council is a direct expression of the electorate in the provinces : as such, it does in principle wield provincial power. Provincial councillors are elected for a term of four years. The council meets in open session. In principle, the council has the final word on all matters of provincial interest, namely : budget and finance, the management of provincial assets, certain police forces operating solely in the province, and the management of provincial services, especially in the spheres of education and welfare. Like the Permanent Deputation which will be discussed farther on, the council is at pains to ensure proper coordination in the management of those boroughs that come under its authority, especially on such matters as non-navigable and non-floatable waterways, the performance of public works and services involving several boroughs and the sharing of the corresponding expenditure between them. Finally, it is the Provincial Council's task to elect the Provincial Senators and to present candidates for the posts of Judge of Appeal, President and Vice-President of the Courts of First Instance.

As the Provincial Council only exercises its powers while in session, and as sessions are for short periods, its authority devolves on the Permanent Deputation when the council is not sitting, except for certain matters specifically reserved for the council. The Permanent Deputation in each province is elected by the provincial council from among its members. The Permanent Deputies are elected for a term of four years and no mandate can be revoked. There are six Permanent Deputies in each Permanent Deputation, headed by the Governor as the King's representative.

Consequently, the central authority of the country is always present in the midst of the provincial authority. Indeed, it is the Permanent Deputation which is the most important cog in the provincial machinery. In contrast to Ministers of the Central government, the Permanent Deputies who are, so to speak, the Executive body of the provincial authority, are not vested with individual competence: the Permanent Deputation may only act as a body, whereas the individual Permanent Deputies who are members of it are powerless to act on their own. The sphere of authority of the Permanent Deputation is both wide and varied.

The Deputation holds both administrative and statutory competence. It is the Permanent Deputation itself that exercises the tutelary authority, with powers of decision, over the local authorities: in the first place, its approval is required for all the important acts of the municipal authorities, and without such approval such acts are null and void. The Permanent Deputation may also order the boroughs to fulfil their legal obligations, if necessary by appointing special commissioners to act on their behalf and in their stead. The Permanent Deputation is also an important ruling body. It pronounces statutory rulings on appeals against decisions made by the municipal authorities. It may either modify them, or annul them entirely on the basis of illegality or inexpediency.

Some mention should be made here concerning the important part played by the Governors of the Provinces. Appointed and dismissed by the King, the Governor is the delegate and the representative of the central authority to the provincial authorities.

Inheritors of the ancient principalities which were formerly a part of the Catholic Low Countries, the provinces have assumed the responsibilities laid on them by the Constituent Assembly and the Legislative with a degree of efficiency and dynamic energy beyond all criticism. Over the last quarter of a century, their traditional administrative tasks have been rounded off by new initiatives. Among the most important of these are : economic expansion, social housing schemes and the cultural infrastructure. The role of the Belgian provinces is becoming more important with each day that passes.

*
**

THE BOROUGHS

It is well known that, when the French Revolution broke out, the "communes" as they then existed were done away with, for various reasons which need not be gone into here. But it was very soon perceived—and this point is still a very important one today—that boroughs cannot be lightly dispensed with.

The institution consisting of a borough, which enables all the people living in its area to be personally responsible for the management of their affairs because those responsible for such management are directly elected by the local citizens and from among themselves, corresponds to one of the prerequisites of the democratic system.

Indeed, democracy presupposes that all decisions are made by the representatives of the people, and that they are so made at a level best fitted for implementing appropriate measures to ensure general well-being in full knowledge of the requirements, necessities and possibilities of the population. Not only political factors, but also administrative, social and economic factors call for borough institutions which alone can make for the harmonious, efficient development of local infrastructures.

Even though the man of today, in order to satisfy a whole series of needs, has to go outside his borough, he nevertheless continues to want various services to be made available in his own local environment so that his day-to-day life may be made pleasant and his material requirements met. Outside his family circle, a man lives his community life primarily within his local entity or his borough. He therefore requires his local administrative institutions to display their legal competence, their administrative capacity and their political influence so that they may procure for himself and his fellow-citizens the material framework and machinery designed to meet the needs of our present-day welfare society.

As a result, the borough as an institution contributes its share to the proper functioning of all the other democratic institutions in the country.

The large number of boroughs in Belgium—2359 at the present time—does however give rise to some serious problems.

In order to remedy this state of things, the central authority took two important measures, separated by a fairly wide interval in time.

THE INTER-BOROUGH ORGANISATIONS

By the end of the 19th century, it became obvious that the creation of inter-borough organisations was necessary to allow the smaller boroughs to join forces in carrying out essential tasks. In this way, a whole series of laws were enacted to provide for the setting-up of inter-borough facilities:

— the law of 6 August 1897 concerning the organisation of medical treatment establishments;

— the law of 18 August 1907 concerning inter-borough associations for water supplies;

— the law of 1 March 1922 concerning inter-borough associations for purposes of public utilities;

— the law of 18 July 1959 providing for special measures with a view to overcoming economic and social problems in certain regions; and

— the law of 26 July 1962 regarding concessions for the building of motorways.

At the present time there are 234 inter-borough associations which may be classified according to their purpose as follows:

34 supplying electricity

20 supplying electricity and gas

17 supplying gas

33 supplying water

10 supplying teledistribution

27 for environmental improvements, etc.

 7 for the building of motorways

12 undertaking other public works

15 for garbage removal and sewerage

13 for culture, sport and tourism

13 engaged in various sectors

33 engaged in the medico-social sector.

These associations of boroughs are, in principle, set up for a specific purpose of direct interest to the boroughs concerned. The creation of an association, a borough's application for membership of such an association, and its statutes, must all be approved by the King. The association may be authorised to undertake, in the King's name, such expropriations as may be deemed necessary for the public weal; it may float loans and receive subsidies from the public authorities.

THE MERGING OF BOROUGHS

For many years now, voices have been raised in Belgium to advocate a reduction in the number of boroughs by means of mergers of two or several of them. The procedure to be followed in such cases was definitively framed by the law of 23 July 1971 governing the merging of boroughs and modifications to their territorial boundaries. Three possible methods are provided for by this piece of legislation:

— a merger, which in principle applies only to boroughs of comparable size and importance;

— a modification of borough limits for the purpose of rectifying certain notable anomalies along the boundary lines;

— annexation, which presupposes the total or partial uniting of one or several neighbouring boroughs, particularly small ones, with a single central borough which will retain its paramount status.

Proposals for mergers, drawn up by the Ministry of the Interior, are submitted jointly by the Minister of the Interior and the Governor of the province to the borough councils concerned and to the Permanent Deputation of the provincial council simultaneously. A statutory ruling on the modification of borough limits is delivered by means of a Royal Decree debated in Cabinet which must be submitted to the Houses of Parliament for ratification.

The process leading to borough mergers began in 1961 as soon as the law of 14 February 1961 went into force. To date, 449 boroughs have been merged.

To complete this survey, we should mention here the law of 26 July 1971 which provided for the establishment of urban areas and federations of boroughs. This law and its effects are discussed under article 108-B of the Constitution.

CHAPTER 1

PARLIAMENT

ARTICLE 32

"The members of both Houses represent the Nation, and not merely the province or subdivision of a province which elected them."

This article dates from 1831 and has never been modified.

Under the old regime, Belgium was not a unitary State: it was a collection of principalities united solely by the fact of being governed by a single ruler. Moreover, the names of the Belgian provinces derive from those ancient political entities. In voting this clause, the Constituent Assembly wished to assert the unity of the Nation and to remind its elected representatives that their task was not merely to uphold the particular interests of their individual constituencies, but to have the country's general interest and that of the entire Belgian population constantly in mind.

In the early days of Belgian independence, the existence of two Chambers signified quite another concept than that which prevails today. In the 19th century, the Senate was called upon to act as a conservative counterweight to the initiatives promoted by a House of Representatives deemed to be too much of the people, despite the status qualification required of all its members. In actual fact, the pre-requisite of a personal fortune imposed on all candidate Senators did not apply to candidate members of the Lower House.

The division of national representation into two assemblies, from a more modern standpoint, provides for a period of examination and reflection between the reading of a bill in both Houses. This waiting period allows the national press and public opinion to make their views known before the final vote after which the bill becomes law.

It is difficult to sum up in a few lines all that the national political mandate entails: its political enhancement, its servitudes, ambitions and multifarious duties.

To give the nation a government is the primordial task incumbent collectively on both Houses as constituted corporate bodies.

The essential function of a Member and a Senator taken individually is to enact laws and vote on the Budget. To do so they must possess full information, supplied in the first place by the Government and also by their own political parties, specialized groups of citizens, the electorate, and finally through their own personal study of the matter in hand. In our present age of advanced technical specialization and wide diversification, this unavoidably leads members to specialize in given subjects.

The work is therefore apportioned according to aptitude, competence and subject-matter.

Members of Parliament must also keep a close watch on what the government is doing. They do this by means of written and oral questions, interpellations, and speeches during budget debates.

All this takes up a great deal of a member's time if he is at pains to ensure efficacious government.

He must also attend meetings of the Committees (at least two in number) to which he has been appointed, take an active part in their work and, if he is the Chairman, report to the House on the project concerned and uphold it in public session. He may also report back to his own Party Committee which meets once a week. He must also reckon with his local political federation and his constituents for whose benefit, in some districts, he will hold a regular weekly meeting.

To the above duties must be added his other obligations: his attendance at the Cultural Council of which he is automatically a member; any other political mandates that may have been entrusted to him with all the servitudes and duties they necessarily entail in the sphere of local or international policies; and it will be seen that the time available to a conscientious member of Parliament is barely sufficient for him to discharge his functions with the requisite efficiency.

ARTICLE 32-B

"For those cases prescribed in the Constitution, the elected members of each House are divided into a French-language group and a Dutch-language group in such manner as is laid down by law."

This is an entirely new article inserted at the third revision; it rounds off Article 32 by rendering its unitary character more flexible.

Consequently, members of Parliament are at one and the same time both the representatives of the Belgian people as a whole, and in specific cases the representatives of their respective language groups.

In the latter capacity, and apart from their competence as members of the Cultural Councils provided for under Article 59-B of the Constitution (see later), both Deputies and Senators are, in the following cases, empowered:

— to table a motivated objection stating that a draft or proposed bill is such as to be gravely prejudicial to the relations existing between the two language groups (see Article 38-B);

— to pass laws requiring a special qualified majority vote (1) (on the extraprovincialization of an area, modifications to the boundaries of language regions, the functioning of the Cultural Councils, the extent of cultural autonomy, cultural co-operation, and regional organization).

The term "elected members" has been selected because the Senate also includes non-elected members: the sons of the Monarch or, failing them, Belgian princes of the Royal House in the direct line of succession (see Article 58). Senators by right do not, therefore, belong to a linguistic group.

In accordance with the Constitution, the legislator has laid down the manner in which the division of Members of Parliament into language groups takes place (Law of 3 July 1971).

This law also includes several clauses relating to the Cultural Councils set up for the French and Dutch speaking cultural communities; these clauses will be dealt with later in the commentary on Article 59-B.

The following belong to the French language group in the House of Representatives and the Senate respectively:

a) Deputies and Senators elected in the French and German speaking regions;

---

(1) Overall two-thirds majority, and simple majority vote by those present and of the "ayes" in each language group.

b) Deputies and Senators elected in the constituency of Brussels, the provincial Senators from Brabant, and co-opted Senators when the latter take oath in French or German. If they take oath in several languages, that which is first used determines their language group.

The following belong to the Dutch language group in the Lower House and the Senate respectively:

a) Deputies and Senators elected in the Dutch speaking region;

b) Deputies and Senators elected in the constituency of Brussels, the provincial Senators from Brabant, and co-opted Senators when the latter take oath in Dutch. If they take oath in several languages, that which is used first determines their language group.

The decision as to which language group any Member belongs is an irrevocable one for the entire duration of the Government in office.

The number of members who make up the respective Cultural Councils is not a determinate one. Indeed, it may vary, for instance in the event of a general election when the decennial census calls for a new distribution of mandates in the regions, or in the event of the death or resignation of a member from a bilingual region whose successor belongs to another language group.

ARTICLE 33

"The sessions of both Houses are public.

"Nevertheless, each House may go into secret committee at the request of its president or of ten members.

"It then decides, on the basis of an absolute majority, whether the sitting is to be resumed in public on the same subject."

This article dates from 1831 and has never been modified. It is indeed a fundamental article, for the publicity surrounding democratic institutions is the best means of control offered to the general public through the medium of the press. Such control is exercised over the institution itself and its elected members alike.

Possible abuses can thus be prevented or, if they occur, can be sanctioned or otherwise dealt with owing to the fact that they can be made public.

It should be noted that the Chambers only resort in exceptional circumstances to the power vested in them by the Constituent Assembly of meeting in secret committee: in practice this is only done when the House is debating its own budget.

The publicity surrounding the conduct of business in both Houses does not depend solely on the fact that the Press and private persons may attend parliamentary sittings; it is also ensured by the publication of an analytical report of each session, parliamentary annals (a verbatim report of each sitting), and all documents connected with the work of the Legislative: draft and proposed bills, committee reports, amendments, etc. These published documents enable both private persons and associations of all kinds to keep abreast of the legislative work in hand. In this way they may make representations in good time to the Members of their constituencies or to their political parties and acquaint them with their views, objections and wishes.

The public nature of parliamentary business may therefore be regarded in this case as a form of participation in the life of the State and of the Nation.

Finally, it should be noted that the rule embodied in Article 33 of the Constitution is equally applicable under Article 59-B of the Constitution where sessions of the Cultural Councils are concerned.

ARTICLE 34

"Each House verifies the powers of its members and pronounces judgment on any contestation that may arise in this regard."

This clause dates from 1831 and has never been modified.

A law dated 17 May 1949 did however institute a prior check on the eligibility of each candidate, to be carried out by the main electoral offices in each constituency, with the right of appeal to the Appellate Courts.

This does not prevent the Houses from investigating the eligibility of candidates in their turn, when the time comes to verify their credentials and to satisfy themselves that electoral procedures have been properly complied with. In practice, it often happens that complaints are lodged with one House or the other, but it is rare indeed for them to be acknowledged as well founded. If the complaint is a valid one, it will generally be acted upon.

This constitutional provision might be open to criticism on the grounds that the members of both Houses thus find themselves called upon to act as both judge and defendant in the matter, or again, that immediately following a general election some members who have not yet been sworn in are called upon to arbitrate on a subject of some delicacy. In actual fact, however, such invalidations occur very rarely indeed, and they are always well founded.

ARTICLE 35

"No person may be a member of both Houses simultaneously."

This clause dates from 1831 and has never been modified, for reasons which will be obvious.

As soon as the Constituent Assembly decided to institute a bicameral system of representation, it was clearly necessary to prohibit any possibility of dual membership of both Houses at once, or the bicameral principle would prove worthless.

As the Constituent Assembly saw it, the conservative Senate was to serve as a counterweight to an excessively democratic Lower House. It should be recalled that in those early days, each candidate Senator had to afford proof of a very high minimum tax rating, a prerequisite not imposed on candidate Deputies. Today, the Senate has lost its conservative character despite the higher age minimum (40 years) and certain other conditions which are hardly justifiable in present circumstances.

The bicameral system is still an excellent one owing to the improvements which can be made to the wording and content of bills as a result of the double reading, and particularly by allowing time for the general public to make its views known between the time when the bill is first tabled and when it is put to the vote.

While the Senate and the House of Representatives enjoy equal powers at the present time, there are still some minor differences in their respective competences, as follows:

— the Senate may not meet at times when the House of Representatives is not sitting (Article 59);

— the House of Representatives alone has the right to impeach Ministers and to arraign them before the Court of Cassation (Article 90);

— the Senate alone may present candidates for the post of Counsellor at the Court of Cassation (Article 99);

— members of the Audit Office are appointed exclusively by the House of Representatives (Article 116).

ARTICLE 36

"A member of either House who is appointed by the Government to any salaried post other than that of Minister, and who accepts, ceases to sit immediately and does not resume his functions save as the result of a new election."

This article dates from 1893 and replaces the 1831 clause worded as follows: "A member of either of the two Houses, appointed by the government to a salaried post which he accepts, must immediately relinquish his seat and may only resume it as a result of a new election."

This provision merely states a principle, for the actual rules governing incompatibility are embodied in the law of 6 August 1931.

The Constituent Assembly of 1831 wished to prevent the government —which, in those days, was still greatly influenced by the King—from granting privileges or favours to members of Parliament, for instance by raising them to Cabinet rank, and thus exercising an influence on their personal judgment and their vote. By 1893, however, the parliamentary system was functioning smoothly so that an appointment to Cabinet rank was no longer dependent on royal favour: indeed, the second Constituent Assembly deemed it right and proper procedure that Cabinet Ministers should be chosen mainly from among members of the two Houses. It therefore inserted this exception in the text of Article 36.

In turn, the legislator has established incompatibility between parliamentary status and salaried posts in the service of the State (such as: magistrate, minister of religion, schoolteacher in State schools with the exception of university professors, barristers officially representing Civil Service institutions, etc.).

On the other hand, a member of either House may also hold office as a Cabinet Minister, a Secretary of State or a university professor.

A parliamentary mandate is incompatible with that of a provincial councillor. But a Deputy or a Senator may also be a municipal councillor, an alderman or a burgomaster (mayor).

ARTICLE 37

"At each session, each House nominates its president, its vice-presidents and makes up its steering committee."

This clause reflects the absolute sovereignty of the national assemblies and their autonomy insofar as the Executive is concerned.

At the opening of each parliamentary session, the senior member in age of each House occupies the presidential (speaker's) chair, while the youngest members act as secretaries. The senior member arranges for the election of the definitive steering committee, namely: the president, the vice-presidents and secretaries. As soon as this has been done, the definitive steering committee takes over from the provisional one.

Without a steering committee, the Houses are not deemed to be properly constituted and would be unable to perform their functions. Consequently, this is an essential formality to be carried out at the start of each new session.

The steering committees of the two Houses generally comprise members drawn from the various political parties, thus making the committees truly representative of each House. Except in very rare cases, the presidents are appointed from among the members of Parliament belonging to the political parties forming the coalition government.

It often happens that the political parties meet beforehand to decide upon the composition of the steering committee and to agree on the names of members to be elected to the committee. In that case, a single candidate is presented for each post and when this happens no vote is taken and the candidates are proclaimed as elected members of the steering committee in terms of the Assembly's rules.

Article 37 therefore confers on each House the privilege of nominating its president, whereas in terms of the fundamental law (during the period 1814-1830), this appointment was made by the King.

Article 37 also stipulates that the duration of the presidential function is equal to that of the Parliamentary session, and will therefore automatically terminate with the dissolution of Parliament or the closure of the session. However, custom dictated by necessity has somewhat tempered this ruling, in the sense that the president is deemed to remain in office up to the time when he is either re-elected or replaced.

We shall see further on that Article 46, providing that "each House, through its own rules, shall determine the way in which it shall exercise its powers", establishes the autonomous nature of the Houses to which we have already alluded, and the sovereignty of the measures they take for the purpose of exercising their powers. Any intervention by the government, or even by the law, in such matters is therefore prohibited. This ruling also applies to the basic status of the president.

Space is lacking to review the very numerous prerogatives conferred upon the presidents of the two assemblies by the *House Rules*. Yet the entire range of rules and regulations in this regard may easily be summed up in a single principle, which is: "The president represents the House, speaks in its name and directs its work in accordance with the Rules."

Thus defined, the task outlines the scope and importance of the presidential function within the framework of the State's highest offices. Indeed, when one compares Articles 25 and 32 of the Constitution according to which "the members of both Houses represent the Nation" from which "all powers stem", one cannot but realize the primacy of the legislative power in the hierarchy of authority. There can therefore be no question of attributing to those who represent the Houses any other than first place in the entire range of public office. This concept is again formulated, with perhaps greater expressive force than strict accuracy, in the title sometimes bestowed on the presidents of the Houses: that of "First citizens of the State". The same concept is upheld by Protocol when, in public ceremonies, the two presidents of the Houses are assigned the first place immediately after the King.

Apart from the powers conferred on these presidents by the House Rules and which, in view of their source, may be regarded as quasi-constitutional powers, custom has considerably broadened their influence generally throughout the State.

Such influence is difficult to define in precise terms. It does not rest on written rules but is based on tradition and custom, the gradual development of which is explained by the authority vested in the office and the personal prestige surrounding those appointed to it. Placed by their peers at the summit of the political structure, politicians themselves who are generally matured and enriched by the invaluable personal experience they have acquired in the performance of important State functions, the presidents of the two Houses of Parliament quite often appear as the supreme arbiters of public affairs.

Thus, for instance, in the event of a ministerial crisis, it is their opinion which is sought before all others by the Head of the State. There is no case on record of this custom having been set aside; indeed it has become a rule, and it may be asserted that any derogation of it would be fraught with serious consequences.

Thus, too, as a general rule, the presidents of the legislative assemblies are called upon to take action with the Government in order to regulate the work of the Houses, or to enlighten Ministers on their temper and attitude, or again to initiate with them some form of action which, while not exactly falling within the scope of their parliamentary prerogatives as such is nevertheless justified by the national interest bound up with such action. Such interventions are invariably characterized by the most perfect courtesy, and because of the lofty opinions by which they are inspired, they are received with equal consideration; and it never happens that they are contradicted by the president's own personal attitude where party conflicts are concerned.

Impartiality is a specific duty imposed on both presidents in the performance of their parliamentary functions. There is no speech at the opening of a session that does not mention this obligation and that does not contain a solemn pledge to obey it. The presidents must acknowledge no party affiliations on the floor of the House. They must solely acknowledge the representatives of the Nation, all of whom are equal in terms of the Rules.

But their statutory impartiality ceases to apply outside the parliamentary precincts. The presidents make it a point of honour to claim their complete political freedom, and they neglect no opportunity of upholding, outside the Houses, those concepts which they regard as vital to the interests of the State. This has rarely earned them reproach, for such liberty is essential to the prestige surrounding the presidential office which must not be entrusted to men of small stature politically. That such freedom of speech and opinion may be exercised without criticism honours our democracy.

The Rules of the House of Representatives define, in Article 5, the *functions* of the president when the latter effectively chairs a sitting, i.e. when the House is working.

The reader's attention should be drawn to the fact that, broadly speaking, the Senate Rules are identical to those of the Lower House.

Article 5 of the House Rules provides that:

1. The functions of the president are: to maintain order in the assembly, to ensure that the House rules are obeyed, to judge whether bills, motions and other proposals are allowable, to ask questions and put them to the vote, to proclaim the results of votes and ballots, to pronounce the decisions reached by the House, to speak in its name and in accordance with its wishes.

2. The president may not speak in a debate except to state a question and to bring the debate back to it; should he wish to debate he must leave the chair and may not resume it until the debate on that subject has ended.

3. The president apprises the House of all messages, letters and other despatches that concern it, with the exception of anonymous missives.

When the president is replaced by a vice-president during a sitting, the latter exercises, *in conducting the debate,* all the powers and prerogatives of the president (Art. 6 of the House Rules).

Finally, the essential task incumbent on the secretaries is to verify proper voting procedure, to call the roll for nominal votes, to count the "ayes and noes" when voting is done by sitting and standing, and to call the roll of members for purposes of a secret ballot. In certain circumstances they may read out texts and messages to the House on behalf of the president (Art. 7 of the House Rules).

In order to review all matters pertaining to the steering committees of the Houses and their functions in a single commentary, it may be well to indicate the task and status of the Clerk of the Assembly, to whom reference is made in the House Rules but not in the Constitution. Articles 85 and 86 of the Rules of the House of Representatives enunciate the duties and responsibilities of the General Secretary of the Assembly in a lapidary but precise manner.

First and foremost, he records the debates and implements the decisions of the Assembly. He assists the president in all circumstances: public sitting of the House, secret committee, steering committee, Presidential conference, and keeps the minutes of all these meetings. He assumes the practical responsibility of organizing the work of the House and its various committees. On behalf of the steering committee, he holds authority over all the offices and services of the House and the staff employed by them.

Elected by the House for an unspecified period, the Clerk continues to exercise his authority over all offices and services in the name of the steering committee, even though the mandates of the latter's members have expired.

The Electoral Code authorizes the Clerk, after a general election, to receive the official reports sent in by the provincial and district offices, as well as all other relevant documents, so as to prepare for a verification of the powers of the newly elected members.

Among the unwritten powers vested in the Clerk, it may be added that while the content of questions submitted for debate in the House does not fall within his competence, his task is not only to supervise the form in which they are tabled, debated and voted upon, but also to record the decisions of the Assembly, register them and implement them as required.

Legislative procedure is his sphere of competence. His duty is to ensure that regulations, rules and customs are implemented, and that they are rightly interpreted. For this purpose he acts as advisor to the president of the House. To those aware of the vital importance of proper parliamentary procedure in the finalization of questions submitted for debate in Parliament, it will be clearly apparent that the political role of the general secretary is a crucial one. The result is that the man holding this office must be totally independent not only of the Executive power, but also of the various political parties. He belongs to the House as a whole, and must be worthy of its trust and that of all its members.

ARTICLE 38

"Every resolution is passed on the basis of an absolute majority of votes cast, except as shall be prescribed by the House and Senate rules with respect to elections and candidatures.

"Should there be an equal number of votes cast on both sides, the proposal under discussion is thrown out.

"Neither of the two Houses may adopt any resolution without the majority of its members being present."

This article dates from 1831 and has never been modified.

The problem which gave rise to debate was whether abstentions should count or not in establishing a majority, since they are in fact admissible in establishing a quorum (sufficient number of members sitting). In 1969 the Senate, and later the Lower House, with an eye to the forth-coming vote on constitutional reforms, laid down in their rules that abstentions cannot be taken into account when calculating a majority vote, meaning that a bill could be passed by 2 votes to 1 and 120 absten-tions, or that a constitutional clause might be adopted by 7 votes to 2 and 140 abstentions—an absurd situation, but quite possible in theory. In fact, however, such situations do not arise.

The quorum of members present at sittings of the Lower House is 107, namely: 212 (total number of Deputies) divided by 2 equals 106, plus 1. If the number of members is an odd one, the figure of one and a half is added, as the number of votes is not divisible. This is the case in the Senate which has 182 members, and in which the quorum is 92, i.e. half the total number plus one.

The general rule governing voting in both Houses and in the Cultural Councils is that any motion is passed by an absolute majority vote. This ruling applies equally to the voting on laws and the voting on decrees.

There are, however, two series of exceptions to this rule:

a) five cases in which two-thirds of the total votes cast are required (qualified majority): the granting of votes to women (1); authorizing the King to become Head of another State; any revision of the Constitu-tion; the creation of new categories of candidates eligible for member-ship of the Senate; and the granting of authority to the King to name his successor;

---

(1) This problem was disposed of by the law of 27 March 1948.

b) six cases in which not only a two-thirds majority must be secured, but also a simple majority in each of the two language groups on condition that the majority of members in each language group are present (special qualified majority): the extraprovincialization of any area; any change in the boundaries of the language regions; definition of the functioning of the Cultural Councils; decisions on so-called "cultural" matters; decisions as to the form which cultural co-operation will take; and regional organization.

In the cases listed under (a), these are matters of crucial importance to the Belgian State. In the cases listed under (b), these are matters regarded as essential to the French and Dutch cultural communities and their relationship to each other.

ARTICLE 38-B

"Except in the case of budgets and laws requiring a special majority, a reasoned motion signed by at least three-quarters of the members of one of the linguistic groups and introduced after the report has been tabled and before the final voting in public session may declare that the provisions of a draft or proposed bill which it specifies are of such a nature as to have a serious effect on relations between the communities.

"In such cases, parliamentary procedure is suspended and the motion is referred back to the Cabinet which, within a period of thirty days, gives its reasoned findings on the motion and invites the House to reach a decision either on those findings or on the draft or proposed bill in such form as it may have been amended.

"This procedure may only be applied once by the members of a linguistic group in respect of one and the same draft or proposed bill."

This clause dates from the Third Revision of the Constitution (1967-1971).

The question here is one of the two guarantees given to the French-speaking minority: its purpose is to prevent any law from being passed by a majority vote of the Dutch-speaking group despite its rejection by a substantial majority of the French-speaking group. The other guarantee is equal representation of the two language groups in the Cabinet (Article 86-B).

As Dutch-speaking members of Parliament are more numerous than French-speaking members, in theory at least there is a risk that a law can be passed by means of a simple majority vote of the Dutch-speaking Deputies and Senators even though it is deemed unacceptable for material or psychological reasons by the French cultural community. The latter then insisted on the institution of a parliamentary procedure designed to eliminate such a risk. Indeed, the passing of any law in such circumstances would seriously threaten relations between the two cultural communities.

Known as "the alarm bell", this procedure does not apply to budgets, for the latter are not laws in the accepted sense of the term even if they are debated and approved as such. Indeed, budgets do not create any general legal precedents.

No motion may be tabled in the event of a bill which is to be passed by a special majority vote, this being either the ordinary majority of votes cast by members of each of the language groups plus a two-thirds majority vote of all members of the House, or the two-thirds overall majority alone.

The motivated objection must, where necessary, be tabled *after* the bill has been examined by the competent committee of the House of Representatives or the Senate and a report on it presented by the parliamentary committee, and *before* it is finally put to the vote in open session. The objection must be motivated and it must clearly and unequivocally set forth the clause or clauses of the bill in question that are likely to be prejudicial to relations between the two communities.

The motion has the immediate effect of suspending parliamentary procedure. The Cabinet, which comprises an identical number of French-speaking and Dutch-speaking Ministers, is apprised of the problem and gives it further consideration. A compromise must then be sought in line with the best traditions of Belgian parliamentary democracy: in the absence of any absolute majority on one side or the other in the country and in Parliament, solutions through some form of compromise must inevitably be found and, in practice, have indeed often proved very satisfactory.

The newly introduced Article 38-B is therefore aimed at ensuring a harmonious relationship between the two great cultural communities, since the French language community obtains a constitutional guarantee eliminating the risk of its subjection to the law of the other community which enjoys a numerical majority, while the Dutch language community has obtained its cultural autonomy through the provisions of Article 59-B.

ARTICLE 39

"Voting is done either by word of mouth or by sitting and standing; all laws generally are voted on by the calling of names and word of mouth. The election and presentation of candidates are voted on by secret ballot."

This article dates from 1831 and has never been modified.

However, the rules of both Houses have been altered to permit the use of push-button voting and signed voting papers. Article 38 of the Lower House rules provides in effect that "of equal validity to the voting procedure by roll-call and word of mouth is the individual vote by means of a mechanical device, and that cast by means of signed voting papers."

Article 38 associates the public nature of parliamentary sessions as laid down by Article 33 with the obligation incumbent on members of both Houses to make known publicly their attitude to all bills submitted for their approval. Such publicity attendant upon all the essential acts performed by members of Parliament enables proper control to be exercised by their electorate.

The election and presentation of candidates are exempt from this ruling because they concern people, which makes the ballots a matter of delicacy rather than of national importance when it comes to prescribing mandatory legal standards governing community life.

The Belgian Houses of Parliament present candidates or make appointments to fill vacant posts at the Audit Office, the Court of Cassation, the Council of State, the Belgian National Railway Board, and the supervisory committee of the Belgian Savings Bank.

Both Houses, apart from their steering committees, appoint their own delegates to international parliamentary assemblies (the European Parliament, the Council of Europe Advisory Assembly, the Western European Union Assembly, and the Benelux Interparliamentary Advisory Council).

As for the Cultural Councils, they are also called upon to vote on decrees by means of a nominative ballot, while the election and presentation of candidates is also handled here by means of a secret ballot (the appointment of members to the Permanent Commission on Language Supervision and to the Boards of the B.R.T. and the R.T.B.—Belgium's two radio and television networks).

ARTICLE 40

"Each House has the right of investigation."

This constitutional clause applied originally to the House of Representatives and the Senate. The Third Revision of the Constitution extends this procedure to the Cultural Councils, within their own sphere of competence of course.

Usually it is the government which provides all desirable data and information to the parliamentary assemblies, but cases or circumstances may arise when the Houses consider it their duty to conduct a thorough investigation of their own.

However, it was not enough merely to state the principle: a law had to be enacted for its implementation (3 May 1880).

In terms of this law, each House exercises this right either as a corporate body or through a commission set up for the purpose. The law confers on the House, its Commission of Enquiry and the Chairman thereof all the powers vested in an examining magistrate: the House or its Commission may summon witnesses and experts and hear their testimony. Witnesses, interpreters and experts called upon to testify to the House or its Commission of Enquiry are bound by the same obligations as those incumbent on them at a hearing before an examining magistrate: should they refuse or neglect to satisfy these obligations, they are liable to the same penalties. They take oath according to the formula customarily used in the Assize Courts. Perjury and false witness are sanctioned by a prison sentence that can go from two months to three years.

This law needed to be completed so as to provide for the Cultural Councils, whose regional competence did not permit them to conduct an investigation save in the region and on such matters as fell within their scope.

The exceptional procedure consisting of a Parliamentary Enquiry, as will be seen hereunder, has been implemented only five times by the Lower House and once by the Senate since the Kingdom was founded.

Parliamentary Enquiries from 1880 up to this date

(Law of 3 May 1880 on Parliamentary enquiries)

I. *House of Representatives:*

1. 5 May 1880: Parliamentary Commission of Enquiry into the moral and material situation of primary education in Belgium, the results of

the law of 1 July 1879 and the means used to hinder the implementation of that law (known as the *Schools Enquiry Commission*)

2. 10 March 1909: Commission of Enquiry into the effects of the law of 21 March 1902 (modifications to laws governing the militia and the pay of militiamen)

3. 17 April 1935: Parliamentary Commission of Enquiry appointed to establish responsibility for the devaluation of the franc, sanctioned by the law of 30 March 1935 and the Royal Decree of 31 March 1935.

4. 8 January 1959: Parliamentary Commission appointed to conduct an enquiry into the riots which occurred in Leopoldville in January 1959.

5. 22 June 1972: Parliamentary Commission of Enquiry into the direct or disguised introduction of advertising matter (text or image) in television broadcasts by the R.T.B., the B.R.T. and Teledistribution.

II. *Senate:*

1 March 1951: Commission of Enquiry into the activities of the Sequestration Bureau.

ARTICLE 41

"No bill may be passed by either House except after being voted on article by article."

This article, which has never been modified, aims at preventing a government from forcing a vote in the Houses on the overall contents of a law containing clauses some of which are satisfactory and others that are unacceptable.

Without this article, the Houses would not possess complete sovereignty in the matter of legislation.

The procedure governing the approval, in public session, of any draft or proposed bill comprises four phases:

— a general debate,

— a debate on the contents, article by article,

— voting on each article,

— voting on the bill as a whole.

Voting on the individual clauses of a bill need not be done by the calling of names system. They are usually subjected to the "sitting and standing" voting procedure which saves a great deal of time.

Nonetheless, a roll-call vote is sometimes taken on a clause deemed to be an essential one, and should a certain number of members request it.

Similarly, a draft or proposed decree can only be passed by either of the Cultural Councils when it, too, has been voted upon clause by clause.

ARTICLE 42

"The Houses have the right to amend and to divide up the articles and amendments proposed."

This article has never been modified.

The right of amendment vested in the Houses arises out of the right of initiative conferred on them in terms of Article 27 of the Constitution.

This right of amendment and of subdivision is also vested in the Cultural Councils insofar as decrees are concerned.

The rules of both Houses lay down the conditions in which the right of amendment may be implemented, both under the heading of legislation and that of the budget. They stipulate in particular that an organic law cannot be modified by means of a budget amendment.

They also stipulate that all amendments must effectively apply to the specific object or clause of the bill which they are designed to modify.

Finally, they state that "in any proposal (bill, motion, etc.) containing various matters (objects), subdivision under separate headings is automatically and by right adopted whenever this is requested (even by a *single* member)."

ARTICLE 43

"It is prohibited to present petitions to the Houses personally.

"Each House has the right to refer the petitions addressed to it back to the Ministers. The latter are bound to provide explanations regarding their contents whenever the House shall request it."

This article has remained unchanged since 1831.

Its first paragraph by no means places any restriction on the right of any citizen to submit a petition to the public authorities, this principle being upheld by Article 21 of the Constitution. It merely forbids them to be laid before the Houses by the petitioner in person, as this would place unacceptable pressure on members of Parliament and would also favour the bolder at the expense of the shyer, more modest members of the public who are content with committing their petitions to paper and sending them in.

The second paragraph should be read in conjunction with Article 88 which provides that the Houses may demand the attendance of Cabinet Ministers. Both clauses establish the responsibility of Ministers towards the Houses.

The same rules obtain insofar as the Cultural Councils are concerned.

ARTICLE 44

"No member of either of the two Houses may be prosecuted or sought out as a result of the opinions and votes he has expressed in the exercise of his functions."

This article dates from 1831 and has never been modified.

It grants Deputies and Senators total immunity with respect to the speeches they make in Parliament and the votes they have cast both in the Houses and in the Cultural Councils. Thus, the nation's elected representatives in the Senate and in the Lower House may speak and act freely with no fear of becoming involved in legal proceedings.

The immunity conferred by this Article covers not only all speeches delivered in Parliament itself (during public sittings, in committee, or in political groups), but also the opinions expressed at Question Time or during interpellations, and even the written questions laid before the government in the Questions & Answers Bulletin. Statements made as members of a Parliamentary Committee of Enquiry are also immune. But no such immunity applies to speeches made outside Parliament, or to articles written for newspapers, or again in cases where a member of the Lower House or the Senate arranges for the publication or general distribution to the public of a speech he has delivered within parliamentary precincts.

ARTICLE 45

"No member of either of the two Houses may, during the session, be prosecuted or arrested as a punishment save with the permission of the House to which he belongs, except in the case of *flagrante delicto*.

"No bodily constraint may be used towards a member of either of the two Houses during the session, save with the same permission as above.

"The detention or prosecution of a member of either of the two Houses is suspended during the session and throughout its duration if the House shall so require."

This article dates from 1831 and has never been modified.

The parliamentary immunity conferred by this article extends to all offences and misdemeanours committed by a member of Parliament during the performance of his parliamentary duties or outside it. The purpose here is not to grant special privileges to a certain category of citizens, but to ensure the proper functioning of the Houses, which certain persons might attempt to perturb by instituting groundless legal proceedings against an inconvenient political adversary.

The immunity can always be waived. It is up to the House to which the member concerned belongs either to authorize the prosecution or to reject it after reviewing the grounds for complaint, and if the action contemplated does not threaten to place obstacles in the way of the proper conduct of business by the House.

Parliamentary immunity runs no risk of becoming a privilege since it is subjected to a threefold limitation:

— the case of *flagrante delicto*, for here it is obvious that there can be no question of political manoeuvring;

— the limitation in time, since the prosecution may go forward when the parliamentary session closes: it has been delayed merely;

— the possibility that the House itself may authorize the legal proceedings to go forward.

ARTICLE 46

"Each House, through its own Rules, shall determine the way in which it shall exercise its powers."

This article sets the seal on the absolute autonomy of each House, which therefore has the right to establish its own rules without any interference from outside, from the other House, from the Executive, or from any jurisdictional body whatsoever. Each House must, of course, obey constitutional prescriptions which it is free to interpret in its own way.

The Rules of the House of Representatives and the Senate are therefore something more than merely internal regulations: they are genuine sources of public law.

It should be noted that this statutory autonomy of each House has not prevented the two representative assemblies from drawing up their Rules along broadly parallel lines. The fundamental principles governing Parliamentary procedure are the same for both Houses.

Both sets of Rules have been the subject of numerous modifications as time went by, in order to bring them into line with the changing necessities of parliamentary work.

Finally, it should be pointed out that the Rules are framed to organize parliamentary activities and particularly the work done in committee, the conduct of public debates, the right of interpellation, the system of written questions and answers, etc.

In obedience to the Constitution which they clarify where necessary, the Rules must enlighten members as to their rights and obligations; they must ensure that the groundwork is properly prepared for debates and that these are arranged in an orderly fashion. They must also— and this is very important—safeguard freedom of speech and the rights of the Opposition, while taking care not to allow the debates to become unruly or be disturbed, thus discrediting the Assembly and consequently the system itself.

In implementation of the Constitution, the Rules must see to the practical organisation of debating and voting on laws and budgets; the way in which parliamentary initiative is used (proposals, motions and amendments); and the control exercised over the Government (interpellations, written and oral questions).

The Presidents of the two Houses are, beyond all doubt, those parliamentarians who are most thoroughly conversant with the Rules, the interpretation and application of which is incumbent on them. They are assisted in this task by the Clerk of the Assembly, whose extensive knowledge not only of the Rules themselves but of jurisprudence in general, is an invaluable adjunct to the office of Speaker.

The Rules drawn up for the Legislative Assemblies enable the Houses not only to settle problems connected with the implementation of the Constitution as it affects the work of legislation and control over the Government, but also disciplinary problems and certain material questions arising out of the organisation and functioning of Parliament (Clerk or Recorder, fiscal department, accountancy committee, library, officials and employees, the House police).

Without going into details concerning the Rules of the two Houses and their material organisation in particular, it seems essential to give a brief indication of the way in which parliamentary business is conducted in the three spheres that are vital to this institution:

1. the framing of laws,

2. the passing of budgets,

3. control and supervision of the Government's acts.

1. *The framing of laws*

When a bill is tabled by the government before the steering committee of one of the Houses, the president refers it to that committee which it considers competent to conduct a preliminary examination of the bill; where necessary the House may be consulted as to such referral. A bill may also be referred to two or several joint committees or to a special committee to be set up on the basis of proportional representation. In each House there are about 23 Permanent Committees, each specialising in a given subject.

The committee thus apprised of the matter sets to work in the presence of the Minister concerned, and where necessary, that of his staff. A chairman is designated who will draw up the final report with the help of the notes taken by the committee's administrative secretary.

The report must contain a summary of the committee's discussions and its motivated conclusions, specifying how the voting went (usually omitting the names of the individual voters) on each clause of the bill, on any amendments that may have been made to it, and on the proposal as a whole (the final vote). In general the various arguments for and against are not recorded in the name of the speakers so as to preserve the confidential nature of the committee's discussions. The report, approved by the president or by the committee if the latter requests it, is then translated, printed and distributed. At this point, the bill is now ready for the public debate.

This opens with a general discussion in which any member may speak for a maximum of half an hour, while the Minister concerned and the chairman of the committee may both intervene when they wish.

Once this general discussion is over, the House begins to study the individual clauses and any amendments which may have been proposed by the committee or by the Government since the report was tabled.

The House votes on each clause and on each of the amendments, if any.

A bill which has been amended in the course of the first reading must be submitted to a second vote.

When each clause has been passed, the House proceeds to take a nominal vote on the bill as a whole.

If it is passed, it is sent to the other House where the same procedure will begin once more.

If the bill is passed *ne varietur*, it is sent to the Minister concerned who takes the necessary steps to have it sanctioned and promulgated by the King (who is the third branch of the Legislative authority and head of the Executive authority).

The document (parchment) containing the law is signed by the president (speaker) and by two secretaries of each House; it receives the royal signature and that of the Minister or Ministers concerned: and finally, that of the Minister of Justice in his capacity as Keeper of the State Seals. Then the law is published in the *Moniteur belge* (official gazette).

If a bill sent over by one House is amended by the other, it must be returned to the assembly which first passed it, for the wording adopted by the two Houses must be absolutely identical.

Parliamentary initiative in the sphere of legislation allows Deputies and Senators to table bills in any of the national languages. The text is then translated by the competent office in the House concerned. Permission to print must be given by the steering committee. When authorization has been given, the bill is printed and distributed.

In the Lower House, the person who tabled the bill and wishes to see it examined in committee must ask for his request to be taken into consideration. In the Senate, this procedure is virtually automatic.

This formality allows the Houses to refuse the request and to block the bill in its initial stage so as to prevent it from being examined. Such cases of refusal have rarely occurred during the last ten years.

If the request is taken into consideration, it is referred to the competent committee by the President in the same way as the bill itself.

In the Senate, a recent reform has established four Permanent Sections which examine, in public session, most draft and proposed bills and Budget proposals. They proceed with a general debate and with a clause-by-clause discussion. Then the Senate will proceed with the voting in full session, the outcome of which will lead to the final decision.

2. *The passing of budgets*

The passing of budgets by parliamentary vote is essential to the functioning of the State, whether the question is one of receipts (the budget of Way and Means) or expenditures.

When the *Rules of the Lower House* were revised in 1962, new arrangements tending to speed up the debate and examination of budgets were adopted. These reforms were of three kinds:

The first, and the most important, is the possibility now given to the Lower House (1) to debate budgets coming from the Senate (where they were initially tabled) in its competent body, namely: the Permanent Committee which comprises all its effective and substitute members.

These debates, in which all members of the House may take part, are held in a special room in the same way as a committee meeting, the only difference being that the press and the general public are admitted and that such debates are published in the Parliamentary Annals and in the Verbatim Reports on Sittings.

The second major reform is the time limit placed on public sittings of the House or the Permanent Committee; in the first place, the *overall* speaking time allotted to each political group for its *official* speakers is limited; and secondly, the number of sittings to be devoted to each budget is limited. These restrictions were established by the Presidential Conference, a new body created out of whole cloth during the 1962 Revision of the Rules and which, in itself, constitutes the third major reform introduced on that occasion.

The Presidential Conference, which consists of the President (speaker), Vice-Presidents, and leaders of the political parties each of whom is accompanied by a delegate from his party, is principally responsible for drawing up the order of work in the House each week before submitting it to the House itself. (2)

---

(1) A reform is now being introduced both to reduce the number of permanent bodies and to extend their competence to include legislative matters.
(2) In the Senate, there is a Committee for Parliamentary work.

This reform, which enables the political parties to state their views in the preparatory stages, prevents the great loss of time formerly experienced during the interminable debates at public sittings which were solely concerned with arranging the order of work.

The Presidential Conference also intervenes in other spheres as an advisory body—especially in connection with requests for recommendations by the Council of State—and it is also a political organ of the House, one which is more influential than the steering committee from which the leaders of the political parties are excluded.

In order to save time, the budgets are shared between the Lower House and the Senate on the alternating principle whereby each House in turn undertakes the initial examination of a certain number of budgets one year, while it becomes the turn of the other House to do so the following year.

The sole exception is the budget of Ways and Means, which is always submitted first to the Lower House.

Except insofar as has been stated above, the procedure governing the examination of budgets is the same as that for the tabling of ordinary bills, but the referral to the various committees is laid down in the Rules themselves, meaning that this does not depend on either the President or the House itself.

Strict rules have been framed to speed up the tabling of the report and the public debate.

Apart from the overall speaking time allotted by the Presidential Conference to each political party, other members not officially instructed to speak are allowed ten minutes each.

Where the individual clauses and amendments are concerned, speaking time is limited to five minutes each.

It should also be added that, save in the case where the Lower House decides otherwise, the budgets voted upon and sent over by the Senate are subjected neither to a report nor to an examination in committee.

3. *Control exercised over the acts of the government*

This is one of the essential tasks incumbent on Parliament which, having placed its confidence in the government when the latter was formed, is equally empowered to demand an accounting at any time on the subject of its policies and the acts performed by its Ministers.

Lack of confidence may take several forms, in particular that of refusing to vote on budgets or the adoption of an order of the day, fully motivated, tabled at the end of an interpellation.

It is obviously difficult for members of Parliament to keep fully informed of all that is going on, except if they ask questions or if, rumours having reached them regarding matters that might weaken their confidence in a Minister, they decide to interpellate him directly.

Questions may be put either in writing or orally, and may even be tabled as matters of urgency.

When the answer has been given, no debate may take place nor any order of the day be tabled.

The Minister thus questioned may reserve his reply, which frequently happens in the case of written questions but almost never in the case of oral ones.

Questions are merely one way of obtaining information, and another way is provided by the debates on budgets during which numerous questions may be raised in connection with the policy pursued by the Minister concerned.

Interpellation is something else again, for it tends to obtain from a Minister not only the information actually sought, but also some justification of the acts he has performed or for which he bears the responsibility, or even an explanation of the absence of any reaction on his part when faced with a particular situation.

If the explanations given do not satisfy the interpellator, he may in serious cases table an order of the day implying lack of confidence, which means that if this order of the day is adopted by the House, the Minister under indictment must resign. This extreme solution occurs only in very rare cases, for the majority benches are usually content—in the event that they do not actually wish to express genuine confidence—with merely tabling an order of the day involving no definite action either way.

The Rules of both Houses contain several clauses specifically dealing with questions, interpellations and orders of the day.

Furthermore, the Rules of the Lower House specify a certain number of cases in which questions are irreceivable: special or personal cases, statistical information, documentation, or legal consultations, the purpose of which is the same as that of an interpellation or a bill already tabled.

SECTION I — THE HOUSE OF REPRESENTATIVES

ARTICLE 47

"Members of the House of Representatives are directly elected by all citizens aged 21 years and over, resident for at least six months in the same borough, and who do not come under any of the causes of disenfranchisement laid down by the law.

"Each elector is entitled to only one vote.

"A law may, under the same conditions, attribute voting rights to women. This law must secure at least two-thirds of the votes cast."

This article, dating from the 1921 Revision of the Constitution, states the principle of universal suffrage pure and simple. The franchise was extended to women by a law of 27 March 1948, passed by a two-thirds majority vote as required by the Constitution.

Formerly, up to 1893, the property assessment system was in force, i.e. only citizens with a specified minimum tax rating were entitled to vote.

The constitutional reform of 1893 introduced universal suffrage qualified by the plural vote, with a maximum of three votes. This was known as the Ability and Property Assessment Franchise (vote capacitaire et censitaire). An extra vote was granted to married taxpayers and land-owners, while two extra votes were granted to persons holding degrees in higher education, and to those who occupied or had previously held certain offices or who were engaged in certain professions.

In the opinion of the Constituent Assembly, the six-months' prior residence requirement was a factor indicating the stability and reliability of the citizen. Today, if an elector has changed his address within this six-month period, he must cast his vote in the borough of his former residence.

As for the legal causes of disenfranchisement, they are few and are subject to a judicial order (such as court sentences for a serious crime, or cases of lunacy).

It should also be noted that voting by proxy or a postal vote is possible in certain circumstances (for enlisted soldiers, invalids, etc.).

For some years now the question has been under consideration of lowering the voting age to 18 years, but this will call for another amendment to the Constitution.

ARTICLE 48

"The constitution of the electoral bodies is regulated for each province by the law.

"Elections are held on the basis of the proportional representation system as specified by the law.

"Voting is compulsory and secret. It takes place in the borough save in exceptional cases to be specified by law."

In 1831 Article 48 read as follows :

"Elections are held on the basis of such divisions of provinces and in such places as the law shall specify."

In 1893 the following text was adopted :

"The constitution of the electoral bodies is regulated for each province by the law.

"Voting is compulsory and takes place in the borough save in exceptional cases to be specified by law."

This modification replaced the provincial divisions by the provinces themselves as electoral entities, and made voting compulsory.

The present wording was adopted in 1920 : it instituted proportional representation and the secret ballot and raised them to the status of constitutional principles.

A secret ballot is an elementary democratic requirement. As for proportional representation, this is a guarantee to minority groups and ensures that the national representation shall faithfully reflect the entire population. According to this voting system, a broad parallel exists between the number of votes gained by each of the various political parties and the number of seats they effectively secure in Parliament; furthermore, there is a coupling system between the lists of candidates up to the provincial level, i.e. from one electoral district to another within the same province.

The following is a brief review of the electoral system presently in force.

1st principle : the elections are held in electoral districts which are coupled up to provincial level; each province has from two to five electoral districts.

2nd principle : the number of seats to be filled in each electoral district is determined by the population figure according to the latest ten-yearly census.

3rd principle : the number of valid votes collected in each electoral district is divided by the number of seats to be filled in the district, which gives the *electoral divisor*. This entitles each party reaching the electoral divisor to one seat.

It also determines the number of seats which goes to each list absolutely. This number is obtained by dividing the number of valid votes by the electoral divisor.

This division gives the electoral quotient of the district.

4th principle : The provincial bureau then proceeds to allocate those seats which have not been attributed at the level of the districts. For this purpose, the electoral figure is calculated (the number of valid votes gained by each list) throughout the entire province.

This electoral figure is, *for each list*, divided by one or more figures higher than the total number of seats which each list has won in the districts.

The results of this division for each list are described as *provincial electoral quotients*.

They are classified in order of their importance.

5th principle : The allocation of seats on the basis of this classification of the provincial electoral quotients is done firstly by bearing in mind the quotients established by the main district office for each list so as to operate this sharing-out according to the remaining fractions. These fractions are obtained by dividing the district electoral quotient by a number immediately higher than the number of seats obtained by each list in the district.

The remaining seats are allocated according to the size of the various fractions calculated.

And now, in the light of two practical examples, we shall proceed to describe the Belgian electoral system.

First example : the allocation of seats to the various lists (no coupling in this instance).

132

Supposing : 4 lists of candidates;
11 seats to be filled.

	List 1	List 2	List 3	List 4
Electoral figures	54,000	40,000	21,000	9,800
To be divided by 1	54,000 1st	40,000 2nd	21,000 4th	9,800
2	27,000 3rd	20,000 5th	10,500 10th	4,900
3	18,000 6th	13,333 8th	7,000	3,266
4	13,500 7th	10,000 11th	5,250	2,950
5	10,800 9th	8,000	4,200	1,960
6	9,000			

The electoral figures (no. of valid votes) amassed by the various lists are successively divided by 1, 2, 3, 4, 5, 6, etc. These quotients are then classified in order of magnitude down to the 11th seat to be filled. The last quotient is the electoral divisor. Each list obtains as many seats as its electoral figure contains the electoral divisor. (1)

List 1 : 54,000 divided by 10,000 = 5 (seats) + remainder,
List 2 : 40,000 divided by 10,000 = 4 (seats),
List 3 : 21,000 divided by 10,000 = 2 (seats) + remainder,
List 4 : 9,800 divided by 10,000 = no seat.

Total : 124,800 votes   11 seats

Second example : the coupling or grouping of lists.

In this case, the overall total of valid votes cast in the district is divided by the number of seats to be filled : the quotient thus obtained constitutes the electoral divisor. The electoral figures obtained by the various lists are divided by this divisor and the results show the number of seats that can be allocated at once.

The electoral divisor is higher than in the example given above (124,800 divided by 11 = 11,345); accordingly, 3 seats remain to be filled in the present instance.

So :

List 1 : 54,000 divided by 11,345 = 4 seats + remainder,
List 2 : 40,000 divided by 11,345 = 3 seats + remainder,
List 3 : 21,000 divided by 11,345 = 1 seat + remainder.

                        8 seats

(1) This apparently complicated system leads to a fairly exact parallel between the number of votes cast and the number of seats allocated. It was worked out by Victor D'Hondt, Professor at the Faculty of Law, University of Ghent (1841-1901).

The three seats which remain unfilled in the districts will be the subject of a further allocation at the provincial level : the electoral figures are divided by 1, 2, 3 and so on if the list of candidates has not yet obtained a seat, by 2, 3, 4 and so on if the list has obtained a single seat, by 3, 4, 5, etc. if it has already won two seats, and so forth. The quotients thus obtained are classified in order of magnitude up to a number of quotients equal to that of the seats which are still unfilled; each useful quotient entitles the allocation of an extra seat. The method of implementation is set out in the Electoral Code.

Therefore, in our second example, there were still three seats which remained to be filled.

This is how their allocation is calculated :

List 2 : 40,000 divided by 4 = 10,000 + remainder, making the 9th seat,

List 2 : 40,000 divided by 4 = 10,000 + remainder, making the 11th seat,

List 3 : 21,000 divided by 2 = 10,500 + remainder, making the 10th seat.

ARTICLE 49

"Para. 1 — The Lower House comprises 212 members.

"Para. 2 — Each electoral district has as many seats as result from dividing its total population by the national divisor, i.e. when the total population of the Kingdom is divided by 212.[1]
"Remaining seats are allocated to those districts with the largest surplus population not yet represented.

"Para. 3 — The distribution of members of the Lower House as between districts (constituencies) is effected in proportion to the population by the King.

"For this purpose, a population census whose results he publishes within six months, is carried out every ten years.[2]

"Within three months following such publication, he determines the number of seats allocated to each constituency.

"The new distribution applies with effect from the next general election.

"Para. 4 — Electoral districts are determined by legislation; this also lays down the necessary qualifications to be on the electoral list and how the electoral procedure shall be conducted."

This article dates from the Third Revision of the Constitution (1967-1971) and replaces the former 1831 wording which was as follows: "The electoral law determines the number of Deputies according to the population figure; this number may not exceed the proportion of one Deputy to every 40,000 inhabitants. It also determines the qualifications necessary to be an elector and how electoral procedures are to be conducted."

Owing to the fact that the population of Belgium had more than doubled in one century, the number of Deputies had also doubled, and this gave rise to much criticism on the part of the general public (108 Deputies in 1847 — 212 in 1949).

This figure has not increased since 1949, but as the population increase varies from one electoral district to another, the number of seats allocated to each constituency has had to be modified at regular intervals

---

(1) Presently 45,200.
(2) In terms of the law of 31 December 1856, date of the first ten-yearly census.

in keeping with the fluctuating population figures revealed by the ten-yearly census in the various electoral districts.

This decision was given material form by the adoption of a new Article 49 of the Constitution.

The reallocation of seats is now done by means of a Royal Decree in terms of this article.

As a result, the redistribution process has become an automatic one and no longer depends on the initiative of the legislator, although the latter retains his right of control over the government. It should be emphasized that this task, which is undertaken by the Executive, merely calls for some simple arithmetic whereby the redistribution of seats is easily calculated. Any division or alteration of electoral districts, however, is still a matter which the legislator alone can handle.

By fixing the number of Representatives once and for all at the figure of 212, the Constituent Assembly has also definitively fixed the number of directly elected Senators at 106, for Article 54 of the Constitution does, in fact, provide that the number of Senators directly voted into office by the electorate shall be equal to half the number of Deputies.

ARTICLE 50

"To be eligible, it is necessary:

"1 — to be Belgian by birth or to have been granted full naturalization,

"2 — to enjoy civil and political rights,

"3 — to be aged 25 years or over,

"4 — to be legally resident in Belgium.

"No other condition of eligibility may be required."

The present text dates from the Second Constitutional Reform (1920-1921). It replaced the 1831 wording which was as follows:

"To be eligible, it is necessary:

"1 — to be Belgian by birth or to have been granted full naturalization,

"2 — to enjoy civil and political rights,

"3 — to be aged at least 25 years,

"4 — to be resident in Belgium.

"No other condition of eligibility may be required."

It should be noted that during the period from 1831 to 1893, while certain citizens were disenfranchised owing to their insufficiently high tax assessment, they could nevertheless be elected to the House of Representatives: they were eligible even though they were not electors (see Article 47).

ARTICLE 51

"The members of the House of Representatives are selected for a term of four years.

"The House is renewed every four years."

This article was adopted in 1921 in replacement of the former 1831 text which read as follows:

"The members of the House of Representatives are elected for a term of four years. Half of them are renewable every two years, according to categories specified by the electoral law. In the event of dissolution, the House is entirely renewed."

The purpose of the old text was to avoid any possibility of a too sudden change, since at least half the Deputies would retain their seats. This wording bears the imprint of the 1831 Constituent Assembly which aimed at maximum stability.

The new article was drafted so as to prevent too frequent elections, even though today it is rare for the Houses to sit for the full period of four years. Quite often an early dissolution of Parliament takes place (Art. 71). It is nevertheless desirable that legislatures should not be too short so as to permit the accomplishment of certain legislative duties.

Inversely, legislatures that last too long would give rise to an imbalance between the official parliamentary majority which remains unchanged and the mentality of the electorate which is continually undergoing a process of evolution, whether fast or slow. A term of four years is a reasonable one.

ARTICLE 52

"Each member of the House of Representatives is entitled to an annual indemnity of 12,000 francs.

"He is furthermore entitled to travel free on all lines of communication that are operated or contracted out by the State.

"The law specifies those methods of transportation which members may use free of charge apart from those mentioned above.

"An annual indemnity, chargeable to the endowment destined to cover the expenses of the House of Representatives, may be attributed to the president of that assembly.

"The House determines the amounts that may be levied on the indemnity under the heading of contributions to the retirement or pension funds it has deemed useful to set up."

This wording dates from the 1921 Constitutional Reform, and the article in question has in fact been modified twice.

In 1831 the wording was as follows:

"Each member of the House of Representatives is entitled to a monthly indemnity of 200 florins (1) for the entire duration of the session. Those members resident in the city where the session takes place are not entitled to any indemnity."

In 1893 the following version was adopted:

"Each member of the House of Representatives is entitled to a yearly indemnity of 4,000 francs (2).

He is furthermore entitled to travel free on the State railways and on those railways which have been contracted out, starting from his place of residence to that city in which the session takes place."

The purpose being obviously to prevent political power from falling into the hands of the wealthy alone, it is necessary to provide for the decent remuneration of those who dedicate themselves to the management of public affairs, especially today when a parliamentary mandate has developed into one of the most time and energy consuming occupations of all. It is also quite understandable that some retirement or pension scheme should be set up for the people concerned.

---

(1) About 26.500 francs at 1974 values.
(2) About 265.700 francs at 1974 values.

The constitutional sum of 12,000 francs has completely lost its meaning owing to the progressive decline in the value of the franc. The House of Representatives has gradually adapted it in step with rising prices. Today, the parliamentary indemnity amounts to 900,000 francs per annum (tied to the cost of living index).

Half of this sum is regarded as a reimbursement of the expenses incurred in the performance of parliamentary duties, and this half is tax-free. The other is a genuine salary.

Members of the House of Representatives may, after an eight-year term, apply for a retirement pension (not a full one) on condition that they have reached the age of 55 years. To obtain the full pension, they must have sat for at least twenty years.

Moreover, in the event they are not re-elected, Members of Parliament benefit from an indemnity for their reclassification or establishment, equivalent to their parliamentary emoluments for a period of nine or eighteen months, depending on their seniority in Parliament.

The growing complexity of the tasks incumbent on members of Parliament requires indeed that they must virtually renounce all other forms of employment. This explains why the indemnity has necessarily been increased, particularly as widespread democratization has brought about the election to Parliament of persons with no private means.

SECTION II — THE SENATE

ARTICLE 53

"The Senate is composed:

1. of members elected on the basis of the population in each province, in accordance with Article 47. The provisions of Article 48 are applicable to the election of those Senators;

2. of members elected by the provincial councils in the proportion of one senator to every 200,000 inhabitants. Every surplus of at least 125,000 inhabitants confers the right to elect an additional senator. However, every provincial council shall nominate at least three Senators;

3. of members elected by the Senate on the basis of half the number of Senators elected by the provincial councils. If the number is an odd one, it is increased by one digit.

These members are designated by the Senators who were elected according to the provisions of 1. and 2. of the present article.

The election of Senators who are elected according to the provisions of 2. and 3. of the present article, is carried out according to the proportional representation system as laid down by the law."

This article has also been modified on two successive occasions.

In 1831 it read as follows:

"The members of the Senate are elected on the basis of the population in each province by those citizens who elect the members of the House of Representatives."

Consequently, there was only one kind of Senator: those who had been directly elected.

In 1893 the provincial senators were added to their number, and the article was modified as follows:

"The Senate is composed:

1. of members elected on the basis of the population in each province, in accordance with Article 47: however, the law may require that the electors be 30 years of age or more. The provisions of Article 48 are applicable to the election of these Senators;

2. of members elected by the provincial councils, on the basis of two senators per province with less than 500,000 inhabitants, three per province with from 500,000 to one million inhabitants, and four per province with over one million inhabitants."

In 1921 the article was adopted according to its present wording, as a result of which a third category of senators was instituted: that of the co-opted Senators. As the provincial councils themselves are elected bodies, the senators appointed by those councils are also genuine representatives of the nation, but at one remove. The co-opted Senators chosen by the directly elected Senators and the provincial Senators are therefore also elected, but at two removes.

It should be recalled that there is also a fourth category of Senators: this comprises Belgian princes of the Royal House in the direct line of succession. (see Article 58.)

*
**

Generally speaking, it may be said that the members of both Houses, whether directly or indirectly elected, are in fact elected according to the system of proportional representation.

The constitutional ruling that allocates at least three seats to provincial senators nominated by each province, whatever the population figure may be in that province, is a derogation of this system in that it favours the relatively underpopulated province or provinces which, because of this population factor, are slightly "under-represented" in the Belgian parliament.

Far from placing the Belgian electoral system on a majority footing, this constitutional ruling does in fact provide an additional guaranteed protection for the geographical minorities in the country.

ARTICLE 54

"The number of Senators directly elected by the electorate is equal to half the number of members of the House of Representatives."

The wording of this article dates from 1893. The original 1831 text read as follows:

"The Senate consists of a number of members equal to half the members of the other House."

Because of the institution of the category of provincial Senators in 1893, it became necessary to specify that Article 54 was concerned solely with the directly elected Senators.

Since the number of members of the House of Representatives was fixed once and for all at the figure of 212 during the Third Constitutional Reform, the number of directly elected Senators is automatically fixed once and for all at the figure of 106 (see Article 49).

On the other hand, and even without the need for a further revision of the Constitution, the number of provincial Senators and, consequently, that of the co-opted Senators, will increase in proportion to the rising population figure in Belgium. At the present time, apart from its 106 directly elected members, the Senate has 50 provincial Senators and 25 co-opted Senators, making a total of 181 Senators, to which must be added a single Senator by right (1). (See Article 58.)

It follows that, in order to calculate the quorum of those present, the figure used as a basis for this calculation is 182.

---

(1) Prince Albert, brother of the King and Heir Presumptive to the Throne.

ARTICLE 55

"The Senators are elected for a term of four years. The Senate is entirely renewed every four years."

This article dates from 1921 and replaces the 1831 wording which read as follows:

"The Senators are elected for a term of eight years; half of them are renewed every four years in accordance with the order of the series laid down by the electoral law.

"In the event of dissolution, the Senate is entirely renewed."

Election for an eight-year term and renewal by halves were provisions aimed at reinforcing the stability and composition of at least one of the two legislative assemblies, a stability already sought for in the case of the Lower House since the latter was also only renewable by halves, every two years during a total four-year term.

The third Belgian Constituent Assembly (1919 to 1921) had observed that the electorate did in fact ensure such stability by re-electing a great many of the outgoing Senators. In those circumstances, it was regarded as a more normal and democratic procedure to provide for a complete renewal of both Houses at least every four years (see Article 71). In that way, the composition of both Houses reflects to a greater extent the will of the Belgian people and its gradual evolution.

ARTICLE 56

"To be elected Senator, it is necessary:

1. to be Belgian by birth or to have been granted full naturalization;

2. to enjoy civil and political rights;

3. to be legally resident in Belgium;

4. to be at least forty years of age."

The above provisions have been modified on two occasions; the present wording dates from 1921.

The 1831 text stipulated that "in order to be elected and to *remain* a Senator", these four conditions had to apply throughout the Senator's term of office.

Furthermore, a 5th clause required the candidate Senator to pay at least 1,000 florins (132,000 francs at today's values) per annum as income tax, including licence dues.

In those provinces where the roll of citizens paying 1,000 florins in income tax did not attain the proportion of 1 out of every 6,000 inhabitants, the list could be rounded out by adding the names of the highest tax-paying citizens in the province until such time as the proportion of 1 out of 6,000 was attained.

In 1893 Clause 5 was replaced by the following text:

"5. to pay to the State Treasury at least 1,200 francs of direct taxes, including licence dues;

or to be either the owner or the usufructuary of real estate situated in Belgium, the rateable value of which amounts to at least 12,000 francs.

In those provinces where the number of these eligible candidates does not attain the proportion of 1 out of every 5,000 inhabitants, the list may be completed by adding the highest taxpayers in the province until that proportion is attained. Citizens whose names are entered in this complementary list are only eligible in the province in which they have their legal residence."

The purpose of Clause 4 (governing age), which has never been modified, is to make the Senate a more weighty and mature assembly.

The purpose of Clause 5 was to recruit Senators from amongst only those wealthy classes of the population, and thus to make the Senate a more conservative body than the Lower House.

These two conditions, and the adjunction of Senators elected by the Provincial Councils and later the co-opted Senators, means that there is, in practice if not in theory, a difference between the two assemblies: the Lower House appears as a more "political" body, while the Senate appears as a "House of Ponderation".

ARTICLE 56-B

"To be elected Senator under provision n° 1 of Article 53, it is also necessary to belong to one of the following categories:

"1. Ministers, former Ministers, and Ministers of State;

"2. Members and former members of the House of Representatives and the Senate;

"3. Holders of a graduation certificate awarded by one of the higher educational establishments, a list of which is laid down by law;

"4. Former superior officers in the Army and Navy;

"5. Regular members and former members of the commercial courts who have served for at least two terms;

"6. Those who have, for at least ten years, performed the office of minister of one of the forms of worship whose members are entitled to a salary chargeable to the State;

"7. Regular members and former regular members of one of the royal academies, and professors and former professors of one of the higher educational establishments, a list of which is laid down by law;

"8. Former provincial governors; members and former members of the Permanent Deputations; former district commissioners;

"9. Members and former members of the provincial councils who have served for at least two terms;

"10. Mayors and former mayors, town councillors and former town councillors of those boroughs which are the chief towns of districts and those with over 4,000 inhabitants;

"11. Former governors-general and vice governors-general of the Belgian Congo; members and former members of the Colonial Council;

"12. Former directors-general, former directors and former inspectors-general of the various ministerial departments;

"13. The owners and usufructuaries of real estate and landed property located in Belgium, the rateable value of which amounts to at least 12,000 francs; those taxpayers who pay at least 3,000 francs in direct taxes annually to the State Treasury;

"14. Those who, with the rank of managing director or similar rank, have been placed for five years in charge of the day-to-day management of a Belgian commercial joint-stock company, the capital of which is paid up in the amount of at least one million francs;

"15. The heads of industrial enterprises permanently employing at least 100 workers, and agricultural enterprises with an area of at least 30 hectares (123,5 acres);

"16. Those who, with the rank of director-manager or some similar rank, have been placed for three years in charge of the day-to-day management of a Belgian cooperative society having at least 500 members over the past five years;

"17. Those who, as effective members, have for five years held the post of president or secretary of a mutual benefit society or federation with at least 1,000 members over the past five years;

"18. Those who, as effective members, have for five years held the post of president or secretary of a professional, industrial or agricultural association with at least 500 members over the past five years;

"19. Those who, for five years, have acted as president of a chamber of commerce or industry with at least 300 members over the past five years;

"20. Members of industrial and labour councils and of provincial agricultural commissions and conciliation boards who have served in that capacity for at least two terms;

"21. Elected members of one of the advisory councils set up alongside ministerial departments.

"A law may create new categories of eligibility; it must be passed by a two-thirds majority vote at least."

This article dates from the Second Revision of 1919-1921.

As we have seen, the general conditions governing eligibility for membership of the Senate were fixed by Article 56, while a 5th clause dating from 1831 and modified in 1893 further imposed a minimum tax assessment. This latter condition was only required of senators directly elected by the Belgian electorate.

It is quite normal that in terms of a system based on two separate and differently constituted Houses, the Constituent Assembly should have sought to operate a number of important distinctions.

In 1893, when a new category of senators was instituted — that of the provincial senators — the then Constituent Assembly inserted an Article 56-B stating that "the senators elected by the provincial councils are exempted from the tax assessment clause; they may not belong to the assembly which elects them, nor have been a member thereof, during the two years preceding the date of their election." We shall find this latter clause under Article 56-C.

The first sub-clause in that new text indicated that the 1893 Constituent Assembly placed far greater confidence in the choice of the provincial councils than it did in that of the electorate. The 1919-1921 Constituent Assembly maintained that difference, since it replaced the tax requirement by a series of alternative conditions regarding senators directly elected by the people and dispensed therefrom those indirectly elected by senators (either those designated by the provincial councils or those co-opted by other senators).

Article 56-B as it stands therefore lays down alternative conditions, in the sense that only one of these need be met. Apart from those which require or presuppose personal means (see No. 13), there are others involving knowledge (see Nos. 3 and 7) or experience (see Nos. 8, 11 and 12). The purpose here was to render ineligible any person who did not already assume certain responsibilities in society. All these conditions are therefore vestiges of the tax assessment and capability systems. In actual fact, however, these provisions today exclude virtually no-one: owing to the progressive devaluation of the franc, most Belgian citizens meet the requirement laid down in No. 13 and are therefore eligible as Senators.

The abolition of Article 56-B was considered by the Constituent Assembly of 1970. The House Commission was in favour of its elimination, but the Senate Commission opposed it, for reasons connected, it would appear, with prestige.

ARTICLE 56-C

"Senators elected by the provincial councils may not belong to the assembly which elects them nor have been a member thereof during the two years preceding the date of their election."

This provision dates from the Third Constitutional Reform (1967-1970) and replaces the 1921 text which read as follows:

"Senators elected by the provincial councils may not belong to the assembly which elects them, nor have been a member thereof, during the year of their election or during the two previous years."

This article had been taken from the old Article 56-B.

The 1921 text, as also that which had appeared under Article 56-B since 1893, laid itself open to two interpretations: in the phrase "during the two previous years", the word "previous" might be taken to mean either "previous to the year of election" or "previous to the day of their election". In the first case, the delay would have to be two years plus the year of election; in the second case, the delay would be two years only.

In order to terminate conclusively the ambivalent interpretation to which this text had given rise in the past when the question was one of verifying the powers of certain Senators, the 1970 Constituent Assembly was at pains to define its exact import by adding the words "during the two years preceding the date of their election." This solution, moreover, corresponded with the interpretation placed on this clause for years past by the Senate when fixing the precise period concerned. The words "during the year of their election" became redundant, since this period falls within the delay of two years preceding the date of election, and they were therefore struck out.

Article 56-C does not, therefore, permit a provincial councillor or a former provincial councillor who has relinquished his office *within less than two years* to take up the post of *provincial* Senator; but he may be either elected directly or co-opted.

ARTICLE 56-D

"In the event of a dissolution of the Senate, the King may dissolve the provincial councils.

"The act of dissolution contains a summons to the provincial electors within forty days, and to the provincial councils within two months."

This article dates from 1921. It should be read in conjunction with Article 71 which allows for an anticipatory dissolution of the Houses.

It is desirable, whenever the Senate is renewed, that the intermediate body which stands between the electorate and the provincial Senators, i.e. the provincial councils, should also be renewed so that the new Senate may reflect public opinion, to the extent that it has evolved since the previous general election, more faithfully and accurately.

ARTICLE 57

"Senators receive no salary.

"They are, however, entitled to the reimbursement of their expenses. This indemnity is fixed at four thousand francs a year.

"They are furthermore entitled to travel free of charge on all line of communication operated or contracted out by the State.

"The law lays down those means of transportation which they may use free of charge apart from the lines mentioned above."

This text dates from 1921; it should be compared with the provisions of Article 52 concerning the indemnity payable to the Deputies. It replaces the 1831 text which read as follows:

"Senators receive neither salary nor indemnity."

In 1831 it was quite understandable that no indemnity should be provided for senators, since these were wealthy men at that time.

By 1921, however, the democratic principle had made sufficient progress for the concept of an indemnity to be agreed.

As a result of progressive devaluation, the stipulated amount of 4,000 francs has subsequently been adapted by the Senate itself without resorting to a further revision of the Constitution.

At the present time, Senators enjoy the same indemnities as those granted to members of the House of Representatives.

Members of the Senate may, after a five year term of office, apply for a retirement pension (not a full one) on condition that they have attained the age of 60 years. To obtain the full pension, they must have held a seat in the Senate for at least twenty years.

ARTICLE 58

"The sons of the King, or failing these, Belgian princes of that branch of the Royal Family which is in the line of succession, are senators by right at the age of eighteen years. They are only entitled to speak and vote at the age of twenty-five years."

Article 58 had been drawn up in 1831 as follows:

"At the age of eighteen years, the Heir Presumptive of the King is a senator by right. He is only entitled to speak and vote at the age of twenty-five years."

The purpose of this article was to provide the future Head of the State with a course of political training by having him participate in the work and debates of a parliamentary assembly.

At the time of the First Constitutional Reform (1893), the present wording was adopted. It extends the right to sit in the Senate to all princes in the direct line of succession.

At the present time, Prince Albert alone benefits from this right. The evolution of political custom and opinion probably explains why his participation in the activities of the Senate is, so to speak, more or less a symbolic one. Prince Albert is, in fact, particularly attentive to all problems connected with Belgium's economic expansion abroad, and for many years now he has personally headed a number of important trade missions to foreign countries. Matters involving urban redevelopment, as well as the state of the nation from the ecological standpoint, are also the subject of his concern and the work he accomplishes in the service of Belgium.

ARTICLE 59

"Any assembly of the Senate which is held outside the time of the session of the House of Representatives shall automatically be null and void."

This article dates from 1831 and has never been modified.

The First Constituent Assembly wished to ensure that the Senate should serve as a counterweight to the House of Representatives. But the pre-eminence of the latter should not be construed as allowing the Senate to act on its own, which would have upset the democratic interplay of powers.

The House of Representatives is in fact deemed to reflect the feelings of the nation at large, all of its members having been directly elected by the people.

In practice, however, this constitutional arrangement has lost all its significance: the sessions of both Houses are closed at the same time, usually on the eve of the opening of the following session.

The 1970 Constituent Assembly has reinforced this rule by extending it to the Cultural Councils, any assembly of which, held outside the period during which Parliament is in session, is automatically considered to be null and void. (See Article 59-B, para. 2, in fine.)

SECTION III — THE CULTURAL COUNCILS

ARTICLE 59-B

"Section 1. There is a cultural council for the French cultural community, made up of members of the French linguistic group of both Houses, and a cultural council for the Dutch cultural community, made up of the members of the Dutch linguistic group of both Houses.

"A bill passed on a majority vote within each linguistic group of each of the Houses, subject to the majority of the members of each group being present and providing that the total votes cast in favour in the two linguistic groups attains two-thirds of the votes cast, shall determine the procedure whereby the cultural councils exercise their powers with particular reference to Articles 33, 37, 38, 39, 40, 41, 42, 43, 44, 59, 70 and 88.

"Section 2. The cultural councils, each in its own sphere, shall determine by decree :

"1. cultural matters;

"2. education, excluding all matters appertaining to the Schools Covenant, compulsory education, teaching structures, diplomas, subsidies, salaries, and the standards governing the student population;

"3. co-operation between the cultural communities and international cultural co-operation.

"A law passed with the majority specified in Section 1, paragraph 2, shall lay down the cultural matters referred to at (1) above, and also the forms of co-operation referred to at (3) of this paragraph.

"Section 3. Moreover the cultural councils, each in its own sphere shall determine by decree, to the exclusion of the legislator, the use of languages for :

"1. administrative matters;

"2. the education provided in establishments which are set up, subsidised or recognised by the public authorities;

"3. industrial relations between employers and their personnel, together with such business instruments and documents as are laid down by the law and regulations.

"Section 4. Such decrees as are promulgated in pursuance of Section 2 shall have the force of law respectively in the French language region and in the Dutch language region and also in respect of institutions established in the bilingual region of Brussels-Capital which, by virtue of their activities, must be considered as belonging exclusively to one or other of the cultural communities.

"Such decrees as are promulgated in pursuance of Section 3 shall have force of law respectively in the French language region and in the Dutch language region except as regards :

"— such boroughs or groups of boroughs which are adjacent to another linguistic region and where the law lays down or permits the use of a language other than that of the region in which they are located;

"— departments whose activities extend beyond the linguistic region in which they are established;

"—national and international institutions referred to in legislation whose activity is common to more than one cultural community.

"Section 5. Initiative is vested in the King and in the members of the cultural councils.

"Articles 67, 69 and 129 are applicable to the decrees.

"Section 6. The law determines the overall credit which is made available to each cultural council which controls the allocation thereof by decree.

"This credit is arrived at in the light of objective criteria laid down by the law.

"Funds of an equal amount are fixed in matters which, by their nature, do not lend themselves to objective criteria. In the light of the same rules, the law determines the proportion of this credit which must be devoted to the development of each culture in the Brussels-Capital territory.

"Section 7. The law decides the measures for preventing any discrimination for ideological and philosophical reasons.

"Section 8. The law sets up the procedure aimed at averting and settling any points in conflict as between the law and the decree, and as between one decree and another. "

Article 59-B was inserted in the Constitution during the Third Revision and was sanctioned on 24 December 1970.

Together with Article 3-B from which, in actual fact, it stems, and with Articles 3-C, 32-B, 59-C and 107-D, Article 59-B gets to the very heart of the linguistic and regional problems to which the Constituent Assembly attached the greatest possible importance.

While the aims of the Third Revision of the Constitution were many and varied, its paramount objective was indeed to ensure harmonious relations between the various linguistic communities in Belgium, and this over-riding concern has had a greater effect on the Constitution than either of the two previous revisions carried out in 1892-1893 and in 1919-1921. Fundamentally important though they were, those two revisions did not in fact overturn the very organisational structure of the Belgian State. The latter remained very much as it had been set up in 1830 and was still governed by the opinions and beliefs prevailing in the society of that time.

Now, in the intervening period, a very profound change had occurred in the outlook and thinking of the people, and this change was not yet reflected in the text of the Fundamental Charter. In point of fact, Belgium comprises two large linguistic communities, one of which in particular—the Dutch-speaking community—has grown increasingly aware of its own importance, and not only in numerical terms. The coexistence of these two great cultural communities within the framework of a single State gave rise to difficulties that became more and more serious as the 20th century advanced, and which raised the delicate problem of the relationship between a centralised administration and the local authorities.

This growing awareness was further strengthened after World War II, to such an extent that all political circles realised the urgent need to rethink the whole question of the fundamental structures of the Belgian State so as to adapt their institutions to meet the cultural, political, social and economic factors that had evolved. In their turn the Walloons who, in particular, had benefited from the industrial progress of the 19th century, felt themselves to be threatened on the economic plane and, furthermore, they were afraid of being relegated to the minority on the political plane if important decisions in all spheres were to continue to be made, according to the principles of pure democracy, at the level of a Parliament in which they were numerically weaker than the members coming from the Dutch-speaking region of the country.

On the practical side, a number of schemes were initiated in an attempt to arrive at a *modus vivendi* between the two communities while, at the same time, preserving their union within the framework of a single State and the special characteristics of each region within its own territory.

As far back as 1936, the Study Centre for State Reform acknowledged that :

"There are in Belgium two main cultural communities. Two "communities" : the word is a modern one; it is based on a very ancient concept, but one which has taken on a completely new psychological significance. It describes the

157

attachment, the very strong bond of all the heart-strings, to a cultural group; it places less emphasis on political and material factors but accentuates the cultural and linguistic ones. It is, in fact, the reflection of a lofty and highly respectable reality. A community is an entity vested with very real rights. An elite can only achieve its full development and fulfil its educational mission if it remains in close contact with the community.

"The reality of such popular communities and that of the nation having been established, the question sometimes arises as to which of them should be given preference. The Commission is of the opinion that no such conflict should arise. Indeed, a State does not worthily perform its task unless it promotes the development of all the moral and material potential proper to the communities of which it is composed. It must protect this development from all attacks, whether they come from without or within. It must even go farther : a State must not merely attempt to satisfy the desires of its people; it must arouse the urge to do better, just as a good parent does his best to educate and train his children.

"Since we have two communities which, on certain essential points, have separate needs, hopes and desires, the State must adapt itself to this duality : it must take care not only to safeguard the common interests of the entire population but, with the same solicitude, the same affection, it must help each community to achieve its full material and intellectual flowering."

Then came the war, which interrupted the research work though it did not put a stop to the legitimate aspirations of each of the linguistic communities—quite the contrary, in fact.

The work was resumed after the Liberation, and in 1948 a new study centre was set up, called the « Harmel Centre » after the man who inspired its creation (1). The legal style and title of this Centre was as follows : "Research Centre for the purpose of finding a national solution to the social, political and legal problems which have arisen in the Walloon and Flemish regions". The final report on the Centre's work was tabled in 1958; apart from its general conclusions, it included an in-depth analysis of four factors : population figures, the economy, political and cultural affairs.

Some of its conclusions regarding the linguistic problem were given material form under the Lefèvre government which took office in 1961, but it is quite certain that the difficult relations between Flemings and Walloons did not arise purely and simply from a question of language. No, the whole problem was on a far vaster scale and involved the social and economic spheres as well.

That is why, in 1963, the Government asked the three traditional political parties to undertake a joint examination of the whole community problem and to suggest means of charting an efficient reorganisation of the State machinery. This joint approach came to be known as the "Round Table Conference". The conclusions arrived at by the Round

---

(1) Pierre Harmel, President of the Senate, former Prime Minister and, among other things, Minister of Foreign Affairs.

Table, set forth in its report of 20 January 1965, made particular reference to cultural autonomy and the insertion in the Constitution of a new Article 3-B designed to regulate the matter.

The first definite result achieved by the Round Table was the tabling, on 3 March 1965, of the first draft of a Statement of Intent to Revise the Constitution.

On July 1, 1966, a law was passed setting up a "Permanent Commission for the Improvement of Community Relations". Among other things, this Commission was given the task of framing definite proposals designed to improve and promote relations between the communities. Set up officially on 20 October 1966, the Commission was headed by a former Minister, Mr. P. Meyers, so that it is also known as the "Meyers Commission" or, again, as the "Thirty-Six Commission" from the number of members of which it was composed.

Nevertheless, in view of the difficulty in reaching any agreement on fundamental points, the Vanden Boeynants government which took office in 1966 suggested that the whole problem of community relations should be set aside for two years. But once again, it was the cultural question which caused this government to topple in 1968.

The forming of the next government, headed by Mr. Eyskens, was a particularly arduous affair because the negotiators ran into community problems every time. Yet the people's will, as shown by the elections, nevertheless reflected the desire of all Belgians to solve this difficulty once and for all. That is why the Eyskens government, which took office in 1968, did not hesitate to tackle the onerous task imposed on it by the critical situation : on 17 October 1968, it tabled some proposed constitutional reforms intended to deal with the community problems afflicting Belgium. The machinery had been put under way, and it would not stop until the job had been done, in particular by the addition and sanctioning of Articles 59-B and 107-D.

A study of the Government proposals tabled in October 1968 took a long time, however, and this is not surprising in view of the importance and complexity of the problems. Thus, for instance, between 1968 and 1970 the Commission on Constitutional Reforms had already met over a hundred times in order to discuss and draft those articles that were due for revision. Meanwhile, and in the light of the Commission's work, the Government for its part had been tabling some complementary proposals on 28 January 1969.

But there were still vast difficulties that had to be surmounted which is why, in September 1969, the government took another initiative designed to push the reforms along. It invited all the political parties represented in Parliament to meet in a working party known as the

"Twenty-eight Group". This group met from 24 September to 13 November 1969 and arrived at some important conclusions even though it left two fundamental problems still unsolved : the status of the boroughs surrounding the city of Brussels from the linguistic and cultural standpoint, and the organisation of the Brussels economic region. To deal with these two specific problems, another commission entitled the "Twenty-four Group" or the "Brussels Working Party" was set up towards the end of November 1969 without, however, reaching any firm conclusion either.

But the government was not prepared to wait for the results, if any, achieved by this latter group, and on 18 February 1970 the Prime Minister made a further statement to Parliament, the tenour of which was reflected in the proposals tabled on the following 4 March. They embodied the conclusions reached following the work of the "Twenty-eight Group" and, according to the Prime Minister, should lead to a "national compromise capable of establishing the unity of the Belgian people on a new and different basis".

It was in fact the proposals tabled on 4 March 1970 that were finally used as a basis for the framing of Article 59-B. On the subject of cultural autonomy, these proposals set out the following points :

CULTURAL AUTONOMY

Proposal for points 1 and 2 : the linguistic regions.

Belgium comprises four linguistic regions : the French-speaking region, the Dutch-speaking region, the bilingual region of Brussels-Capital, and the German-speaking region.

Every borough in the Kingdom is part of one of these regions.

The bilingual region of Brussels-Capital extends over the territory of the nineteen boroughs forming the administrative district of Brussels-Capital.

The boundaries of these regions may not be altered or rectified except by an Act of Parliament passed by a special majority vote.

Proposal for point 3 : the cultural communities.

Belgium comprises three cultural communities : the French-language cultural community, the Dutch-language cultural community, and the German-language cultural community.

Their organisation and prerogatives are determined in accordance with the principles laid down by the Constitution.

Proposal for point 4 :

a) *the organs of the cultural communities.*

An Act of Parliament, passed by a special majority vote, is to institute the organs of the French cultural community and those of the Dutch cultural community, and shall determine their composition. Only elected representatives of the Nation may be members thereof.

The same Act shall empower those organs to regulate by means of decrees having the force of laws :

1) those cultural matters as it shall specify, within the sphere and in the manner it shall determine;

2) the use of languages in accordance with the stipulations of Article 23.

It shall also determine the way in which all discrimination on ideological or philosophical grounds shall be prevented, and the way in which discrepancies and conflicts as between one decree and another, or as between a decree and the law of the Kingdom, are to be settled.

b) *the use of languages.*

Section 1. The use of languages is optional.

It can only be regulated by laws or decrees, and then only in respect of :

1) the armed forces, legal and judicial matters, acts by the legislative authority, and royal or ministerial edicts and decrees;

2) administrative matters;

3) education, in the scholastic establishments set up, subsidised or recognised by the public authorities;

4) all business instruments and documents required by the laws and regulations;

5) social relations between employers and their personnel.

Section 2. The official languages are :

—French, in the French language region;

—Dutch, in the Dutch language region;

—French and Dutch on an equal footing in the bilingual region of Brussels-Capital;

—German in the German language region, without prejudice to the additional use of French in such cases as shall be determined by the law.

Section 3 : Acts of Parliament passed by a special majority vote shall regulate the use of languages in those matters enumerated under Section 1 above :

1) For those matters listed in Para. 1 of that section, throughout the Kingdom;

2) For those matters listed in Paras 2 to 5 of that section :

—in the bilingual region of Brussels-Capital and in the German language region;

—in those boroughs or groups or boroughs adjacent to another linguistic region where the law prescribes or permits the use of another language than that of the region in which they are located;

161

—for those departments whose activities extend beyond the linguistic region in which they are established;

—for national and international institutions which, because of their activities, must be considered as common to both cultural communities, and which are designated by law;

—for departments and institutions established abroad.

Section 4 . The decree shall regulate the use of languages in the matters enumerated under Section 1, paras. 2 to 5, in the unilingual regions, save only for those matters reserved for an Act of Parliament as specified in Section 3.

Much progress had been made between 1968 and 1970, and this can be readily seen by consulting the table (see "Annexure") which retraces the development of the wording between the original text of 17 October 1968 and the final text of 24 December 1970. Even so, in order to simplify matters, this table does not show the various minor amendments put forward either by the government or by Parliament and which were tabled either in commission or at public sittings of the Houses.

In the eyes of the Government, the proposed wording should settle three points :

— cultural autonomy;

— the guarantees to be granted both from "the community standpoint and from the ideological and philosophical standpoint";

— economic decentralisation, which should go hand in hand with cultural autonomy.

In order to achieve cultural autonomy, the Government proposed that the two linguistic communities should be enabled to make decisions on cultural matters, this term being understood in its widest sense and to include education as well.

With this aim in mind, the Government suggested that the two communities should be provided with bodies which, by means of decrees sanctioned and promulgated by the King, would regulate cultural matters.

At the same time it provided for guarantees ensuring that the two communities would be able to develop freely, each according to its own special characteristics, within the framework of a unitary State, and that neither of them should have the feeling that it was in the minority. The same guarantees were to be granted to the ideological and philosophical minorities within each Community.

The Government thus hoped "to ensure, by means of appropriate guarantees, the brotherly co-operation of Flemings and Walloons within the framework of a State whose main strength lies in their unity".

162

The Government's solution, and in the final analysis that adopted by Parliament, was aimed at putting an end to the conflict once and for all. But has it?

It is quite certain that the sudden interruption of the Constituent Assembly's work by the dissolution of Parliament on 24 September 1971 has left a very great many problems unsolved. Indeed, the revision procedure had been put in hand in 1965, resumed in 1968, and after many hesitations, had been suddenly speeded up in 1970 and completed rather abruptly in 1971.

It is therefore obvious that the revised texts, and Article 59-B in particular, will continue to raise problems for the legal experts because they are but imperfect translations of the real intentions of their authors and because the interruption in the work of the Constituent Assembly has allowed vague terms, lacunae and even apparent contradictions to stand in the wording. Thus, for instance, the normative or legislative function has been completely overturned by the appearance of the "decree" concept. As we shall see farther on, the new categories of enactments which have been introduced into the constitutional articles raise new problems connected with the legal priorities of such legislation.

Be that as it may, however, it cannot be denied that the redistribution of powers, especially those connected with cultural autonomy within the framework of Article 59-B, marks a very important stage indeed in the evolution of institutional affairs in Belgium.

After thus reviewing the genesis of the wording, but before proceeding to analyse it in detail, some attention should be paid to certain preliminary questions which were raised in the course of the debates.

There were two questions of principle and one question of expediency.

The first question of principle concerned the actual scope of the wording in the articles to be added to the Constitution.

Nobody indeed disputed the need to enshrine the principle of cultural autonomy in the Fundamental Charter. But the problem was whether the Constitution should be restricted merely to a statement of principle, or whether it would be preferable for it to go into details regarding the practical way in which such cultural autonomy should be organised. In its statement of intent to revise, tabled in 1965, the government chose to abide by the conclusions reached at the Round Table and merely stated a principle, considering that the creation of Cultural Councils endowed with a wide measure of autonomy and individual powers and prerogatives did not call for a revision of the Constitution since the ordinary legislative procedures would be quite sufficient for the purpose. From this standpoint, Article 3-B would simply have been rounded off by an additional clause stating that "the French language region and the Dutch language region have been granted their cultural autonomy."

But the evolution of political thinking, especially as a result of the general election held on 31 March 1968, led the Government to propose a far more detailed wording. This new procedure, however, did not fail to arouse criticism on the part of certain members of Parliament who considered that the Constitution should merely lay down that a law might create cultural councils endowed with statutory authority. This, then, would have been a kind of "framework law", the actual organisation of their cultural autonomy being taken care of by a law which, if necessary, could be subjected to a qualified majority vote.

On the other hand, the majority of members felt that such a law, even if it were passed on the basis of a qualified majority vote, would not offer sufficient guarantees for the two linguistic communities. As we know, it was this latter opinion which finally prevailed, and which led to the elaboration of one of the longest and most detailed articles in the Constitution.

The detailed regulation of cultural autonomy in the wording of the Constitutional article having been accepted as opportune, another and even more fundamental question of principle was raised, namely, the way in which this detailed regulation could be achieved. Important legal and political objections were raised, and the former especially are vital to our understanding of the text.

The legal objections were mainly of two kinds :

1. There was a contradiction between the proposed text, according to which Senatorial Councils were to be set up, and Article 32 of the Constitution which states that "the members of both Houses represent the Nation, and not merely the province or subdivision of a province which elected them."

2. A second legal objection concerned Article 26 of the Constitution, an unmodified article which states that the legislative authority is exercised collectively by the King, the House of Representatives, and the Senate. Now, the decrees mentioned in the revision proposals, which were not to be subjected to the legal controls laid down in Article 107 of the Constitution, were tantamount to actual laws having a limited territorial scope. If they were to be framed by the Cultural Councils alone and not by Parliament, then this would constitute a violation of Article 26 of the Constitution.

The political objections, while they are important in their way, are of less interest to us in our review of the exact scope and implications of Article 59-B.

To the first objection, the Government replied that the cultural councils, while they were originally to consist of Senators alone, were indeed deliberative assemblies separate from the Senate, and that it would consequently be possible to allow them legislatory powers. Indeed, those Senators would not assemble and debate under the heading of Parliament. The Constitution would thus institute a plurality of office, without however confusing the two functions. If, then, a member of Parliament should vote in favour of a decree to be implemented on a regional basis, he would not be doing so as a representative of the Nation : it would be because he would also be a member of the cultural council.

The second objection was a far more basic one and involved the actual interpretation of Article 26 of the Constitution and the scope of the decrees. During the parliamentary work in preparation for the statement of intent to revise tabled in 1965, the government had proposed that an Article 26-B should be inserted in the Constitution so as to permit the Constituent Assembly to authorise the Houses to delegate their powers to certain commissions or sections. But the members considered that the Legislative Assembly alone was empowered to legislate.

Here, on the contrary, the question was of quite another kind since two new bodies were to be set up in the form of Senatorial Councils. The latter were not, therefore, one of the branches of the Legislative Authority or a part of one of these branches, indeed they were two new entities separate and distinct from the Senate.

The Government justified its proposal by interpreting the term "legislative" which appears in Article 26 as being of purely formal significance. In other words, the Government was inspired by the idea that the legislative function is not a monopoly vested in the Legislative Authority, but that it can be exercised by an official body other than that authority. Taken in its material sense, the concept of law refers to its content, but the Constitution contains no definition of that concept in its material significance. Furthermore, still according to the Government, the Legislative Authority is vested with residual competence, meaning all forms of competence not specifically attributed to another authority. Yet this residual competence is indeterminate and residual matters may be restricted by the Constituent Assembly. As an example, the government pointed to the way in which the Constituent Assembly of 1831 acted when, in terms of Articles 31 and 108 of the Constitution, it gave the Provincial and Municipal Councils genuine statutory powers within the boundaries of their respective territories, and where exclusively provincial or municipal interests were concerned. The Government believed that the Constituent Assembly of 1970 could also act along the same lines by acknowledging statutory powers in respect of those bodies which it would be necessary to set up in order to achieve cultural autonomy. In doing so, the Constituent Assembly would not be obliged to alter Article 26 of the Constitution. In consequence, and still according to the government's view, the term "legislative" which appears in Article 26 does not refer to any general and mandatory norm, which would indeed be a material definition of what law is, but solely to those decisions made in obedience to certains forms, according to parliamentary procedure as regulated both by Chapter 1, Heading III of the Constitution and by Article 69 of that same Constitution.

Without questioning the objective at stake, certain members of Parliament nevertheless criticised the Government's reasoning. In particular, they claimed that while the statutory function is exercised by several bodies, the norms established by the Legislative authority are the source of all the others. Thus, the King may take statutory measures, but only in implementation of the laws. Similarly, the provincial and municipal institutions also wield statutory powers, but supervision has been organised to prevent them from overstepping their prerogatives. It is a different matter with the decrees which will have the force of regional laws, since this would have the effect of withdrawing supervisory powers from the Executive, the possibility of other courses of action from the Legislative, and the possibility of verifying the legality of such measures from the Judiciary. Those same members of Parliament, while they criticised the Government's reasoning, nevertheless considered that a genuine justification of the measures decided upon lay in the fact that the cultural councils would remain subordinate to the Legislative authority, firstly because their powers would remain restricted to linguistic and cultural matters, and secondly because if the decrees were not to be subjected to some form of supervision, they would indirectly remain subordinate to the control of those bodies forming the national sovereignty.

In any event, the objection that the project conflicted with Article 26 of the Constitution was waived, and the debate was indeed a very useful means of clarifying these concepts.

A question of expediency was also examined during the debates. Indeed, it will have been noticed that in the wording originally proposed, the intervention of the Council of State and the conditions attendant upon such intervention were explicitly provided for so as to establish a form of preventive control prior to the promulgation of the decrees. Subsequently it was deemed more opportune to omit this procedure from the constitutional article but, while respecting the original intention, to leave it up to the legislator to settle the question. As will be seen farther on, this was effectively done by means of the law of 3 July 1971 providing for the distribution of members of the Legislative Assemblies into linguistic groups, and laying down a number of measures surrounding the cultural councils for the French cultural community and for the Dutch cultural community. A Section III of this law does in fact deal with the procedure aimed at preventing and reconciling the conflicts arising between the law and the decrees, and as between one decree and another.

A few more words concerning the final presentation of Article 59-B.

We already know that, initially, all the contents of this article, together with other measures, were included in a modified version of Article 3-B and in a modification to Article 23. The Senate Commission decided however, during the debates, to split up the contents of Article 3-B and to spread them over a certain number of new articles so that the matters originally dealt with in Article 3-B would be better located in their proper places. And so it happened in particular that the cultural councils came to form the subject-matter of Article 59-B and Article 59-C.

Furthermore, on 3 July 1970, the Government proposed that Article 23 of the Constitution should be left unmodified even though the modification had already been adopted by the Senate on 25 June 1970. As the wording of Article 23 was now to remain unchanged, the government was led to include the proposed modification in the new article 59-B so that, apart from the Legislative, the cultural councils could also regulate the use of languages by means of decrees and in certain spheres. Where cultural autonomy was concerned, the modification to Article 3 did in fact provide that the cultural councils should regulate by means of decrees the use of languages in the unilingual regions in such spheres as : administrative matters; education in those establishments set up, subsidised or recognised by the public authorities; social relations between employers and their personnel together with the business instruments and documents required by the laws and regulations, with the exception of those prerogatives which were still to be exercised by the Legislative.

The time has now come to comment in detail on the text of this vitally important article.

1. *The number of cultural councils*

In terms of Section 1, there is a cultural council for the French cultural community and a cultural council for the Dutch cultural community.

Originally, one of the proposed texts provided that there should be two cultural councils, one for each community. A commissioner pointed out, however, that Article 59-C also provided for the creation of a cultural council for the German language region. Any wording that merely mentioned two cultural councils might therefore be regarded as contradictory to Article 59-C. That is why the wording now explicitly provides not that there are two cultural councils, but that there is one for each of the two cultural communities.

Furthermore, it happened several times during the debates that the question was bandied about of setting up a fourth cultural council for the Brussels region. Faced with the difficulty of defining that region, most members agreed that a special institution for Brussels should be provided for, one that would take account of the peripheral boroughs benefiting from certain linguistic facilities, without however creating a special cultural council for the purpose. During the discussion, the Minister for Community Relations underlined the fact that Article 126 of the Constitution was to be modified and would provide a solution for the Brussels area that would be based on measures enacted for the benefit of other great urban centres within the framework of Articles 108 and 108-B of the Constitution.

This solution was agreed upon, and was included not under Article 126, but in a new article 108-C, sections 4, 5 and 6 of which provide for the existence of a French committee for culture and a Dutch committee for culture within the urban district to which the capital city of the Kingdom belongs.

II. *Denomination of the new bodies*

The question of how the new bodies were to be named was also raised. Certain members indeed pointed out that a Royal Decree of 7 February 1938 had created two cultural councils, one French-speaking and the other Dutch-speaking, whose competence was a purely advisory one. As this decree had not been abrogated, there were therefore two cultural councils already in existence, and this might lead to confusion if the same name were to be used in the Constitution to designate new bodies which, unlike the old, would be vested with normative powers. The protagonists of this idea therefore proposed to call the new bodies not "Councils" but "Assemblies". This term, they believed, would indicate more aptly that their membership consisted of elected representatives, and this would preclude any confusion with a board of advisors appointed by the King.

Apprised of the question, the Senate nevertheless retained the term "Council" which is a more traditional one from the standpoint of Belgian administrative law. In point of fact, the advocates of this term maintained that it is habitually used by all the bodies which are vested with normative powers on the regional plane, for instance : the Provincial Council, and that there could be no confusion possible between a small administrative body acting in a purely advisory capacity, whose existence was not even recorded by the Constitution, and the new bodies to be set up.

The term "Council" was therefore adopted.

III. *Composition*

Originally, the Government's wording provided for two Senatorial Councils.

Why had the choice of members been restricted to Senators only ?

In principle, the Government considered that normative powers could only be granted to parliamentarians, and the Senate was chosen because of its special features which had been called for on several occasions. This was a new departure, and one that was part and parcel of the redistribution of tasks between the two Houses, not only where community problems were concerned, but also in regard to the modernisation of the State. The choice of the Senate is explained by its own special methods of election on various levels : Senators who are directly elected, Provincial Senators, and co-opted Senators. In this way, the choice of the Senate would bear more closely in mind the various tendencies of the Belgian people.

This initiative was not, moreover, such a revolutionary one since, in strictly limited and specifically designated matters, the Constitution had already divided certain definite powers between the two Houses. Thus, the impeachment of Ministers is a monopoly of the Lower House; the appointment of councillors to the Court of Cassation is the prerogative of the Senate.

After receiving the assent of the Senate Commission, this composition of the new Councils was nevertheless criticised because certain members considered that no distinction in principle could be made between the Lower House and the Senate. Various systems were then put forward :

—the composition of the Councils to be restricted to a certain number of Deputies and Senators belonging to the same linguistic group for the corresponding cultural community;

—the composition to be extended to all the members of the same linguistic group but considered solely within the framework of their own House;

—the composition to include all the members of the Lower House and the Senate belonging to the same linguistic group;

—the Councils to be composed of members from both Houses; each of the Houses to designate such members according to a system of proportional representation; etc., etc.

Another amendment was aimed at allowing the Legislative far greater latitude in making its own decision about how the cultural councils should be made up, by providing that a law passed on the basis of a special majority vote would determine in particular the composition of each Council.

This was the text finally adopted by the Senate on 17 June 1970.

But this method was again called in question during debates in the Lower House. Certains members in fact considered that as the Legislative Assemblies were to transfer part of their authority to the cultural councils, it was unthinkable that a certain number of Deputies or Senators would have no further say in the matter. The Prime Minister supported this view which made it possible to come up with a solution to the difficulties surrounding the number of members of which the cultural councils should be composed, the distribution of members as between the Lower House and the Senate, and representation on the basis of political parties and regions. The Prime Minister also considered it opportune that all parliamentarians should continue to participate in the exercise of legislative authority on cultural matters.

That is how the text came to be adopted which provided that each cultural council should comprise members of the corresponding linguistic group belonging to both Houses.

During the debates, another problem had been raised. Some members thought that the cultural councils should be composed not only members of Parliament, but also of delegates from the most representative cultural associations in each linguistic region. This solution was, however, set aside for a fundamental reason. The majority considered in fact that the cession by Parliament of part of its prerogatives was so vitally important that such normative powers could only be granted to bodies consisting of members elected by the nation at large. They pointed out that in England, for instance, the Chancellor of Arts enjoyed wide powers in disposing of the funds made available to him by the State, but on the other hand he had no normative powers whatever. According to the majority, the power of deciding what policy must be implemented must therefore remain in the hands of persons directly elected by the Nation. That is why the cultural councils are composed solely of elected members.

Yet another problem came to the fore : that of deciding whether the new text was such as to restrict the authority of the Legislative, for instance by preventing it from organising each of the two councils in obedience to the bicameral system. The majority considered that the way in which the text was worded and the spirit in which the debates had been conducted precluded such a possibility. The cultural councils, therefore, must each sit in an assembly that comprises both Deputies and Senators, and their internal arrangements must not be such as to divide them into two sub-assemblies, one for the Deputies and the other for the Senators.

IV. *Operating methods within the cultural councils.*

These operating methods were also the subject of lengthy debate, and the proposals submitted for revision were radically modified during the discussions.

It was as a result of the communication made to Parliament on 18 February 1970 that the Government put forward, on 4 March following, the proposals reproduced above (see pages 160 to 162).

In order to establish the special majority, the Government suggested one of the three following methods, depending on the matter concerned :

—a majority vote in each of the linguistic groups of the Lower House and the Senate;

—at least two-thirds of the votes;

—at least two-thirds of the votes and the presence of two-thirds of the members during the debate.

The discussion ranged principally over the question of whether a special majority was necessary or not. Certain members thought that if a special majority was required, this would end by rendering any genuine cultural autonomy pointless, because the institution of such autonomy would once again be subjected to the agreement of a quasi-constitutional majority.

On the other hand, others considered that the armistice to the language war, which was the primary target of Article 59-B, would be ruined from the start if a law voted on the basis of a simple majority could be imposed on a very large majority of representatives of the French-speaking community as a result of a positive vote by the representatives of the Dutch-speaking community plus a small number of French-speaking members.

Finally, Parliament deemed it logical to require a special majority, seeing that certain prerogatives were being withdrawn from the two Houses and entrusted to other bodies.

Article 59-B provides moreover that a certain number of constitutional clauses applicable to the two Houses are to be extended to cover the operating procedures of the cultural councils. These are :

— the public nature of their sittings;

— the appointment of their steering committees;

— the need for an absolute majority vote in decision-making;

— the method of voting on decrees;

— the right of amendment;

— the right of investigation;

— the rules pertaining to petitions;

— parliamentary immunity;

— the commencement date of sessions and their duration;

— the presence of Ministers;

— the ban on meeting outside the period when the House of Representatives is in session.

In connection with this last ruling. it is important to refer hereunder to the commentary on Article 71 in which the question is dealt with regarding the effect of a dissolution of Parliament on the existence of the cultural councils. In this respect, moreover, certain members considered that there could be no objection to the cultural councils meeting at times when the House of Representatives was not in session. The majority, however, did not support this point of view and and felt that it would be unthinkable for members of the Lower House, once Parliahad been dissolved, to continue to sit on the cultural councils and make decisions of a legislative nature. The reference to Article 59 was therefore retained in the final text.

In order to be complete, it should be mentioned that a law of 21 July 1971 has regulated the functioning of the cultural councils in detail. Their functioning is, moreover, similar to that of the Houses, to such an extent that certain clauses of the law are merely a restatement of the constitutional articles applicable to Parliament, but adapted for the benefit of the cultural councils.

In particular, Clause 21 of this law provides that "each cultural council draws up its own rules", which has been done for both councils. In framing these rules, each cultural council nevertheless preserves its independence, so that certain rules are not identically the same for each council. Thus, for instance, the Dutch-speaking cultural council ignores the formality of a second reading of a proposed decree. Yet these are only minor differences which do not affect the general operating methods of each council.

Each council comprises various bodies :

—the plenary assembly, all sittings of which are public ones;

—the steering committee, consisting of a chairman, three vice-presidents and four secretaries elected by the council. This steering committee is the body which takes charge of the everyday management, organisation of work, and appointment of personnel in the councils;

— the clerk, or recorder, who is elected by the council from outside its members. He attends all meetings of the Council and the steering committee and directs its services under the authority of the chairman;

—the committees, which may be of several kinds :

a) the permanent committees, specially qualified to handle the matters referred to them;

b) the special committees, set up for a definite purpose;

c) the accountancy committees which deal with the internal finances of the councils.

The work of the councils may be classified under three main headings :

a) the examination and voting of decrees;

b) the examination and voting of cultural budgets;

c) the audition of "requests for explanations", which to some extent corresponds to "question-time" in the national Parliament.

When a draft or proposed decree is tabled, the text is referred to the competent committee which, after examining it, reports back to the plenary assembly so that the debate and the final vote may take place. The examination of the budgets submitted to the council is handled by the "committee on general policy and the budget" which distributes the work among the specialised committees, who then report back. After that, the committee on general policy and the budget prepares a digest of the reports to be used for the debate in the plenary assembly.

As for the "requests for explanations", these may be tabled by any member of the council. The Cabinet Minister competent to deal with the question is given notice of it and the matter is debated in public session. However, unlike the procedure with regard to parliamentary questions, the debate cannot end in a motion of confidence or of no-confidence but only in a recommendation.

Let us recall two other essential clauses in the law of 21 July 1971 :

In terms of clause 6, "each cultural council meets as of right on the third Tuesday of October each year, unless it has been convened previously by the King.

The King pronounces the session closed.

The King has the right to call an extraordinary general meeting of both cultural councils or of one of them."

According to clause 7, "any assembly of a cultural council held outside the period during which the Legislative Houses are in session, is automatically null and void."

V. *Competence ratione materiae*

A. In cultural matters

In the government proposal of 17 October 1968, a list of matters was given in paragraph 4 which largely stemmed from the conclusions reached by the Round Table Conference with regard to the competence of the cultural councils.

As far as language is concerned, a distinction had been made by the Government between the specifically cultural aspect, such as spelling, and the use of the language itself. The cultural councils would have been competent to deal with both aspects, but because of the existence of linguistic minorities within each Community, their powers would have been curtailed to some extent where the actual use of the language was concerned. It was for these reasons that the Government deemed it preferable to settle the latter point by modifying Article 23 of the Constitution. As we have already seen, Article 23 was in point of fact left unchanged.

With regard to education, the agreement of 12 June 1968 annexed to the Government statement had enumerated in detail those matters which must remain under the jurisdiction of the national Legislative Authority. It was, however, difficult to circumscribe those matters with any precision. The list would have been too long for it to have been included in the Constitution, and the delicate nature of such matters required a great deal of circumspection in dealing with them. That was why the Government text provided that the Legislative Authority itself should grant the cultural councils powers to regulate education in such spheres as are specific to the regions.

Moreover, the Government text left it to the Legislative to modify and add to the list of matters enumerated. The Government laid great stress on the fact that the word "modify" did not mean that the competence of the cultural councils could in any way be curtailed or diminished. This term was used solely to permit their competence to be adapted or further clarified. Similarly, the list could not have been completed except by the addition of matters of a similar nature.

These initial proposals were put forward by the Government and clarified on 28 January 1969.

There is no doubt that these clauses, which are essential to establish the competence of the cultural councils, were the subject of lengthy debate.

The first question raised was whether a list of cultural matters should be inserted in the Constitution or not, and on this point opinions were very much divided. Certain members of Parliament, for instance, pointed out that the enumeration of such matters in a law threatened to make the fact of cultural autonomy subservient to the whim of essentially changeable political majorities.

Others, however, considered it necessary to define in the constitutional article the competence of the cultural councils, both ratione loci and ratione materiae. This point of view won acceptance at the outset, and thereafter ensued a very long debate on the various matters listed. The main points at issue were above all the question of education, which is so important in Belgium, and the question of cultural relations with other countries.

The perspective altered, however, between 1969 and 1970 so that after the Government communication of 18 February 1970, the initial text was drastically revised, after which it only contained the following :

— cultural matters;

— education, excluding all that appertained to the Schools Pact, compulsory school attendance, the educational structure, diplomas, subsidies, salaries, and the standards governing the student population;

— co-operation between the cultural communities and international cultural co-operation;

— the use of languages in the unilingual regions in accordance with the proposed modification of Article 23 of the constitution which had not then yet been withdrawn.

In this state the text was adopted by the Senate and passed to the House of Representatives. Speaking to the members of the Lower House Committee, the Minister for Community Relations stated that cultural matters included in particular those matters listed in the government's first proposal but that, in the course of the debate, the Senate had considered that constitutional articles should be couched in concise terms and be statements of principle merely. Consequently, the list of cultural matters should be left to the discretion of the Legislative and be established by means of a law passed on the basis of a special majority vote. Here again, the most hotly debated questions were those connected with education and international cultural co-operation. With particular reference to education, the work of the Lower House parliamentary committee clarified the following principles :

The following might be placed under the jurisdiction of the cultural councils :

1. For State schools and free schools subsidised or recognised by the public authorities :

— the definition and supervision of compulsory school attendance;

— curricula and "streaming", together with their syllabus and timetable, but only to the extent that this matter is not included among the conditions whereby diplomas are acknowledged since this matter is reserved for the national Legislative;

— the organisation of school inspection;

— diplomas required of the teaching staff;

— promotional work;

— school vacations and holidays;

— and, more generally, everything connected with improving and promoting school attendance.

2. For State schools :

— organic rules and regulations of day and boarding schools.

With regard to international relations, the Minister for Community Relations emphasized that the constitutional text could not modify the prerogatives of the Executive as set out by Article 68 of the Constitution. The Executive authority would therefore remain competent to conduct negotiations for the purpose of framing and concluding cultural agreements. It would retain the right of initiative where the signing of such agreements was concerned. The problem, however, was to establish which body would be competent to approve such agreements. It might indeed happen that the views of the two main cultural communities on the subject of cultural relations with other countries differed from one another both with respect to the principle of signing an agreement and the extent to which Belgium should contribute to it. The government therefore believed that two kinds of agreement should be taken into account : firstly, those involving all Belgians even though their degree of involvement might vary; and secondly, those affecting one of the cultural communities only, to the exclusion of the other. In the final text, all reference to article 68 of the Constitution was, however, deleted. It was merely stated that a law passed on the basis of a special majority vote would not only determine cultural matters in detail but would also define the forms co-operation should take, especially on the international plane.

Here it is necessary to recall that as far back as 1965, the government had proposed a revision of Article 68 of the Constitution so as to permit a more accurate definition of the rules governing parliamentary approval of certain categories of international agreements, together with greater flexibility in the approval procedure.

On 11 May 1971, the government tabled a bill in the Senate steering committee in implementation of Article 59-B with respect to international cultural co-operation. Clause 5 of this bill was worded as follows : " Any draft treaty pertaining to cultural co-operation which affects mainly the French cultural community or the Dutch cultural community shall be submitted to the cultural council of the cultural community concerned for its opinion. This shall be done by the Minister responsible for Foreign Affairs. No treaty pertaining to cultural co-operation of a kind likely to place an additional burden on the budget of the French or the Dutch cultural community may be approved by the Legislative Assemblies unless it is backed by a favourable recommendation from the cultural council of the cultural community concerned."

The Government explained the scope of this clause as follows :

"Clause 5 is aimed at implementing the constitutional article which empowers the Legislative to chart the forms which international cultural co-operation shall take. When drafting this clause, article 68 of the Constitution as it now stands (i.e., unrevised) was borne in mind.

The contents of Clause 5 of this bill are in fact based directly on Article 68 according to which "those treaties that might affect the State or individually become binding on certain Belgians only become effective after they have received the consent of both Houses."

The procedure proposed by the Government in Clause 5 is designed to ensure the participation of the cultural councils when cultural agreements are being entered into.

Two conditions of a formal nature are required :

1) for any treaty which affects chiefly one cultural community, the opinion of the cultural council concerned is necessary. Such opinion shall be laid before the Executive before the latter signs the treaty.

2) for any treaty likely to place an additional burden on the budget of one of the cultural communities, the favourable opinion of the cultural council concerned is necessary. Such opinion shall be referred to Parliament prior to the latter's approval of the treaty.

The two procedures outlined above are not mutually exclusive; should occasion arise, they will both be applied in respect of one and the same treaty.

Finally, the government wishes to make it clear that Clause 5 of this bill will possibly have to be revised if and when a modification is made to Article 68 of the Constitution which the Preconstituent Assembly has stated to be revisable. "

When this clause was debated in the Senate Committee, several commissioners pointed out that the text was not in accordance with the terms of the new wording of Article 68 of the Constitution as revised and already adopted by the Committee, even though it had not yet been approved by Parliament. Therefore, the Committee unanimously decided to strike out Clause 5 and to pass a new text later on, the new wording to be the subject of another bill and to be drawn up on the basis of the new Article 68 when it had been modified and approved.

As a matter of fact, the revision of Article 68 never happened since Parliament was dissolved on 29 September 1971, and the dissolution put a full stop to Parliament's mission as a Constituent Assembly, for the new Houses which met as a result of the general election on 7 November 1971 did not rank as a Constituent Assembly.

Thus, the problem of the relationship between a vital point of Article 59-B and the still unmodified Article 68 remains unsolved even today.

It should also be stressed that during the debate, certain members wished to have it written into the Constitution that the competence of the cultural councils should also embrace the mass communications media such as radio and television. This proposal was not adopted, so that the text finally accepted by both the Lower House and the Senate was not further modified.

The law to be passed on the basis of a special majority vote referred to in Section 2 of Article 59-B was resorted to on 21 July 1971. It is entitled " Law governing the competence and functioning of the cultural councils for the French cultural community and for the Dutch cultural community."

Clause 2 of this law defines the cultural matters referred to in Article 59-B, Section 2, para 1 of the Constitution. These matters are :

1) the defence and promotion of the language;

2) the promotion of training for research workers;

3) the fine arts, including the theatre and motion pictures;

4) the cultural inheritance, museums and other cultural and scientific institutions;

5) libraries, gramophone record libraries and similar facilities;

6) radio and television broadcasting, with the exception of official government communications and commercial publicity;

7) youth policies;

8) permanent education and cultural animation;

9) physical education, sport and open-air activities;

10) leisure and tourism.

The same clause adds that : "The competence of the cultural council to regulate cultural matters comprises the power to enact decrees pertaining to the infrastructure. "

It is interesting to refer back to the parliamentary working papers in order to see how the Government justified its choice of matters.

The Government began by recalling that it had to choose between two methods : either a detailed enumeration of those matters, or a statement of general headings.

The first presented a disadvantage in that it might be thought to constitute a definitive list. The second and more flexible method would necessarily require subsequent interpretation.

The Government chose the second method. Furthermore, in clarifying the kind of cultural matters selected, it took care to state that such clarifications were to be construed as examples only.

This is what the parliamentary paper has to say about it :

1. By "the defence and promotion of the language", the following should be understood inter alia : linguistics, spelling, terminology, encouragement in the correct usage of the language, the distribution of literature within the country and abroad, and the definition of conditions surrounding the granting of subsidies, awards, grants and scholarships.

2. "The promotion of training for research workers" comprises in particular the definition of conditions surrounding the granting of subsidies, awards and scholarships; and the setting up of institutions for the sole purpose of encouraging research training.

3. The concept of "fine arts, including the theatre and motion pictures" must be taken in its widest sense : literature, music, theatre, ballet, cinema and the plastic arts. Competence in this sphere includes, inter alia, the definition of conditions surrounding the granting of subsidies, prizes, awards, grants and scholarships; the setting up of funds, academies and any other institutions for the practice of the fine arts and literature, and protection for the recognised status of professional artist.

4. The heading "the cultural inheritance, museums and other cultural and scientific institutions" covers a very wide field.

The concept of "cultural inheritance", which refers to both the movable and immovable patrimony, comprises inter alia : regulations surrounding the export of works of art; the obligation to deposit, with a public institution set up for the purpose, one or several copies of each and every publication printed according to the typographical, phonographical or chemicographical process; the compulsory preservation of radio or television recordings that are of interest to the history of civilisation; the obligation to inventory and to deposit the archives and personal records of legally constituted bodies; the definition of rules surrounding the deposit of archives and personal records belonging to private persons; the preservation of monuments, beauty-spots and places of historic interest; the regulation of signs and advertising displays on public monuments and in places and beauty-spots of historic interest and in their immediate vicinity, as well as along highways of tourist interest; the definition of conditions surrounding the granting of subsidies for the acquisition and preservation of monuments, beauty-spots or places of historic interest.

By "museums and other cultural and scientific institutions" is meant : the creation of museums, the definition of conditions surrounding the granting of subsidies for the creation, acquisition and preservation of buildings and collections; the reception of visitors, prospection (excavations); the drawing up of inventories and the organisation of loan facilities; the conditions under which collections may be ceded on loan; etc.

5. "Libraries, gramophone record libraries and similar facilities" : these terms refer to every kind of collection made available to the public : libraries, including mobile libraries, newspaper and magazine collections, recordings both sound and visual. This competence includes the conditions surrounding the granting of subsidies for the setting up and preservation of such institutions, the acquisition of works, the promotion of personnel training (e.g. librarians), etc.

6. "Radio and television broadcasting". This heading should notably cover the creating of radio and broadcasting stations, to the exclusion of radiotelegraphy and radiotelephony or other forms of radio communications which are not regarded as coming within the cultural sphere as conceived by the Constituent Assembly. Such institutions shall comprise all the requisite facilities, including the technical and administrative departments, so long as they are not regarded as being common to both the cultural communities; such competence shall in any case include the right to appoint members of the bodies set up to manage the broadcasting stations, as already envisaged during the preparatory work for the law of 18 May 1960 governing broadcasting, which is now in force (Senate, 1959-1960 session, Report no. 119, p. 12).

7. "Youth policies"—this term does not refer to schooling, but to general education and training for young people, whether organised or not, to the exclusion however of the legislation surrounding child welfare (penal, social and civil legislation); it comprises the definition of conditions surrounding the granting of subsidies for the socio-cultural education of young people, indemnities for the social promotion of youth, etc.

8. "Permanent education and cultural animation" comprises everything which contributes to the full cultural development of adults in the widest sense of the term, such as the associations set up by the citizens themselves on their own initiative, the conferences, lectures, night classes, family training institutes, social and civic training facilities, the organisation of community development, to the exclusion however of schooling and scholastic education in the traditional sense.

9. "Physical education, sport, and open-air activities" comprises both professional and amateur sport, to the exclusion of regulations governing betting, sporting results, boxing matches and the ban on doping; the concept of open-air activities includes camping and caravaning.

10. Under the heading "leisure and tourism", these matters should be considered from the widest angle without taking the time factor into account (at the end of the working day, during the week-ends or the holidays). They comprise among other things : non-professional artistic performances (theatre, music, the plastic arts, etc.), pastimes and hobbies regardless of whether they are technical, scientific or artistic; tourism from one-day outings to holiday excursions. This competence comprises the definition of conditions surrounding the granting of subsidies and awards, the setting up of institutions, the promotion of personnel training, etc.

180

11. The competence vested in the cultural council to regulate cultural matters comprises the power to enact decrees pertaining to the infrastructure. To avoid any doubts on this subject, the bill explicitly states as much under Clause 11.

To understand this text, it is necessary to bear in mind that the Government did not originally foresee the exception made in this law with respect to radio and television broadcasting, and it added a clause 11 dealing with the infrastructure pertaining to the various matters listed.

Is it necessary to state that this circumscription of the matters in question was the subject of lively debates in Parliament ? Nevertheless, the text of Clause 2 of the law of 21 July 1971 makes it clear that the Houses stuck fairly closely to the Government wording, apart from the two alterations we have just mentioned.

B. In linguistic matters.

We have already seen that from the linguistic standpoint, the Government originally considered that a distinction should be made between the "cultural" aspect and the "language usage" or semantics aspect, and that the latter was to be regulated by a modification to Article 23 of the Constitution. In this modification, the Government laid down the following principles :

1) maintenance of the principles enshrined in the 1831 Constitution regarding the optional character of the use of the languages spoken in Belgium, and maintenance of the competence vested in the national Legislative to regulate their use solely in those matters explicitly set forth in the Constitution;

2) insertion of the following new principles :

a) to provide the Legislative with a possibility of intervening in future, for instance with regard to foreign business enterprises established on Belgian territory;

b) to define in the Constitution itself the official language of each of the four linguistic regions;

c) to provide that the linguistic laws may no longed be modified save by a majority vote in each of the linguistic groups of the Lower House and the Senate;

d) to define the competence vested in the national Legislative on the basis of the following norms :

— for the entire Kingdom : legal and judicial affairs and the armed forces;

— for the region of Brussels-Capital and the German language region : all matters;

— for those boroughs specifically designated in which the use of a language other than that of the region is provided for : all matters;

— for those departments whose activities extend to another linguistic region or to one of the boroughs mentioned above : all matters.

e) and consequently to define the competence vested in the cultural councils :

— *ratione loci* : French language region or Dutch language region, excepting only those boroughs or departments in which the national Legislative alone is competent;

— *ratione materiae* : administrative matters, education, regulation of the use of languages by private business enterprises and employers within the same limits as those laid down in respect of the Legislative.

As we have seen, it was finally decided not to modify Article 23 of the Constitution, so that Article 59-B had to be rounded off by means of a Section 3 designed to indicate the competence vested in the cultural councils where the use of languages was concerned. The Government proposal gave rise to little debate, with the sole exception of social relations. Certain members did not immediately grasp the exact scope and significance of the term. Others considered that, in this sphere, the human viewpoint should prevail and that the promulgation of excessively rigid decrees should be avoided, especially with regard to those enterprises located near the linguistic boundary, in which the personnel employed could obviously come from either region. Other members, on the contrary, felt that the concept should be understood in a very wide sense, especially in order to deal with the growing number of cases where foreign business and industrial enterprises had established themselves both in Flanders and in Wallonia.

After a lengthy debate in Parliament, the proposal submitted by the Government was accepted.

VI. *Scope of the decrees*

We have already seen that a fundamental objection had been raised regarding the scope of the decrees in terms of Article 26 of the Constitution.

Nevertheless, it should be pointed out that the Government never departed from its original theory, according to which such decrees should have the full force of law. It should also be stated that the parliamentary work is so clear that there can no longer be any doubts on this score.

Thus, to a Parliamentarian unable to grasp the difference between a decree and a law, another member replied that a decree "is regional in character and restricted as to content". Another said that as far as he was concerned, the cultural reform proposed was not unconstitutional, because "what is being created is not really a kind of Legislative authority in the sense of Article 26 of the Constitution, but another kind of authority—to use a well-worn term, it is a normative authority."

We could quote any number of instances, but it is sufficient to recall in this context the clarifications which the Government put forward when it tabled the bill which was to become the law of 21 July 1971 already referred to.

Although this point was not in dispute, the Government restated the principle that the two new bodies set up under the Constitution were vested with the same competence as that enjoyed by the Legislative authority on the matters specified. The cultural councils, so long as they remain within the limits of their competence as defined in Article 59-B, are therefore empowered to modify or abrogate existing legislation, to prescribe any obligation that could not be imposed except by the Legislative authority, and to take any measures coming within the competence of that authority.

The Government stressed, however, that the Legislative authority was to retain its residual competence for the entire territory of the Kingdom and that, in contrast, the cultural councils had no competence other than that explicitly vested in them by the Constitution, such competence being moreover restricted *ratione loci*. It followed, according to the government, that the cultural councils are incompetent whenever a constitutional article has expressly reserved certain matters for the law to regulate, the law signifying in this case an Act of Parliament in terms of Article 26 of the Constitution.

Thus, for instance, the cultural council will not itself be competent to frame penalties for infringements of its decrees, since Article 9 of the Constitution lays down that no penalty may be established nor inflicted save by virtue of a law. (1)

To conclude, it must be admitted that as Article 26 remains unchanged, the term "law" must be taken in its purely formal sense, namely : as an act regularly performed by the authorities referred to in the said Article 26.

---

(1) In order that the Cultural Councils might be qualified to sanction infringements of their decrees by means of penalties, it was necessary to enact a piece of legislation. This provision is embodied in Clause 22 of the law passed on 3 July 1971, whereby the Cultural Councils may, within the limitations imposed on their competence, establish penalties for infringements of their decrees, penalties which may not exceed a six months' prison sentence or a fine of five thousand francs.

The decree, on the other hand, belongs to the normative function. It has the same weight as a law when considered from the material standpoint. Formally, however, it is by no means a law since it is enacted by an authority whose powers are limited by the Constitution itself, *ratione loci* and *ratione materiae*.

Were it necessary to provide further confirmation of this point of view, this can be found in the fact that the decree escapes the supervision of the Judiciary as provided for under Article 107 of the Constitution. The first proposals put forward by the Government did, moreover, make an explicit reference to this fact; but this explicit statement was quite rightly judged to be supererogatory and was therefore omitted.

The foregoing was clearly stated by that eminent statesman, Mr. Pierre Harmel, President of the Senate, during the opening session of the Upper House on 8 October 1974, and he expressed it in these terms :

"Similarly, in the spheres of cultural autonomy and provisional regionalisation, we shall take care to preserve the rightful sphere of action of the new Assemblies in all their integrity. But we know that the Ministers entrusted with these duties remain politically answerable to Parliament; we must therefore permit such control to be exercised.

"One might criticise the number and variety of all the assemblies in which members of Parliament, and Senators in particular, are called upon to take part ! It is true that we shall have to sit in turn in the Senate, the Cultural Council, the Regional Advisory Council, and that some of us, over and above these duties, will be members of the European assemblies. All that is transitional. Parliament wished it so during the period when the Council of Ministers of the European communities remains composed of delegates from the national governments, and as long as the national Ministers in charge of cultural and regional affairs remain answerable to both Houses.

"Thus, Parliament's task remains a vital one, at the hub of the new distribution of powers. Both Houses retain their residual powers of debate : everything which our laws do not expressly detach from the central trunk towards the branches formed by other deliberative bodies remains within the sphere of authority of Parliament itself; and everything that is so detached still does not escape our political vigilance, and will remain subject to it throughout the transitional period which Europe and our own regions are undergoing.

"It is very important that the Senate should be watchful and ensure that its powers and prerogatives continue to be exercised to the full."

184

VII. *Competence ratione loci*

This question has been dealt with in Section 4 of Article 59-B, which makes a distinction between the two kinds of matters coming within the competence of the cultural councils : the strictly cultural matters referred to in Section 2, and the linguistic matters referred to in Section 3.

A. In cultural matters :

In obedience to the objective pursued by means of the institution of the cultural councils, it is logical that each of these should be only competent in that language region for which it was set up.

However, in this connection arises the particularity of Brussels-Capital, where both the French language community and the Dutch language community have specifically cultural interests to defend. That is why the decrees are also applicable to those institutions set up in this region which, because of their activities, must be considered as belonging exclusively to one or other of the two cultural communities.

In its proposals, the Government pointed out that by the term "institutions", it was referring not only to legally constituted bodies whether of an official or a private nature, but also to all organisations established in the region of Brussels-Capital which depended on such bodies.

We have already said that certain members of Parliament would have liked to see a third cultural council created for the Brussels area, but there were such obstacles in the way that the majority gave up the idea. That was the only difficulty which arose in respect of this clause.

B. In linguistic matters :

Remember that the text pertaining to this subject only appeared in Article 59-B on 1 December 1970 when the proposal to modify Article 23 had been abandoned. This wording also gave rise to little difficulty. Some members were nevertheless anxious to know whether, in the boroughs which had been granted linguistic facilities and depending on the agreement of the cultural councils, special measures might be taken for the benefit not only of foreigners but also that of fellow-countrymen who did not speak the language of that borough.

The then Minister of Community Relations referred the members in question back to the text of Article 59-B, Section 2, 3rd paragraph, according to which the cultural councils are empowered to regulate co-operation between the cultural communities. He emphasized, moreover, that the law applies on the subject of the use of languages in those boroughs which have been granted linguistic facilities, and that the Legislative may take legal measures on the basis of a simple majority vote.

The wording of Section 4, para. 2 of Article 59-B therefore requires no further explanation.

VIII. *The right of initiative*

This question is regulated by Section 5 of Article 59-B. This section presented little difficulty and was hardly debated at all. At the most, the original text—which was far more explicit—was altered and simplified by the Government with reference to Articles 67, 69 and 129 of the Constitution.

By the reference to Article 67, as in the case of Acts of Parliament the King is empowered to issue regulations and edicts for the implementation of decrees without being able either to suspend them, or to exempt them from being implemented.

By the reference to Article 69, he also has the power to sanction and promulgate the decrees.

By the reference to Article 129, the decrees only come into effect when they have been published according to the prescribed forms. Clause 7 of the law of 3 July 1971 which contained in particular certain measures affecting the two cultural councils, has laid down the formula for the sanctioning and promulgation of the decrees and the obligation to publish them in the *Moniteur Belge* (official gazette) together with a translation in the language used for the decrees of the other cultural council. In terms of Clause 9 of that same law, the decree becomes mandatory, as in the case of laws, on the 10th day following its publication, unless some other period of time has been formally stated.

IX. *Financial means.*

This question is regulated by Section 6 of Article 59-B.

The importance of the problem will explain the lengthy debates which took place on the subject.

In its initial proposals, the Government had already provided that each council would be qualified to determine by decree the cultural budget for its own community, within the limits of an overall credit voted by the Houses. Some members considered, however that if true cultural autonomy was to be achieved, then the councils should not have to rely on a credit to be allocated by Parliament on its own. Complete autonomy involves the power to have independent financial means at one's disposal.

But the discussion mainly centred on the amount of the credits which were to be allocated to each community. Some members wished to write the method of sharing out the overall credit into the Constitution itself; others upheld the concept of an equal amount for each community, subject to those matters for which objective criteria could be established being reviewed separately. Yet others were mainly concerned at the minimum quota which was to be reserved for the Brussels-Capital region.

During the debate, some members also pointed out that, in fact, it would not be the council that determined the cultural budget : it would only be allocated an overall credit and its competence would therefore be restricted to designating those cultural activities to which the credit would be devoted. Its competence lay solely in its right to use the credits placed at its disposal, so that the wording would have to be modified.

Finally, the commission rallied to the concept of objective criteria to be determined by law, together with that proportion of the overall credit to be set aside for the cultural institutions established within the territory of Brussels-Capital. Even so, certain members maintained their opposition to the rule of equality under the heading of credits.

Here an important fact should be mentioned.

In the Government proposals of 4 March 1970, it was laid down in particular that a law passed on the basis of a special majority vote could attribute to each region the power necessary to levy taxes. In that case, each cultural council would indeed have been vested with genuine autonomy. The proposal was, however, opposed for various reasons : the creation of an extra range of taxes; Parliament's exclusive right, in terms of Heading IV of the Constitution, to levy taxes; the risk of a continuing movement towards a federal system whereas the kind of cultural autonomy aimed at was one in which the communities, while autonomous in certain respects, would nevertheless remain part of a unified though regionalised Belgium, in which there should continue to be a national budget divided between the communities, together with a national Government whose work was not to separate the communities but to organise proper co-operation between them. This point is an extremely important one because everything connected with taxes remains the sole prerogative of the national Parliament, and it is therefore Parliament's job to include in the national budget a grant or endowment for each community.

In the initial stage, acting on the Government's proposal, the national Parliament determines the overall credit, i.e. the total amount of credits to be made available to each cultural council. This overall credit is partly calculated on the basis of objective criteria as determined by law (population figure, number of people benefiting from the cultural policy, the number of projects on the programme, etc.), and partly on the basis of those matters which do not lend themselves to any objective criteria and for which endowments of equal amounts must therefore be provided (for instance, in the case of radio and television broadcasting).

When the overall credit is voted, each cultural council determines by decree the various purposes for which its overall credit is to be used, depending on what cultural policy it aims to pursue.

With particular reference to the Greater Brussels area, and within the framework of the overall credit allocated to each cultural council, the national Parliament determines what proportion is to be appropriated for the development of each of the two cultures in the territory of Brussels-Capital. The question here is one of a guaranteed minimum amount, which may if desired be increased by each cultural community as it thinks fit. The sums thus decided upon are allocated to the two Committees for Culture, the French and the Dutch, set up within the Greater Brussels Area, in implementation of Article 108-C of the Constitution.

X. *Ideological and philosophical guarantees*

This question is dealt with under Section 7 of Article 59-B.

It must be remembered that in acknowledging their cultural autonomy, the Government wished at the same time to provide for guarantees in order that the two communities should be enabled to develop freely without feeling that they were being placed on a minority footing within the framework of such autonomy.

The Government also wanted to avoid any risk of seeing ideological or philosophical minorities being relegated to a status of inferiority within each community.

That is why two principles were stated in the proposal dated 17 October 1968 :

1. a law must be passed on the basis of a special majority vote in order to lay down the guarantees to be granted to ideological and philosophical minority groups;

2. a preventive measure was provided for, through the intervention of the Council of State and the special qualified majority vote, so as to prevent either of the cultural councils from acting in contravention of the guarantee law.

Many amendments to the Government's wording were put to debate, and at one time there was even a project to write the principle of respect for minority groups into the text of a modified form of Article 6.

However, a ban on any discrimination in cultural matters was maintained in Article 59-B, although the recourse to a special majority vote was omitted.

During the debates, moreover, the Prime Minister had emphasized how difficult and arguable this question was, and he recalled the importance of the constitutional guarantee afforded by a parity government; in his opinion, this was indeed one of the first and greatest guarantees surrounding the proper functioning of the system and the protection of minority groups.

The law referred to under this heading in Article 59-B was passed on 3 July 1971. In particular, it contains the following measures:

CHAPTER II

Measures pertaining to the cultural councils
for the French cultural community and the Dutch cultural community

Section 1

Measures designed to prevent any discrimination
on ideological and philosophical grounds

Art. 4

A motivated motion, signed by at least one-quarter of the members of a cultural council and tabled after the submission of the report and before the final vote in open session, may state that the measures contained in a draft or proposed decree which it designates, and of which that cultural council has been apprised, contain some form of discrimination on ideological and philosophical grounds.

Art. 5

The presidents of the Legislative Chambers and of the two cultural councils, meeting as a body, shall rule on the admissibility of the motion on the basis of the provisions of Article 4.

In the event of a vote divided two against two, the motion shall be admissible.

A decision of admissibility shall suspend the debate on the measures concerned.

In that case, the draft or proposed decree, together with the motion, shall be referred to the Legislative Chambers which shall rule on the content of the motion.

Art. 6

The debate on the measures designated by the motion may not be resumed by the cultural council until such time as each of the Legislative Chambers has declared the motion to be unfounded.

Furthermore, on 15 July 1971, the leaders of the three traditional parties signed a cultural pre-agreement, the text of which is reproduced hereunder :

The undersigned parties,

Having taken note of the Prime Minister's statement during the Senate debate on the bill of 7 July 1971 providing for the organisation of cultural autonomy, confirm in particular :

— firstly, that in terms of Article 4 of the law of 3 July 1971, a motivated motion, signed by at least one-quarter of the members of a cultural council and tabled after the submission of the report and before the final voting in open session, may state that the measures contained in a draft or proposed decree which it designates, and of which that cultural council has been apprised, contain some form of discrimination on ideological and philosophical grounds;

— secondly, that in respect of each of the cultural matters enumerated in Article 2 of the draft, the competence of the cultural councils must be understood and interpreted in the light of the clarifications contained in the statement of intentions and in the very detailed reports prepared by Mr. Van Bogaert;

Desirous of permitting every trend of opinion in our society to contribute to the development of culture within a democratic system;

Bind themselves to apply and implement the following principles :

1. The cultural policy must notably promote, by all suitable means, understanding and co-operation based on mutual respect as between the persons, groups, organisations and institutions of different ideological and philosophical tendencies.

2. The cultural councils, the provincial and municipal councils and all other authorities vested with normative or statutory powers must take care to ensure that all ideological and philosophical tendencies shall be represented and shall participate in the charting of their cultural policies.

3. No law, decree, edict or regulation shall be enacted that contains any form of discrimination on ideological and philosophical grounds.

The undersigned parties therefore consider that the Act of Parliament provided for in terms of Article 59-B, Section 7 of the Constitution must be passed as soon as possible, and they therefore undertake and bind themselves :

1. To define in an agreement the practical directives that shall be valid for the entire country, and that must be respected by each and every institution entrusted with the implementation of a cultural policy.

These directives shall be framed for the purpose of preventing any persons, groups, organisations or institutions :

a) from being treated in a privileged or discriminatory manner owing to their ideological and philosophical views, bearing in mind the legitimate demands of national security and those of law and order;

b) from perpetrating any abuse of authority by virtue of their size, numerical importance or influence;

2. To define the terms and conditions whereby such practical directives can be related to the principal means that an autonomous cultural policy must have at its disposal.

The undersigned are referring in particular to such means as :

a) subsidies;

b) other forms of benefits and advantages;

c) the use of cultural infrastructures and public offices;

d) the composition of advisory councils and committees;

e) the composition of managing and administrative bodies;

f) the status of personnel performing cultural tasks.

3. To provide for such means as may guarantee the accomplishment of the objectives in view.

4. to proceed immediately with the designation of their delegates.

5. to work diligently for the signing of an agreement within the shortest possible period of time, and at the very latest by 30 November 1971.

ADDENDUM TO THE CULTURAL PRE-AGREEMENT OF 15 JULY 1971

At all events, within the year following the institution of the cultural councils, decrees shall be enacted to cover all the important credits, particularly with respect to their size and their allocation, that are connected with cultural autonomy (cultural section). These decrees are subject to the implementation of Article 4 of the law of 3 July 1971.

Brussels, 15 July 1971.

From this text, a reference will be noted to a cultural agreement that was to be concluded within the shortest possible period of time, and by 30 November 1971 at the very latest.

The new agreement was actually signed on 24 February 1972 by representaties of all the Belgian political parties with the exception of the Volksunie. This cultural compact was made law on 16 July 1973 at which time it was sanctioned by all the political parties without exception, both the traditional parties and the linguistic ones. The full text of this law is given hereunder :

CHAPTER 1 — *Scope of implementation*

Art. 1. In implementation of Article 6-B and 59-B, Section 7, of the Constitution, the decrees enacted by each of the cultural councils may not contain any form of discrimination on ideological and philosophical grounds, nor constitute any infringement of the rights and liberties of ideological and philosophical minorities.

Art. 2. The following are subject to the provisions of the present law : all measures taken by the public authorities in respect of the cultural matters referred to in Article 2 of the law of 21 July 1971 governing the competence and functioning of the cultural councils, as well as in the sphere of international cooperation as defined in Article 59-B, Section 2, para. 3 of the Constitution.

The said cultural matters do not comprise those measures pertaining essentially to penal law, social law, fiscal law and economic regulations.

The term "public authorities" should be construed as follows : the Executive authority, the provincial authorities, the interprovincial associations, the municipal authorities, the authorities in charge of urban areas and federations of boroughs, the intermunicipal associations, the French and Dutch cultural committees in the Greater Brussels area, and the public offices and departments subordinated to those authorities.

CHAPTER II. — *General principles pertaining to participation in the charting and implementation of cultural policies*

Art 3 - Para. 1 : The public authorities must associate the users and all ideological and philosophical tendencies with the charting and implementation of cultural policies according to the terms and conditions laid down by the present law, and on condition that they accept the principles and the rules of democracy and that they comply therewith.

Para. 2 : The concept of an ideological tendency is founded on a certain notion of life or of the way in which society should be organised.

The representation of such tendencies is based on their presence in the ranks of a representative assembly of the corresponding public authority.

Para. 3 : The representation of the users is based on the existence of representative organisations which are officially approved within the geographical jurisdiction and competence of the public authorities or the cultural organisation.

The criteria governing the acknowledgement of representative organisations may only be established by means of a law or a decree as the case may be.

Their representative nature depends on a range of criteria; acknowledgement may not be withheld on the basis of a single one of these criteria, and especially not on the basis of the number of members or supporters of such an organisation.

Para. 4 : For the purpose of implementation of the present law no person, organisation, or institution may, without its expressed agreement, be regarded as belonging to a given ideological or philosophical tendency.

Art. 4. Any public authority, any body set up by a public authority or on its initiative, any organisation or person which has at his or its permanent disposal any infrastructure belonging to a public authority, and subject to the provisions of Article 5 hereunder, shall abstain from any form whatsoever of discrimination, exclusion, restriction or preference for ideological or philosophical reasons the effect of which would be to nullify or compromise the free exercise of rights and liberties, and the sanctions or benefits accruing from the implementation of laws, decrees and regulations.

Art. 5. —No public authority may permanently place an infrastructure at the disposal of any entity belonging to an ideological or philosophical tendency unless that authority is in a position, within a reasonable period of time, to confer a similar benefit on any other organisation which may request it.

This conferral may in no case be postponed for a period in excess of that which remains before the renewal, by means of an election, of the body representing the public authority which makes the decision.

If the public authority has but one infrastructure available, it may only place it at the disposal of the various ideological or philosophical tendencies on a rota basis.

CHAPTER III. — *Participation in the charting of cultural policies*

Art. 6. The public authorities must associate in their work of charting and implementing their cultural policies all those representive organisations which are officially recognised, and all ideological and philosophical tendencies.

For this purpose, they shall have recourse to appropriate bodies and structures, whether existing or to be instituted, designed for consultation or concerted action.

Art. 7. These consultative bodies shall be so composed as to ensure adequate representation of all ideological and philosophical tendencies as well as of the associations of users, and to avoid the unjustified predominance of any one tendency or range of users' associations claiming to belong to the same tendency.

The recommendations and opinions laid before the public authorities may comprise notes compiled by minority groupings.

CHAPTER IV. — *General principles surrounding participation
in the management and administration of cultural bodies*

Art. 8. Para 1 : In implementation of Article 3 of the present law, the public authorities must associate the users' associations, together with the various ideological and philosophical tendencies, in a advisory capacity or with the right to speak and vote, and on the basis of an equitable and effective democratic representation, in the management of the cultural institutions set up by the public authorities or subordinate to them.

Para. 2 : The right of participation in a managing, administrative or consultative body is based on the following :

— either on the existence of a representative users' organisation within the area covered by the competence of the public authority concerned;

— or on the presence of a representative membership belonging to the ideological or philosophical tendency concerned within the representative assembly of the public authority in question.

Art. 9. The bodies set up for the management or administration of the infrastructures, institutions or cultural services created by the public authorities or subordinate to them, are subject to the provisions of Article 17 hereunder. They must be composed according to one of the three following forms of representation :

a) the proportional representation of all political tendencies existing within the public authority or authorities concerned. In this case, the managing or administrative body must be assisted by a permanent advisory committee on which all organisations representing the users and all philosophical and ideological tendencies are represented; this advisory committee has the right to be kept completely informed regarding the acts and deeds of the managing or administrative body.

b) an association of delegates of the public authority or authorities concerned with representatives of the users and the various tendencies. In this case, the rules governing representation must obey the principle of proportional representation where the delegates of the public authorities are concerned, and insofar as the users and the various tendencies are concerned, the measures provided for under Article 3 of the present law.

c) an association of specialists or users within an autonomous body, whether or not the latter has been endowed with a legal status, to which the public authorities concerned have entrusted management or administration. In this case, the provisions of Articles 3 and 6 hereof are applicable.

CHAPTER V. — *Guarantees pertaining to the cultural activities of the public authorities and the cultural organisations*

Art. 10. The rules governing official recognition and the granting of subsidies in cash or in kind for the benefit of regular cultural activities may only be established, as the case may be, in terms of a law, a decree or a debate in the representative assembly of the public authority.

In the absence of any such arrangements, the granting of any subsidies and advantages must be the subject of a specific budget entry.

Art. 11. When the question is one of recognised organisations whose activities are for the benefit of a whole cultural community, the decree shall provide that the financial intervention on the part of the public authorities shall simultaneously consist of the following :

— the subsidising of a nucleus of officials;

— the annual granting of an inclusive subsidy destined to cover operating expenses;

— the granting of subsidies on the basis of work effectively performed.

The conditions and the procedure surrounding official recognition are defined by a law or a decree as the case may be.

Art. 12. The provisions of Articles 10 and 11 of the present law do not apply to those subsidies intended to promote new ventures of an experimental nature. In this case, the initial subsidies may only be granted during a maximum period of three financial years; the decision to grant such subsidies must be the subject of a motivated recommendation from a competent advisory body.

CHAPTER VI. — *Special guarantees pertaining to individual promotional schemes*

Art. 13. In the sphere of art, literature and science, any intervention or promotion on the part of the public authorities is to be based exclusively on artistic, aesthetic and scientific criteria.

The equal rights of all citizens, irrespective of their personal convictions, must be ensured, with particular reference to the granting of prizes, awards, scholarships, loans and any other allocations, participation in sporting events and cultural activities, and the promotion of research work.

Art. 14. Any public authority which grants subsidies or other forms of encouragement to persons, organisations or bodies whose activities are of a cultural nature, must publish each year, as an annexure to its budget, a detailed list of the beneficiaries together with an indication of the funds or advantages granted to them.

CHAPTER VII. — *Guarantees pertaining to the utilisation of cultural infrastructures*

Art. 15. Any cultural organisation or group which has been officially approved, whether or not it claims allegiance to any ideological or philosophical tendency, may utilise the cultural infrastructure managed under the aegis of a public authority which is suitable for such utilisation by virtue of its nature and the statutes governing its establishment.

Art. 16. The rules defining the terms and conditions of utilisation shall be based solely on the material characteristics proper to the cultural infrastructure under consideration.

Art. 17. The programming or content of the activities which take place within the framework of the cultural infrastructure may not give rise to any intervention on the part of the public authorities nor of the managing and administrative bodies, except with respect to those measures bound up with penal law, social law, fiscal law, or economic regulations, and without prejudice to constitutional guarantees.

CHAPTER VIII. — *Guarantees pertaining to the utilisation of means of expression*

Art. 18. Each ideological and philosophical tendency represented in a cultural council must have access to the means of expression dependent on the public authorities of the community concerned.

Art. 19. The radio and television broadcasting stations must, in the composition of their administrative and managing bodies, abide by the proportional representation of the political groups within each of the cultural councils.

The managing and administrative bodies must be assisted by a permanent advisory committee comprising representatives of all the recognised users and all ideological and philosophical tendencies. This committee is entitled to receive full information concerning the acts and deeds of the administrative and managing bodies.

CHAPTER IX. — *Guarantees pertaining to personnel*

Art. 20. — With regard to those members of the personnel who perform cultural functions in cultural establishments and organisations, their recruiting, designation, appointment and promotion, both as regards statutory and temporary personnel and those members of the staff engaged under contract, must be carried out in obedience to the principle of equal rights, without any ideological or philosophical discrimination and in accordance with the rules governing their respective status, bearing in mind the need to ensure a balanced distribution of the posts, offices, functions and responsibilities among the various representative tendencies, a minimal representation of every tendency, and to prevent any monopoly or unjustified predominance of any of these tendencies.

CHAPTER X. — *Concerning the Permanent National Committee for the Cultural Pact*

Art. 21. A National Committee for the Cultural Pact has been set up whose task is to supervise that the measures enacted by the present law are being complied with.

For this purpose, the committee receives all complaints regarding infringements of the provisions of this law that may be lodged by any party having a recognised interest or who believes himself to be the victim of prejudicial treatment.

Art. 22. The committee consists of twenty-six effective members and twenty-six substitute members, divided into thirteen Dutch-speaking and thirteen French-speaking effective members and into thirteen Dutch-speaking and thirteen French-speaking substitute members.

The French-speaking effective and substitute members are elected by the cultural council of the French cultural community; the Dutch-speaking effective and substitute members are elected by the cultural council of the Dutch cultural community; and in both cases such election is based on the proportional representation of the political groupings of which each Council consists.

Furthermore, the committee comprises two effective and two substitute members appointed by the council of the German cultural community. These members have the right to speak and vote whenever the committee is apprised of a complaint involving the German language region.

All these committee members are appointed for a term of four years.

Those parties not represented on the committee may designate one French-speaking, Dutch-speaking or German-speaking member to act in an advisory capacity, on condition that such a party is represented in the cultural council of the community concerned. The appointment is made by the political group of the cultural council concerned.

It is ruled that membership of the committee is incompatible with any elective mandate.

The credits necessary to cover the operating expenses of the committee are set aside in each of the budgets of the Ministry for Dutch Culture and the Ministry for French Culture on a fifty-fifty basis.

The committee is assisted by State officials placed at its disposal by the Government.

Art. 23. The mandate of the committee members expires three months after the Legislative Chambers have been renewed as a result of a general election.

The committee appoints two chairmen from among its members, on the basis of an absolute majority vote of the Dutch-speaking members on the one hand and the French-speaking members on the other hand.

The committee appoints from among its members as many vice-chairmen as there are political parties represented on it, from among the Dutch-speaking members on the one hand and the French-speaking members on the other hand.

Art. 24. Para. 1 : The committee investigates the complaints laid before it. It hears the complainant and the authority indicted by the complaint; it may undertake on the spot hearings of all witnesses and reports and request communication of all information and documents which it deems necessary for the proper investigation of the affair, and receive all statements in testimony. It shall do its utmost to conciliate the parties.

Para. 2 : Failing any settlement by conciliation, the committee, in open session, shall put forward a motivated recommendation on the grounds of the complaint, if necessary accompanied by another recommendation addressed to the authority concerned requesting it either to agree to the formal nullification of the decision made, or to take any necessary steps to ensure compliance with the provisions of the present law.

This recommendation is issued within sixty days of the receipt of the complaint, but this period shall not cover the months of July and August.

The recommendation is notified to the complainant, to the authority in respect of which the complaint had been lodged, and where necessary to those other authorities vested with trusteeship or supervisory powers, and in every case to the competent Minister for Culture.

Art. 25. The complaint must be lodged with the committee within a period of sixty days from the date on which the public authority's decision under indictment was made public or notified to the complainant. This period begins on the day on which the complainant is apprised of the decision in the event that the latter has neither been made public nor notified to him.

When the complainant has the right of appeal to the administration section of the Council of State in respect of the facts which are the subject of his complaint, the official period set for the introduction of his request for nullification is suspended.

The complainant then benefits from a further sixty-day period in which to refer the matter to the Council of State, this period commencing at the end of the month following notification of the committee's recommendation, or at the end of the period during which such recommendation should have been made.

Art. 26. The permanent committee shall submit an annual report on its activities to both Houses of Parliament and to the cultural councils.

CHAPTER XI. — *General provision*

Art. 27. Any acts or regulations which run counter to the provisions of the present law and which emanate from public authorities subordinate to trusteeship or supervisory bodies, may be suspended or nullified by those bodies."

The main point here is the setting up of a National Committee for the Cultural Compact whose task is to supervise and ensure compliance with the terms of the law. Any complaints may be laid before this committee in respect of infringements of the law, on condition that such complaints are lodged by an interested party or one who considers himself to have been injured in some fashion. The committee, however, is only vested with advisory powers though its opinion may in some cases be accompanied by a recommendation addressed to the authority concerned, asking the latter either to confirm that the decision under indictment has been nullified, or to take all necessary steps to ensure compliance with the law. The committee does however have an efficient weapon at its disposal in the form of the annual report on its activities which is submitted to both Houses of Parliament and to the cultural councils.

XI. *The settlement of disputes*

This question is dealt with in Section 8 of Article 59-B.

It will be recalled that the Government, in its initial proposals, had provided for a fairly complicated procedure designed to prevent any conflict as between the law and the decree, or as between one decree and another. It might indeed happen that a draft or proposed decree went beyond the jurisdiction and competence of a cultural council. Similarly, some decrees might be incompatible when the sharing of competence as between the French language cultural council and the Dutch language cultural council had not been respected. That is why the Government wished to write into the Constitution itself the full details of a preliminary procedure to be undertaken before the Council of State.

As we have seen, the Government's proposals were subjected to a lengthy debate and, in the final analysis, the Constituent Assembly reached the conclusion that it would neither be possible nor desirable to write such precise and detailed arrangements on so delicate a subject into the Constitution itself.

That is why Article 59-B, in its final form, retains solely the principle that a procedure should be laid down by a law voted on a simple majority basis. An amendment aimed at making a special majority vote necessary was unanimously rejected by the Commission for Constitutional Reform set up in the House of Representatives, and finally the present wording, which is far more concise, was also unanimously adopted by the Senate Commission.

During the debate it was agreed that while the procedure would not be laid down in the Constitution itself, the principle of creating a third Chamber within the Council of State was nevertheless to be retained. This Chamber would be specially entrusted with the task of settling conflicts and contradictions either as between national legislation and decrees or between the decrees themselves. The legal arrangements for this purpose were included in the law of 3 July 1971 already mentioned above. The actual wording is as follows :

"Prevention of conflicts

"Art. 10 — With the exception of proposed cultural budgets, all draft and proposed decrees are submitted for the motivated recommendation of the legislation section of the Council of State. The recommendation is to be annexed to the statement of motives.

"Cabinet Ministers and the presidents of the cultural councils may request a motivated recommendation from the legislation section on any draft or proposed decree and on all amendments to such draft or proposed decrees.

"The presidents of the cultural councils are required to seek such recommendation whenever at least one-third of the members of the council concerned request it according to the procedure laid down by the rules of that council.

"The request for a recommendation is referred to the French-speaking or the Dutch-speaking chamber of the legislation section depending on whether the language used in preparing the draft or proposed decree or the amendment thereto is French or Dutch.

"Art. 11. — When, according to the recommendation made by the legislation section of the Council of State, a draft or proposed decree or an amendment thereto oversteps the competence of the cultural council, then the measure under indictment may not be adopted by the cultural council until it has secured a favourable vote in the Legislative Chambers.

Settlement of conflicts

"Art. 12. — Para. 1 : The Council of State comprises a section set up to deal with conflicts of authority. It examines conflicts as between the law and a decree and as between a decree issued by the cultural council of the French cultural community and a decree issued by the cultural council of the Dutch cultural community.

"Para. 2 : The section dealing with conflicts of authority consists of :

"1) the first president, or a president and three members of the Council of State appointed by the first president;

"2) four assessors and four substitute assessors.

"Half of the number of magistrates referred to under 1) together with half the number of assessors and substitute assessors referred to under 2) must show proof, by submitting their degrees, that they have passed their graduation examinations as doctors or bachelors of law in the French language, while the other half of those officials shall show similar proof that they have passed such examinations in the Dutch language. Furthermore, they must also show proof of a thorough working knowledge of the other national language.

"The conditions governing the appointment of assessors in the conflicts of authority section are the same as those governing the appointment of assessors in the legislation section of the Council of State.

" The King appoints the assessors and substitute assessors for a term of five years which is renewable, or for the term which remains to be served until they have reached their seventieth year of age.

"The following are applicable to the assessors and substitute assessors of the conflicts of authority section : Clause 38, para. 2 and Clause 54, Section 3, para. 2 of the law of 23 December 1946 covering the institution of a Council

199

of State, modified by the law of 3 June 1971. The following are applicable solely to the assessors : Clause 39, paras. 2 and 3, to the extent that the items on the agenda involve the conflicts of authority section, together with Clause 40, para. 2.

"The King determines the emoluments accruing to the assessors and the substitute assessors.

"Para. 3 : A substitute assessor may only sit when the titular assessor is prevented from doing so.

"Para. 4 : The procedure in the conflicts of authority section is identical to that followed in the administration section. The King may however modify it.

"The language of the procedure is the same as that which is applicable in cases referred to the bilingual chamber of the administration section.

"Para. 5 : Rulings are delivered on the basis of a majority vote.

"In the event of an equal number of votes for and against, that of the first president or of the president of the section is the deciding vote. Mention shall be made in the ruling of the equality in the number of votes cast.

"Art. 13 : The Council of Ministers (the Cabinet) shall apprise the conflicts of authority section should it consider that there is a conflict or the possibility of a conflict. Such a request is signed by the Prime Minister.

"Art. 14 : The conflicts of authority section of the Council of State is competent to rule, on a prejudicial basis, on all questions pertaining to a contradiction as between a law and a decree or as between decrees of the French cultural council and those of the Dutch cultural council, and which have been referred to it by the courts and tribunals, or by any other jurisdiction.

"Each jurisdiction shall refer the prejudicial matter to this section whenever it considers that a reply to this question is necessary in order to make its decision.

"The referral decision suspends procedure and prescription and is without appeal.

"When the request comes from an appellate jurisdiction, it suspends implementation of the decision appealed against, except in cases where provisional implementation automatically takes place.

"Art. 15. — The rulings delivered in terms of Articles 13 and 14 above become mandatory except in the event of their nullification by Parliament within ninety days of the notification of such a ruling by the Registrar of the Council of State to the President of each of the Houses of Parliament; the Registrar shall also simultaneously notify it to the Prime Minister.

"Within thirty days of such notification, the Cabinet shall lay its motivated opinion on the ruling before Parliament.

"The decision of both Houses must be made within sixty days either of the date on which the Cabinet's opinion is tabled, or of the date on which the thirty-day period allowed for its transmission has expired.

"Such periods are suspended from the first day of July until the second Tuesday in October each year, as also during the time when Parliament is not in session.

"Art. 16. — The Recorder of the House which has pronounced on the ruling shall notify the House's decision to the Registrar of the Council of State.

"Art. 17. — When both Houses of Parliament have pronounced their nullification of the ruling, the Registrar of the Council of State shall notify both decisions, together with the original ruling, to the jurisdiction which referred the matter to the Council in the first place, so that it may issue its prejudicial ruling.

"Art. 18. — When one of the Houses of Parliament has not pronounced its nullification, or when the ninety-day period has expired without Parliament having exercised its right to nullify the ruling, then the Registrar of the Council of State shall notify the ruling to the jurisdiction which referred the matter to the Council in the first place, so that it may issue its prejudicial ruling.

"He shall mention on such notification that the ruling has become mandatory.

"Art. 19. — The decision of both Houses of Parliament to annul a ruling or, failing annulment, the ruling itself, goes into effect on the tenth day following its publication in the *Moniteur belge* (official gazette).

"Art. 20. — When a prejudicial question such as that referred to in Article 14 is raised for the first time before the Court of Cassation, either by the parties concerned or ex officio, the Court shall refer the matter to the Houses of Parliament for their decision.

"This request suspends the course of prescription.

"The decision of Parliament goes into effect on the tenth day following its publication in the *Moniteur belge* (official gazette).

"Art. 21. — The King shall submit to the Houses of Parliament or to the competent cultural council, as the case may be, a bill or decree aimed at the abrogation or the alignment of the measure referred to the Council of State either with its ruling or with the decision made by Parliament. "

As we may see, the above law has therefore created two kinds of guarantees :

— a prior guarantee, since in terms of Article 10, para. 2, Cabinet Ministers or the presidents of the cultural councils may seek the opinion of the legislation section of the Council of State on any draft or proposed decree or amendment thereto.

In matters coming within his competence, therefore, should any Minister entertain doubts regarding the admissibility of a decree, all he has to do is refer the matter to the Council of State.

— a subsequent guarantee. Indeed, in terms of Article 13 of this same law of 3 July 1971, the Council of Ministers (Cabinet) apprises the conflicts of authority section of the Council of State whenever it considers that a conflict exists or that there is a possibility of conflict.

It should also be remembered that, in terms of Article 14, the conflicts of authority section of the Council of State is competent to rule, on a prejudicial basis, on questions pertaining to the contradiction between a law and a decree, or between decrees issued by the two cultural councils, when such matters are referred to it by the courts and tribunals or by any other jurisdiction.

In theory, therefore, an overstepping of competence can be ruled out. But in reality, such an overstepping always remains possible should the various authorities not make use of the means placed at their disposal for the prevention of it.

Basically, the situation differs little from that which arises in the event of an unconstitutional law. Parliament might also vote an unconstitutional law just as the cultural councils might overstep their competence. There is but a single restriction placed on the cultural councils; while there is no means of verifying the constitutionality of laws insofar as Parliament is concerned, this is not so with respect to the cultural councils since the conflicts of authority section of the Council of State may always be apprised a posteriori of cases of conflict.

It should moreover be stated that the question as to whether a Constitutional Court (which does not exist in Belgium) should be set up, was raised on several occasions during the debates. Some members, however, pointed out that such a Court would be in contradiction with the traditions of Belgian public law according to which the ultimate right to interpret the Constitution is vested in Parliament alone. That is why, in the law of 3 July 1971, the last word has been left to Parliament, and the rulings delivered by the Council of State only become mandatory if they have not been annulled by the Legislative Chambers within a period of ninety days. But we must remember that the Government for its part did not oppose the setting up of a Constitutional Court.

XII. *Co-operation between the cultural councils.*

Finally, again in order to maintain a certain form of co-operation within the framework of the cultural autonomy created by Article 59-B, clause 4 of the law of 21 July 1971 provides that each cultural council shall comprise a committee whose task is precisely to promote co-operation between the two cultural communities, the French and the Dutch.

These committees, meeting in joint session, form the "combined co-operation committees". Clause 4, which is so vital to the harmonious functioning of the new institutions, is reproduced hereunder :

CHAPTER III. — *Co-operation between the cultural Communities*

Art. 4. — Para. 1 : Each cultural council comprises a committee whose task is to promote co-operation between the French cultural community and the Dutch cultural community.

This committee is made up according to the system of proportional representation of the political groupings. It comprises fifteen members, including the president and the vice-president of the cultural council.

Para. 2 : The committees referred to in Para. 1, meeting in joint session, form the combined co-operation committees.

During the session, the combined co-operation committees shall hold at least two sittings. The latter are chaired in turn by the president of one cultural council and the other; the first sitting shall be chaired by the older of the two presidents.

The combined co-operation committees may request those Ministers responsible for cultural matters to be present, as also any other Minister.

The combined co-operation committees shall frame their own internal rules.»

Coming now to the end of this lengthy explanation of the machinery set up to provide for cultural autonomy, it is now necessary to emphasize that the two cultural councils which have been set up do indeed constitute the genuine cultural parliaments of the two communities, both French-speaking and Dutch-speaking. Their permanent nature is guaranteed by the fact that, as institutions, their existence is written into the Constitution, while their competence and operating procedures may not be altered or modified save in terms of a law passed on the basis of a special majority vote.

Yet the sovereign powers of each council are nevertheless subjected to certain limitations, which are :

— those matters acknowledged as coming under their jurisdiction;

— the amount of the overall credit allocated to them;

— the fact that ministerial responsibility may not be implicated within the councils;

— where necessary, the intervention of the national Parliament when there is a question of protecting minority groups, or when conflicts of authority arise.

It is useful, moreover, to recall that the cultural councils do not have an Executive. The authority entrusted with the implementation of laws is also responsible for the implementation of decrees, i.e. the Executive authority as laid down by the Constitution. The King issues the regulations and edicts necessary for the implementation of the decrees, without however being empowered either to cancel them or to decide that they shall not be implemented.

Furthermore, if the courts and tribunals find themselves faced with conflicts of authority, they are not qualified to rule on them but may solicit the opinion of the conflicts of authority section of the Council of State. This section will rule on a prejudicial basis, pending a final decision to be made by Parliament.

It is certain that the two cultural councils have not yet acquired sufficient experience to be able to carry out their task without hesitations or misgivings. Thus, for instance, certain decrees contain legal errors, such as a clause entrusting the King with their implementation whereas such a formula is redundant in legal terms, the King being constitutionally responsible for the implementation of decrees as well as laws. But those are minor details which can easily be put right when the cultural councils have had an opportunity to acquire a wider measure of experience in their work.

The fact remains that, from now on, the two cultural councils have come to join the House of Representatives and the Senate so as to form the new parliamentary institution.

The following table will provide a clearer picture of the new parliamentary set-up in Belgium :

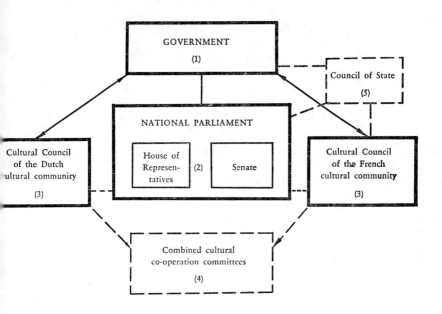

(1) Within the Government, there is :

— a Minister of National Education and a Minister for Culture for the French-speaking part of the country;

— a Minister of National Education and a Minister for Culture for the Dutch-speaking part of the country;

— cultural appropriations in the budgets of other Ministries.

(2) The national Parliament (bicameral) votes laws and budgets (or budget appropriations) for non-cultural purposes, plus the major part of the National Education budget covering those educational credits subjected to the provisions of the Schools Pact.

(3) Each cultural council (unicameral) consists of French-speaking Deputies and Senators on the one hand and of Dutch-speaking Deputies and Senators on the other. It votes decrees and, in the form of a budget decree, the French culture and Dutch culture budget as well as cultural credits included under the headings of other government departments. Part of the National Education budget comes under its jurisdiction.

(4) The "combined committees" consist of the two cultural co-operation committees set up respectively within the French cultural council and the Dutch cultural council.

(5) The Council of State must (in respect of draft bills and decrees) or may (in respect of proposed decrees and amendments) be apprised of requests for a recommendation as to whether Parliament or the cultural council are competent to enact such measures; it rules on conflicts as between the law and a decree or as between decrees issued by the French council and the Dutch council.

ARTICLE 59-C

"There is a council for the German cultural community. The law determines its composition and jurisdiction."

This article was adopted during the Third Revision (1967-1971) and formally enacted on 24 December 1970.

There can be no better way of summarising the aims of both Parliament and Government than by reproducing the justifications put forward by the latter when it tabled the bill that was to become law on 10 July 1973, as will be discussed farther on.

In setting out its motives, the Government stated as follows :

"In the course of the recent revision of the Constitution, the Constituent Assembly particularly wished the Fundamental Charter to embody full recognition of the essential components of the Belgian reality today : thus, it acknowledged the existence of three cultural communities, four linguistic regions, and three socio-economic regions.

In this way, the German-speaking population of Belgium now sees its existence constitutionally acknowledged and guaranteed. The boundaries of the German language region benefit from the same immutability as the other linguistic boundaries, for any modification thereto is also subordinated to an Act of Parliament passed on the basis of a qualified majority vote.

Not content with acknowledging the linguistic regions, the Constituent Assembly also wished to ensure that the three cultural communities, backed by the three national languages, should each expand and prosper according to its own innate talents and virtues, and that they should provide adequate solutions to their own specific problems. Indeed, the Constituent Assembly believes that the cultural wealth of Belgium consists of the autonomous development of her cultural communities without, of course, prejudice to their co-operation and mutual enrichment. The Government is in complete agreement with this view."

The Government added that such had been the justification for the cultural autonomy vested in the French and Dutch-speaking cultural communities, and that such was also the justification for Article 59-C which, in accordance with this principle, created a council for the German cultural community.

Formerly, the Commission for Institutional Reform had already provided that a cultural institution for German-speaking Belgians would be set up by Royal Decree.

It was to materialise this intention, as we have seen in connection with Article 59-B, that the Government included among its proposals of 17 October 1968 a paragraph 8 under Clause 3-B which read as follows :

"There is, for the German language region, an advisory cultural council the composition and jurisdiction of which are determined by law."

During the general debate on the original text of this Clause 3-B, the wording suggested by the Government gave rise to some controversy. Some members in fact expressed their regret and even their bitterness at the fact that the Government had not proposed a degree of cultural autonomy for the German language region that would be as complete and extensive as that granted to the two other language regions. In particular, they wished the German language cultural council to be vested equally with powers of decision.

Other members, however, did not support this opinion because they felt that it would not be possible to set up a German language cultural council on the model of the other two councils since the German language region did not have enough members of Parliament to represent it. Now, as we already know, Parliament had considered that the power of voting decrees should not be bestowed on any persons other than those elected by the people. In practice, therefore, it was necessary to ensure the full flowering of German culture, but solely through the channel of a council whose composition and functioning should be determined by law.

The then Minister for Community Relations, moreover, clarified the intentions of the Government : full respect for the German language was to be legally guaranteed; the expansion of cultural activities in the region would be encouraged by the use of the German language in all main means of communication and in education; the necessary prerequisites for the development of a genuine cultural life were to be made available to the region. The government text, which had already been reworded in the proposals dated 28 January 1969, was therefore allowed to stand.

Nevertheless, the notion that the German cultural council must not be placed on a footing of inferiority was gaining ground, and on 20 May 1970 the Senate Commission proposed a new text which read as follows :

"There is a cultural council for the German cultural community. The law shall determine the composition of the council, the conditions governing the presentation and election of its members, and the way in which they shall perform their functions. The law shall make the Council competent to settle those cultural affairs as it shall specify, and shall regulate the way in which the Council co-operates with the other communities."

Later on, the majority in Parliament came to the conclusion that it would not be possible to ensure the cultural autonomy of the German language region in the same way as had been done for the two other communities. The territorial and numerical importance of the German language community was far inferior to that of the two other communities, and while it was necessary to provide a status of cultural autonomy for the German language region, some solution sui generis would nevertheless have to be sought in keeping with the special problems affecting that region. This latter theory finally won the day, with the result that, in the final analysis, Parliament reverted to a wording that was far more similar to the Government's proposals, and one which left it to the Legislative to define the competence and functioning of the Council for the German cultural community, without resorting to a law passed on the basis of a special majority vote.

Meanwhile, as we have seen, the clause in question had been withdrawn from the original Article 3-B in order to become the new Article 59-C of the Constitution.

It was by means of the law of 10 July 1973 that the Legislative performed the constitutional task prescribed under Article 59-C. Its main clauses are reproduced hereunder :

CHAPTER I. — *Territorial jurisdiction*

Art. 1. The Council of the German cultural community, hereinafter referred to as the Council, has a jurisdiction extending over the German language region as defined in clause 5 of the laws governing the use of languages for administrative purposes.

CHAPTER II. — *Composition of the Council*

Section 1 — General provisions

Art. 2. The Council consists of 25 members.

Art. 3. When they are not members of the Council, the following are entitled to attend sittings in an advisory capacity :

i) Members of the House of Representatives and Senators elected in the electoral region of Verviers, who are legally resident in a borough of the German language region, and who have taken the constitutional oath either exclusively in German, or with German as their first language;

ii) Senators elected by the Provincial Council of Liège, together with Senators elected by the Senate, on condition that they comply with both of the conditions laid down in (i) above;

iii) Provincial councillors elected in the districts of Dison and Spa, on condition that they comply with both of the conditions laid down in (i) above.

Art. 4. To be a member of the Council, it is necessary :

i) to be Belgian;

ii) to enjoy civil and political rights;

iii) to be aged 21 years or over;

iv) to be legally resident in a borough of the German language region for a period of at least one year prior to the day of appointment;

v) to enjoy electoral rights in the electoral district stipulated in Article 7.

Art. 28. The Council, acting either on its own initiative or at the request of the Presidents of the Legislative Chambers or of one or several Ministers, gives its opinion on problems relating to the matters enumerated in Article 59-B, paras. 2 and 3, of the Constitution, and in Clause 2, paras. 1 and 3 to 10, of the law of 21 July 1971 regulating the competence and functioning of the Cultural Councils set up for the French-language cultural community and the Dutch-language cultural community.

The Council determines the procedure according to which its opinions are framed and presented.

Art. 29. Ministers shall submit the following to the Council for its motivated opinion :

i) draft bills, organic and statutory decrees pertaining to matters referred to in Art. 28 and which apply to the German language region, together with amendments thereto;

ii) draft bills tending to modify the present law, together with amendments thereto.

The Council gives its motivated opinion on bills and amendments thereto which correspond to the conditions laid down in i) and ii) above, and which have been brought to its attention by the President of one of the Legislative Chambers, or by a Cabinet Minister.

Failure to give an opinion within a period of 60 days from the date on which the Council was notified, is deemed to signify agreement.

Art. 30. Within the limits and according to the method stipulated by each law, the Council regulates, for the German language region, those cultural matters referred to in Art. 28 together with education, excepting only those matters withdrawn by article 59-B, para. 2, (ii) of the Constitution from the competence of the two other cultural Councils.

Art. 31. The Council enacts the statutory decrees pertaining to the financing of cultural activities.

In particular, within this framework it determines the conditions surrounding the granting of subsidies, awards and grants or scholarships to private persons, institutions and associations.

Art. 32. A Commission has been set up under the Council for the official German translation of laws and regulations; it is known as the "Ausschuss für offizielle deutsche Übersetzung der Gesetze und Erlasse".

It is composed of three members appointed by the Council from among candidates having special aptitudes in the sphere of judicial and legislative matters together with a thorough knowledge of the German language and German legal phraseology.

The Council frames the conditions of appointment and defines the functioning of this Commission together with the emoluments of its members. The Council supplies the Commission with the material means necessary to accomplish its task.

The term of office of members of this Commission is four years and is renewable.

Art. 33. Draft translations of official documents referred to in Art. 32, when approved by the Council, are ratified by the King. These translations are published in the "Memorial des Rates der deutschen Kulturgemeinschaft".

Art. 34. Clause 8 of the law of 30 July 1963 governing the use of languages in education is replaced by the following clause :

"In those scholastic establishments located in the German language region, and under the conditions laid down by the Council for the German cultural community, part of the syllabus may, starting from the third year of primary education, be taught :

a) in French in the German language primary, secondary and higher education establishments;

b) in German in French language primary schools.

The statutory decrees of the Council for the German cultural community referred to in Para. 1 are to be submitted by the Government within six months for ratification by the Legislative Chambers.

They shall only become effective when they have been made mandatory by law."

Art. 35. The Council may only make decisions on the matters provided for under Art. 34 when they have sought the opinion of the directors of scholastic establishments and the parents' associations that may exist in such establishments. These opinions must be annexed to the Council's debates.

Failure to make their opinions known within a period of ninety days from the date on which those directors and associations have been notified shall be deemed to signify agreement.

Art. 36. The Council gives its opinion regarding the appointment of the official responsible for radio and television broadcasts in the German language. In this, it takes over the prerogatives of the Advisory Commission on German language Broadcasting.

Art. 37. In exercising the attributions vested in it in terms of the present chapter, the Council is called upon :

i) to set up public offices, subject to ratification by law;

ii) to delegate one or several of its members as directors or auditors on the board of any public body whose activities are connected with one or several of the matters coming within the jurisdiction of the Council;

iii) to take any and all initiatives aimed at promoting co-operation with the other cultural communities.

Art. 38. The Council may inflict penalties sanctioning any infringement of its decrees. These penalties may not exceed those applicable in the police courts.

Art. 39. Dating from the entry into force of the decrees enacted by the Council in terms of the present law or of the laws referred to in Art. 30, any provincial and municipal regulations which may conflict with them shall cease to be applicable within the limits laid down in Art. 1.

Article 107 of the Constitution is applicable to decrees enacted by the Council. Under Clause 12 of the coordinated laws governing the Council of State, a para. 2 is to be inserted, reading as follows :

"The administration section shall, in the same way, settle difficulties concerned with the respective competence of the King, the Cabinet Ministers, and the Council for the German cultural community."

Art. 40. The Council draws up its own internal rules.

CHAPTER V. — *Concerning the implementation of the Council's debates*

Art. 63. The Cabinet Minister whose competence includes, for the German language region, those matters which are the subject of a statutory decree, is entrusted with the implementation of that decree.

The other decrees are implemented by the committee.

CHAPTER VI. — *Concerning appeals and trusteeship measures*

Art. 64. The Cabinet Minister whose competence includes the matter concerned may suspend the implementation of any decree enacted by the Council or the committee which runs counter to the law.

The decree of suspension must be issued within ten days of the Minister's receipt of the decree in question.

It is notified immediately to the Council and the committee who may either justify their act or withdraw it.

If, within forty days of the Minister's receipt of the act whereby the authority concerned has taken cognizance of the suspension, the King has not annulled the decree, the latter shall go into effect.

Art. 65. The Council's steering committee is competent, subject to authorisation by the Council, to institute appeals referred to in Clause 14 of the coordinated laws governing the Council of State against the acts and regulations referred to in that article and which have been framed in infringement of the Council's prerogatives.

Art. 66. The internal rules shall determine the method whereby the steering committee shall institute the legal action referred to in Art. 65.

In the sphere of elections, Article 6 lays down as follows : "The Council is renewed simultaneously with the House of Representatives. Its members are elected by the voters of boroughs forming part of the German language region referred to in Art. 1 and who meet the conditions required to elect members to the Houses of Parliament." As for the financial means which must be available to the Council for it to perform its tasks, it is useful to review Articles 67 and 68 as follows :

Art. 67. Every year, in the Budget for Cultural Endowments, an appropriation is made specifically to cover the activities of the Council for the German cultural community; the Council's operating expenses are chargeable to the Endowment Budget.

Art. 68. Furthermore, the Council may receive :

i) Subsidies from the provinces and the boroughs and from the federations of boroughs existing within the German language region;

ii) Donations and legacies to the Belgian State with the proviso that they be used for the Council's activities;

iii) The fruit of loans contracted in the name of the Belgian State with the permission of the Minister of Finance.

Finally, seeing that it was not possible to hold an election immediately, the law contains a series of transitional measures designed to permit the Council to be set up until the end of the legislative session in course at the time when the law went into effect.

Among this range of measures, a certain number are worthy of mention owing to the light they shed on the way in which the problem of cultural autonomy has been solved in the German language region.

I. *Territorial jurisdiction*

Of necessity, this jurisdiction had to be circumscribed by the German linguistic region itself as determined by Article 5 of the coordinated laws of 18 July 1966 governing the use of languages for administrative purposes.

This territorial delimitation was, in fact, the outcome of combining Article 3-B of the Constitution, which divided the territory of Belgium into four linguistic regions, with Article 3-C acknowledging the existence of three cultural communities, and with Article 59-B which determined the territorial jurisdiction of the Cultural Councils set up for the French and Dutch language cultural communities respectively.

During the parliamentary debates, the question of the "Eastern Cantons" was frequently raised. However, it should be stated at once that this concept does not entirely cover that of the German language region as governed by the Council for the German cultural community.

Any vagueness in the use of either term might well be productive of errors.

The German language region, as defined in the coordinated laws governing the use of languages for administrative purposes, comprises in fact the Cantons of Eupen and St.-Vith together with the boroughs of Elsenborn, Rocherath, Bullange, Bütgenbach and La Calamine.

In contrast, the concept of the "Eastern Cantons" seems not to appear in any legal act or document. There is however a reference to it, used for descriptive purposes in a portion of legislation dealing with the aftermath of the war of 1940-1945.

Thus, a law of 27 July 1953 defining the effects of the application of German law in that part of Belgian territory which was wrongfully annexed to Germany in May 1940, specifies the boroughs to which it applied by referring to the concept of annexation in implementation of the decisions made by the Reich on 18 May and 23 May 1940.

This law related not only to the Cantons of Eupen and St.-Vith already mentioned, but also to the Canton of Malmédy as a whole and to a number of other boroughs or parts of boroughs belonging to other Cantons, and even to other provinces.

The following list will serve to compare those boroughs which form the German language region with those affected by the law of 1953 and which, informally, are included in the general term of "Eastern Cantons".

GERMAN LANGUAGE REGION	EASTERN CANTONS
Province of Liège	*Province of Liège*
Canton of Eupen	Canton of Eupen
Eupen	Eupen
Eynatten	Eynatten
Hauset	Hauset
Hergenrath	Hergenrath
Kettenis	Kettenis
Lontzen	Lontzen
Neu-Moresnet	Neu-Moresnet
Raeren	Raeren
Walhorn	Walhorn
Canton of St.-Vith	Canton of St.-Vith
Saint-Vith	Saint-Vith
Amblève	Amblève
Crombach	Crombach
Heppenbach	**Heppenbach**
Lommersweiler	Lommersweiler
Manderfeld	**Manaderfeld**
Meyerode	Meyerode
Recht	Recht
Reuland	Reuland
Schoenberg	Schoenberg
Thommen	Thommen

GERMAN LANGUAGE REGION	EASTERN CANTONS
Province of Liège (cont'd)	*Province of Liège* (cont'd)
Canton of Malmédy	Canton of Malmédy
	Malmédy
	Bellevaux-Ligneuville
	Bévercé
Bullange	Bullange
Bütgenbach	Bütgenbach
Elsenborn	Elsenborn
	Faymonville
	Robertville
Rocherath	Rocherath
	Waimes
Canton of Aubel	Canton of Aubel
	Aubel
	Clermont
	Gemmenich
	Hombourg
La Calamine	La Calamine
	Montzen
	Moresnet
	Sippenaken
	Canton of Limburg
	Limbourg
	Baelen s/Vesdre
	Bilstain
	Goé
	Henri-Chapelle
	Jalhay
	Membach
	Welkenraedt
	Canton of Spa
	Sart
	Canton of Stavelot
	Stavelot
	Province of Limburg
	Canton of Fouron-St.-Martin
	Remersdaal
	Province of Luxemburg
	Canton of Vielsalm
	Beho
	Petit-Thier

N.B. 1. In the above list, reference is made to electoral cantons and not to judiciary cantons.

2. Apart from the Cantons of Eupen, Malmédy and St.-Vith, the Eastern Cantons do not necessarily comprise the entire territory of the boroughs named, but only those parts of the boroughs in question that were annexed to Germany. (Cfr. Art. 1 of the law of 27 July 1953.)

It was to that purely descriptive concept that members of Parliament frequently referred subsequently when they spoke of "the eastern part of the country", "the Eastern Cantons" and so forth. Quite recently, a law of 25 July 1974 concerning the change of first or Christian names by people born in the territories annexed by Germany in 1940, once again took as a basis the concept outlined in Article 1 of the law of 27 July 1953.

This shows that while the concept of the "Eastern Cantons" has no official existence in law, it is nonetheless used to describe a series of cantons or boroughs in terms of a historical fact : the annexation of part of Belgium's territory in 1940.

It is nevertheless necessary to mention another locution which has recently made its appearance and which resumes the concept of the "Eastern Cantons" even though the latter are not specifically designated. In the Government which took office early in 1973, there was a new appointment : that of "Secretary of State for the Eastern Cantons". His functions, moreover, have never been clearly defined since a Royal Decree of 8 October 1973 merely restricted itself to acknowledging his competence in those cultural matters referred to in the law of 10 July 1973.

II. *Composition of the Council*

In its definitive form, the Council comprises 25 members elected by the inhabitants of the German language region. These members, moreover, must respond to certain conditions laid down in Article 4 of the law of 10 July 1973.

Certain other persons may, however, also attend sessions of the Council in an advisory capacity, even when they are not members. These people are members of Parliament who are considered as belonging to the German language region, together with certain provincial councillors.

We have already seen that, at its inception, the Council for the German cultural community did not have a membership composed according to the normal rules, because it was necessary to resort to the special transitional measures provided for in the law so as not to delay the setting up of the Council.

The definitive system only came into effect on 5 April 1974, as a result of the special elections which had taken place on 10 March previously so as to ensure the direct election this time of the requisite number of Council members in terms of Article 2 of the law.

III. *Prerogatives of the Council*

a) Matters

From the standpoint of matters coming under its jurisdiction, the Council is vested with the same competence as the Cultural Councils for the French and Dutch language communities. In this regard, there is therefore absolutely no difference between this and the two other language regions.

b) Powers

The special characteristics with which this Council has been endowed have determined two kinds of powers which are acknowledged in respect of it :

1) Advisory powers

— the Council intervenes first by means of opinions or recommendations, either on its own initiative or at the request of the President of one of the Houses, or that of one or several Ministers;

— this opinion or recommendation must obligatorily be sought by Ministers who are required to lay before the Council all draft bills and organic or statutory decrees involving cultural matters for the German language region, together with all draft bills that tend to modify the organic law instituting the Council.

2) Statutory powers

Furthermore, the Council wields certain statutory powers to the extent that, for the German language region, within the limits and according to the methods defined in each law, it regulates cultural matters and education, with the exception, however, of those matters which the Constitution has withdrawn from the competence of the two other cultural councils.

According to the authors, by the term "statutory powers" should be understood the competence to establish general legal norms applicable without distinction to all persons who find themselves in specific de facto conditions. Furthermore, the Council is competent to enact statutory decrees pertaining to the financing of cultural activities, in particular by fixing the conditions governing the granting of subsidies, awards and scholarships both to private persons and to institutions or associations.

It was this question of what powers should be acknowledged in respect of the Council which gave rise to much of the debating. Indeed, certain members of Parliament, wishing to place the Council on a footing of complete equality with the other two cultural councils, would have liked to see it vested with full powers of decree. They argued that Article 3-C of the Constitution recognises three cultural communities placed on the same footing : the French, the Dutch and the German. However, the majority considered that powers of decree could not be granted to the Council for the German cultural community. By settling the question in two separate constitutional articles : n°ˢ 59-B and 59-C, the Constituent Assembly was at pains to make a distinction between the two systems while granting the Council for the German cultural community a degree of competence fully equal to that of the other two councils. The Council for the German cultural community does not, therefore, possess the legislative or normative powers acknowledged in respect of the other two councils. The Constituent Assembly alone would have been able to grant it the power to make decisions having the force of regional laws. It was notably the small numerical importance of the German-speaking Belgian population : about 63,000 inhabitants spread out over some 25 boroughs, that justifies the difference in the Council's prerogatives. Furthermore, the majority considered, quite logically from their standpoint, that it was impossible to grant powers of decree to an assembly which did not consist of members of Parliament, but only of people elected to it regardless of whether they were members of Parliament or not.

That is why the powers acknowledged in respect of the Council for the German cultural community are powers of a sui generis nature. The competence of the Council for the German cultural community must therefore be delegated to it by Parliament. There can consequently be no question of any sovereign power since the Legislative has the right to recall any powers it has granted. Moreover, the Cabinet Ministers exercise a kind of trusteeship within the framework of their own competences, and in particular they may suspend implementation of any regulation issued by the Council for the German cultural community in the event that such a regulation is counter to the law. Any annulment thereof must, however, be pronounced by Royal Decree.

IV. *Other questions*

The operating rules of the Council only differ very slightly in principle from what has been laid down for the other two cultural councils. Thus, for instance, the Council's statutory decrees must be published in the *Moniteur belge* (official gazette) and they come into force on the 10th day after such publication unless some other measure intervenes. Thus, again, Article 57 has provided for measures designed to protect minorities so as to prevent any discrimination on ideological or philosophical grounds. Thus, finally, the Budget for Cultural Endowments must contain an appropriation exclusively designed to cover the activities of the Council for the German cultural community.

The Legislative has therefore done its utmost, while bearing in mind the special nature of the Council for the German cultural community, to establish it along the same lines as the other two cultural councils. Even so, it happens that important questions have either been lost sight of or intentionally omitted, without it being possible to give any definite reasons for these lacunae. Thus, the law of 10 July 1973 is silent regarding any incompatibility that might exist between one of the functions of president, member of the steering committee, or member of the Council, with any other form of public office. This question did not arise in respect of the other two cultural councils because they are composed of members of Parliament and hence a matter of incompatibility is settled, so far as they are concerned, by Article 36 of the Constitution. It may therefore happen that a member of the cultural council for the German cultural community may at the same time hold some other public office. This is indeed an anomaly which has perhaps escaped the attention of the legislators. The same goes for the question of duplication between the attendance tokens and the indemnities granted to members of the Council, the President and members of the steering committee and, on the other hand, any other emoluments received for the performance of a public office. Such duplication has not been settled by the Legislative either.

Finally, some attention should be given to what happens to the Council for the German cultural community in the event that Parliament is dissolved. The question will be handled in detail farther on under Article 71, but it is as well to point out here and now that, as an organic body, it seems that the German Cultural Council could continue to meet validly even though a dissolution of Parliament takes place.

Despite these particularities, it must be acknowledged that the Constituent Assembly has taken full account of the existence of the German-speaking population of Belgium and that it has done its best to ensure that they too shall benefit from the setting up of an institution whose specific task it is to take charge of their special interests and thus afford them a measure of protection identical to that acknowledged in respect of the two other cultural communities.

CHAPTER II

THE KING AND HIS MINISTERS

Section 1 — THE KING

ARTICLE 60

"The constitutional powers of the King are hereditary in the direct line of natural, legitimate heirs of H.M. Leopold George Christian Frederick of Saxe-Coburg, from male heir to male heir, in order of primogeniture, to the perpetual exclusion of female issue and descendants thereof.

"Shall be deprived of his right of succession any prince who marries without the consent of the King or of those people who, failing him, exercise his powers in the cases laid down by the Constitution.

"However, he may be relieved of this disqualification by the King or by those who, failing him, exercise his powers in the cases laid down by the Constitution, on condition that both Houses agree thereto."

The text presently in force dates from 1893 and replaces the 1831 wording which was as follows:

"The constitutional powers of the King are hereditary in the direct line of natural, legitimate heirs of H.M. Leopold George Christian Frederick of Saxe-Coburg, from male heir to male heir, in order of primogeniture, to the perpetual exclusion of female issue and descendants thereof."

The principle of a representative constitutional monarchy with hereditary powers was adopted by the National Congress on 22 November 1830 by 174 votes to 13.

By Decree of 29 January 1831, the King bears the title of King of the Belgians.

The patronymic title of Duke of Saxony and Prince of Saxe-Coburg and Gotha has fallen into abeyance since World War I, although it has never been officially renounced.

Article 60 established the rules of succession to the Throne.

This text contains two separate rulings:

1. Princes who are in the line of succession to the Belgian throne must be direct descendants of Leopold I, but may not descend in the female line.

The exclusion of women from the Throne has been much criticized in recent years by women's associations who have emphasized its discriminatory character, and who refer to the Declaration of Human Rights.

Furthermore, the descent must be both legitimate and natural: this clause therefore rules out not only any children born out of wedlock, but also all adoptive children.

Royal powers are not, therefore, included in the King's family inheritance. An adoptive son would certainly be a member of the Royal Family, but he would not be in the line of succession.

As the order of succession has been laid down by the Constitution, the King is powerless to alter it except in terms of the powers of initiative which, under certain circumstances, are acknowledged in his regard by Article 61.

2. A second ruling which is an exception to common law is: that an heir to the Throne who wishes to retain his right of succession must secure the Royal permission to his marriage, however old he may be and even though he himself is not the King's son, but a prince who is nevertheless in the line of succession. Such royal permission must be covered by the countersignature of a Cabinet Minister responsible to both Houses. Arising out of this, the nation's representatives do in fact have an indirect say in the choice of their future Queen. A commission has proposed that these provisions be extended by analogy to embrace the question of the King's own marriage, since such a union is far more important from the political standpoint than that of a Crown Prince.

This point, debated in the Lower House on 6 February 1950 with no definite conclusion being reached, remains unsettled, but in actual fact the consent of the Government is necessary in the case of the King's own marriage.

Article 60 also empowers the King to intervene in the event of disqualification. In fact, according to the third paragraph of the article, the King or those persons who exercise his constitutional prerogatives may relieve the prince concerned of this particular disqualification. In this case, therefore, the King has genuine powers of initiative, though not an exclusive one since the Royal decision must not only be countersigned by a Cabinet Minister (Article 64), it is also subject to the consent of both Houses on the basis of a simple majority vote. This ruling provides additional confirmation that the King has no powers save those formally granted to him under the Constitution (Article 78).

ARTICLE 61

"Should there be no male descendants of H.M. Leopold George Christian Frederick of Saxe-Coburg, the King may nominate his heir with the consent of both Houses, expressed in the manner prescribed by the following article.

"If no nomination has been made according to the method outlined above, the throne shall be vacant."

This article matches the text adopted in 1831 with the exception that the word "he" was replaced by "the King" when the Constitution was revised in 1893.

This article provides for two eventualities: political adoption, and the vacancy of the throne.

1. *Political adoption:*

Apart from the powers of initiative vested in him by Article 60, the Constitution attributes a further prerogative to the King: the power to intervene in the transmission of the monarchy. However, this prerogative also is subjected to certain conditions.

Political adoption has been provided for so as to prevent, if at all possible, the throne from becoming vacant should there be no direct male descendance. The heir adopted by the King for political reasons and with the assent of both Houses may claim the right of succession, though he need not actually be a blood relation of the Royal Family.

This provision confirms, *a contrario,* the principle that the order of succession laid down by the Constitution may not be arbitrarily modified by the King.

In such a case, the majority required in Parliament is that of two-thirds of all votes cast, two-thirds of the members being necessarily present in each House at the sitting. This is known as a reinforced majority.

2. *Vacancy of the throne:*

The procedure has been laid down by Article 85 of the Constitution and will therefore be examined in its right place. To date, there has never been any time when the Belgian throne has been vacant.

ARTICLE 62

"The King may not simultaneously be the Head of another State except with the consent of both Houses.

"Neither of the Houses may debate on this subject unless at least two-thirds of its total number of members are present, and the resolution is only passed if it secures at least two-thirds of the total number of votes cast."

This article dates from 1831 and has never been modified.

Its origins are to be found in the importance which the Constituent Assembly acknowledged in respect of the fundamental responsibilities attributed to the King. The latter owes his entire life to the Nation, and may not withhold any part of it in order to devote himself to governing another State. It is also a fundamental guarantee that there shall be no risk of partiality on the part of a Sovereign called upon to reign over two different States.

That is why no union, even a purely personal one, may be concluded between two States without the consent of Parliament. Even so, it is still necessary for the latter to secure a majority vote of at least two-thirds of the votes cast, with two-thirds of the total number of members of each House present at the sitting.

This article came into real effect in 1885 when King Leopold II became Head of the Independent Congo State. It was a personal union that came to an end when the Congo became a Belgian colony by Act of Parliament dated 18 October 1908. The Congo (now the Republic of Zaïre) became independent in 1960.

ARTICLE 63

"The King's person is inviolable; his Ministers are responsible."

This article dates from 1831 and has never been modified.

It establishes the political status of the King. The inviolability of the Head of the State is threefold: penal, political and civil.

From the penal standpoint, the King may neither be prosecuted nor condemned for any penal offence. His freedom from responsibility covers crimes and misdemeanours as well as petty offences, and the Constitution has provided for no derogation of this rule.

From the political standpoint, the King must be sheltered from all responsibility for two reasons: to ensure the permanent nature of his royal function which is not limited as to time; and to preserve the hereditary character of the monarchy. Consequently, whether he acts as Head of the Executive by signing Royal Decrees, or as the third branch of the Legislative power by sanctioning a bill passed by both Houses, the King remains invulnerable to all criticism. The Cabinet Minister (or Secretary of State) who has advised the Head of the State and who, by his countersignature, has covered the Royal Act, is alone responsible.

Finally, from the civil standpoint, the King is protected from any legal actions brought against him in the civil courts except insofar as the private legal obligations arising out of his personal estate are concerned. Consequently, the King may not be personally summoned or subpoenaed; in such cases he is represented by the Administrator of the Civil List. The King is nevertheless required to respect all contracts pertaining to the management of his personal estate.

Finally, any legal judgments pronounced may not be enforced in respect of Crown property since this belongs to the State and is merely placed at the King's disposal; they may however be enforced in respect of his private and personal assets.

It will be seen, therefore, that the King's own responsibility can never be invoked. According to the Constitution, the King wields no personal power and he is consequently unable to act alone in the political sphere, regardless of whether he does so directly or indirectly.

Not only "the King can do no wrong", but "the King is incapable of doing wrong."

This constitutional ruling is absolute and covers every sphere in which the King may intervene.

The result, as parliamentary events in Belgium have underlined on several occasions, is that "the power which is maintained through heredity and inviolability" can only be in the nature of a moderating influence. The inviolability acknowledged in respect of the King guarantees the permanent character of the Monarchy, while the fact that in no circumstances can he lay himself open to any criticism reinforces his prestige and his predominant position above all political, social, economic or philosophical dissensions.

ARTICLE 64

"No act of the King's is effective unless it is countersigned by a Minister who, in so doing, renders himself responsible therefor."

This article dated from 1831 and has never been modified.

It is the essential clause completing that which absolved the King from all political responsibility (Article 63).

In terms of the principle of inviolability, the King has no personal power and may not therefore act alone.

Consequently, it is necessary for his every act to be covered by a person politically responsible to Parliament. Such responsibility is normally assumed by means of the countersignature of at least one Cabinet Minister or Secretary of State.

Thus, every political act of the King is actually a collective one entailing the intervention of at least two people:

— firstly, the King who represents permanence but who is, at the same time, absolved of all political responsibility;

— secondly, a Minister who assumes responsibility but who is not necessarily a permanent factor in the life of the nation.

The King's incapacity to act alone covers primarily all deeds by the Royal hand: the signing of decrees, acts of Parliament and Orders-in-Council. By the decision of the first Constituent Assembly, any Royal Decree that is not countersigned by a member of the government is *ipso facto* invalid.

But constitutional custom has extended this rule until it embraces any and every act of the King's which might have political repercussions either directly or indirectly. This applies, for instance, to all proclamations made by the Head of the State to the armed forces or the civilian population; to his public speeches; and to all public attitudes and decisions he may adopt. In default of a formal countersignature, it is necessary for a Cabinet Minister to be present at the King's side as proof that this member of the Government is assuming full responsibility for the words spoken by the King. The same is true of audiences granted by the Head of the State, of meetings between the King and foreign Heads of State, and State visits made by the King to other countries.

The ministerial responsibility covered by Article 64 is above all a political one, in the sense that a Cabinet Minister is thereby fully responsible to Parliament and should the act he covers not meet with approval, he would have no option but to resign his post.

*
**

The overall contents of Articles 63 and 64 should not lead to the over-hasty conclusion that the King's incapacity to act alone confines him to the role of a mere figurehead and prevents him from giving rein to his personal views. According to a famous formula, the King retains his right " to be consulted by his Ministers, to encourage them, and to warn them."

He has the unquestionable right to be consulted by his Ministers on important political problems, and to make his opinions known to them at that time.

He also has the right to encourage them by his suggestions and his heartening support in the midst of all the difficulties with which they have to contend.

Finally, he has the right to warn them and to advise them against making any hasty or ill-considered decisions, pointing out the adverse consequences these might have for the country at large.

The King's role is far from passive. He is moreover assisted in his task by a Privy Council that enables him to rely on the opinions of private colleagues selected without regard for their political affiliations. The origins and the composition of the King's Privy Council derive purely from custom, and the members of the Council have neither power nor responsibility in public affairs. The King is free to choose his Councillors but Cabinet Ministers, who are consulted unofficially, may advise against the appointment of any person they consider unfitting. The task of the King's Privy Council is to keep the Sovereign informed and to promote contacts with his Ministers. The Privy Councillors therefore have no right to judge whether a Minister should be received in audience or not, nor to establish contacts with officials without the agreement of the Minister concerned.

Through his threefold action on his Ministers, the King may therefore play a positive part in the political orientation of his country. But this action, which can only take the form of private discussions between the King and his Ministers, must remain covered by the veil of constitutional secrecy. The King's part in the final decisions must remain confidential. This constitutional secrecy is binding on the King and his Ministers alike. In other words, while the King must preserve absolute discretion concerning his discussions with his Ministers, the latter may never "uncover the Crown", i.e. expose the King's hand in affairs. This fundamental rule has moreover been emphasized on a number of occasions by the Council of State. (1)

The King's influence, veiled though it be in constitutional secrecy, may thus have a greater or lesser effect depending on the Monarch's own personality, wisdom and experience.

It is therefore desirable to lay great stress on the undoubted psychological importance of the Monarchy within the context of Belgian society. The King represents not only tradition and permanence, but also modern ways and ideas and the faculty of adaptation to the evolutionary process. This is entirely due to his position at the centre of things, which enables him to direct the attention of his fellow-citizens to the major problems of a general nature that involve not only the present generation, but those of the future.

---

(1) The Council of State is the highest administrative jurisdiction in the land (see Art. 94).

ARTICLE 65

"The King appoints and dismisses his Ministers."

This article dates from 1831 and has never been modified.

The laconic terms in which it is framed illustrate yet again that the Belgian Constitution is primarily a fundamental charter which, in the main, only sets out general principles. Article 65 does not in fact provide any details as to how the King may exercise the power of appointment and dismissal thus conferred on him. This is where established custom is called upon to complete and to adapt to existing circumstances those principles which are concisely stated in the Constitution. Thus, constitutional custom defines the task of the Head of the State but it may only be upheld insofar as it does not run counter to the spirit or the letter of the Constitution.

The part played by custom in the practical implementation of the Constitution is readily understandable, for initially the Constituent Assembly could not foresee the growing influence of the various pressure groups, and above all the development of parliamentarianism, a political system whereby the political parties forming the majority decide how the Government is to be formed.

Usage has thus developed in parallel to the ever growing complexity of political affairs, and serves to compensate for the brevity of the constitutional text.

At the present time, from the strictly legal standpoint, Article 65 means that the appointment of members of the Government (Prime Minister, Cabinet Ministers and Secretaries of State) is a matter for the King alone. The Royal Decree of Appointment, which must of course be countersigned by a Minister, requires no prior or subsequent authorization from any quarter, not even Parliament. The Decree, so to say, gives material form to the trust bestowed by the King on the person or persons named therein.

In actual fact, however, the procedure is far more complex. The formation of a government is, to a growing extent, the outcome of many complex processes, the Royal Decree being merely the final step in the whole complicated procedure. The growing strength and power of the political parties are matched by a corresponding shrinkage of the King's scope for action. In actual fact, however, the King's role is just as important as it has always been, but the royal power is now directed towards a different end. The King has gradually come to be the arbiter of national reconciliation who must reckon with the will of the Nation while being careful to preserve the stability of its institutions from the effects of too-frequent shifts in the Parliamentary majority.

This evolutionary process has become more marked, especially since the introduction of universal suffrage in 1919 has—with a few rare exceptions — made it impossible to form a government whose authority is guaranteed by the backing of a single political party enjoying an absolute majority in Parliament. Generally speaking, therefore, they have been coalition governments, the outcome of compromise, whose very existence depends on a parliamentary majority. It so happens that Parliament's approval is vitally necessary in such cases and this limits to some extent, or at least influences, the Monarch's choice. At the present time, the Government appointed by the King is therefore in haste to secure a vote of confidence in Parliament regarding a political programme that is generally submitted to the Houses in the form of a statement, normally read by the Prime Minister.

The political parties and other influential bodies such as the big trades unions have usually paved the way in order to secure the vote of confidence. It is they who determine the various points set out in the programme, the compromises arrived at between the political parties forming the new Government, what members should be called upon to become Cabinet Ministers and Prime Minister in particular, and how the ministerial portfolios should be allocated.

The new trend in the royal task first became apparent in 1847 when Leopold I was forced to abandon a unionist policy in order to form a homogenous liberal government (1). While the King's role has thus changed somewhat on the surface, his personal influence nevertheless remains vast in the formation of a government, for indeed it is he who, faced with the growing development of political parties with widely varying programmes, must help to select a majority that will gain the confidence of Parliament and thus be able to govern the country. It is there that his essential role actually lies, and not in the personal appointment of Ministers, for this is largely a formality arising out of the parliamentary majority which has been worked out.

The procedure leading to the formation of a government therefore comprises several phases:

1. The King consults a number of persons, such as for instance: the outgoing Prime Minister, the Speakers of the House and Senate, the Chairmen of the Cultural Councils, possibly some Ministers of State, the Chairmen of the political parties, the Governor of the National Bank, the leaders of the great trades unions, former Ministers or Members of Parliament whose influence is still to be felt, etc.

---

(1) The policy of unionism pursued during the first years of Belgium's independence was based on the agreement of all political parties to share in the management of public affairs by setting up a government which, of its very nature, reflected the unity of all Belgians.

2. Then comes the possible nomination of an Informant charged with reporting back to the King on the possibilities of setting up a viable government (this procedure emerged for the first time in 1935).

3. A Former is then appointed, that is, a person whom the King entrusts with the task of forming a new Government.

4. The Government is then formed on the basis of a specific programme and with the certainty of obtaining a Parliamentary majority, or at least the neutrality or tacit support of those parties not represented in the Government.

5. The various Ministers are appointed by Royal Decree.

6. In some cases, they are approved by the political parties represented in the Government.

7. Finally, approval and vote of confidence by both Houses.

It is therefore only in the actual appointment of Ministers that the King wields his constitutional powers, but the foregoing explanation immediately makes it clear that this final act is in fact merely the outcome of a more or less lengthy and arduous procedure.

Formally speaking, it is necessary to distinguish between a Royal Decree appointing one or several Ministers and one that sanctions the formation of a new Government.

It may indeed happen that one or several Ministers have to be replaced as the result of resignation, death, or a personal impeachment by Parliament. In this case, it is the Prime Minister in office who submits the candidate's name for the King's approval and who countersigns the Royal Decree of Appointment.

On the other hand, if the entire Government resigns, the King appoints the Prime Minister in accordance with the information that comes to light during the procedure outlined above and which is supplied by the political parties who now hold the parliamentary majority. The Royal Decree appointing the new Prime Minister is usually countersigned by the outgoing Prime Minister. This is a basic formality arising out of Article 64, and one which guarantees the essential inviolability of the King. His countersignature does not, of course, imply that the outgoing Prime Minister endorses the policies of his successor in office, especially as the latter may be drawn from the ranks of the former Opposition.

But if the outgoing Prime Minister should refuse to countersign the Royal Decree appointing his successor, it is understood that the latter would be entitled to countersign his own appointment. In fact, that is precisely what would happen in the event of the death of a Prime Minister in office.

At the same time as he appoints the new leader of the Government, the King signs another decree by which he accepts the resignation of the outgoing Prime Minister. This second Royal Decree is countersigned by the new Prime Minister.

Subsequently the other members of the Government are appointed by the King and the Royal Decree is countersigned by the new Prime Minister.

*
* *

Article 65 also confers on the King the power of dismissing his Ministers. From the standpoint of parliamentary logic, such dismissal can only be the result of a loss of confidence, either on the part of the King or that of Parliament.

Here again established custom plays a very important part and the dissolution of a government is virtually always caused by a breakdown in the majority that supported it in Parliament.

The loss of royal confidence by a Government is a relatively rare occurrence, for the King may not withdraw his confidence from a government in office except in a case where he deems that the Cabinet is no longer acting in the best interests of the Nation. It is abundantly clear that such a hypothesis has rarely come to light, for its effect would be to expose the Crown and to bring the King under suspicion of pursuing his own personal policies. The King's will must therefore always be covered by constitutional secrecy, and in reality the King acts far more frequently by exercising his constitutional right to warn or to advise his Ministers.

Loss of Parliamentary confidence occurs more frequently, and can be manifested at any time during a term of office. In this eventuality, the King is more or less obliged to accept the Cabinet's resignation if Parliament has formally voted a motion of no-confidence.

As stated above, the fall of a Government is usually the result of a breakdown in the parliamentary majority. This may be due to any number of causes, ranging from the erosion of power to irreducible opposition regarding fundamental matters included in the Government's programme or which have arisen during its term of office owing to various circumstances.

Without any question of pursuing a personal policy, the King is free to accept or refuse a Government's resignation, depending on whether he considers the proposal to be justified or not. In actual fact, since 1944 the King has on six occasions refused to accept a government's resignation because, in nearly all cases, he considered that disagreements between the political parties in office were not sufficient proof that Parliament had lost confidence in them.

In most cases, however, the King bows to the arguments advanced by the Prime Minister, accepts the Government's resignation and embarks on his round of consultations. He may furthermore reserve his reply and seek the advice of influential persons before formally accepting the resignation. And in 1968 it even happened that he changed his mind and cancelled his agreement to the resignation of the Government in office.

*
**

Until a new Government is appointed, the outgoing Government Ministers and the Prime Minister in particular remain responsible for the King's acts. Their responsibility only terminates with the appointment of the new Prime Minister and members of his government.

This is where the concept of a "caretaker Government" comes in. It is a concept unknown in constitutional law, but which has come to occupy a very important place owing to custom. It is in fact the usual thing, when a Government has resigned for any reason, for the King to instruct it to act as "caretaker" in the handling of day-to-day business pending the formation of a new government.

Perhaps this concept should be analysed in depth.

It should first be made clear that it does not arise when one or several Ministers resign from a Government that continues in office. In this case, either the King waits for their successors to be named so that the appointment of the latter may coincide with the dismissal of the former, thus avoiding any hiatus; or if it proves difficult to replace them, those Ministers who are still in the Cabinet take over the supervision of the Ministries abandoned by their outgoing colleagues until such time as the posts are filled. In this case also, the concept of "caretaking" is inapplicable.

It should be noted in passing that neither does it apply to subordinate offices, the holders of which retain their prerogatives until such time as their replacements are appointed.

The concept would therefore seem restricted to the sole eventuality of a government that resigns as a body, whatever its reasons for doing so may be.

It would also seem to rest on two fundamental principles that define and delimit its application:

— firstly, the principle of continuity of power. It is clearly important that the country's affairs should continue to be managed despite the resignation of the government;

— secondly, the restrictions placed on the actual scope of that power. This principle obtains especially if Parliament is dissolved at the time of the Government's resignation. Indeed, in such a case, parliamentary control can no longer be exercised and if the Government continued to wield its full authority, it might come to be even more powerful than it is normally when its work is subjected to parliamentary control. This concept of "caretaking" has raised a number of problems.

*
* *

In the first place, there is the problem of its legal status. In other terms, should a caretaker Government be subjected to control exercised by a legal administrative body, in the event the Council of State, or is this concept a purely political one deriving solely from parliamentary procedure?

As far as Belgium is concerned, the first solution was adopted since on two occasions—in 1963 and in 1968—the Council of State was required to pronounce on the validity of an administrative act performed after a Government's resignation duly accepted by the King but not yet sanctioned by Royal Decree.

In a ruling of 15 March 1963, the Council of State effectively acknowledged that no constitutional provision restricts the powers of Ministers during the period preceding acceptance of their resignation.

In a ruling of 10 May 1968, the Council of State similarly confirmed that "it cannot be accepted that the Minister has exceeded his powers, considering that during the period preceding his resignation following a general election, he remained fully competent to decide, on the basis of a properly conducted promotional procedure, which of the candidates should be given preference."

Whatever the theoretical considerations may be, the question certainly seems to have been resolved from the legal angle, and all acts regarded as day-to-day business, performed by a "caretaker" Minister or Government, may therefore be sanctioned by the Council of State.

The problem is still however a delicate one, for the task confronting an administrative judge called upon to decide the exact extent to which the Government is competent to act may, on numerous occasions, necessitate a thorough enquiry in the political sphere.

As already stated, the point at issue is indeed to prevent the caretaker Government from exercising powers that are virtually a great deal wider than those vested in it while it was actually in office.

*
* *

The most important problem is to arrive at a precise definition of a concept that is largely based on tradition, the practical implementation of which depends essentially on circumstances as they arise.

Positively speaking, it may be said that day-to-day business is mainly that which involves decisions to be made within the framework of the ordinary supervision and management without which public departments and services would cease to function. It therefore refers to decisions which would normally arise in ordinary conditions and which are not such as to compromise the future. This implies decisions on purely routine matters, those made at a lower echelon, those which represent merely the continuation or the final outcome of current procedures, and those taken to implement matters undertaken jointly with other departments.

Such, for instance, are decrees appointing civil servants to posts of the lowest rank; those implementing legal procedures in special cases, such as retirement, superannuation, etc.

Day-to-day business could also include matters that are normally outside the direct province of the Government such as, for instance, the negotiation of collective bargaining agreements between employers and workers. Their validity remains unaffected by the resignation of a government even though they must be sanctioned in due course by a royal decree.

A third and far more delicate category involves matters of urgency. A state of urgency or of emergency does indeed create an exceptional case which has the effect of giving the authorities greater powers than they would normally wield.

This concept, however, is one that is very difficult to handle for it involves not only a broadening of the Government's powers but also the possible threat to the vital interests of the Nation if no decision were to be made. This would be the case, for instance, if, at an international meeting on important monetary questions, the Minister of Finance was required, along with his colleagues from other countries, to make certain decisions imposed by force of circumstance.

Those are, in general, the kind of affairs which might be described as day-to-day business and which remain the responsibility of an outgoing Government on a caretaker basis.

Negatively speaking, the following could not therefore be regarded as day-to-day business, for instance:

— matters that are indubitably political in character, especially those involving new departures or which imply a definite political choice owing to the composition of the outgoing Government;

— the recruiting of new staff of any kind, apart from cases where it is necessary to replace officials who have retired, died or resigned and where it is necessary to do so at once in order to maintain the continuity of public service. There is indeed the risk that during these interim periods, the caretaker Ministers may take advantage of the situation to increase the staff of their ministries by appointing persons of their own political affiliations;

— promotions to the higher echelons of public offices and special services, such as for instance the appointment of General Secretaries, Public Prosecutors, Attorneys-General, Lieutenants-General in the Armed Forces, etc.;

While they are individual ones, all these decisions are affected by the importance of the posts to be filled and are thus obviously political in character. Consequently, they threaten to compromise the responsibility of the incoming Government.

The same goes, moreover, when the question is one of approving a transaction, granting a concession, etc. when such transactions or concessions may have important repercussions on the national economy, or when they involve new budgetary appropriations that might place the incoming Government in an intolerable position; and so forth.

A college of jurists gave a considered opinion in January 1974 that a Government which has resigned, but whose resignation has not yet been accepted by Royal Decree, may not table in either House any Statement of Intent to Revise the Constitution. To embark upon procedures tending to modify the fundamental law goes far beyond the scope of the day-to-day business which can still be handled by a Cabinet which has now *ipso facto* become a caretaker administration, for such a Statement is a particularly weighty political matter.

From this catalogue of simple examples it becomes abundantly clear that the notion of caretaking is one that, above all, revolves around the concept of political integrity and a wholesome respect for the rights of all citizens.

It would also appear that the King runs the risk of becoming personally involved, and thus of "exposing the Crown", when during the interim period he agrees or refuses to sign the decrees submitted to him by Ministers of the outgoing Government.

If he agrees, he is automatically covered by the ministerial counter-signature.

On the other hand, the King might well find himself being asked by the caretaker Government to accomplish a certain act, and consider it his duty to abstain from performing it. His responsibility in this case is a matter of appearance only, for any abstention on the part of the Monarch is equally covered by ministerial responsibility. Faced with the King's refusal to sign a decree, the Minister may in effect try to convince him that he should sign; or he may yield to the King's reasons. If their disagreement persists, a Minister who does not wish to see his political responsibility engaged must resign on personal grounds.

Another important question concerns the role of Parliament during a crisis.

Three possibilities arise in this connection:

1. The Government resigns, and at the same time Parliament is dissolved. In this case, the caretaker Ministers will be responsible, either personally or through their successors in office, to the new Parliament that follows the general election.

2. Parliament is dissolved legally, while the Government remains in office.

In this case, the government has not formally resigned, but parliamentary control is no longer being exercised, and cannot be until the new Parliament meets.

3. The Government resigns, whereas Parliament is not dissolved. In this case, Parliament remains theoretically free to perform its usual functions. It is certain, however, that it cannot do so to the fullest extent. In effect, it can no longer control a government which has resigned by means of questions and interpellations; however, in exceptional cases, proposals and bills which have no political implications have, on occasion, been examined by Parliament in the presence of an outgoing Minister. This was notably the case when laws granting provisional credits to the Government were debated.

Briefly, then, Parliament must in principle abstain from all business that necessarily involves some form of political co-operation with the government. Yet, to ensure the continuity of public services, it must still vote on the budget and the Armed Forces contingent, so that the State may at least be able to count on the availability of the funds it requires in order to function, and to call up the militiamen for their military service. In practice, the Prime Minister—with the King's agreement—instructs his colleagues as to what business may still be submitted for the King's signature, and the Speakers of the Lower House and the Senate will suspend all parliamentary activity until such time as a decision is made regarding the permanence or otherwise of the Government.

To conclude: recent events have shown that the royal task has changed both as to purpose and method, and that the King is now coming to play an increasingly important part as initiator and arbiter of national reconciliation.

The nomination of a person to form a Government might appear as a political act performed by the King in violation of the constitutional rule that states his irresponsibility. On the legal plane, however, this is not so, for the outgoing Prime Minister in particular remains responsible for all acts of the King's.

ARTICLE 66

"He confers rank in the Armed Forces.

"He appoints persons to posts in the general administrative departments and those connected with external relations, except in such cases as are laid down by law.

"He does not make appointments to other offices except under the express ruling of a law."

This article dates from 1831 and has never been modified.

It contains three rulings that differ in scope according to their frame of reference.

In actual fact, the question here is one of implementing Article 29 of the Constitution and this article defines how the King's administrative function is exercised in certain spheres.

In principle, Article 66 confers a specific power on the King in such a way that any interference in these matters on the part of the Legislative would be tantamount to an intrusion in the affairs of the Executive. Furthermore, with reference to these matters, the article signifies that the royal signature is required, which implies that it is forbidden to delegate such powers to a Minister.

In fact, however, administrative practice has somewhat tempered the formal constitutional ruling.

1. In the first place, the King has the right to confer rank in the Armed Forces without any apparent restriction being placed on his powers. The fact remains that in terms of Article 118 of the Constitution, this right can only be exercised in accordance with the law governing armed forces recruiting and promotions.

2. The King also has the right to appoint persons to posts in the general administrative departments and those connected with external relations. In this instance, however, the Constitution provides that an exception to the rule may be established by an Act of Parliament.

a) The King therefore has the right to appoint, in particular, the ambassadors through whom he establishes diplomatic relations. The Head of State is kept informed of all diplomatic discussions undertaken with foreign countries.

b) The King also has the right to appoint persons to posts in the general administrative departments, i.e. central government offices and their outlying departments. This right is being exercised to an increasing extent within the framework of general statutes established by royal decree so as to exclude arbitrary appointments or promotions.

From the theoretical standpoint, the authors have often wondered whether the legislator was entitled to define the status of civil servants in lieu and on behalf of the Executive. Numerous arguments have been advanced for or against the exclusive competence of the Executive during the past century, and Belgian parliamentary history reveals that on several occasions bills or draft bills have been tabled for the purpose of establishing a general civil service statute. The first of these bills was tabled in 1894, and was followed by others in 1895, 1900, 1935, 1936 and by a preliminary draft bill prepared by administrative departments during the years 1935-1936.

More recently, the Civil Service Association has upheld the principle of a legal statute governing civil service executives in Government offices on the grounds that the general status of civil servants, which they regarded as being too much influenced by the trade unions, did not deal in a sufficiently precise manner with those officials appointed to high responsibilities in the functioning of government offices. However well founded this more or less theoretical argument may be, the status of all civil servants is currently defined by Royal Decree of 2 October 1937, since modified on various occasions and basically altered in 1964. Without rejecting the principle that this status should be legally defined, its authors considered at the time that more or less justifiable interventions in parliamentary debates threatened to overturn a statute the provisions of which form an organic whole.

They also considered that a recourse to legislation might take up too much time whenever decisions had to be made quickly, and they were also of the opinion that a law constituted a legal method less fitted to regulate details of implementation even though the latter are equally important. This, however, has not prevented the Legislator from intervening in Government administrative departments where statutes were concerned. This is necessarily so in the matter of pensions in terms of Article 114 of the Constitution. The question of dual appointments has also been settled by a 1935 decree having the force of law, which would automatically call for Parliament's approval if it had to be revised.

The Legislator has also intervened on behalf of certain categories of citizens judged worthy of special interest: war veterans and war victims, colonial employees whose career was abruptly terminated in 1960 owing to the accession to independence of the Belgian Congo, and the establishment of a regular status for temporary staff. In the latter cases, however, it must be admitted that while Parliament itself has laid down rules that should in principle come within the province of the Executive, it has done so in many cases because it desired to extend those rules beyond government offices to embrace their subordinate administrative services.

c) The constitutional ruling provides for exceptions as laid down by law. It would, however, be a betrayal of the Constitution to consider that this provision enables the Houses to reserve all appointments to themselves. Any derogation must be an exceptional one, or the constitutional principle is overthrown.

3. On the other hand, where all other posts are concerned the rule is set aside, in the sense that the King's right is only vested in him under the express ruling of a law. This clause is directed mainly at the subordinate offices—provincial and municipal—in respect of which the Legislator has generally stipulated that personnel are chosen for these posts by the local authorities.

The clause also applies to all bodies connected with the public services, or in other words the State-controlled organizations. Every law setting up one of these has generally stated which authority has powers of appointment. A law was indeed passed on 16 March 1954 authorizing the King to define the statutory framework governing personnel employed in a great many State-controlled organizations, and there was some discussion at the time as to whether this provision would effectively empower the King to appoint all employees in such organizations. But the Council of State then ruled that the law of 16 March 1954 continued to restrict the King's powers in terms of the organic laws governing the establishment of such bodies. Thus the Council of State adopted a restrictive position, acknowledging in respect of the King only the power to define the status of the personnel and that of altering the legal provisions aimed solely at regulating such status. On the other hand, his powers do not extend to authorizing him to alter the legal provisions providing that an executive body is competent to appoint or dismiss personnel. The Council of State deemed that these powers of appointment and dismissal did not only affect the status of the personnel; primarily they contributed to defining the full extent of the organization's autonomy. Thus, where the State-controlled organizations are concerned, the King remains bound by prior legal provisions, few though they be, which sanction the right of an executive body to appoint its own personnel.

The Council of State also ruled that the King's power was subordinated to yet another restriction connected with the establishment of the statute itself. In defining the status of personnel employed in the State-controlled organizations, the King remains bound by prior legal provisions such as, for instance, consultation with the executive bodies concerned. These formalities have in most cases been stipulated for the purpose of ensuring that the organization's autonomy shall be respected and that its specific needs shall be borne in mind.

In a more general way, it should also be noted that the increasingly general recourse to statutes has had the effect of placing shackles upon the King's authority. This fact must be interpreted as a disciplinary rule which the Executive imposes on itself in order to forestall any risk of arbitrary practices. It so happens that the recruiting of civil servants is no longer done by any method save that of competitive examinations and that every appointment must be based on the examination results. In other cases, a right to present candidates has been introduced. Where high-ranking posts in Government departments are concerned, yet a third protective procedure has been set up, which calls for the mandatory discussion of each candidate by the Cabinet.

ARTICLE 67

"He issues the regulations and decrees necessary for the implementation of laws, without ever being able to suspend the laws
themselves nor exempt them from being implemented."

This article dates from 1831 and has never been modified.

It is of capital importance in the proper functioning of all institutions
for it establishes the principle of the legal priority of the Legislative
over the Executive. Thus, it is the Legislator who must define the principle of the law, the details of which are worked out by the Executive in
terms of the statutory powers vested in it. So the King's powers may
only be exercised within the framework of the law.

It is, however, an undoubted fact that the Executive thereby still wields
considerable influence, for the implementation of laws covers a very
wide field indeed. The King may moreover delegate part of his
authority in the making of minor decisions which, in this case, take the
form of ministerial decrees.

Warned by experience of earlier historical events, the Constituent
Assembly deprived the King not only of power to suspend laws, but also
of power to exempt persons from implementing them. Consequently, the
King may not suspend the implementation of laws either by the citizens
at large or by any category of citizens, unless such power of exemption
has been specifically conferred on him by Act of Parliament.

Above all, he may not grant any suspension of, or exemption from, the
law in respect of private persons, especially as it is clearly stated in
Article 6 of the Constitution that all Belgians are equal in the eyes of
the law.

Should the King exceed the statutory powers thus granted to him, the
corresponding sanction is provided for under Article 107 of the Constitution, in terms of which the courts and tribunals must refuse to implement decrees that are not in accordance with the laws.

In actual fact, however, the implementation of Article 67 is far more
complicated.

1. Apart from the power vested in the King to issue the regulations and
decrees necessary for the implementation of laws, the King does in fact
have a general power of police, in terms of which he may issue a decree
even in the absence of any law. This was a highly controversial question

in the old days, but this royal power was confirmed by the Court of Cassation in 1922. In terms of the general power of police, the King may issue general decrees necessary for the maintenance of law and order, public hygiene and peace. While the controversy continues on the theoretical plane, the question does however seem to have been settled pragmatically by a law of 5 June 1934 which amounts to a genuine act of constitutional interpretation insofar as Article 67 is concerned. It provides notably for sanctions regarding police decrees that are not obeyed and thus indirectly acknowledges the legal validity of such decrees. It should also be noted that the decrees and regulations issued by the King in the general police sphere are themselves subject to the validity control laid down under Article 107 of the Constitution.

2. Other phenomena have appeared in the political life of Belgium as a result of exceptional circumstances which have influenced the evolutionary development of constitutional law.

a) First of all, there are the royal decrees issued in accordance with what are known as the "special powers" laws. The special powers laws originated in periods of crisis which may occur even in times of peace. In this case, Parliament feels rather powerless when faced with the extent, the technical nature and the urgency of the problem to be solved, and it waives its own authority in favour of the Executive whose reaction is usually much faster. The special powers thus granted by the Legislative therefore amount to an intentional broadening of the Executive's competence.

The decrees issued in terms of special powers are therefore truly the work of the Executive. It is obvious that in so delegating its authority Parliament surrounds the concession with a certain number of conditions, as for instance that which obliges the Government to have any decrees issued in terms of special powers ratified by the Houses.

Another precaution normally taken is that of rendering a Cabinet debate mandatory. Similarly, Parliament generally sets a definite term for such delegation of authority; and finally, the authority thus delegated is often a restrictive one involving specific matters only.

The basis for such delegation of authority has been found in Article 78 of the Constitution, in terms of which the Legislative is free to transfer this or that specific problem within the province of the statutory power. The royal decrees thus issued are as valid as an Act of Parliament, but they are not decrees having the force of law, and still less, *a fortiori*, are they laws. They therefore remain subject to the control of legal validity laid down in Article 107 of the Constitution even though the judge may not rule on the opportunity, the necessity or the utility of the measures decreed.

They may alter existing laws, but they themselves may not be altered later on save by Act of Parliament.

If they are confirmed, as often happens, by subsequent Act of Parliament, the Legislative then appropriates them for its own use in the future, so that such decrees do not lose their status of Royal Decrees but from that point on they escape the control procedures laid down by Article 107 of the Constitution.

b) Another phenomenon consists of the decrees having the force of law, or "decree-laws", which themselves are subdivided into two categories:

— the decree-laws issued in wartime owing to the fact that the Government is faced with the material impossibility of summoning both Houses. These decree-laws were issued by the King during the 1914-1918 War, or by Ministers meeting in Council during the 1940-1945 War;

— the second category comprises decree-laws issued by the King in implementation of the so-called "extraordinary powers" laws.

The first category arises out of circumstances due to *force majeure* or Acts of God, whereas the second depends on the urgent need for quick action.

The validity of such decrees having the force of law (decree-laws in short), especially those falling into the first category, has been the subject of lengthy discussion by the authors. In any case, necessity being the mother of invention, it was obvious that in wartime, when one or several branches of the Legislative had lost all liberty of action, the branch that had managed to retain its freedom to act had to be able to take the measures necessary to safeguard the vital interests of the Nation.

In 1914-1918 Parliament found it materially impossible to meet and so the King, who had remained in the unconquered part of the country, alone exercised all the prerogatives of the Legislative. It goes without saying, however, that the King could not do so except in cases of evident need and urgency.

The position was quite different in 1940-1945, since the King was deprived of the possibility of reigning and his authority, in terms of the Constitution, then devolved on his Ministers meeting in Council. Furthermore, as Parliament was again unable to meet, the Cabinet which was already acting for the King also found itself exercising the constitutional powers of the Legislative.

Such decree-laws remain decrees for form's sake since they are issued by the Executive; but they are just as valid as actual laws since the Executive has legally taken over from the Legislative. They are not assimilated to any laws but by their very nature they are equivalent to law. Of necessity, therefore, they are exempted from the validity controls provided for in Article 107 of the Constitution, and furthermore they require no ratification in Parliament since they constitute regular acts by the legislative authority.

The second category concerns the decree-laws issued in terms of the laws governing "extraordinary powers". In this case, the question is no longer one of Parliament finding it physically impossible to meet, but rather one of the moral impossibility of exercising its prerogatives. The validity of such acts lays itself open to discussion and has indeed been debated, but the acts exist. Indeed, in this case Parliament is not prevented from sitting normally but it considers that the necessity, complexity and urgency of the measures to be enacted in special circumstances are such as to impel it to increase the power of the Executive and to stand aside while the latter takes action. In deciding that they find themselves more or less in the moral impossibility of accomplishing their tasks, the Houses of Parliament realize that they may be reproached with sanctioning their own removal from the seat of power. That is why the practice in question has sometimes been criticized as unconstitutional by the authors, for the Legislator has no right to renounce his own authority. These "extraordinary powers" laws are generally passed in very special circumstances, such as the disturbed events in 1939 and in 1945.

Neither are these decrees to be regarded as genuine laws, though they are assimilated thereto. Consequently, the validity control laid down in Article 107 of the Constitution is waived and subsequent ratification by Parliament is not required.

The Courts of Law are entitled, however, to verify that the decrees thus issued are indeed within the limits which the Legislative has placed upon the King's powers.

These powers vested in the King remain exceptional ones, but it is not up to any other authority to assess the necessity and urgency dictating such exceptions.

There is a third category of provisions which must still be dealt with, though these do not actually constitute exceptional measures as is the case with the two previous categories. These are the so-called "lois-cadre" (framework laws) in which the Legislative, when it feels stifled by the complex ramifications of the task confronting it, is content with passing a law tracing merely the fundamental aims and broad outlines of what is to be done, surrounded by a few rules as to how it is to be done, and instructs the Executive to work out the precise methods of implementation. Some of these framework laws provide simply that the King shall have the power to regulate the matter in question.

It is immediately clear that this procedure is a far more correct one since it is simply an application of Article 78 of the Constitution and the transfer of authority to the Executive is handled in a stable and permanent fashion. Among the framework laws enacted, the following should be mentioned: those regarding tolls; the operation and policing of the railways; road traffic and the highway code; those extending the family allowance system to employers and non-salaried workers; etc.

Under this heading, the royal decrees issued in implementation of the framework laws retain the character of ordinary royal decrees subject to the rulings of common law.

A dual sanction therefore guarantees respect of the Constitution: the first being the ministerial responsibility of those Ministers who countersign the decrees of implementation; the second being the provisions of Article 107 of the Constitution.

These adventitious developments arising out of Article 67 only serve to prove yet again that this article is indeed the legal foundation-stone of the parliamentary system.

ARTICLE 68

"The King commands the armed forces on land and sea, declares war, makes treaties of peace, alliance and commerce. He advises the Houses of the contents thereof as soon as the interest and security of the State permit, enclosing all relevant documents.

"Commercial treaties and those which might affect the State or individually become binding on Belgian citizens, only become effective after they have received the consent of both Houses.

"No cession, exchange or addition of territory may take place save under a law. In no case may the secret clauses of a treaty render the public clauses null and void."

This article dates from 1831 and has never been modified.

Its wording is fairly complex, so that it is important to set it out in a more orderly fashion in order to analyse clearly what prerogatives have been acknowledged by the Constituent Assembly in respect of the Executive.

1. *International relations:*

In contrast to other Government business, the Constitution acknowledges that the Executive plays a predominant part in the sphere of international relations.

We have already seen that the King appoints the persons employed in external relations, save for legal exceptions (Art. 66). But furthermore the Executive is, in principle, solely responsible for relations with foreign countries. In this sphere, therefore, its role is a vitally important one.

The Minister of Foreign Affairs is politically responsible for diplomatic relations.

Negotiations with foreign countries often end in the signing of treaties; the power of making such treaties is acknowledged by the Constitution to rest with the King. The limits laid down in Paras. 2 and 3 of Article 68 should be interpreted restrictively.

The King's sole obligation is to inform Parliament of the treaties concluded, but only when, for reasons connected with the interest and security of the State, the Government judges that the time is ripe to do so.

Generally speaking, the King thus wields a threefold power:

— he has the right of diplomatic legation and conversation which represent the ordinary day-to-day activities of embassies;

— he makes international treaties;

— it is who directs diplomacy in wartime, i.e. he has an equal right to declare war or to make peace.

The Constitution however has tempered somewhat the vital role played by the Executive but, as already stated, these restraints are restricted to certain matters and are subject to strict interpretation.

a) In the first place, the approval of Parliament is required in the event of cession, exchange or addition of territory. This is fully understandable since it represents merely the application of Article 3 of the Constitution which has, so to speak, stabilized the boundaries of the State except in case of legal intervention.

b) The secret nature of treaties or clauses thereof may be necessary in certain circumstances.

The Government is not bound to disclose such secret clauses if the interest and security of the State command otherwise. At the very most, the Constitution provides that the secret clauses of a treaty may not invalidate the public ones.

c) Other treaties require the consent of both Houses, without such consent affecting their validity. These include:

— commercial treaties governing trade relations and which regulate customs tariffs in particular;

— treaties that may affect the State. It is obvious that, generally speaking, every treaty has some financial repercussions. That, however, is not the sense in which this clause should be understood: it is aimed primarily at all treaties likely to have a *direct* impact on the State budget;

— again, all treaties that are individually binding on Belgian citizens, i.e. which are capable of modifying their personal rights, such as for instance the status of marriage in international law;

— another constitutional article also requires parliamentary intervention. This is Article 121 which will be dealt with in due course, and which covers the case of a treaty authorizing a foreign army to enter Belgium;

— there is also some question as to whether the approval of both Houses is required in the event of a treaty modifying the internal laws of Belgium. This would be the case, for instance, when certain formalities are imposed by an internal law in certain circumstances whereas an international treaty would dispense those liable under such law from obeying it. Basing their opinion on a strict interpretation of the Constitution, the authors ended by acknowledging that in this case the King may act alone in terms of Para. 1, since the exceptions stated in the following paras. allow no latitude of interpretation.

Nevertheless, it is obvious that should such an eventuality arise, the Government will be answerable to Parliament, as indeed it is for all treaties.

⁂

Paragraph 2 refers to the "consent" of both Houses.

Some people have wondered what legal character Parliament's intervention may have. It is admitted in principle that Parliamentary consent does not affect the external validity of any treaty that may be concluded, meaning that the latter remains valid insofar as the contracting States at the international level are concerned. The consent of Parliament is only required so that the treaty may receive internal validity, i.e. without such consent, Belgian citizens are not individually bound by such a treaty and cannot be legally constrained to submit to it.

It should be added that the Constitution has provided neither for the publication nor the promulgation of treaties. As a general rule, Parliament's consent takes the form of a law, the wording of which is very simple and generally amounts to a single clause stating that such-and-such a treaty will come into force with effect from such-and-such a date. In this case, the law is usually completed by an annexure giving the full wording of the treaty in question.

It should also be added that any authentic interpretation of a treaty is outside the competence of Parliament, since it is primarily an act of the Executive. Consequently, and for the same reasons, Article 107 of the Constitution does not apply in such a case; the Judiciary's control cannot in fact be legally exercised owing to the fact that such a treaty cannot be construed as a decree or as a general, provincial or local regulation.

⁂

In connection with Article 68 and especially its provisions concerning international treaties, an important problem has arisen in recent years because of the proliferation of such treaties. Indeed, apart from international relations which have become considerably more widespread—a fairly generalised process of evolution—Belgium, like other nations, has become involved in a number of international institutions such as the United Nations, the E.E.C., the E.C.S.C., NATO and a number of other European organisations. The principle of national sovereignty has now to a certain extent been subordinated to that of supranationality.

It was to take account of this new fact and the inevitable adaptation of the Constitution in keeping with international realities that the government, as a result of the conclusions laid before it by the Commission for Institutional Reforms, had in particular proposed that Heading III, Chapter III of the Constitution be revised by the insertion of an Article 107-B designed to settle the question of conflict between an international treaty and national domestic law.

In the Statement of Intent to Revise published in the *Moniteur Belge* (official gazette) of 17 April 1965, the Houses had supported the government in this view and proposed that Article 68 should also be modified.

The dissolution of Parliament on 24 September 1971 interrupted the work of the Constituent Assemblies and thus left the work of revision unfinished, so that the Constitution had not in fact been altered to meet the new international realities. Only Article 25-B, which was passed on 20 July 1970, now authorised the delegation, by means of treaty or a law, of certain specific powers to institutions set up under international civil law.

On the other hand, Article 68 among others was still unchanged, and allows certain lacunae and inadequacies to persist.

It should, however, be noted that jurisprudence has attempted to compensate for the absence of any Article 107-B by advocating the primacy of international law over national domestic law. But this jurisprudence has not yet been confirmed, and the only evidence of it is to be found in a ruling delivered on 27 May 1971 by the Court of Cassation.

To understand the import of this ruling, it is useful to recall briefly the broad outlines of the way in which jurisprudence and the concepts of theorists have evolved in regard to possible contradictions between an international treaty and domestic law.

Whether the question was one of a law predating a treaty or a law passed subsequently to it, up until 1963 jurisprudence usually settled the problem on the basis of a purely temporal criterion. It was in 1925 that the Court of Cassation upheld the theory by examining whether or not the treaty was of later date than the legal provisions with which it conflicted. The most recent of the two was then given preference, for it was supposed to embody the latest expression of the will of the legislators. Apart from a few unimportant exceptions, this then was the theory commonly admitted in law.

However, this theory began to be set aside from 1963 onwards, starting with an address by the Attorney General of the Court of Cassation. The Attorney General, on this occasion, upheld the notion that "because of the growing number of normative treaties, the ceaselessly expanding spheres they embrace, and the difficulty with which the Legislator today has to contend in attempting to discern possible contradictions between a new law and treaties that are already in force", it was necessary for the Court of Cassation to revise its position regarding a solution to any conflict between an international treaty and domestic law. The Attorney General only made one reservation: "if a constitutional text required the courts and tribunals to apply the domestic laws even if the latter were in contradiction to a treaty previously approved and published and which is still in force; or if a law, either in its general clauses or in a special clause referring to a definite matter, formally stated such an obligation, then the courts and tribunals would be constrained to obey such a requirement even though the question was one of treaties having the specific characteristics of those treaties instituting the European Communities. But, in the absence of any such written requirement", the jurisprudence creating such an obligation... could not be justified". This new theory has been restated with growing force by the Court of Cassation which, through its Attorney General, urged Belgian justice to give priority to international treaties in cases when these conflicted with national domestic law. In 1968 for instance, in an address delivered on 2 September, the Attorney General stated that "the international judicial order and the national judicial order are not separate, but must be regarded as spheres of the general judicial order. They are subjective aspects of one and the same judicial order. Law is law, one and indivisible, or it is not law... The superiority of international law must be sanctioned for reasons of social ethics. It must also be sanctioned because a superiority of the national law would mean the condemnation of international law, for it would give form and substance to the constant threat hanging over the general nature of the latter by making it impossible for the rules of international law to achieve or to maintain that general nature. It means that if international law was not given priority over domestic law, it would cease to exist." And this consideration led the Attorney General to reach the following conclusion: "It is our earnest desire that a revision be undertaken to adapt the Constitutional clauses relating to international law to fit the great process of evolution leading to the establishment of world equilibrium which itself is founded on the law of solidarity... If, however, the Constituent Assembly does not carry out a positive constitutional reform in this direction, and one which is becoming increasingly necessary, then it will doubtless be up to each judge to adopt a definite attitude in favour of this ultimate objective."

As we know, the Constituent Assembly indeed omitted to proceed with such a reform, but on the other hand the Court of Cassation put some of these principles into practice by means of its ruling of 27 May 1971.

This ruling, although the only one of its kind to date, deserves to be studied in detail.

Firstly, it is a reminder that a treaty is not a law, but that it is solely an act accomplished by the Executive power. It is the treaty itself which is binding on the contracting parties, and not the consent given by Parliament in the form of a law. The form itself matters little, and Parliament might very well restrict itself to sanctioning the treaty by means of a resolution. In its ruling, the Court of Cassation confirms these principles by stating that "even when the consent to a treaty, as required by Article 68, para, 2, of the Constitution is given in the form of a law, the Legislative power, in accomplishing this act, is not exercising a normative function." Such a reminder of these principles has thus had the effect of waiving the prior application of a purely temporal criterion founded on the commonly admitted equivalence between a treaty and a law.

By waiving the temporal criterion, the Court of Cassation has thus invited that a solution be sought in a priority criterion, i.e. in whether or not international law is superior to domestic law.

The Court of Cassation has not hesitated to attribute superiority to international law by virtue of its very nature, and has even gone so far as to uphold the view that the Judiciary must acknowledge such primacy, which it had not hitherto done on the grounds of the separation of powers.

The Court of Cassation has nevertheless laid down certain criteria that must be met by the rule of international law if the primacy of the latter is to be recognized. The Court requires:

a) a norm of international law;

b) its publication in the domestic judicial order;

c) the existence of its direct effects in that same judicial order.

And even more: the ruling of the Court of Cassation makes absolutely no distinction between whether the rule of law is truly international, or whether it derives from the European Community.

Nor does the ruling operate any distinction between the fact that the conflict between domestic law and international law may, or may not, be intentional on the part of the Legislator.

Finally, the ruling emphasizes that the effect of international law is not to render the domestic law null and void; but solely to record that its effects are decisive to the extent that the domestic law is in contradiction to a directly applicable clause of an international regulation. The solution to the conflict does not lie in cancelling the domestic law, but only in the fact that the latter may not be upheld in opposition to a treaty.

Let us once more recall that the Constituent Assembly did not confirm this theory. The drafting of the text which should have ended by becoming Article 107-B was, moreover, an extremely delicate and complicated task.

Many problems therefore remain acute, particularly the following: Does the priority, thus asserted, of the international rule of law apply to the unwritten law of nations? May domestic jurisdictions exercise any control over the procedure according to which the norms of international law laid down by supranational authorities are framed? May a simple recommendation coming from a supranational authority render a domestic law without effect? Does the rule of international law also enjoy priority over constitutional rulings? These are only some of the problems which the interruption to the work of the Constituent Assembly has left unsolved.

2. *Command of the Armed Forces:*

In terms of Para. 1, the King commands the armed forces on land and sea. It is, of course, now necessary to add the Air Force which did not exist when Article 68 was drafted in the year 1831.

It is also the King who declares war and who makes peace treaties. Here again, to preserve his inviolability, the King's decisions must be covered by the Minister of National Defence.

This clause has given rise to some controversy regarding the exact scope and extent of the royal powers. Some authors have thought that in commanding the armed forces, the King need not be covered by ministerial responsibility, whereas others were of the opposite opinion. The former pointed to the precedents established in 1831, 1914 and 1939 when the Head of the State assumed the effective command of the armed forces.

The latter, on the other hand, considered that in the event of defeat, the King acting alone would be deprived of the shield of royal irresponsibility and would run the risk of being exposed to personal criticism.

In fact, at the time of the precedents set in 1831 and in 1914, those Ministers who were in the King's train covered the military decisions he was called upon to make.

In any event, the government remains answerable for the conduct of military operations and the authors are unanimous in upholding the notion that because of the development in military techniques, the Head of the State should no longer, in modern warfare, assume personal command of operations, for he might then find himself under the overall command of a foreign general.

It is also useful to point out that the Executive may not use the armed forces as it wishes, and that in this case it is bound to secure parliamentary consent, since in terms of Article 119 of the Constitution, which will be dealt with in its proper place, an Act of Parliament decides the yearly armed forces contingent.

ARTICLE 69

"The King sanctions and promulgates the laws"

This article dates from 1831 and has never been modified.

It will be recalled that in terms of Article 26 of the Constitution, the legislative power is exercised collectively by the King, the House of Representatives and the Senate in such a way that in terms of Article 27, the initiative belongs to each of these three branches.

Here again, the King's influence may be felt since his right of initiative under cover of the Government is no more restricted than that of the other two branches of the Legislative. Bills may therefore be tabled by the Government with royal permission and with the countersignature and the responsibility of one or several Ministers.

The right of initiative implies, of course, the right of amendment.

By promulgation must be understood the act whereby the Head of the State attests to the existence of a law properly voted by Parliament and renders it enforceable. By sanction is understood the King's approval given to a law properly voted by Parliament.

In actual fact, both sanction and promulgation are the subject of one and the same act, since the formula generally adopted is as follows:

"The Houses have adopted and We sanction the following... We promulgate the present law..."

Furthermore, in terms of Article 69, the King might theoretically refuse to sanction a bill passed by the Houses.

In practice, however, the King may no longer exercise his power of veto by refusing to sanction a law voted by Parliament. Both sanction and promulgation therefore automatically ensue when a bill is passed by Parliament.

If the Government abandons a bill which it has tabled itself, or if it opposes the adoption of a proposed parliamentary initiative, it does so through the majority which supports it in Parliament. This is how it may prevent a vote that it does not want, or no longer wants. Through this procedure, there is no need to resort to the refusal of the royal sanction to a bill that has already been passed.

It should also be recalled that Article 129 of the Constitution regulates publication of the law. In this regard, it should however be pointed out that the Executive retains a certain freedom of action, in the sense that if the Legislative has not set a certain period or a specific date for the coming into force of the law, the responsible Minister may delay its enforcement by postponing the date of publication.

Finally, it should be remembered that in terms of Article 59-B, Para. 5 of the Constitution, the King also sanctions and promulgates the decrees voted by the Cultural Councils.

ARTICLE 70

"The Houses automatically meet every year on the second Tuesday in October, unless they have been convened previously by the King.

"The Houses must sit during at least forty days every year.

"The King pronounces the closure of the session.

"The King has the right to convene the Houses in an extraordinary session."

In its initial form, this article dates from 1831. The first para. was, however, modified during the Third Constitutional Reform on 30 June 1969. The 1831 wording effectively provided that the Houses were to meet on the second Tuesday in November. The month of November was altered to October in 1929. The reason for the change was that the late start of the Parliamentary session made for delays in examining the budgets. By advancing the opening of Parliament by one month, the Constituent Assembly hoped to avoid, or at least noticeably reduce, occasions when it was necessary to resort to provisional credits.

Since 1963 it has been legally necessary for budgets to be tabled in both Houses on 30 September of the year preceding that to which they refer. Of these, at least the Budget of Ways and Means must be approved by both Houses prior to the first day of the following January. This was virtually impossible when the opening date of Parliament was set in November.

In order to fully comprehend the wording of this article, it may be necessary to recall the exact meaning of some of the fundamental concepts used therein:

The term *session* refers to the period during which Parliament is legally capable of meeting and of performing its function.

The term *sitting* refers to the effective meeting of Parliament for purposes of debate. These sittings can obviously be held only within the period of a session.

The term *legislature* refers to the time which elapses between the date when Parliament first meets and that when its powers collectively terminate.

Convening of the Houses: The first Constituent Assembly provided for the automatic opening of the Parliamentary session so as to prevent any abuse of power by the Executive in the event that it alone was free to convene Parliament.

With the same purpose in mind, it provided for a minimum duration of forty days for each session seeing that, whatever happens, certain duties are incumbent on Parliament, in particular the Budget vote and the armed forces contingent vote.

Convening in extraordinary session: On the other hand, the Constituent Assembly acknowledged that the King may convene the Houses in extraordinary session during the parliamentary recess, should imperative and urgent circumstances warrant it.

In certain cases, such as those foreseen by Article 71 or 82 which we shall examine in due course, the competence of the Executive is indeed linked and the latter is under a constitutional obligation to convene the Houses.

Closure: Again, it is the King who is empowered to close the session. In practice, however, the King only does so with the agreement of the two parliamentary assemblies.

The closure of Parliament is therefore sanctioned by a royal decree covered by ministerial responsibility.

In reality, a custom has grown up progressively whereby Parliamentary sessions are only closed on the eve of the opening of the new session. In this way, the Houses are theoretically in permanent session, and the government which may desire them to convene during a recess no longer has to call for the convening of an extraordinary session. A summons is simply sent out to all members by the Speakers of the two Houses.

ARTICLE 71

"The King has the right to dissolve the Houses, either together or separately. The act of dissolution contains a summons to the electorate within forty days, and to the Houses within two months."

This article dates from 1831 and has never been amended.

But, as has already been the case with other articles, the tendency of this one has been modified during the passage of time and under pressure of circumstances.

Briefly, Article 71 comprises three distinct rules:

1. *A right:* the King's right to dissolve the Houses;

2. *Methods:* the King may dissolve both Houses together, or either of them separately;

3. *A condition:* a summons to the electorate and to the Houses within a certain period. This condition therefore has the effect of binding the Sovereign's competence, in the sense that the moment the King dissolves at least one of the Houses, he is obliged to summon the electorate within the specified period.

As it has done on many occasions, the Constituent Assembly has attempted by means of Article 71 to establish a balance between the Legislative and the Executive. As the legislator is free to give or withhold his confidence to any Government, the Executive is equally free to dissolve Parliament when it finds itself in serious conflict with the latter.

Originally, the act of dissolution was therefore an appeal to the electorate to settle a dispute between the two branches of political authority. By imposing a formal condition, however, the Constituent Assembly has averted any risk of the King's availing himself of the opportunity thus afforded to seize personal power.

In accordance with Article 64, the Royal Decree of Dissolution must of course be countersigned by a responsible Minister. A Minister will not, however, assume such responsibility save in agreement with the parliamentary majority or, in exceptional circumstances, with the very manifest support of the general public.

As previously stated, the implementation of Article 71 has been tempered somewhat by force of circumstance, so that in this case also it is apparent that custom plays a very important part alongside the Constitution itself.

A closer study should now be undertaken of the various concepts bound up with Article 71.

First of all, the power to dissolve Parliament is acknowledged in respect of the King by the Constitution. This, of course, also embraces all those authorities which exercise the royal powers in terms of the Constitution, as laid down in Article 60, para. 2.

At the present time, the King's inviolability is covered by the Prime Minister whose function has progressively developed until it has become a fundamental institution in the life of the country. Because of this evolutionary process, it has become accepted practice for the Prime Minister to be one of the countersignatories of the Act of Dissolution since he is virtually the prime mover of the government in office.

His endorsement is not an absolute rule, however, since all that is needed is a Royal Decree countersigned by any Cabinet Minister.

Another institution which the Constitution only recognized in two of its articles—articles 79 and 82—has also evolved as the years passed: this is the Council of Ministers, or Cabinet. It has therefore been wondered whether the Council of Ministers had any special part to play in the dissolution of Parliament. Neither the Constitution nor any particular law have attributed any specific competence in this field to the Council of Ministers.

Yet it is in this sphere that custom again exerts a tremendous influence on procedure since except for the single Act of Dissolution of 29 April 1950, virtually all the Royal Decrees of Dissolution had invariably been debated by the Council of Ministers. (We shall see later on what the position has been in recent years.) The formula adopted has perhaps undergone some modifications in the course of time, but it has had no fundamental effect on the part played by the Council of Ministers. Thus, at the first dissolution in 1833, the decree was issued "on the basis of the report and on the recommendation of" the Council of Ministers. Subsequently a different formula was adopted: the decrees were issued "on the basis of the report" or "on the proposal" of a Minister and "on the recommendation of the Council of Ministers".

This was generally the case during the reign of Leopold II: a single Minister, usually the Minister of the Interior, countersigned the decree. This procedure was gradually stabilized and during the reigns of Albert I and Leopold III, the decrees were usually proposed by the Minister of the Interior on the recommendation of the Council of Ministers.

It was during the Regency of Prince Charles (1944-1950) that the Prime Minister first appeared as one of the proposers of the decree, generally backed by the Minister of the Interior, but invariably with "the recommendation of the Ministers who have debated the proposal in Council".

Following the precedent set in 1950 which broke with a long tradition (even though the tradition was subsequently reinstated), the authors wondered whether the part played by the Council of Ministers might not progressively lose its importance in years to come.

It would nevertheless seem that the highest authorities in the Kingdom will do their utmost to preserve established custom, for it is an extremely delicate matter for the King to agree to a dissolution of Parliament when certain parties in office, who are consequently represented in the Cabinet, do not agree that such dissolution shall take place. The fact remains that the precedent of 1950 has been followed by the case of the Royal Decree of 30 January 1974 which was issued on the sole recommendation of the Prime Minister and the Minister of the Interior while the Council's agreement was not formally recorded in the decrees.

To the King's right to dissolve Parliament corresponds the Sovereign's equal right to refuse a proposal of dissolution. Several cases may arise: the King may find himself in disagreement with a single Minister as opposed to the Government as a whole; he may be in disagreement with part of the Government; or again he may disagree with the entire Cabinet which would naturally represent the most serious situation since, in this case, the King might be at risk of exposing the Crown by calling on the country to judge between himself and the Government in office. But in any event, the principle of inviolability implies that the King's refusal must be covered by a Minister. In reality, his refusal to proceed with the dissolution of Parliament against the Government's recommendation is such a serious matter that it has happened only on very rare occasions in Belgian history and the most recent case dates right back to 1846.

As we have seen, the act of dissolution is of necessity a royal decree, in implementation of Articles 64 and 71 of the Constitution. It is usually dated and signed by the King. At the same time, it is countersigned by one or more Ministers.

Furthermore, still in terms of Article 71, it must contain a summons to the electorate within forty days, and to the Houses within two months. That is a guarantee intentionally inserted by the Constituent Assembly to avert the danger of an alienation of power, so that the Executive may not remain without proper control being exercised. A decree of dissolution that did not contain such a summons would automatically be null and void.

Finally, as with every other official act, to be valid the decree must be published in the proper way. In practice, it is notified to the two Houses and published in the "Moniteur Belge" (official gazette).

The question has also arisen as to whether such a decree should necessarily be submitted to the legislation section of the Council of State. According to established jurisprudence, the only decrees excluded from legal verification by the Council of State are those which are not general in character and which do not arise out of the legislative function.

Since the law of 23 December 1946 came into force, providing for the setting up of the Council of State, one decree of dissolution has been submitted for the recommendation of that supreme assembly—that of 19 May 1949—whereas two subsequent decrees invoked the principle of urgency.

At all events, the practice is by no means an established one since again, in the last case to date, the royal decree of 30 January 1974 makes no mention either of any consultation with the Council of State or of any urgency in the step decided upon.

As stated above, the right of dissolution was intentionally included from the start by the Constituent Assembly so as to counterbalance the right vested in Parliament to overthrow the Government.

In actual fact, the motivations leading to an act of dissolution have become extremely varied.

It will be recalled that the Constitution has foreseen two cases of automatic dissolution: when the Throne falls vacant in terms of Article 85, and when there is a Statement of Intent to revise the Constitution in terms of Article 131.

It is not possible to review in detail all the causes of dissolution which have arisen since 1831. It should however be pointed out that since that date, only three dissolutions have taken place in the spirit which motivated the Constituent Assembly, the last of which occurred in 1864. Indeed, in the eyes of the Constituent Assembly, dissolution was primarily a means of settling conflicts arising either between the two Houses, or between the Legislative and the Executive.

But many other reasons have come to be added as time went by. This was the case when dissolutions took place in the absence of any disagreement, but solely because Parliament no longer represented the will of the people, or again under pressure from the political parties. It may indeed happen that the parties in office are faced with such disagreement on fundamental matters that a parliamentary majority in support of the government no longer exists. It may also happen that the parties in office have agreed among themselves to propose that the King shall dissolve Parliament at a time when they consider a general election is likely to strengthen their majority in Parliament.

The effect of the Act of Dissolution is therefore to terminate the legal existence of the Lower House, or the Senate, or both together. At once the Houses cease to be official bodies, meaning that they immediately lose their authority and prerogatives, and individual members revert automatically to the status of private persons who, as such, are no longer representative. That is why an act of dissolution is necessarily coupled with a general election.

So the concept of dissolution must be carefully distinguished from kindred concepts such as closure, which puts an end solely to one of the Parliamentary sessions but not to the legal existence of the assembly itself; or prorogation (adjournment) which merely suspends a Parliamentary session for a certain period of time; or again the concept of conditional dissolution, such as the case laid down in Article 79 of the Constitution in the event of the King's death.

Article 71 has provided for the possibility of dissolving only one of the Houses.

The Constituent members discussed this point at great length, especially in regard to the Senate where a number of members were very hostile to the possibility of dissolving that Assembly. The majority of Congress members considered that attitude a far too dangerous one because the Senate, should it be thus shielded from all risk of dissolution, would be in a position where it might gain undue ascendancy over the House of Representatives—a development which the Constituent Assembly was determined at all costs to prevent.

In actual fact, cases when only one of the two Houses has been dissolved are extremely rare in the history of Belgium. It should also be pointed out that in terms of Article 59 of the Constitution, the Senate may not meet outside the period when the House of Representatives is in session, on pain of its proceedings being declared null and void.

It has also been wondered what the position of members of Parliament was in the event of dissolution.

Many authors have taught that the decree of dissolution not only terminates the legal existence of both Houses; it also terminates the individual mandate of each Member. An obvious exception to this rule is contained in Article 79 of the Constitution in the event of the King's death, in which case the Houses, even if they are outgoing ones, must automatically meet. Today, however, it is considered more reasonable to abide by Article 239 of the Electoral Code, in terms of which: "The mandate of members of the Legislative Chambers normally comes to an end:

— for those members of the House of Representatives and the Senate who are directly elected, on the date set for the ordinary meeting of the electoral bodies called upon to provide for the replacement of outgoing representatives and senators;

— for senators elected by the Provincial Councils, on the date set for their replacement;

— for senators chosen by the Senate, on the eve of the first ordinary or extraordinary sitting of the new Senate."

In other words, the Nation may not remain without representation, and so parliamentary mandates only terminate when the new mandates come into effect.

It should be noted in passing that as far as the acquisition of parliamentary status is concerned, the elected member is invested with this status as soon as the election results are proclaimed, and he therefore benefits from parliamentary immunity even before he takes oath. His status is, however, a conditional one until the validity of his election has been verified and confirmed.

From this principle, now universally admitted, come several practical consequences:

1. Each member of Parliament continues to benefit from the immunity laid down by Article 44 of the Constitution, an immunity which is in fact a perpetual one and continues even when his mandate comes to an end for all matters pertaining to that mandate;

2. On the other hand, he may only benefit from his inviolability for the duration of a parliamentary session, even though he may invoke it even before he has been sworn in as prescribed by Article 45 of the Constitution.

Once the session has come to an end, he may therefore no longer claim inviolability and from then on he may be prosecuted and arraigned like any other citizen;

3. Finally, remaining a member of Parliament, he continues to benefit from the indemnity provided under that heading, even when the dissolution of Parliament has been pronounced.

In January 1974, the dissolution of Parliament took place for the first time in the history of Belgium since the Cultural Councils came into existence.

We know that article 59-B of the Constitution has provided for the existence of a Cultural Council for the French-speaking community, and a Cultural Council for the Dutch-speaking community. Furthermore, Article 59-C provided that the task of deciding upon the composition and competence of a similar Council for the German-speaking community should take the form of a law. Parliament discharged that task by voting the law of 10 July 1973.

What then happens to the Cultural Councils when Parliament is dissolved?

1. *French and Dutch language Cultural Councils:*

According to Article 59-B of the Constitution, these two Cultural Councils are composed of members of the two language groups in each House, so that it would seem that once Parliament has been dissolved, both of these two Cultural Councils are automatically dissolved as well.

Article 59-B has not, however, foreseen this eventuality, and while Article 71 itself gives the King the right to dissolve the Houses, it says nothing about the Cultural Councils; furthermore it must be interpreted to the letter so that the King is not empowered to dissolve the Cultural Councils at the same time as he dissolves Parliament.

Nevertheless, a law of 21 July 1971 has defined the competence of these two Councils, and here we should cite Clause 6 of that law which stipulates the periods during which each of the two Councils should meet. It also empowers the King to pronounce the closure of a session and also to convene either or both of the Councils to meet in an extraordinary session. But here again, there is no question of giving the King power to dissolve the two Councils. As for Clause 7 of that same law, it provides that "any assembly of a Cultural Council which is held at a time when the Legislative Houses are not in session shall automatically be null and void". The conclusion is therefore that while the King has no formal power to dissolve the two Cultural Councils in question, the latter may not legally meet at any time when Parliament is not in session.

As the act of dissolution automatically terminates the legal existence of Parliament and therefore ends the session, it follows that the French and Dutch language Cultural Councils may not officially meet when the Houses are dissolved.

2. *Council for the German cultural community*

This case is quite different.

We have already seen that in terms of Article 59-C, it is up to the law to determine the composition and competence of this Council.

This law was passed on 10 July 1973. It provides that the German Cultural Council shall comprise 25 members elected by voters in the boroughs forming part of the German language region, on condition that these voters are enfranchised as electors to the Legislative Houses. Clause 6 of the law also stipulates that the Council must be re-elected at the same time as the House of Representatives. As it was not possible to organize an election immediately, and as furthermore it was a matter of urgency that the German Cultural Council should take its place alongside the other two Councils, some transitional measures were adopted for the initial composition of the new Council. Clause 72 of the law of 10 July 1973 stipulates that this temporary composition of the German Cultural Council was only valid until the termination of the legislature in course at the time when this law went into force.

It should be remembered that the legislature is the time during which an assembly is legally in existence. As a result, the dissolution of Parliament having terminated the legal existence of the collective legislature represented by the two Houses of Parliament, the members of the German Cultural Community Council ceased to be so by the act of dissolution itself, and could therefore no longer meet. Special elections had therefore to be arranged in order to reinstate the German Cultural Council, and in terms of Clause 6 of the law mentioned above, that election had to take place simultaneously with the general election held to renew the House of Representatives. This was effectively done, since a Royal Decree of 1 February 1974 summoned the electorate to elect a new German Cultural Council.

That, however, was a condition relating to the transitional period. In an organic system the situation would be more complicated for, in contrast to the other two Cultural Councils whose case was reviewed earlier on, one might wonder whether the German Cultural Council was still authorized to meet after the dissolution of Parliament. In effect:

a)   the law of 10 July 1973 has no clause similar to clause 7 of the law of 21 July 1973 which provides for the automatic invalidation of all meetings of the French and Dutch language Cultural Councils outside the Parliamentary session;

b) in contrast to those two Cultural Councils, the German Cultural Council is not composed exclusively of members of Parliament, but of members elected directly to it, so that the dissolution of Parliament need not therefore have any effect on their membership.

The problem remains open, and to prevent all future complications a special provision should be made, failing which the German Cultural Council might hold valid meetings even though Parliament has been dissolved.

From this survey, it is easy to conclude that the dissolution of Parliament has gained an importance quite other than that intended by the 1831 Constitution. According to the Constituent Assembly, such dissolution was to ensure that a balance was struck between the Executive and the Legislative powers, each of these having its own means of action where the other was concerned. Today, however, political realities are quite different. Conflicts between those two powers have become very rare for, on the one hand, the Government may normally rely on a parliamentary majority in order to promote its policies, and on the other, the Houses exercise a less detailed control over the work of the Government owing to the growing importance of the part played by the political parties and the great trade unions.

It has thus become very infrequent for the Government as such to find itself with a minority in Parliament. In fact, the Government has become increasingly answerable to the political parties and, through them, to the electorate.

It was therefore quite natural for the process of dissolution to change as well. We have indeed seen that the reasons for a dissolution are now connected far less with a conflict between the two branches of authority than with a breakdown in the parliamentary majority. The fact remains that dissolution is still a very tricky weapon to handle.

ARTICLE 72

"The King may prorogue Parliament. However, such adjournment may not exceed one month in duration, nor be repeated during the same session, without the consent of the Houses."

This article dates from 1831 and has never been modified.

By prorogation (adjournment), as already stated in reference to Article 71, is understood the suspension of a Parliamentary session for a certain period of time.

Again pursuing its objective of striking a balance between the powers, the Constituent Assembly has granted the Executive the prerogative of postponing parliamentary debates, but it has surrounded this prerogative with strict conditions governing the length of the period and further recourse to it.

The article was originally conceived in case troubles, either internal or external, might make it impossible for parliamentary debates to be conducted in a peaceful and orderly manner.

In fact, since the year 1858, the King has never made use of the prerogative thus vested in him.

The article has really lost its entire significance, since as both Houses are in permanent session, there is no closure even during the parliamentary recess. The session is only closed at the opening of the following one.

In practice, it is possible for the Government to adjourn the Houses by asking the Speakers not to reconvene them.

If the Government has a majority in Parliament, this majority will support its wishes in a spirit of solidarity, and the Houses will therefore not reconvene.

If, on the other hand, the Government does not succeed in convincing its majority, or if it no longer has a majority in the Houses, it must be inferred that it has lost the confidence of Parliament and it will be forced to resign.

ARTICLE 73

"He has the right to reprieve or commute the sentences delivered by judges, except in regard to what has been laid down for the Ministers."

This article dates from 1831 and has never been modified.

Here we touch on the jurisdictional function acknowledged in respect of the King, for the Constitution has reserved the prerogative of clemency to the Head of the State.

The principle of the separation of powers is respected since justice has been done, the sentence pronounced and put into effect. At the most, the sentence will not be implemented, and this comes within the competence of the Executive.

It is barely necessary to recall that here again, the right of reprieve exercised by the Head of the State must be covered by the ministerial countersignature.

Royal clemency is therefore able to soften the rigours of penal law or a judicial sentence.

By a decree of 16 October 1951, the Court of Cassation has moreover confirmed that "conditional discharge neither cancels nor modifies the sentence, but merely suspends its material implementation".

Article 73 provides for either a complete reprieve or for a sentence to be commuted. The King may not, therefore, call off a prosecution nor shield the accused from the course of justice.

It goes without saying that such measures of clemency call for an individual examination of each specific case.

A single exception is provided for: that of Ministers, as stated in Article 91 of the Constitution.

It should be emphasized that the right of reprieve may never be delegated by the Head of State to one of his Ministers. To avoid all confusion, a careful distinction must be made between the right of reprieve and amnesty.

Reprieve differs from amnesty in four ways:

1. Reprieve is an individual measure granted to a specific person mentioned by name, whereas amnesty is a general ruling applicable to all

those who have suffered under the same law so that, indirectly at least, it is a criticism of the principle surrounding the law itself.

2. Reprieve is a measure which is left to the appreciation of the Executive, whereas amnesty necessarily calls for an Act of Parliament.

3. Reprieve consists in suspending the total or partial enforcement of the sentence, whereas amnesty cancels out the indictment itself and thus terminates all proceedings.

4. Reprieve means that the sentence and all it entails are still in the files, whereas amnesty automatically wipes out the sentence so that no record of the charge is preserved in criminal files.

ARTICLE 74

" He has the right to mint coinage in implementation of the law."

This article dates from 1831 and has never been modified.

The first part of this article reflects the ancient regalian law pertaining to the royal prerogatives, by virtue of which the sovereign alone was competent to act in monetary matters. It is immediately obvious that such a privilege has long been obsolete, which is why the second part of Article 74 provides that Parliament alone has the right to mint coinage and issue currency.

It should be remembered that in the days when the Belgian constitution was promulgated — in the year 1831 — the currency in circulation consisted almost entirely of coinage. By the term currency, in the economic sense of today, we understand the coins and treasury notes held by persons outside the banking system, the sight deposits in national currency built up in national institutions by residents other than the merchant banks, and possibly their other financial assets on call at less than a year's term.

The constitutional provision under Article 74 is now implemented by the law of 12 April 1957 governing the monetary statute, modified by the law of 3 July 1972 pertaining to monetary parity.

The parity of the currency unit in Belgium is in principle determined by law. However, in case of emergency, it may be modified by royal decree enacted on a proposal by the Minister of Finance after a debate in the Council of Ministers (Cabinet); the Minister of Finance only tables such a proposal after consultations with the National Bank of Belgium. The decision, accompanied by a statement of motives and the recommendation of the National Bank, is immediately communicated to both Houses of Parliament by the Finance Minister.

The parity of the Belgian franc is expressed in the prescribed forms laid down by the International Monetary Fund set up by the final act of the United Nations Monetary and Financial Conference held at Bretton Woods, and is sanctioned by the law of 26 December 1945.

The law of 3 July 1972 provides that the parity of the Belgian franc is 0,0182639 grammes of fine gold though this has not yet officially gone into effect. In practice, Belgium has communicated to the I.M.F. a "central rate" corresponding to that parity figure, and which temporarily plays a part analogous to that of parity.

All the gold coins minted prior to the entry into force of the law of 12 April 1957 have ceased to be legal tender among private persons or to be acceptable in payment by public and treasury offices.

The use of banknotes only began to develop in Belgium to any considerable extent during the second half of the 19th century, after the setting up of the National Bank in 1850 and the *de facto* monopoly granted to it of issuing paper money. The latter came to be more and more widely used, and its acceptance as legal tender was imposed in 1873. Thus, the law of 1957 merely confirmed this state of things by providing that notes issued by the National Bank of Belgium were to be treated as legal tender by all public and treasury offices and by private persons, any contradictory agreements notwithstanding. This provision may not be invoked by the National Bank with regard to the bearers of its notes.

Temporarily, the National Bank has been dispensed from the obligation of refunding its notes in coinage. By means of a decree debated in the Cabinet, the King may rescind this dispensation. Subject to the same formalities, he may define other conditions governing the exchange or payment of notes issued by the National Bank.

From the foregoing, it will be seen that the holders of banknotes are theoretically entitled to claim a refund of the amount shown on those banknotes in hard cash : that is why each banknote is marked "payable at sight".

The organic law governing the National Bank provides that it must cover the sum of its notes in circulation by means of readily convertible assets. Furthermore the law of 1957, modified by the law of 9 June 1969, obliges the Bank to cover its sight obligations (essentially the banknotes in circulation) at the rate of at least one-third of the total sum involved, by means of its gold reserves, its gold credits with international financial institutions, and by the rights which the Belgian State holds as a member of the International Monetary Fund and which, insofar as the Bank is concerned, are reckoned as its own assets in terms of the law.

Finally, there is also the treasury currency : the 50 and 20 franc notes and the coinage. Those notes do not bear the inscription "National Bank of Belgium" nor are they marked "payable at sight". In fact, they are not banknotes but treasury notes.

Treasury currency is issued on behalf of the Treasury by the Monetary Fund, set up in 1930. There is a legal limit set for the issue of small change, which includes all the treasury currency except for the so-called "even" money which are the 25 centime coins : in terms of the law of 21 May 1973, the issue of small change may not exceed 12 thousand million francs. In actual fact, the amount issued is determined by the requirements of the public. When these requirements are lower than the issue, the surplus goes back to the National Bank; if the latter's assets are in excess of 700 million francs, the Treasury takes back the excess amount.

ARTICLE 75

"He has the right to confer titles of nobility, without ever being able to grant privileges on that account."

This article dates from 1831 and has never been modified.

The abolition of titles of nobility was a consequence of the Declaration of 1789 according to which all men were free and equal in rights.

A strict application of the principles of equality would involve the complete eradication of all titles of nobility.

The Constituent Assembly was at pains to find some compromise between the principles propounded by the Old Regime, in which heredity was very important, and the Republican principle of equality as between all citizens.

That is why it maintained the King's prerogative of conferring titles of nobility, while at the same time prohibiting the granting of any privilege on that account, so that such titles are purely honorific ones.

The illegal use of titles of nobility is actionable under the Penal Code.

ARTICLE 76

"He awards military decorations in obedience to the prescriptions of the law in this respect."

This article dates from 1831 and has never been modified.

Yet again, when taken to extremes, the principle of the equality of all citizens tends to eliminate all honorific distinctions.

However, the Constituent Assembly was not prepared to go to such extremes, and it has acknowledged in respect of the King a right to confer military decorations, while again tempering this prerogative by subjecting it to the formal sanction of the legislator.

The institution of orders and decorations is not therefore a disclaimer of the principle of equality between citizens, since the term "orders" does not refer to certain social classes enjoying a greater or lesser degree of privilege: the distinctions are purely honorific ones.

It should be pointed out that the Constitution only deals with military orders and decorations and does not refer to civil ones. The authors have wondered on occasion whether the conferring of honorific distinctions on civilians was acceptable in terms of the Constitution; while the controversy remains unsettled, in practice the conclusion is an affirmative one since the government has the power to institute civil orders and distinctions and to confer them.

Furthermore, it is the Executive alone who, in terms of Article 66, lays down the terms and conditions attendant upon the granting of civil decorations.

It is surprising to note that the Constituent Assembly was more concerned with the Armed Forces than with the Administration, since it gave the legislator the right to establish standards governing the granting of military decorations. Does this difference stem from the Constituent Assembly's abiding interest in the Armed Forces or, conversely, from its ingrained suspicion of them? The question remains open.

The principal national orders are: the Order of Leopold, instituted by the law of 11 July 1832; the Order of the Crown and the Order of Leopold II, instituted respectively by decrees enacted by the King and Sovereign of the Independent Congo State on 15 October 1897 and 24 August 1900, which were later included with the other national orders when the Congo was taken over by Belgium.

A statutory regulation issued on 15 July 1952 and later amended, governs the bestowal of national orders and decorations on officials and employees of the Civil Service.

It should also be noted that a Royal Decree of 21 July 1867 instituted a civil decoration designed as a reward for services to the nation in the course of a long career in provincial, municipal, electoral or benevolent bodies, and for outstanding acts of courage, humanity, or devotion above and beyond the call of duty. A Royal Decree of 15 January 1885 extended the scope of such civilian awards to embrace all civil servants.

ARTICLE 77

"The law fixes the amount of the civil list for the duration of each reign."

This article dates from 1831 and has never been modified.

The term "civil list" refers to the budget placed at the King's disposal to enable him to face up to the expenditures incurred in discharging his royal function.

The Constitution lays down two rules in this respect:

1. the civil list must be established by the legislator. Thus, it is up to the nation's representatives to fix the sum which is to be paid annually by the State to the person who is the Head of it;

2. the amount of the civil list must be established for the entire duration of each reign. In doing so, the Constituent Assembly desired to place the King above all sordid, or at least rather delicate, arguments that might be prejudicial to the dignity of his office.

The Constitution specifies no particular sum. Originally, the yearly amount was set at 1,300,000 francs for the reign of Leopold I. When Baudouin I came to the throne, a law of 16 July 1951 fixed the yearly amount of his civil list at 36 million francs.

The major part of the civil list goes to pay the salaries and pensions of officials in the Royal Household and to maintain the royal palaces and help finance State occasions.

But the depreciation of currency due to inflation has posed the problem of revising the figure decided upon at the start of the reign. As far back as 1927, a so-called interpretative law introduced a coefficient designed to compensate for the dwindling purchasing power of the civil list.

Following World War II, more complex solutions were adopted. While they are not in accordance with the letter, they do at least conform to the spirit of Article 77.

In obedience to the Constitutional principle, it would undoubtedly have been preferable to operate a distinction between those items in the civil list which remain stable, and those that fluctuate due to changing economic conditions.

It should also be recalled that Article 77 does not prevent such endowments from being allocated to other members of the Royal Family, even though there is no constitutional requirement in this respect. In this way, the Prince of Liège—heir presumptive to the Throne—today benefits from a yearly endowment. The fact is that such a grant is not based on any decision made in implementation of the Constitution; it is a special measure decided upon by the Legislative.

ARTICLE 78

"The King has no other powers save those formally vested in him by the Constitution and the special laws passed in accordance with the Constitution itself."

This article dates from 1831 and has never been modified. It will be apparent, however—and this point has already been made concerning Article 67—that the tendency of the article has been altered somewhat in the course of time.

Like many others, the wording of this article is excessively laconic, and the preparatory work sheds little light on its scope since the provisions were adopted practically without discussion.

As it stands, however, this article does reveal various rulings :

1. It serves firstly to confirm article 25, according to which all powers stem from the Nation. In other words, the Nation represented by its constituent and legislative powers predates the Monarchy, and the King is only king by the favour of the Constitution. While the Executive Power is sovereign in its own sphere, and on an equal footing with the two other Powers, the Constitution nevertheless asserts the pre-eminence of the Legislative Power; and this is the second ruling of the article.

2. In actual fact, the Executive may only hold those powers which are expressly acknowledged as vested in it by the Constituent Assembly and the Legislative. Its competence is therefore an attributory one, whereas the Legislative, conversely, wields residual powers. In other words, the Constitution has divided the attributions of sovereignty between the three powers of the nation, but it has restricted the law courts to the Judiciary and has limited the King to exercising solely those powers formally vested in him by the Constitution itself or by laws enacted in implementation of it.

Consequently, everything which is not specifically regulated by the Constitution is automatically a matter for Parliament to decide.

Basing their opinions on that residual competence, some authors would have liked to broaden considerably the scope of Article 78 in order to justify the adventitious accretions that that grown up around it in the course of time. In connection with Article 67, it has already been pointed out that Article 78 had been resorted to in order to justify not only the "framework laws" (lois de cadre) but the decrees having the force of law and the royal decrees enacted in terms of the special powers laws.

As we have seen, that ruling may serve as a basis for the framework laws since in this case the legislator retains his normative function; all he does is to apply purely and simply the provisions of Article 78.

The question is more debatable in the matter of royal decrees enacted under the so-called special powers laws, for in this instance the legislator is transferring part of his own authority to the Executive.

An appeal to Article 78 is extremely questionable in the case of the decrees having the force of law enacted in time of war, or in terms of the special powers laws.

Indeed, it is not the legislator's prerogative in constitutional terms to waive part of his own authority, and this has already been confirmed by the Court of Cassation itself by a ruling of 6 February 1891 in which the Court states that while the Nation holds sovereign authority, the prerogatives delegated to the three ruling powers may not in any circumstances be sub-delegated.

Legally speaking, therefore, the term "special laws passed in accordance with the Constitution" must be interpreted restrictively, since those laws may never run counter to the Constitution itself.

We have, however, pointed out that these are merely theoretical justifications advanced *a posteriori* to explain certain procedures that went beyond the normal framework and scope of the Constitution but which were in fact dictated by force of circumstance.

In reviewing the following articles, moreover, we shall see that the residual competence vested in the Houses has been invoked on more than one occasion to justify the intervention of the Legislative at times of crisis.

ARTICLE 79

"At the death of the King, the Houses shall meet unconvened by the tenth day at latest following the date of decease. If the Houses have been dissolved previously and a summons has been included in the act of dissolution for a time which is later than the tenth day, the outgoing Houses will resume their functions until those which are to replace them can meet.

"If only one House has been dissolved, the same rule shall be followed in respect of that House.

"Dating from the death of the King and until the oath of office is taken either by his successor to the throne or by the regent, the constitutional powers of the King are exercised, in the name of the Belgian people, by the Ministers meeting in Council and on their own responsibility."

This article dates from 1831 and has never been modified.

With Article 70, it constitutes the second case in which the Houses meet automatically and by right without having been convened.

In view of the gravity of the circumstances, the Constituent Assembly has provided for an extra guarantee: if there has been a prior dissolution of Parliament and a summons to the electorate has been issued, the outgoing Houses resume their functions. The same rule applies if only one House has been dissolved.

It is, of course, essential that the country should continue to be governed.

That is why, from the moment of the King's death up to the moment when his successor or, failing him, the regent takes the oath of office, the King's constitutional powers are wielded by the Ministers meeting in Council, but solely in the name of the Belgian people in whom the fundamental sovereignty is vested.

This provision leads to various consequences:

1. The death of the King does not automatically bring about the accession to the throne of his successor, for the latter must first take the oath of office before he can mount the throne.

2. Belgian law recognizes a period lasting from the death of the King to the installation of his successor: this is known as the interregnum.

3. Article 79 confirms the fact that a dissolution of Parliament or of one of the Houses does not put an end totally to the mandate of their

members since the latter may be called upon to sit again; only a new election and the installation of the newly-elected members conclusively terminate their status as elected representatives of the Nation. This question has been reviewed in previous pages in connection with Article 71.

A noteworthy point too is that prior to the Third Revision (1967-1971), this was the first time the Constitution referred to the Council of Ministers (Cabinet) as an institution. Until quite recently, therefore, the Council of Ministers only existed, theoretically at least, in very exceptional circumstances.

It should also be pointed out that the term "Ministers" as used in this article refers both to the Prime Minister and to the other Cabinet Ministers, exclusive of the Secretaries of State.

It has been wondered whether all the Cabinet Ministers should be present in the Council for the latter's proceedings to be valid.

By a decree of 3 June 1946, the Court of Cassation solved the problem negatively by ruling that while authority is, in principle, exercised by all the Ministers meeting in Council, the fact that certain of them may be prevented from attending a meeting cannot be construed as an obstacle to the wielding of the sovereign authority thus vested in them.

Finally, it should be noted that the third para. of Article 79 was implemented in 1940 when King Leopold III found himself placed in the impossibility of reigning.

ARTICLE 80

"The King comes of age on his eighteenth birthday.

"He does not ascend the throne until he has formally taken the following oath before both Houses meeting together:

"I swear to observe the Constitution and the laws of the Belgian people, to maintain national independence and the integrity of the territory."

This article dates from 1831 and has never been modified.

Not only does it lay down the procedure governing the installation of a new Head of State, it also asserts the primacy of the elected Houses before which the future King must take his oath of office before he ascends the throne. Thus, this article yet again confirms that the Head of the Belgian State is above all a constitutional monarch.

In connection with this article, there has been some question as to the precise moment when a reign began and when it ended.

From Article 79, we already know that Belgian constitutional law recognizes a period of interregnum. Consequently, the King only begins his reign when he has finished taking the oath of office. This ceremony therefore takes on a twofold importance: it marks the moment at which the King may begin to perform his royal task, and at the same time it binds the King's conscience before the entire Nation.

In practice, the King assumes this title immediately on the death of his predecessor; hence he already benefits from the privilege of inviolability even though he may not yet undertake any legally valid act.

On the other hand, a reign only comes to an end with the death of the King, for even the impossibility of reigning, permanent and definitive though it may be, entails no more than the establishment of a regency.

It should be pointed out however that while the King may not unilaterally modify his own powers by, for instance, abandoning part of his authority, he is still entitled to abdicate on condition that the act of abdication is countersigned as usual by a responsible Minister. Thus during his reign, the King may not renounce any of the individual constitutional powers vested in him, but he may renounce the entire range of his prerogatives. That is what happened on 16 July 1951 when King Leopold III abdicated by means of an act signed by himself and countersigned by the Prime Minister, the Presidents (Speakers) of both Houses, the President of the Court of Cassation, and the Attorney General of the Court of Cassation.

The Constitution has also set at 18 years the age at which the King attains his majority. This was in derogation of common law which stipulates the legal coming of age at 21 years. The purpose of this clause was to avoid unnecessarily prolonging a regency, which is always an extremely difficult period since it does not correspond to the normal situation intended by the Constitution. This provision, however, will gradually lose its importance since many parliamentary attempts have already been made to bring down the legal age of majority under common law from 21 to 18 years.

Finally, it should be emphasized that the wording of the oath itself refers back to Articles 67 and 68 of the Constitution.

ARTICLE 81

"If, on the death of the King, his successor is a minor, the two Houses shall meet in a single assembly in order to arrange for the regency and the guardianship of the new King."

This article dates from 1831 and has never been modified.

It has, in fact, never been implemented since, in every case when a King has died, his successor was already of age.

The article retains however its whole importance since it establishes one of the three cases when the two Houses meet in a single assembly:

1. the election of a Regent (art. 81, 82, 85),

2. the election of a King (art. 85),

3. the taking of the oath by the Head of the State, be he King or Regent (art. 80 and 83).

These derogations of the fundamental bicameral principle are justified by the desire to avoid all differences of opinion between the two Houses in matters of extreme importance or in circumstances that brook no delay.

It should be noted that the two Houses reach their decision by means of a simple majority vote and not by a qualified majority.

We shall also see that parliamentary practice, founded on the residual competence of Parliament, has added further cases beyond the three listed above when the two Houses may meet in a single assembly (cfr. Art. 82 and 83).

ARTICLE 82

"If the King is unavoidably prevented from reigning, the Ministers, after establishing that impossibility, shall immediately convene both Houses. Arrangements are made for the regency and guardianship of the King by both Houses meeting together."

This article dates from 1831 and has never been modified.

As previously stated, the Constituent Assembly has envisaged various eventualities in which there would be no King, or in which the King would be incapable of reigning. One of them is the case of the King's minority, dealt with under Article 81; in this instance there is a King, but the royal function is assumed by a Regent.

Article 82 has provided for another hypothesis: that of the King being unavoidably prevented from reigning.

The case envisaged by the Constituent Assembly was that of physical impossibility, as evidenced by the preparatory work on this article. From this standpoint, however, it has never been implemented.

On the other hand, force of circumstance has once more broadened the scope of the article: this happened in 1940 when King Leopold III was in occupied Belgium, a prisoner of the enemy, whereas his Government had sought refuge in Great Britain.

The Government felt itself obliged to interpret the implications of Article 82 by extending it beyond the impossibility of reigning for reasons of health. The Ministers meeting in Council—since Parliament no longer existed—began by taking note of this impossibility, as is proved by a decree of 28 May 1940 in which the Council of Ministers invoked Article 82 of the Constitution and the fact that the King was "in the power of the invader".

Later, because the Houses could not meet until September 1944, namely, until the Occupying Army had left the territory, the Cabinet again exercised the constitutional powers of the King in implementation of Article 79.

The Government confirmed this in the decrees having the force of law which it was forced to enact from London, since those decree-laws invoke both Articles 26 and 82 of the Constitution and the impossibility of convening the Legislative Houses. All power both Executive and Legislative was thus concentrated solely in the hands of the Government, since this was the only branch of authority to remain free.

It should also be added that, as Parliament could not be convened, it was not until it was able to meet for the first time in 1944 that the Houses could arrange for a regency by electing Prince Charles, brother of the King, to this office. The latter exercised the constitutional powers of the Head of the State until 1950.

*
* *

An important question is that of ascertaining at what moment the King's incapability of reigning comes to an end. This question arose with a great deal of immediacy in connection with King Leopold III. In this sphere also the Houses exercised the residual competence already mentioned, and by a law of 19 July 1945 they stipulated that it was their business jointly to announce that the impossibility of reigning had come to an end. That law formally provides that, as King Leopold III had been unavoidably prevented from reigning owing to the enemy occupation of Belgium, he could only resume his constitutional powers "when Article 82 of the Constitution has been implemented and when, after a debate of the Houses meeting together, it is formally established that the impossibility of reigning has come to an end."

It is however necessary to be extremely cautious in handling such a provision since, while the Constitution has provided for guarantees that the King may not of his own accord either cease from exercising his prerogatives or prevent the Houses from meeting normally, it is equally necessary to avoid any abuse of authority on the part of Parliament itself for the purpose of preventing the King from effectively performing his constitutional functions by leaving him in the juridical position of being unable to reign. This very delicate situation occurred in Belgium between 1945 and 1950 at which time, doubtless for their own good reasons, the Houses fell back on the law of 19 July 1945 and refused to admit that the impossibility of reigning had ceased as far as the King was concerned. It was only after a number of developments arising out of a conflict between the parties on both sides, a conflict which ended in a referendum the results of which were published by ministerial decree of 20 March 1950, that Parliament finally acknowledged, by a decree of 20 July following, that "the impossibility of reigning insofar as His Majesty King Leopold III was concerned, had come to an end."

The referendum was not a measure provided for under the Constitution but one which, in this case also, had been decided upon by Parliament in terms of its residual competence. It was organized on 12 March 1950 on the basis of a law of 11 February previously, and it gave the following results: out of a total of 5,236,740 ballot papers deposited in the urns, there were 151,477 blank or invalidated papers; 2,933,382 votes in favour (i.e., stating that King Leopold III should resume the exercise of his constitutional powers); and 2,151,881 votes against the motion.

In any event, the decree of 20 July 1950, itself based on the law of 19 July 1945, created a new precedent.

It should also be noted that in Article 82, the term "Ministers" refers to the Prime Minister and the other Cabinet Ministers, exclusive of the Secretaries of State.

ARTICLE 83

"The regency can only be conferred on one person.
"The regent does not assume his office until he has taken the oath laid down in Article 80."

This article dates from 1831 and has never been modified.

It will be recalled that a regency may be set up in two cases:

1. Should the throne become vacant (article 85),

2. Should the King be unavoidably prevented from reigning. This eventuality may occur in two ways:

a) either in the case of his minority (art. 80),

b) or in the case of an impossibility justified by another reason (art. 82), which in principle is a physical one.

It should also be recalled that here too the Regent is appointed by the two Houses meeting together, in pursuance of Article 82.

In order to maintain unity of decision, the Constituent Assembly set aside the hypothesis of a regency exercised by several people.

Furthermore the Regent, like the King, is a constitutional Head of State, especially inasmuch as he derives his authority from the sovereign choice of Parliament. It is therefore quite understandable that he should take the same oath as the King prior to assuming the office.

There have been two official regencies in the course of Belgian history, though in reality there have been three.

On 24 February 1831 Baron Surlet de Chokier was elected Regent pending the designation of a King by the National Congress. The second Regent was Prince Charles who, on 20 September 1944, was appointed to that office during the period when his brother, King Leopold III, was unavoidably prevented from reigning.

In actual fact, however, Parliament—once again in terms of its residual competence—conferred what were tantamount to powers of regency on the then Crown Prince, today King Baudouin I. It was indeed a law of 10 August 1950 which provided that "the exercise of the King's constitutional powers is hereby conferred by the Houses meeting together, and in accordance with the declaration of His Majesty the King on 1 August 1950 and on the basis of Articles 82, 83 and 84 of the Constitution, on the Heir Presumptive to the Throne... Prince Baudouin, who shall henceforth bear the style and title of Crown Prince." Article 2 of that same law provided that the Crown Prince should exercise the said constitutional powers as soon as he had taken the oath prescribed by Article 83 of the Constitution, and the Houses were convened in single assembly on 11 August 1950. On that same date the two Houses issued a decree stating that "the exercise of the King's constitutional powers was conferred on Prince Baudouin." Also on that date, a royal decree enacted the new formula surrounding the implementation of rulings and judgments of the courts, tribunals, etc. The functions of Crown Prince came to an end with the formal abdication of King Leopold III on 16 July 1951.

ARTICLE 84

"No alteration to the Constitution may be made during a regency."

This article dates from 1831 and has never been modified.

The Regent exercises all the constitutional powers vested in the King.

One single power is withheld from him: that is the constituent power of which the King forms one of the three branches.

This exception was judiciously provided for in 1831 owing to the fact that it is the Constitution which establishes the status of the King.

The Constituent Assembly wished to avert any risk of a Regent's being tempted to take advantage of his temporary and exceptional position in order to set off a political crisis and prevent the King from defending his rights, as for instance during the latter's minority.

ARTICLE 85

"When the throne is vacant, the Houses shall convene in a joint session to make temporary arrangements for the regency until the Houses meet again after they have been entirely renewed; this meeting shall take place at latest within two months. The new Houses, meeting together, shall make definite arrangements in regard to the vacancy."

This article dates from 1831 and has never been modified.

The case of the throne falling vacant is of course a very serious circumstance indeed, since it means that a new dynasty must be sought.

That is why the choice of the new dynasty has been entrusted to the Houses, completely renewed as a result of a general election, which are to meet within a certain period and to debate the matter in joint session.

Here again, no qualified majority vote is required. It was indeed a decree by the National Congress of 28 January 1831 which established the election procedure for the Head of the State.

It should also be pointed out that Article 85 has never yet had to be implemented as the throne has not been vacant since 1831.

Article 85 concludes the series of constitutional articles dealing specifically with the King.

It is therefore permissible to draw certain conclusions. The survey in the preceding pages serves principally to demonstrate that the articles so laconically worded by the Constituent Assembly in 1830 on the basis of certain concepts of the powers of the State, have not aged with the passage of time precisely because of their concision, though they may have acquired new overtones down the years.

As the Constituent Assembly had indeed intended, it emerges that the Executive power is a very real one, acting in complete freedom even though its competence and scope are strictly defined in the constitutional texts and though it does in this way depend to some extent on the Legislative power.

In point of fact, the law remains the supreme standard and thus Parliament retains its *de jure* primacy.

Nevertheless, and with all the intentional guarantees, it has become clear in many instances that the Executive itself may initiate action as well as the Legislative. Thus the Executive retains a *de facto* primacy which compensates for the *de jure* primacy of Parliament. This mainly becomes evident in extremely grave and exceptional circumstances such as wartime, or serious events that justify the use of special powers.

It has also been seen that while the evolution of the Legislative power and especially the growing part played by pressure groups, the political parties in particular, have apparently given the impression of a shrinkage, or at least a certain effacement of the royal powers compared to those wielded in the 19th century, the King's role nevertheless remains an important one. It has simply altered in method, and the King's function, though it may appear less brilliant in the eyes of the country, has gained an added scope that is principally evident in the permanent contacts and discussions between the King and his Ministers under cover of constitutional secrecy; the King retains his prerogative, in the daily course of government, of being consulted by his Ministers, of encouraging them and of warning them.

The result is that the King's role is still a vital one in the life of the country.

SECTION II — THE MINISTERS

ARTICLE 86

"No person may become a Minister if he is not Belgian by birth or unless he has been granted full naturalisation. "

This article dates from 1831 and has never been modified.

It will be seen at once that this article imposes no conditions governing age or ability on appointments to Cabinet rank. Only the following are excluded from serving as Cabinet Ministers:

— foreigners,
— Belgians by marriage,
— Belgians granted ordinary naturalisation.

Conversely, the following may be Ministers:
— Belgians by birth.
— foreigners who have been granted full naturalisation.

It should be noted that in terms of Article 91-B of the Constitution, the term "minister" embraces not only all Cabinet Ministers but also the Prime Minister and the Secretaries of State.

The conditions surrounding appointment to government posts are therefore particularly wide. This is a consequence of Articles 6 and 25 of the Constitution in terms of which all Belgians are equal in the eyes of the law, and that all power fundamentally stems from the Nation.

On the basis of these texts, can a woman who fulfils the minimal conditions imposed become a Minister or a Secretary of State ? Indeed she can, and in recent years we have seen women appointed to Cabinet rank.

The first time when a woman was appointed a Cabinet Minister was on 28 July 1965. This was Mme. De Riemaecker-Legot who, until 19 March 1966, was a member of the Harmel Government as Minister of Family Affairs and Housing. She retained this post, moreover, in the following Government headed by Mr. Vanden Boeynants which remained in office until 17 June 1966.

After that, it was necessary to wait until 1973 before women were again appointed to ministerial rank. In the Leburton Government which took office on 26 January 1973 we find two women, though they did not actually hold Cabinet rank. They were designated as Secretaries of State. Mme. Verlackt-Gevaert was appointed Secretary of State for Family Affairs and the other, Mme. I. Petry, became Secretary of State for Co-operation in Development. During the Cabinet reshuffle which took place in the Leburton administration on 23 October 1973, these two women were eliminated from the ranks of the Government.

But in the Tindemans Cabinet which has now been in office since 25 April 1974, Mme. H. De Backer-Van Ocken has been appointed a full Minister in charge of Dutch Culture and Flemish Affairs.

*
**

One may also wonder whether, in view of the laconic drafting of Articles 65 and 86, Cabinet Ministers need actually to be members of Parliament.

Here again, practice has provided an answer to the question since on several occasions, governments have included "extra-parliamentarians" within their ranks, chosen generally on account of their technical competence when those governments found themselves facing difficult problems. On the theoretical plane, the answer must also be an affirmative one in view of the minimal conditions set by Article 86 and the equality of all Belgians proclaimed by Article 6.

Yet in this sphere also, custom has played an extremely important part, varying in extent according to the ideas prevailing at the time.

Theoretically, we know that in terms of Article 86, amplified moreover by Article 87, the King's choice may be an extremely wide one. In reality, however, events have restricted or extended the royal prerogative in such a way that the powers of the Head of the State are bounded by the customs in force at the time when he is called upon to make his choice.

Thus, in theory there is nothing that obliges the King to select the leader of a political party to head his Government, or to choose as Ministers people who are members of Parliament—Deputies or Senators—or again, to refrain from broadening his choice to include persons drawn from outside Parliament.

This freedom in principle of the King's has however become more and more restricted owing to the growing importance of the political parties and the change in the function of Parliament owing to the increasingly apparent rift between the majority and the opposition parties.

Indeed, as previously stated, the governments are coming to rely more and more on a parliamentary majority—an incidental majority that rallies round a basic programme which has been accepted by the leaders of the parties in office. In practice, therefore, the King is bound to choose his Prime Minister and the members of his Cabinet from the parties forming the majority, on pain of seeing his government deprived, either from the outset or during its term of office, of the confidence necessary to ensure that it functions.

Even within the parties themselves, the King's choice is virtually limited to a few particularly influential people, again for the same reason, i.e. so that the Government's programme may be successfully implemented with the support of the majority parties. This explains a fact which has often been apparent in recent years: that the same people are members of successive governments, even though they may be appointed to different posts.

Similarly, the King is usually brought to select as Prime Minister a leading politician from that political party which holds the most seats in the House of Representatives. This is not an absolute rule, but here again the support of the most powerful party presupposes that the Government will enjoy the backing of this party in Parliament.

Finally, owing to the development of linguistic problems, the King is also brought to choose a person who can rely on the support of members of Parliament belonging to the two language communities of the nation. It would, for instance, be increasingly unacceptable for a Prime Minister to be conversant with only one of the national languages, without being able to speak, let alone understand, the other language.

To these practical limitations imposed on the King's choice corresponds moreover the distrust of the political parties with regard to "extra-parliamentary" technical experts, for the parties fear that their political importance may thereby be sapped to the advantage of a progressively established technocracy.

The fact is, therefore, that the appearance of "extra-parliamentarians" as Cabinet Ministers, while not impossible, is growing more and more improbable; and the difficulty is so to speak heightened by the terms of Article 86-B of the Constitution.

The result is that the very wide possibility of choice acknowledged in respect of the Monarch is in fact extremely restricted since the King must reckon with the political circumstances of the moment, the distribution of parliamentary seats among the various parties, the influence of certain persons within those same parties, and finally, the subtle balance that must be struck between all the varied interests that come into play.

ARTICLE 86-B

"With the possible exception of the Prime Minister, the Cabinet comprises an equal number of French-speaking and Dutch-speaking Ministers."

This clause was inserted in the Constitution on 24 December 1970 during the Third Revision.

As it is worded, the scope of this article is threefold:

— it provides for official constitutional recognition of the Prime Minister;

— similarly, it provides for official constitutional recognition of the Cabinet, or Council of Ministers, not merely in exceptional circumstances (Art. 79) but on a permanent basis.

— finally, it imposes linguistic equality within the Cabinet as between the French-speaking and Dutch-speaking Ministers, with the exception of the Prime Minister, any members of the Government coming from the German-speaking region, and the Secretaries of State.

Consequently, this is a clause which, though couched in simple language, takes on great importance and significance and therefore merits a detailed explanation.

*\
* *

THE PRIME MINISTER

Prior to the insertion of Article 86-B in the Constitution, the title and function of Prime Minister were valid solely as a matter of custom and tradition, without any particular legal status being attached to them. The title itself is, moreover, of fairly recent date, since it was practically unheard-of during the 19 th century. The development of the function of Prime Minister is indeed bound up with the evolution of political affairs in Belgium.

It is a fact that in 1831, Article 65 of the Constitution was still fully effective, and Ministers were really and truly the King's Ministers since the Sovereign was free to choose them without regarding them as an entity, a genuine body politic placed at the head of affairs of State. So it happened, for instance when the first administration was set up under the new monarchy, that the decrees of appointment of four Ministers were countersigned by the fifth Minister, whose own Decree of Appointment was countersigned by an outgoing Minister belonging to the last administration of the regency period. Furthermore, each Minister was in charge of a department; but it was only with the disappearance of unionism in 1847 that the preponderance of one Minister over the others became an increasingly important factor in political life.

Even the terminology remained vague, for during the 19th century we find such terms as "Head of the Cabinet", "Head of the Administration", "Leader of the Government", "Leader of the Administration", or "President of the Council" being used unofficially. None of these titles was officially confirmed, and none of them appears, for instance, in the Decrees of Appointment. In actual fact, such a title was bestowed on the man who formed the Government and who countersigned the Decree of Dismissal of his predecessor and the Decrees of Appointment of his colleagues.

The title of Prime Minister appears for the first time officially in a report drawn up by the Council of Ministers on 24 March 1894. But some authors had already been using it for several years previously, while taking care to point out that the title had no official validity. It should be noted in passing that this term is inspired by the English parliamentary system, in contrast to that of "President of the Council" which was far more widely used on the Continent.

Yet several years were still to pass before the title of Prime Minister received official sanction. Its first appearance was somewhat premature, for the term was first used officially in a Royal Decree of 21 November 1918, the preamble of which referred to a proposal made by the Prime Minister. Subsequently, several Royal Decrees made use of the formula and alluded to the countersignature of the Prime Minister even though this title had not been officially created. Only when a Royal Decree was passed on 20 November 1920 was this particular title officially conferred on the Head of the Government.

The authority of the Prime Minister is not, however, defined in any document, for right up to 1929 the Prime Minister remained at the head of an important Department such as the Interior, Foreign Affairs, Finance, Justice, etc. Thereafter, Prime Ministers were often in charge of a Government department, and it was not until after the end of World War II that a Prime Minister was more frequently seen to have no other function. Even so, it should be noted that while a Prime Minister may not be in charge of a specific department, he very often assumes responsibility for a matter of great immediacy and importance. Thus, we have seen a Prime Minister dealing with the coal problem, or in charge of economic coordination, or again in charge of coordinating scientific policies.

All this goes to show that the process of evolution has been a slow but steady one, and that it was to some extent bound up with the parallel evolution of various political institutions.

The prerogatives of the Prime Minister have also developed gradually over the years, and moreover they vary constantly as circumstances dictate. They therefore depend essentially on a *de facto* situation, and arise more out of custom than out of any legal rulings.

Their variable nature does not, however, detract from the constantly increasing importance of the function of Prime Minister, a function which has progressively become an institution to the point where it has now been officially acknowledged by the Constitution.

It seems important to define here what exactly are the powers and prerogatives of the Prime Minister.

a) *Political prerogatives*

1) Article 65 has already underlined the vast importance of the Prime Minister in both the formation of a Government and in its resignation. It should be recalled in particular that the Prime Minister is not necessarily the leader of any political party, but he is generally a member of the political party which has the largest parliamentary majority. This practice stems from the fact that it is vitally necessary for the Prime Minister to be able to count on Parliament to support his Government. Nor is the Prime Minister necessarily the person designated by the King to form a Government. This point was confirmed in 1950 when a Government was formed by the Minister of Foreign Affairs, in which the latter did not become Prime Minister.

However, in most cases it is the man who forms the Government who becomes its Prime Minister, and his task is thus a crucial one since he must build up a Cabinet that he knows will enjoy the confidence of Parliament. His choice of colleagues is therefore restricted in two ways: firstly, by the need to secure the support of the majority party in Parliament; and secondly, he must be able to count on the confidence of the Head of State. It is also the Prime Minister who draws up the Government statement outlining the programme worked out by the political parties in office, and who reads this statement to both Houses in order to secure the assent of the majority and the requisite vote of confidence.

2) We have also pointed out, in connection with Article 71, the important part played by the Prime Minister in the dissolution of Parliament. More and more frequently in fact, it is he who countersigns the Decree of Dissolution.

3) Again, it is the Prime Minister who is generally regarded as the Government's spokesman to the nation. In obedience to the phenomenon

created by the growing development of the mass media, particularly the press, radio and television, it is his job to keep the country informed of the Government's policies by means of broadcasts or press conferences. Such press conferences have indeed become an established custom after each Cabinet meeting.

4) It is also the Prime Minister who is called upon to act, so to speak, as the universal joint or middleman between the various parts of the political machinery.

For instance, it is he who will be charged with speaking in parliamentary debates on general policy so as to explain the Government's action.

It is also his task to make sure that unity is preserved within the Cabinet and to coordinate the work of the various Ministers within the framework of the established programme and in obedience to the agreement reached between the Government and the majority parties.

In most cases, he is the Cabinet's automatic choice of spokesman when it comes to dealing with the majority parties themselves in cases where a conflict might occur or when it becomes necessary to supply additional information on the established programme. Again, it is he who is called upon to tackle problems of vital importance as and when they arise. In this event, he will do so in co-operation with the Cabinet Minister directly responsible for such matters.

Finally, the Prime Minister is the natural channel of communication between the King and his Government. He fulfils this function by means of increasingly regular visits to the Head of State in order to report on the development of Government policies and such questions as may be of particular interest to the Sovereign.

b) *Head of the Government*

The Prime Minister, whom we have thus shown to be the driving force behind the Government in office, discharges this function mainly by assuming the presidency of the Council of Ministers (the Cabinet), the Government Council, and the restricted Ministerial Committees. These positions of leadership, particularly effective in the coalition governments which are the rule and not the exception in Belgium, enable the Prime Minister to play his part as prime mover of the Government, guardian of Cabinet unity as between Ministers belonging to different political parties, and supervisor of the right and proper implementation of the Government's programme.

c) *Administrative powers*

As we have said, the Prime Minister these days is usually relieved of the burden of heading a government department. However, he would find it impossible to perform his functions in the proper manner were he not assisted by administrative services.

1) The most important of these is the Office of the Prime Minister. A Royal Decree of 25 November 1918 instituted a Prime Minister's Office for the first time. It differs little from the departmental staffs that assist other Cabinet Ministers save that, owing to the numerous specific tasks incumbent on the Prime Minister, it is usually larger than the rest. Indeed, if he is to perform his coordinating task efficiently, the Prime Minister must be able to rely on the co-operation of specialists able to advise him on the main questions confronting the Government. Recently, in fact, we witnessed the appearance of *two* Offices of the Prime Minister: a general policy office, and an office dealing specifically with economic and social affairs.

2) Apart from his Office, other administrative services have been placed under the authority of the Prime Minister.

Firstly, there is the Chancellery, headed by a Director General. This comprises three sections: one whose main task is to help the secretary of the Cabinet in his specific duties connected with the compilation of the minutes of all Cabinet meetings and the notification of decisions reached by the Cabinet; another which is responsible for assembling information and documentation, especially where the press is concerned; and the third consists of administrative offices in charge of personnel management, accounts and office equipment and supplies.

Then there is the economic research and coordination department, also headed by a Director General. As its name implies, this service acts as a coordinating body in all branches of Government activity except for purely administrative problems. It also provides the administrative secretariat of the Ministerial Committee for Economic and Social Coordination.

Finally, there is the Main Supervisory Committee which is directed by the Prime Minister but whose actual operations do not fall within the Premier's province; it is to some extent an independent body. This Committee, which is headed by a high-ranking magistrate of the Court of Cassation, has its own administrative offices. The Main Supervisory Committee was set up by a Royal Decree of 30 October 1910 within the Ministry of Railways, Posts and Telegraphs in order to deal with certain irregularities noted in the Railways Administration. Later on, the Committee's competence was extended to cover all the Ministries, and its official status was defined by a Royal Decree of 28 December 1921, which in turn was amended by another Royal Decree of 12 November 1932. However, it was not until a final Royal Decree was issued on 16 February 1940 that this Committee was made part of the Office of the Prime Minister, precisely on account of its wide general competence.

Its functions and powers are threefold. Firstly, as its name indicates, the Committee has a supervisory function which rather gives it the character of an administrative police force whose task is to pinpoint fraudulent dealings and infringements of regulations, especially those relating to contracts, supplies and undertakings in which the State's interests are involved. Then the Committee also wields certain powers in the matter of claims and disputes, in terms of which it is required to submit a motivated recommendation, at the request of the parties concerned, on disputes that may arise between works contractors and public departments. Finally, the Committee's authority also extends to the survey and examination of important questions such as the preparation of general specifications pertaining to public works and business transactions on behalf of the State. Officials of the Main Supervisory Committee have recently been awarded the status of employees or officials of the Criminal Investigation Bureau.

From time to time the Prime Minister has also been in authority over administrative departments of a general nature. These include the General Administration Department, the Permanent Recruiting Secretariat, and the General Selection and Training Directorate.

Apart from the last-mentioned which was only set up in 1961, the two other departments came into being as a result of the Civil Service reforms proposed in 1937 by Mr. L. Camu, Royal Commissioner for Administrative Reform. In fact, they were set up by Royal Decree in 1939.

The conclusions reached by the reform proposal had in fact made it clear that, over and above the functional role of the various Ministries, it was necessary to provide for institutional coordination as well, so as to avoid a state of anarchy and to lay down general rules of a uniform character, applicable to all State employees, on such matters as their administrative status and emoluments. This, in principle, is the work of the General Administration Department whose essential task is to work out the general regulations applicable to State employees and to ensure that they are implemented and coordinated. The scope of this department has grown as time went by, especially since 1961 when social programmes or collective agreements were periodically signed between the Government and the major unions banded into a Common Front, similar to what happens in the private sector when collective labour bargaining agreements are negotiated. The General Administration Department has also, for some years now, been in charge of a central computer destined to become the operational factor in a national register of all citizens.

The Permanent Recruiting Secretariat in turn has the task of upholding the impersonal, objective nature of recruiting procedures and, as occasion may arise, those governing the promotion of State employees by means of upgrading examinations or tests. Its organizers were determined to avoid any political or other forms of arbitrary selection for appointments and thus ensure that all Belgians enjoyed equality of access to posts in the civil service.

The General Selection and Training Directorate only came into being in 1963 as a modification of the department run by the General Probation Manager which had been set up by Royal Decree of 13 December 1961. In terms of the Royal Decree of 12 December 1963, the prerogatives of the General Selection and Training Directorate are as follows : to promote the application of adequate methods of selecting personnel for recruiting or promotion; to ensure or provide for the basic and advanced training of State employees; to set up a centre of research and documentation on administrative structures and practices; and finally, to promote the best possible use of personnel. This department is specifically entrusted with the task of organizing and supervising the probation period of university-trained candidates for posts in the administrative departments of the State.

These services are also placed under the authority of a Director General, with the exception of the Permanent Recruiting Secretariat which is headed by a Permanent Secretary assisted by two Deputy Permanent Secretaries.

It was to ensure the efficiency of these departments, and particularly that of the first two, that it was deemed opportune at the time to place them under the direct authority of the Prime Minister.

However, owing to the growing burden of responsibility incumbent on the Prime Minister and to certain political circumstances of the time, it has happened that these services were placed at certain periods under the authority of other Cabinet Ministers.

Thus, in 1946, they came under the Minister for the Budget; in 1961 under the Minister of the Interior; while since that date they have generally been managed either by a Minister-Under Secretary of State or a Secretary of State for the Civil Service. Since the official creation of the Secretaries of State, they have been managed by a Secretary of State under the supreme control of the Prime Minister.

At the time when the revision of the Constitution was under discussion, the question of the Prime Minister was raised. The Commission for Institutional Reform was thus brought to examine this question, and it recorded several conclusions. In particular, it considered that the functions of the Prime Minister need not be specified in a constitutional clause, but that the Prime Minister was called upon to bear the special burden of the Government's collective responsibility, without however eliminating the individual responsibility of each Minister in his own sphere of competence.

It had in fact been wondered whether the time had not come to frame in legal terms the pre-eminent role of the Prime Minister insofar as his colleagues were concerned, and to define the scope of his power and prerogatives.

In restricting itself to formulating recommendations instead of definite proposals, the Commission for Institutional Reform has maintained the traditional line of civil law in Belgium, for alongside statute law and the Constitution in particular, there is also custom and tradition, the essential nature of which has been underlined on various occasions and which makes it possible to preserve great flexibility and adaptability in necessarily varying circumstances. The fact remains that, indirectly perhaps but beyond all doubt, the Constitution has officially recognized the Prime Minister in its Article 86-B, and has thereby acknowledged his function in the light of a genuine institution.

On the basis of this rapid survey, it is permissible to draw certain conclusions regarding the way in which the function of Prime Minister has evolved, and the growing importance of that function.

The increasingly broad development of the Prime Minister's function is, from the historical standpoint, due to the convergence of two factors which combine, in the person of the Prime Minister, powers and prerogatives that were formerly exercised by the King himself and by the other members of the Cabinet.

The causes of such a process of evolution have been pointed out on many occasions.

First of all, there is the mutation which has occurred in the exercise of the royal power, which has changed in form and content as time went by, as we have shown notably in those constitutional articles dealing with the King.

Then there is the growing complexity of State business, with the State coming more and more to intervene in all fields of the everyday life of its citizens, to such an extent that some form of coordination was obviously necessary.

Finally, there is the evolution of the parliamentary system itself and the virtually permanent existence of coalition governments, the cohesion of which can only be maintained through the action of a powerful personality acceptable both to Parliament and to those political parties which form the majority.

At all events, the importance of the Prime Minister's function needs no further demonstrating, and it must now be reckoned as an essential cog in the political and administrative machinery. Its importance may of course vary, depending on the composition of successive Cabinets. Thus, in a one-party Government, the Prime Minister's task will be relatively easier since the Premier can then rely on an absolute majority in Parliament and will not have to worry about preserving the unity and cohesion of his Cabinet. On the other hand, when a Government consists of members of several political parties, the Prime Minister will enjoy immense prestige but his task will be a very difficult one, and his means of action will indeed be very much more restricted, precisely owing to the fact that cohesion and unity of outlook will be difficult to maintain in a Cabinet whose members hold widely different political views.

In point of fact, it is in the bipartite governments—which are, moreover, most frequently encountered in Belgium—that the Prime Minister has to strike a careful balance between the prestige that surrounds his function and the means of action at his disposal. His work of coordination is indeed made easier when the question is one of ironing out any conflicts that may arise between the two parties in office, and the field open to his manoeuvres is correspondingly much wider. It is, in fact, when bipartite governments have been in office that the Prime Ministers of the day have witnessed a definite growth in the importance of their function.

The Deputy Prime Minister

In connection with the Prime Minister, it is necessary to say something about a second function which has progressively become separated from the ordinary ministerial posts in the course of a process of evolution which has been slower, but has run parallel to that of the Prime Minister. This is the Deputy Prime Minister.

As in the case of the Premier, the function of Deputy Prime Minister has grown up largely out of custom and tradition, without its scope having been defined in any legal terms. It has not been officially recognized by the Constitution, but its growing importance deserves to be studied within the context of the various ministerial powers and prerogatives.

It was in 1925 that this function became apparent, more or less for the first time, although the title of Deputy Prime Minister did not appear in the Royal Decree of Appointment of the Minister concerned. The experiment did not last long, though, and it was not until 1939 that there was once more a post of Vice-President of the Council of Ministers, though the holder of that post still did not receive the corresponding title.

This second experiment came to an end with the outbreak of war; and was not resumed until the period 1948 to 1950. During the years 1949 and 1950 in particular, the post of Vice-President of the Council of Ministers was held by the Minister of National Defence who, for the first time, was sometimes referred to by that title.

Then the post vanished once more during the two one-party governments that held office between 1950 and 1954.

Since 1954 the function has become a traditional one, but it was still necessary to wait until 1961 before the holder of this post was officially given the title of "Deputy Prime Minister".

The 1973 experiment served merely to reinforce the institution, for reasons which will become apparent hereunder. In the two governments of 1973-1974, there were in fact two Deputy Prime Ministers, and when the first of those governments was formed, there was even some question at a certain point of designating a Chief Deputy Prime Minister. Reactions to this new formula were, however, both numerous and adverse, for there was nothing to justify such a complicated system wherein the hierarchy of government was carried to extremes, save only a matter of political expediency.

Like the Prime Minister, the Deputy Prime Minister has been entrusted either with an important Ministry such as Foreign Affairs, Finance, National Defence, the Interior, or Economic Affairs, or with a special task arising out of the requirements of the moment: administrative reform, coordination of economic policy.

However, in contrast to the function of Prime Minister, the rule here has operated the other way, in the sense that the Deputy Prime Minister is generally placed effectively at the head of a specific government department.

Furthermore, he does not have a special office to assist him in his task as the Prime Minister does, but like the Prime Minister he does have two departmental staff sections at his disposal: one section to look after the affairs of the Ministry in his charge, and the other to handle matters specifically relating to his function as Deputy Prime Minister.

As already stated, the function of Deputy Prime Minister has never been defined in legal terms, and the title itself only appeared quite recently in the Royal Decrees of Appointment. In fact, the function of Deputy Prime Minister stems from the same exigencies as that of the Prime Minister, namely: the substantial increase in the tasks which are now incumbent on the Prime Minister, and the frequency of coalition governments as a result of the evolution of the parliamentary system. The reasons are so evident that it was precisely during the one-party governments of 1950 to 1954 that no Deputy Prime Minister could be found in the Cabinet.

In the case of coalition governments, most of which are two-party governments, the Deputy Prime Minister is, so to speak, the Prime Minister's opposite number in the other majority party. He is consequently responsible for his own party in the Cabinet, and at the same time he is the Cabinet's spokesman to the party to which he belongs. Thus, his function makes for easier relations within the Government itself, and makes it possible to avoid any direct confrontation between the parties forming the Cabinet since, if a conflict or an argument should arise, it is sufficient for the Prime Minister and the Deputy Prime Minister to reach an agreement as being co-responsible for their own parties. The latter is therefore the co-former, so to speak, of the Government in the sense that he is usually the man who was entrusted by his party with conducting the negotiations leading to the formation of the Government in the event that his party does not hold the function of Prime Minister in its gift. In most cases, he is the man who has discussed the programme with the Prime Minister, who has committed his party to that programme and who, when the Government takes office, has the job of smoothing out difficulties and ensuring good relations between the two political parties forming the majority.

It is therefore permissible to sum up the Deputy Prime Minister's function as follows:

1) He is generally in charge of an important Government department;

2) He is the Prime Minister's opposite number in all discussions between the parties forming the majority;

3) He helps the Prime Minister to accomplish the onerous tasks incumbent on him. In this capacity notably, the restricted Ministerial Committees (which will be reviewed in detail farther on) often meet with the Deputy Prime Minister in the chair, and this enables the Prime Minister himself to carry out his other tasks.

It is precisely the fact that the Deputy Prime Minister usually belongs to the other wing of the parliamentary majority forming a two-party Government which complicated the issue when the 1973 Government was formed. In actual fact, at that time there were three parties in the majority, and to ensure that all three were properly represented in the Cabinet, two Deputy Prime Ministers were appointed, each from a party different from that of the other and from that to which the Prime Minister belonged.

As previously stated, there was even some question of creating the post of Chief Deputy Prime Minister. Because of the fact that the regionalist concept had made great progress in the general way of thinking, the Brussels region might have felt itself insufficiently represented at the head of the Government since the Prime Minister was drawn from the French-speaking element and the two Deputy Prime Ministers from the Dutch-speaking element. In response to this concern, there was even some thought of appointing a third Deputy Prime Minister belonging to the Brussels region, but in order to establish a definite chain of command and to prevent the parcelling up of the Deputy Prime Minister's function, with all the friction that this would inevitably cause, it was proposed to nominate a Chief Deputy Prime Minister.

This idea was abandoned, however, for the complications arising out of such a system were clearly discernible and this kind of superimposition of inadequately defined functions would only have ended, in the short term, in paralysing the Government's ability to act.

One fact at least must be singled out and borne in mind as a result of this experiment, which is: that while it is historically justified by the growing complexity of government business, the function of Deputy Prime Minister is very definitely a matter of political expediency.

The Council of Ministers, or Cabinet

Article 86-B acknowledges indirectly, not only the existence of the Prime Minister, but also that of the Council of Ministers, or Cabinet, as a permanent political institution.

The question does not however take on the same aspect as that of the Prime Minister, because the Council of Ministers already existed in legal terms and in institutional practice:

On the legal plane, the Belgian Constitution had already acknowledged the existence of such an entity in Article 79 which provided that, during an interregnum, the constitutional powers of the King were to be wielded by the Ministers meeting in Council and under their responsibility.

Without alluding to the concept of "Council", the Constitution again refers to the part played by Cabinet Ministers as a body in Article 82, that is: when the King is unavoidably prevented from reigning. Indeed, we have seen that in such a circumstance, it is incumbent on the Ministers to convene the Houses immediately, so that Parliament may take the necessary action to provide for a trusteeship and a regency.

In connection with Article 82, it has also been pointed out that the same constitutional ruling had been invoked by the Government in 1940 when the King was a prisoner of the enemy invader. Similarly, by means of a new and extensive interpretation, the Ministers wielded the constitutional powers of the King in obedience to the spirit of Article 79 until such time as the two Houses of Parliament, after the army of occupation had been driven out, were once more able to meet and elect a Regent. Even so, right up to 24 December 1970, those were the only cases when the Council of Ministers was constitutionally in existence.

In fact, the legal existence of the Council of Ministers had already been acknowledged in many legal documents, so that its existence in legal terms predated that of the Prime Minister himself, and that in contrast to the function of Prime Minister, the existence of the Council of Ministers as an institution was acknowledged and sanctioned mainly through the channel of legislation.

Thus, the law of 29 October 1846 governing the organization of the Audit Office already provided that, in the event that the Office refused to approve an order for payment, the reasons for such a refusal were to be examined at a meeting of the Ministers in Council, and that the Ministers should then decide whether the order should be passed for payment on their own responsibility. This example, which dates back to the very first years of Belgian independence, is far from being an isolated one, for a number of subsequent pieces of legislation have provided for the intervention of the Council of Ministers, not only in the laws governing special or extraordinary powers but in many other sectors as well.

Moreover, already in 1831, the National Congress had voted budget appropriations allowing for credits for the secretariat of the Council of Ministers, and when the very first dissolution of the House of Representatives took place on 28 April 1833, the Royal Decree of Dissolution referred to "the report and the recommendation of Our Council of Ministers". In connection with Article 71, it has already been pointed out above that, except in two cases, the Council of Ministers was always referred to in the Royal Decrees of Dissolution. In parallel to the evolution of the Prime Minister's function, it happens more and more frequently that laws and regulations, even those enacted by Royal Decree, mention the intervention of the Council of Ministers.

Whatever the case may be, the Council of Ministers was, until the latest Revision of the Constitution (1967-1971), a product more of custom and tradition than of the Constitution. Until 1914, the Cabinet did in fact meet rather infrequently because, generally speaking, the governments were formed from a single political party, so that it was only necessary for the Cabinet to meet in cases where its intervention was stipulated either by law or by regulation. The development towards meetings at much shorter intervals—at the present time there is a Cabinet meeting at least once a week—began after 1918 when governments came more and more to be formed on a coalition basis.

To avoid any misunderstanding, it is moreover necessary to distinguish between several kindred concepts which have sometimes become confused in practice.

In the strict sense, the Cabinet is a Council presided over by the King. Such Councils were frequently held during the reign of Leopold I. This practice, however, fell off progressively during the reign of Leopold II, and by the time Albert I ascended the throne they occurred very seldom indeed.

Later they became a matter of extreme rarity both during the reign of Leopold III and during the Regency.

The progressive disappearance of Councils presided over by the King is part and parcel of the general way in which political institutions have evolved over the years in Belgium. On the one hand, as we have seen, the exercise of the royal powers has undergone a mutation to the point where the King has less and less to do with the day-to-day conduct of public affairs; on the other, too-frequent meetings of Cabinet Ministers in the presence of the Sovereign carried with them a danger of "exposing the Crown" through indiscretions that had become all too likely as the news media grew in scope and importance. It is, however, the concept of a "Council of Ministers" that has finally won acceptance, for if the King no longer takes the chair at Cabinet meetings, theoretically he is still entitled to do so.

Alongside the concept of a Council of Ministers, that of a "Cabinet Council" has sometimes come to the fore. It became fairly widely accepted in 1918 and subsequent years and was bound up with the official appearance on the scene of a Prime Minister. At that period, the term was used to operate a distinction between the Council of Ministers presided over by the King, and Ministers meeting under the chairmanship of the Prime Minister.

Quite recently—and the question will be referred to again under Article 91-B—yet another concept appeared: that of a "Government Council". As the Secretaries of State do not constitutionally form part of the Council of Ministers, this novel term has been used to distinguish between ordinary Cabinet meetings and plenary meetings of the Government to which the Secretaries of State are effectively admitted.

Finally, we shall allude farther on to a fourth concept: that of a "Crown Council".

At the present time, the Council of Ministers is still devoid of any genuine legal status. Its prerogatives and its functions stem largely from custom and tradition, and shortly after a new government is formed, it generally happens that the Prime Minister sends a circular round to all his colleagues indicating the way in which he would like the Cabinet to meet. It usually begins by defining the prerogatives of the Cabinet by specifying those matters on which its agreement is required, those on which its opinions are requested, and those on which verbal information must be supplied. The circular also formulates practical instructions regarding internal and external procedure, and particularly the way in which files should be submitted for examination. It ends by defining the operating rules of the Cabinet, with particular reference to the frequency of its meetings, the notice to be given when submitting matters for examination, and the way in which notifications and decisions are to be transmitted.

Today, the Council of Ministers is at one and the same time a political entity and an administrative entity.

As a political entity, it charts the broad outlines of the Government programme and supervises the implementation of that programme.

As an administrative entity, its task is to make decisions on important matters affecting one or several ministries.

Thus, for instance, its agreement is required:

1) for all bills tabled in Parliament;

2) for all proposed royal or ministerial decrees when its intervention is mandatory in terms of a law or regulation;

3) for debates dealing with the work of the Audit Office;

4) for framing rules and quotas concerning decorations to be awarded in the national orders;

5) for the personal award of higher decorations when there is a derogation of existing rules, or in any cases not provided for in the rules;

6) for decisions regarding the official attendance of a member of the Government charged with representing it at a ceremony or other event;

7) for decisions as to whether the Government will sponsor some important venture.

Similarly, the Cabinet's opinion is sought by means of a document, explanatory note or verbal communication, on all questions that may engage the responsibility of the Government as a whole.

Finally, verbal information is supplied to the Council of Ministers:

310

1) on the development of topical events affecting Belgium's relations with foreign countries and which are likely to have a definite impact on Belgian public opinion;

2) on projected appointments or promotions to top-ranking posts in the administration, the diplomatic service, public offices, and the various special institutions such as higher education, the armed forces, the gendarmerie and the magistrature.

The *de jure* interventions of the Council of Ministers have therefore become extremely numerous, and since 1945 especially, a very great number of laws and royal decrees have formally required a debate in the Cabinet so as to work out the methods of implementation laid down by those laws or decrees.

It is obvious that the increasing burden of work incumbent on the Cabinet has been detrimental to the personal responsibility of each Minister in his own sphere of competence.

Generally speaking, the Cabinet's increasing involvement has developed from the need to provide sufficient guarantees to all citizens. Consequently, this development too is bound up with the existence of coalition governments, for the Cabinet thus enables all its members to exercise reciprocal control and supervision over each other.

So, before it was actually sanctioned by the Constitution, the Council of Ministers had become one of the most important Belgian political institutions, especially where the day-to-day management of public affairs was concerned. That is why the Cabinet now meets at least once a week, and its discussions may last for several hours, depending on the number of items on the agenda or the gravity of some of the problems which have to be dealt with.

In connection with the Prime Minister, we have stressed that one of his main tasks is to take the chair at Cabinet meetings in place and on behalf of the King, within the framework of evolving political institutions.

According to the principle of Cabinet solidarity which makes for cohesion in coalition governments, questions debated in Council are not voted upon. It would seem that voting has only taken place once, during the Cabinet meeting of 10 March 1947 when a difference of opinion arose between members of the Government regarding an increase in the price of coal. This was, moreover, an error from the legal standpoint, since the Council of Ministers is not a debating assembly and has no real powers of decision apart from those cases laid down by the Constitution or by the law. There can therefore be no question of arriving at a majority or a minority, and the Cabinet is not constitutionally authorized to act on behalf of any individual Minister when, by means of his countersignature, he collaborates with the King in accomplishing an act in terms of the executive authority.

In the same way of thinking, the minutes of Cabinet meetings are not made available to Ministers, and they are also forbidden to make notes during the meeting since the question can only be one of an exchange of views, the actual decision being, in the final analysis, a matter for the Executive.

Prior to 1914, no minutes were ever made of such meetings which, as we have seen, were held far less often. The custom of keeping the minutes only became established after 1918 when the function of Prime Minister came to the fore. This can be explained by the growing volume of affairs laid before the Cabinet and the fact that the Ministers belonged to different political parties. Thus, the minutes were useful as an accurate record of the results of discussions. Initially, they were fairly detailed, but the disadvantages of such a system were not long in making their appearance.

That is why, at the present time, the minutes are far more laconic in character and are restricted to a summary of the discussions and decisions reached, the various opinions being outlined without, however, mentioning the names of the Ministers who expressed them. Historians of Belgian politics may find this regrettable, but it must be realized that the Cabinet is mainly engaged in practical work and not in writing history.

The minutes are generally typed in six copies destined for the Head of State, the Prime Minister, the Secretary of the Cabinet, the State archives (2 copies), and the last copy is cut up so that relevant excerpts may be added to the files concerned. Furthermore, Cabinet discussions also give rise to the drafting of a series of notifications on the various problems on the agenda. These notifications are transmitted to the Ministers concerned.

All the material work necessitated in particular by the compilation of the minutes and notifications is done by the Secretary of the Cabinet, assisted as we have said by one of the Chancellery sections, and in particular by the Director General of those services. The function of Cabinet Secretary is thus of essential importance. The secretary is present as a silent spectator at all Cabinet meetings, and by the very fact of his attendance he is conversant with all the discussions and the way in which decisions are reached. This post must therefore be entrusted to a person who, apart from his total discretion which is absolutely essential, enjoys the confidence not only of the Prime Minister but also that of the rest of the Cabinet. That is why, instead of choosing a permanent civil servant from the ranks of the administration, the post of Cabinet Secretary is usually held by the Prime Minister's Principal Political Private Secretary. To date, there have been only two exceptions of very brief duration when this post was held by a person not on the staff of the Office of the Prime Minister. In 1973, the growing complexity of the work load undertaken by the Prime Minister and the enormous range of problems examined by the Cabinet even gave rise to the creation, in the Office of the Prime Minister, of a special appointment as Cabinet Secretary independently of any other work, with the rank however of Principal Private Secretary.

Let us recall in passing that the effective presence of all Cabinet Ministers at the meeting is not required for its discussions to be valid (cfr. Article 79).

The ever more important place occupied by the Council of Ministers in the functioning of Belgian institutions has inevitably raised the question of what legal scope its intervention may have.

Constitutionally, it is the King, under cover of the ministerial countersignature, who alone may exercise the prerogatives vested in the Executive authority. The Cabinet may not, therefore, take the King's place in decision-making. Theoretically, its discussions can only be in the nature of an act in preparation for a decision, the actual making of which is finally a task to be accomplished only by the Executive authority as such.

The growing frequency of Cabinet meetings and interventions by the Cabinet have, however, been stages in an evolutionary process destined unavoidably to raise certain problems.

It is admitted today that when the Cabinet has been vested with a specific power, it is a genuine power of decision-making. But such cases are extremely rare and are the result either of a formal constitutional ruling (Article 79) or a direct intervention on the part of the Legislative (such as the law of 29 October 1846 with regard to the Audit Office).

Apart from those cases, discussions in the Cabinet are merely a formality of an advisory nature leading to the final decision. But here again, it must be ascertained whether or not the formality is a substantial one, the omission of which might invalidate the final act. In 1948 the Council of State issued an opinion in which it pointed out that "the Council of Ministers only has specific powers in the case of the Throne becoming vacant, or of a conflict with the Audit Office, or when an Auditor withholds approval of appropriations for expenditure. Apart from these cases, the Council of Ministers merely makes a recommendation for the benefit of the Head of State." Some authors have taken this ruling at the letter and have considered that an omission to discuss a matter in the Cabinet, where this procedure has not been specifically demanded by the Legislative, cannot invalidate the final decision.

The answer to this problem must however be rather more ambiguous, and in the event of a conflict, it is up to the Council of State to examine whether the requisite discussion is or is not a matter of substantial form, the omission of which may lead to the invalidation of the final decision. In each individual case, the Council of State will bear in mind the intention of the authors who have imposed a Cabinet discussion, particularly by examining whether such a discussion was not insisted upon precisely in order to provide an additional safeguard for the rights of all citizens. In connection with the legal scope of Cabinet discussions, it is necessary to mention a practice which grew up after the 1914 war, gradually became general, and has now become an established custom. At the end of each Cabinet meeting, a government spokesman—usually the Prime Minister—normally makes a statement to the news media (press, radio and television). In that statement, he informs reporters of what decisions have been adopted by the Cabinet on the most important problems that have been discussed. This communiqué is aimed at informing the nation of the solutions agreed on, but while it undoubtedly illustrates the democratic nature of Belgian politics, the procedure still remains a questionable one from the standpoint of the constitutional ruling, since it might mistakenly lead citizens to think that genuine and legally binding decisions have been made whereas, as we have seen, the question is merely one of a consensus of opinion reached within the Government—a consensus which still has to receive the royal sanction before it becomes a definite decision.

In conclusion, we may infer from the foregoing that the Council of Ministers has come to occupy a preponderant place in Belgian political activities, and by acknowledging its existence in two places (Article 86-B and Article 91-B), the Constitution has merely sanctioned a custom that dates back to the first days of independence.

The reasons for the increasingly important part played by the Council of Ministers have been underlined. On the one hand, there is the need to ensure a proper degree of cohesion on the political plane between members of coalition governments. On the other hand, there is the need for centralization on the administrative plane, seeing that the various Government departments form a political entity and that the decisions made by one Minister may not run counter to the work of another Ministry nor have any profound repercussions on the way in which it functions.

The growing burden of State business has had the effect of vastly multiplying the number of Cabinet meetings, in such a way that the institution sometimes appears to be growing more and more unwieldy and, as has already been pointed out, has even made it necessary to institute a post of Cabinet Secretary quite apart from the other members of the Cabinet. Attempts have been made to render the Cabinet less cumbersome. These will be reviewed farther on, but let us now indicate that on 4 October 1961, a Royal Decree stipulated that in cases where a Cabinet discussion is required by a Royal Decree the modification of which does not depend on the law alone, it may be replaced by a discussion in the General Policy Committee or in the Ministerial Committee for Economic and Social Coordination. This represented an initial attempt to lighten the burden of work incumbent on the Cabinet. As we shall see, it was followed by a number of other attempts, but the fact remains that no ideal solution has yet been found and that it all depends essentially on the circumstances prevailing at the time.

Linguistic equality in the Cabinet

The main effect of Article 86-B has been to impose the condition of linguistic equality in the Cabinet.

Here again, the Constitution has done no more than sanction one of the customs arising out of the complex nature of national affairs.

The existence of numerous special but powerful interests, the very clearly defined character of the various regions and particularly the linguistic regions, the individualistic mentality of the Belgian people—all these factors have played an increasingly important part in the composition of governments.

Even before the Constitution came into play, successive governments had to contend with numerous proportional factors so as to be truly representative of all the regions in the country. There is, for instance, the geographical proportioning so that the main provinces and cities are represented in the Cabinet.

Then there is the political proportioning, meaning the balance to be struck in allocating Cabinet posts between those parties forming the parliamentary majority, since Belgian governments are usually coalition ones.

Sometimes there is even the need to strike a balance between different trends within the same political party when the latter has a conservative wing and a rather more progressive wing.

There must also be a proportional number of Ministers from both Houses of Parliament in order that the Cabinet shall not be composed solely of members of the Lower House or of Senators.

Finally, and above all, there is the linguistic proportioning in order that each language region in the country shall be equitably represented in the Cabinet.

The need to ensure that all these balances are struck so that the Government shall be fully representative of the majority in Parliament which itself is representative of the will of the electorate, has brought about a steadily growing number of Ministers to the point where, in 1973, a government was formed consisting of 22 Ministers and 14 Secretaries of State.

Originally, custom dictated chiefly the linguistic distribution of Ministers into equal numbers of French-speaking Ministers and Dutch-speaking ones. The equality thus achieved is an expression of national solidarity as it must exist between the two great cultural communities. At the same time, it provides a guarantee that the interests of the minority formed by the French-speaking region will be safeguarded. The law had already imposed such parity arrangements in the appointment of top-ranking officials; the Constitution has merely extended this concept to include the Ministers themselves.

Such equality is, moreover, essential because the Council of Ministers is called upon to arbitrate in conflicts which arise between the linguistic groups in Parliament and in the Urban Area Council of Brussels-Capital (cfr. Articles 38-B and 108-C).

The Commission for Institutional Reform had underlined that the traditional balance struck between the number of French-speaking Ministers and Dutch-speaking Ministers must be maintained. It added that this custom, dictated by political wisdom, should not be the subject of a constitutional clause. The Constituent Assembly, however, felt it necessary to go further, and it therefore imposed linguistic equality within the Cabinet.

Article 86-B mentions the language in which the Ministers express themselves. It does not go into details, nor does it require proof of that means of expression.

The question might become an important one if the Government were to include any extra-Parliamentary Ministers. This matter has already been put forward in connection with Article 86. As is known, some governments have included Technical Ministers in charge of special responsibilities such as finance, national defence, social problems, etc.

However, these are exceptions to the rule, for the parliamentary system does not welcome persons chosen from outside the political parties forming the majority.

An exception to this equality ruling has been made in respect of the Prime Minister, and this is justified on several counts:

1) The lofty function of Prime Minister makes it desirable that he should not be regarded merely as a representative of one of the cultural communities, but that he should truly be the Prime Minister of the entire nation. Absolute equality in the Cabinet is not, however, precluded, as is indicated by the use of the word "possible", but had this prerequisite been imposed, the result would have been that the Government would invariably have had to consist of an even number of Ministers.

2) A practice had already grown up whereby the Head of the Government was left out of any calculations designed to achieve linguistic equality within the Cabinet.

As it is worded, Article 86-B is therefore primarily a protective measure adopted for the benefit of the French-speaking population, seeing that Dutch-speaking members are, numerically speaking, in the majority in both Houses of Parliament.

In connection with Article 86-B, it should also be emphasized that this Constitutional ruling only imposes linguistic equality as between French-speaking and Dutch-speaking Ministers, without reckoning with any members of the Government who may come from the German-speaking region. A citizen belonging to the German cultural community might therefore become Prime Minister or a Secretary of State (since linguistic equality is not required for the latter in terms of Article 91-B); he might also become a full Minister though he would not count when the time came to establish the requisite linguistic equality.

The restricted Ministerial Committees

We have referred on several occasions to the problems surrounding the structure of the Government, particularly as a result of the growing burden of business incumbent on the Cabinet, a burden which is itself caused by the increasing complexity of the tasks the Government is called upon to tackle, coupled with the frequency with which coalition governments are formed. We mentioned notably an attempt made in

1961 to relieve the Cabinet by entrusting some of its prerogatives either to the General Policy Commission or to the Ministerial Committee for Economic and Social Coordination.

Such attempts have been made in increasing numbers in recent years, and this is one of the reasons, as we shall see later on, which led to the appointment of Secretaries of State (cf. Article 91-B).

Now, the complexity of affairs goes hand in hand with a more technical approach to them, so that only Ministers who are conversant with the technical aspects are able to discuss them.

It was for this reason as much as to improve the way in which such problems were dealt with that the Government has come to resort ever more frequently to Ministerial Committees or Commissions comprising a small number of Ministers only.

Occasional attempts have been made to classify these Committees or Commissions in order of seniority, i.e. according to the length of time they have existed. In fact, such Committees are constantly changing according to the problems which arise, the various tendencies of the parties in office, and the circumstances prevailing at the time.

It is true that certain Committees or Commissions have lasted a very short time because they were set up solely for the purpose of dealing with a specific problem. Such, for instance, was the case of the Ministerial Committee in charge of ethical problems set up in 1973 to examine the problem created by an abrogation or possible attenuation of the penal sanctions imposed in cases of abortion. The same is also true of the restricted Ministerial Committees set up within the last ten years or so for discussions with the major trade unions banded into a Common Front, on the charting of social programmes or collective agreements for the benefit of State employees.

Even those Ministerial Committees that are able to claim many years of uninterrupted existence have often seen changes in their objectives, and sometimes their titles have been altered as well.

It should moreover be pointed out that, generally speaking, the essential task of these Ministerial Committees is to clear away the undergrowth surrounding technical problems before the question is submitted in clear, accurately defined terms for the approval of the Cabinet.

In most cases, the Committees or Commissions set up to look into a specific problem have no legal status, and their operating methods, together with their composition, are decided upon as the circumstances dictate.

Apart from these essentially temporary committees there are, however, other restricted ministerial committees the competence of which has been defined by royal decree.

Up till the last few years, the royal decrees which instituted them were fairly extensive ones, with clauses which decided such questions as their chairmanship, number of members and how these were to be chosen, their competence and prerogatives, their purpose and functioning, etc.

By a royal decree of 1 March 1972, however, there was a return to a more simplified wording in order to gain in flexibility what might be lost in legal precision.

In this way, the royal decree of 1 March 1972 sanctioned the existence of six ministerial committees and provided for the continuance of a seventh. The text merely summarised the competence of each, and left it to the Prime Minister to settle questions of chairmanship, secretariat and operating methods.

Under pressure of circumstances, and particularly from the standpoint of the practical implementation, even in successive stages, of Article 107-D of the Constitution dealing with regionalisation, the Government which took office on 25 April 1974 made a fundamental distinction between these ministerial committees by confirming the nationwide competence vested in some of them. In reality, of course, they merely represent a continuation of previously established ministerial committees.

The royal decree of 30 May 1974 which replaced that of 1 March 1972 provided for the organisation of ministerial committees competent to handle national matters.

It makes two important modifications to the situation as it previously existed :

1) Firstly, it defines with precision the role of these committees by stipulating that they do not have any inherent, autonomous authority but that they are chiefly called upon to fulfil a technical function, so that they may not, in their work, in any way replace the official authority of the Government. Thus, Article 1 of the said royal decree restates that the ministerial committees "prepare the groundwork for debates in the Cabinet, without prejudice to the powers of advisement or agreement that may be vested in them by legal or statutory rulings".

2) Another important modification has been carried out by a reallocation and regrouping of competence and the abolition of two previously existing ministerial committees: that dealing with Foreign Policy, and that of Public Investment.

In this way, the royal decree of 30 May 1974 leaves only five ministerial committees with nationwide competence in existence.

The time has now come to take a closer look at the respective competence vested in each of these five committees.

1) The first of them is the *Ministerial Committee for Economic and Social Coordination.*

According to the royal decree of 1 March 1972, the task of this committee was to frame the technical basis of the Government's economic, financial and social policy and to coordinate its implementation.

In terms of the new royal decree of 30 May 1974, this Committee has been vested with threefold competence since, apart from the prerogatives already allocated specifically to it, it has now inherited as well a part of those formerly vested in the Ministerial Committee for Foreign Policy and a part of those vested in the Ministerial Committee for Investment.

Article 3 of the Royal Decree of 30 May 1974 defines the new prerogatives and duties vested in the Ministerial Committee for Economic and Social Coordination as follows :

This Committee "with due regard to the requirements of proper coordination, rules on the economic, financial and social aspects of Government policy, including that relating to Europe and to foreign countries in general.

"It charts the programmes of public investments, works out the timetable thereof, and decides on the methods of implementation."

a) This Committee has already had a fairly lengthy existence since it dates back to a royal decree of 26 August 1938 which set up the first "Ministerial Committee for Economic Coordination" within the Cabinet. The purpose of this Committee was to achieve, in the economic sphere, a degree of systemised coordination that should be as complete as possible not only at Ministerial level, but on the administrative plane as well. Several reorganisations made since that time, especially just after World War II by means of a Regent's Decree dated 1 May 1947, have had the effect of clarifying and reinforcing the tasks of this committee.

Furthermore, the first Ministerial Committee set up to deal with social matters was instituted by a royal decree dated 7 January 1953 which itself was modified by another royal decree dated 29 May 1956. This was the "Interministerial Committee for Family Affairs" whose task was to coordinate family policies between the various Ministries according to their respective spheres. This Committee, which was chaired by the

Prime Minister and which included the Ministers of Finance, Public Health and Family Affairs, Labour and Social Security, and two other Cabinet Ministers appointed by the Prime Minister, was competent to make recommendations on :

— draft bills or decrees pertaining to family allowances when these contained provisions likely to have a moral or material incidence on families;

— occasions when the Prime Minister considered that a draft bill or decree submitted for Cabinet discussions contained provisions likely to have a moral or material incidence on families;

— occasions when Ministers specifically requested it to do so because they considered it necessary to refer back to the Committee.

Consequently, this Interministerial Committee was first and foremost an advisory body.

It was by means of a royal decree dated 2 June 1961 that a Ministerial Committee was set up for the first time to combine the economic and social fields.

This was the Ministerial Committee for Economic and Social Coordination. Five specialised sub-committees were placed under its authority :

— the Committee for Finance and the Budget;

— the Committee for Economic Expansion and Regional Policy;

— the Committee for Public Investment and Transportation;

— the Committee for Social and Family Policy, which replaced the Interministerial Committee for Family Matters which has just been reviewed above;

— and finally, the Committee for External Economic and Social Policy.

Subsequently, the new system was maintained even though the names and responsibilities of the five sub-committees were sometimes altered and adapted to a certain extent.

The end result was therefore a pyramid structure, the apex of which was the Cabinet, the middle layer being the Ministerial Committee for Economic and Social Coordination, and the base being the five sub-committees. This apparently quite logical structure was, however, ultimately revealed as being impractical, for it was difficult to avoid a certain overlapping of competence.

Which is why a more flexible and pragmatic organisation was instituted in 1966. This made it possible, as and when the need arose, to set up *de facto* sub-committees whose competence could thus be more easily tailored to fit the special problems each was called upon to deal with. While it was still the most important working tool in the process of preparing for Cabinet debates, the Ministerial Committee for Economic and Social Coordination thus reverted to the status of just another ministerial committee equal and parallel to the others.

We pointed out earlier on that, without losing any of its former prerogatives, the Ministerial Committee for Economic and Social Coordination had in fact benefited from the reallocation and regrouping of responsibilities provided for by the royal decree of 30 May 1974.

b) Indeed, the Ministerial Committee for Economic and Social Coordination took over the responsibilities of the Ministerial Committee for External Policy, which itself was merely an offshoot of one ot the five sub-committees which were actually answerable to the first-mentioned Committee.

This Ministerial Committee for External Policy, first known as the Committee for External Economic and Social Policy, was specially entrusted with the international aspects of Belgium's economic and social policies. The Committee had, in particular, to oversee the implementation of a foreign trade development policy and was appointed to frame the instructions intended for Belgian representatives delegated to the international organisations and to conferences dealing with economic, financial or social affairs.

A Ministerial Committee for Co-operation in Development was first set up by royal decree dated 15 January 1962. Its competence was defined as follows : "The Committee charts the nation's general policy in the sphere of co-operation in development and oversees its implementation; to this end, it coordinates the activities of the Government departments concerned. It examines draft bills and decrees pertaining to general policies in the sphere of co-operation in the development of the emergent countries. It works with the Committee for Finance and the Budget in examining budget proposals pertaining to co-operation in development." These responsibilities were progressively taken over in 1965 by the Committee for External Economic and Social Policy, and in 1966 by the Ministerial Committee for Economic and Social Coordination.

However, as the economic construction of Europe proceeded apace, as Belgian foreign trade expanded and co-operation in development gained steadily in scope in a world that was becoming interdependent and interrelated, it appeared increasingly important to pay special attention to all international affairs, the effect of which on the economy and social life of the nation is growing with each day that passes. That was why the Ministerial Committee for External Policy was organically instituted in 1967.

In the royal decree dated 1 March 1972, it is laid down that the Ministerial Committee for External Policy is entrusted with the task of blue-printing the technical basis of Government policy on all matters in which the international aspect predominates. Furthermore, it wields a certain degree of authority regarding the organisation of co-operation with the developing countries.

These are the responsibilities which have just been transferred to the Ministerial Committee for Economic and Social Coordination so as to avoid any duplication or lacunae in the implementation of Government policies.

c) The Ministerial Committee for Economic and Social Coordination has, finally, also inherited a wide measure of the responsibilities formerly vested in the Ministerial Committee for Investment, which has now been wound up.

Indeed, owing to the vast importance gained by investment policies, the royal decree of 1 March 1972 had withdrawn from the competence of the Ministerial Committee for the Budget those questions pertaining to State investments, tenders and purchases. According to the royal decree of 1 March 1972, the Ministerial Committee for Investment was given the task of charting these investment programmes, working out their time schedules and framing their conditions of implementation, while it was at the same time competent to make statutory recommendations regarding State contracts or those entered into on behalf of the State.

The first of these tasks was entrusted to the Ministerial Committee for Economic and Social Coordination, while the others were transferred back to the Ministerial Committee for the Budget as we shall see farther on.

At the present time the Ministerial Committee for Economic and Social Coordination is headed, like the four others, by the Prime Minister. It comprises the Ministers of National Defence, Finance, Foreign Affairs and Co-operation in Development, Public Health and Family Affairs, Social Security, Foreign Trade, Employment and Labour, Communications, the Middle Classes, Public Works, and Economic Affairs, as well as the Ministers and the Secretary of State for Regional Economy and Territorial Development and for Housing, and the Secretary of State for the Environment. Those are the permanent members, who may be joined by certain other Ministers or Secretaries of State whenever certain matters particularly affecting the latter come under examination.

2) The *Ministerial Committee for the Budget* appeared for the first time in 1926 when it was styled the "Treasury Committee". At that time, its task was to work out the measures necessary for the public treasury and to control State expenditure. This Committee soon acquired a very real authority, for it had been vested with powers of decision in some particularly important fields such as the establishment of budgets, State contracts for supplies and public works, subsidies and personnel expenditures. It was seconded from 1930 on by the Committee for the Budget, which consisted of civil servants and was entrusted with the prior study of all matters submitted for its appraisal.

The Treasury Committee was abolished in 1936 and its duties transferred to the Committee for the Budget. The latter, which was now headed by the Prime Minister, saw itself given a paramount role in the preparation of the budget and in overseeing its implementation.

Its title has been altered several times as the years went by. Thus, in 1961 it was known as the Ministerial Committee for Finance and the Budget; from 1965 to 1972 as the Ministerial Committee for Budget Management and the Civil Service; until finally, by the royal decree of 1 March 1972, it regained its original title of Ministerial Committee for the Budget.

In terms of the royal decree of 30 May 1974, the Ministerial Committee for the Budget "rules on the budgetary and administrative aspects of Government policy".

Furthermore, it exercises the prerogatives formerly vested in the committee for Finance and the Budget by the royal decree of 5 October 1961 providing for the organisation of administrative and budget controls.

Finally, it has regained part of the responsibilities which had been withdrawn from it and entrusted to the Ministerial Committe for Investment, for once again it has been made competent to give statutory recommendations on all matters connected with State tenders and contracts.

This extremely important committee now comprises, apart from the Prime Minister who chairs it, the Ministers of National Defence, Finance, Public Health and Family Affairs, Employment and Labour, Communications, the Middle Classes, National Education (for the French-speaking region of the country), and Public Works, together with the Secretaries of State for the Civil Service, the Budget and Scientific Policy, Territorial Development and Housing, and finally the Secretary of State attached to the Minister of Economic Affairs.

3) The *Ministerial Committee for Institutional Reform* has, so to speak, taken over from the Ministerial Committee for Community

Relations set up in 1968, which in 1972 became the Ministerial Committee for Institutional Problems.

Political life in Belgium has been entirely dominated, for a number of years now, by linguistic and community preoccupations. It was therefore essential that this moral encumbrance be removed at the earliest possible date and that acceptable solutions should be found for the thorny problems dividing the Belgian people so that the nation could settle down and join forces once again.

That is why the Government, in 1968, gave priority in its programme to seeking for solutions that could be applied speedily and all-embracingly to the community quarrel.

A Ministerial Committee for Coordinating Institutional Reforms had already functioned for a few months in 1960-1961. It had been set up by a royal decree dated 2 January 1961 with the task of framing general directives aimed at the reform of the State's institutions, of examining draft bills and organic or statutory decrees drawn up for the purpose of achieving that reform, and of searching for solutions to institutional problems involving the centralised and decentralised institutions of the State and other public authorities. However, this Committee did not survive the Government of the day.

In terms of the royal decree of 1 March 1972, the Ministerial Committee for Institutional Problems, which had replaced its predecessor in charge of community relations, was given the task of examining all measures aimed at the implementation and the application of the revised Constitution and corresponding institutional renovations.

The Ministerial Committee for Institutional Reform was virtually a carbon copy of the foregoing, though it operated under another name, for in terms of the royal decree of 30 May 1974 it "rules on all measures aimed at the implementation and the application of the revised Constitution and corresponding institutional renovations".

Apart from the Prime Minister who heads it, the following are members of the Ministerial Committee for Institutional Reform : the Ministers for Brussels Affairs, Finance, Public Health and Family Affairs, Justice, Foreign Trade, the Interior, Employment and Labour and Walloon Affairs, Communications, the Middle Classes, Dutch Culture and Flemish Affairs, plus the two Ministers specially entrusted with Institutional Reform.

4) The *Ministerial Committee for the Environment* first saw the light as a result of the royal decree of 1 March 1972. Its creation was due to the new problems which have arisen, particularly throughout the

Western World, with regard to the protection of natural beauty-spots, historic monuments and the campaign against pollution.

The decree of 1 March 1972 defined its responsibilities as follows : to frame general regulations designed to combat pollution; to propose corresponding public investment programmes and the conditions governing State intervention where necessary; and to coordinate the implementation of the measures decided upon.

The royal decree of 30 May 1974 confirmed the existence of this Committee while simplifying the definition of its responsibilities. It provides in fact that "the Ministerial Committee for the Environment rules on all measures bound up with the law prohibiting pollution of the natural environment and the valorisation of the latter".

This Committee comprises, once again apart from the Prime Minister who heads it: the Ministers of Finance, Public Health and Family Affairs, the Interior, Employment and Labour, Agriculture and Public Works, together with the Minister and the Secretary of State for Regional Economy, Territorial Development and Housing, and the Secretary of State attached to the Minister of Economic Affairs to deal specifically with environment problems, and finally, of course, the Secretary of State for the Environment.

Furthermore, during its meeting of 31 May 1974, the Cabinet decided to set up an Interministerial Commission for the Environment comprising a delegate from practically every Government department and Secretariat of State, to be headed by the Secretary of State for the Environment, the secretaryship being assumed by personnel from the Office of the Prime Minister.

The task of this new Commission is to promote work at the level of the various personal staffs of the Ministers concerned as well as within the public administrations involved in problems created by the Environment and to ensure proper coordination between existing or approved organisations in this sphere. To some extent, this Interministerial Commission is a preferential working tool for the Secretary of State for the Environment since, through the channel it provides, he can establish direct contact with all the Ministers affected in any way by the problem. And it is easy to guess that all the Cabinet Ministers without exception are involved in one way or another in the essential question of protecting the environment.

5) Finally, it is necessary to mention the *Ministerial Committee for Scientific Policy.*

Its origins must be sought in a royal decree dated 17 January 1957 which set up, under the presidency of King Leopold, a "National Commission for the Study of Problems facing Belgium and the Overseas Territories as a result of scientific progress and their economic and social repercussions". Two years later, on 12 January 1959, King Leopold handed the then Prime Minister the final report drawn up by the Commission. This document contained 19 recommendations to the Government, particularly with regard to the organisation of scientific research in Belgium and the need for a national research policy, scientific policies in the Congo and Ruanda-Urundi; higher education; the Academies; water problems; mineral deposits; natural oil and gas; the exploitation of offshore resources; and increased forestry production.

In one of these recommendations (the fourteenth, pertaining to the organisation of scientific research in Belgium and to the need for a national research policy), the Commission proposed in particular "the setting-up of a Ministerial Committee for the Coordination of Scientific Research which, headed by the Prime Minister, would comprise those Ministers of Government departments most closely involved in scientific research and higher education, plus the Minister of Finance, and which would be the paramount organ of Government policy in this sphere."

This "Ministerial Committee for Scientific Policy" was set up by royal decree dated 16 September 1959 covering the organisation of scientific policy.

The Ministerial Committee for Scientific Policy frames and implements the Nation's scientific policies and, to this end, it coordinates the work of all the Government departments concerned. For the benefit of the Cabinet, it charts the broad outlines of the budget programme as far as scientific policies are concerned. As circumstances dictate, the Cabinet submits for the appraisal of the Committee those draft bills or decrees affecting the Nation's scientific policies.

The Ministerial Committee for Scientific Policy which, like the other ministerial committees, is headed by the Prime Minister, comprises the Ministers of Finance, Public Health and Family Affairs, Agriculture, French Culture, National Education for both linguistic regions, Public Works and Economic Affairs, together with the Secretary of State for the Budget and for Scientific Policy, and the Secretary of State for Regional Economy in the French-speaking region.

*
* *

We have already mentioned that the royal decree of 1 March 1972 had considerably simplified the procedure originally laid down in specific royal decrees issued in respect of each of the Committees.

In terms of the royal decree of 1 March 1972, duly confirmed by that of 30 May 1974, it is the Prime Minister who decides upon the composition of each of the Committees and who appoints its chairman.

In fact, we have seen that up to now the Prime Minister has reserved to himself the chairmanship of all five committees.

It is the Prime Minister, too, who convenes each Committee and who draws up its agenda.

Again, he organises the secretaryship of the committees. In actual fact, the secretariat is generally handled by one of the Prime Minister's Principal Private Secretaries in accordance with their competence.

Those members of the Government who are not appointed to sit on a committee are invited to attend any meetings during which matters falling within their competence are to be examined.

The decisions made in committee are notified to the Minister or the Secretary of State concerned.

The royal decree of 1 March 1972 also provided that the Prime Minister should oversee the implementation of all decisions reached by the committees, and that the agenda and minutes of these meetings should be circulated to all members of the Government. These provisions have however vanished from the latest royal decree of 30 May 1974, so that the Prime Minister may, from now on, dispense with the necessity to communicate all the agendas and minutes of the meetings to all members of the Government, and distribute them solely to those Ministers or Secretaries of State directly concerned.

The minutes are, however, invariably addressed to the Head of the State, the secretaries of the committees, certain officials directly concerned by the decisions made and who are specifically designated by their Ministers (particularly the Budget Administration).

Furthermore, two copies are destined for the State Archives, and the remaining copy is for clipping so that excerpts may be appended to the files of the matters dealt with.

Proper coordination in the work of the various Ministerial Committees is ensured by the Principal Private Secretaries of the Prime Minister who are assisted, depending on the problems handled, by Chancellery departments or the Economic Survey and Coordination Office.

Apart from the above-mentioned Ministerial Committees which are competent on a nationwide scale though each is restricted to its own particular sphere, some Governments have also instituted what were tantamount to genuine Inner Cabinets. These generally comprised Ministers with the widest experience and personal influence. In most cases they were set up so as to entrust a small team, but a strong one from both the technical and the political standpoint, with preparing the groundwork for the Cabinet by ruling on the general direction to be imparted to overall policy as well as on the budget options entailed. These Inner Cabinets were thus naturally brought to examine mainly the most important as well as the most delicate problems owing to their possible political repercussions and their effect on public opinion. Thus, in 1961 there appeared an Inner Cabinet on General Policy; in 1965 a Committee for Political Coordination; and in 1966, an Inner Cabinet not otherwise designated.

A royal decree of 29 October 1973 pursued the same line by setting up, within the Cabinet, a Committee for General Policy. This Committee was entrusted with framing the main directives for Government policies, and in cases where these involved fundamental options, with determining what orientation should be imparted thereto.

The decree of 30 May 1974 has in this respect reverted to the former style of Inner Cabinet on General Policy and has included it among the Ministerial Committees wielding nationwide competence.

According to this decree, "the Inner Cabinet on General Policy rules on the broad orientations and the fundamental options of Government policy, including international policies and those relating to co-operation in development". At a first glance, this formula is very close to that enunciated in the royal decree of 29 October 1973 quoted above.

On taking a closer look, however, we find that a vast change has been made to the competence vested in the Inner Cabinet, because international policies and co-operation in development policies are specifically mentioned as being part and parcel of general Government policy. This change has occurred mainly as a result of the disappearance of the Ministerial Committee for External Policy whose responsibilities have thus been reallocated between the Inner Cabinet on General Policy for matters of a general nature, and the Ministerial Committee for Economic and Social Coordination where economic and social questions are concerned.

According to a notification from the Prime Minister dated 7 June 1974 prior to the enlargement of the Government which took place on 11 June following, the Inner Cabinet on General Policy comprises the following members : the Prime Minister himself as chairman, plus the Ministers of National Defence, Finance, Public Health and Family Affairs, Employment and Labour, and Public Works.

Furthermore, the Inner Cabinet on General Policy has taken over the responsibilities formerly entrusted in 1961 to the similarly-named body, with reference to preparations for Cabinet debates.

As can be seen, the phenomenon consisting of restricted Ministerial Committees has taken various forms depending on the composition of the Government in office. Such composition has indeed influenced the appointment of Ministers designated to sit on the various committees for, apart from those Ministers who are competent to do so because of the special responsibilities vested in those committees, the latter have often been set up so as to strike a political and linguistic balance. As an example of this, the Committee for General Policy instituted in 1973 comprised four Social-Christian Ministers, three Socialist Ministers and two Liberal Ministers who, from the linguistic angle, could be broken down into five French-speaking and four Dutch-speaking Ministers.

Similarly, the present Inner Cabinet on General Policy comprises four Social-Christian Ministers and two Liberal Ministers who, on the linguistic plane, are divided equally into three French-speaking and three Dutch-speaking Ministers.

In conclusion, we perceive from this brief survey that the Ministerial Committees have all been created according to the requirements of the moment where the coordination of Government action was concerned in such essential spheres as: financial and budget policy, the proper functioning of the Government administration, economic policy, social policy, scientific policy, foreign policy including co-operation with the developing countries, and Belgium's linguistic and regional problems. It can also be seen from the permutations and combinations taking place in these so-called permanent committees that the problems surrounding Government structural organisation have not yet been given a stable solution. It is even doubtful whether any such solution will ever be possible since the degree of acuteness with which those problems arise is essentially variable.

The most noteworthy phenomenon which has come to light since the present Government took office on 25 April 1974 consists of a dual reinforcement and a dual concentration of authority.

Firstly, reinforcement in the person of the Prime Minister himself, since it is he who, in practice, assumes the leadership of all the Ministerial Committees vested with nationwide competence.

Then, reinforcement of the powers vested in certain Committees especially as a result of the disappearance of the Ministerial Committee for External Policy and the Ministerial Committee for Public Investment.

Thus, it is now up to the Inner Cabinet on General Policy to rule on the great options facing Belgium in the field of international policy, and particularly the country's relations with the European Communities. It is hardly necessary to emphasize the importance of this new orientation when one remembers that the head offices of those communities are all located in Belgium.

It should also be stressed that the intervention of these Committees is sometimes mandatory in cases where this is laid down either by the law or by a royal decree, but such an obligation is more to be construed in the light of Government discipline rather than as an actual formality the omission of which would vitiate the decision made or sanctioned by royal decree.

*
* *

The Ministers and their Ministeries

A Minister is usually the head of an important department of the General Administration of the Kingdom which is charged with assisting him in performing his ministerial task. These important departments, usually known as Ministries or, less accurately, as Ministerial Departments, have grown in number as time went by. Belgium has not escaped the great currents of the twentieth century which have led the political systems of the Western European countries towards an ever more socialised brand of democracy. The number and the titles of Government ministries reflect this trend. Apart from those Ministries whose main task is to administer the higher interests of the State, others have come to join them in course of time for the special purpose of meeting social or economic needs of a general nature or which are specific to certain classes of the population. As the number and the names of Ministries have not been definitively fixed by the Legislator, changes have occurred very frequently and they are often a clear illustration of the special preoccupations of each successive Government. That explains why interministerial coordination, which has devolved through the process of evolution on the Cabinet and on the Prime Minister himself, has now become a matter of constant and acute concern.

It was because of the relationship normally established between Ministers and their Ministries that we have witnessed the arrival of new Government departments on the political scene.

In 1831 there were only five Ministries in charge of administering the supreme interests of the State: War, Finance, Foreign Affairs, the Interior, and Justice.

As a result of new necessities and the appearance of Ministers entrusted with the task of meeting them, new Ministries were set up, usually by detaching one of the essential branches of an existing department.

Thus, from the main trunk, we have witnessed the separation of a Ministry of Public Works which, since 1837, included a special Railway Administration; a Ministry of Agriculture, a Ministry of Industry, a Ministry of Education and Schooling, etc.

Some of these new Ministries were themselves split up to make other ones, such as for instance the Ministry of Communications which arose out of the Railway Administration and the Posts, Telegraphs and Telephones Department.

The question here, however, was one of administrative departments called upon to deal with permanent needs, so that they are still with us today.

In other cases, requirements that were essentially temporary in character gave rise to the creation of other Ministries, such as for example the Ministry of Food Supplies and the Ministry of Reconstruction. Those temporary Ministries only had a brief span of existence, though this factor raised some serious problems when they were done away with, particularly in connection with the resettlement of their staff.

The increase in the number of Ministries has often been criticized, and in particular the Commission for Institutional Reform underlined at the time that the number of Ministers should be restricted, especially through the regrouping of government departments and the creation of Secretaries of State. The work of regrouping them is however very difficult of accomplishment, for while it would theoretically lead to greater coordination, in practice it would make the task of the coordinating Minister more complicated, to the point where he might have to reconcile divergent interests all by himself. Furthermore, the administrative apparatus might become too heavy to be directed by a single man, even if he were to be assisted by Secretaries of State. It should be pointed out that, apart from his department, a Minister may also rely on the help of a private departmental staff that is political in character. This office consists firstly of his personal secretariat and then of a certain number of assistants, backed by an executive staff and entrusted with the task of directly aiding the Minister in the performance of the duties assigned to him.

On the basis of present regulations, the private departmental staffs of Ministers may not comprise more than seven members: one Principal Private Secretary, one Private Secretary, three advisors or special executives, one attaché or secretary to the departmental staff, and one personal attaché or secretary. Derogations of this fixed number may however be granted by the Prime Minister, eventually after consulting the Deputy Prime Ministers. In actual fact, the departmental staffs of Ministers are often in excess of the number laid down by the regulations. The reasons for such increases in numbers are many and varied: the growing burden of affairs incumbent on the Minister who has to deal not only with the management of his Ministry but also with the obligations imposed by parliamentary work at public sittings and in committee, the numerous meetings of the Cabinet and the restricted ministerial committees, the contacts he must necessarily make with the professional organizations and in particular with the trade unions set up for State employees. To all these must be added his political obligations to the party he represents, to his electorate, and so on. Finally, a word must be said about the more or less intentional slowness displayed in some cases by the administration in carrying out the Minister's intentions and implementing the programme he has assigned.

Based on examples in other countries, the existence of Ministers' departmental staffs has often been criticized, or at the very least the number of people employed in them. But the above-mentioned reasons— which are by no means exhaustive—make it essential for Ministers to be able to rely on their personal staff, for without such direct assistance from people who are supposed to share his political ideals, no Minister could acquit himself properly of all the varied obligations incumbent on him.

Whatever the case may be, a new trend is coming rapidly to the fore, especially with the appearance of the Secretaries of State. Indeed, in recent Governments, there has no longer been that sustained relationship between Ministers and their Ministries, so that the appearance of Ministers entrusted with important but inevitably temporary interests has no longer automatically given rise to the creation of new departments. This break in the parallel bond between Ministers and their Ministries has moreover caused some concern in Parliament, but in reply to a parliamentary question on 23 November 1973, the Prime Minister said unequivocally that "care must be taken to avoid all confusion between the ministerial function, which implies responsibilities in a clearly defined and restricted sphere, and the partitioning into Ministries of services placed at the disposal of members of the Government in order to assist them in the accomplishment of their mission". The Prime Minister went on to stress, moreover, that "a degree of coordination in the policy to be implemented and a concerted approach to the decisions which are to be made must take place between those members of the Government whose provinces either dovetail or overlap" and that such coordination and concerted approaches can be settled by means of an internal protocol signed by the Ministers concerned. This question was raised notably in regard to the "regional" Ministers, i.e. those Ministers in charge of Walloon, Flemish and Brussels Affairs. Indeed, this was a case where certain Ministers, by virtue of their prerogatives, might appear as Superministers in the eyes of some of their colleagues, since their authority enables them to call upon the co-operation of several Government departments and to involve themselves in matters coming within the province of those Ministries.

It is interesting in this connection to mention another statement made by the Prime Minister in answer to a parliamentary question put to him on 19 February 1973. The Prime Minister stressed that the prerogatives of the regional Ministers had been defined in a document approved by the Cabinet and thereafter made public. The document reads as follows:

"The Ministers for Walloon, Flemish and Brussels Affairs are a prefiguration of a regionalized Belgium.

"They have been given the task of devoting special attention to their own region, to make themselves conversant with the needs, requirements and aims of their inhabitants, and to channel these demands towards the Ministers and the Secretaries of State who are competent to deal with them on the technical plane. As of now, their task is to act as liaison officers between the Government and the individual regions according to the conditions laid down hereunder.

"Within the Government, provision will be made for a separate concerted approach between the Walloon members wielding a regional competence at the initiative of the Minister for Walloon Affairs; and between the Flemish members wielding a regional competence at the initiative of the Minister for Flemish Affairs; this for the purpose of establishing a common line of conduct in the matter of business to be handled from a regional standpoint, until such time as the Executive Committee of the regional councils shall assume this task.

"With regard to competence, the question is therefore specifically one of tasks that can be circumscribed in geographical terms.

"Where Brussels is concerned, the Minister in charge of Brussels Affairs shall establish contacts with those of his colleagues who have special problems relating to or involving Brussels.

"That same Minister shall also be competent to deal with housing, territorial amenities and regional economy in the Brussels area. This relates particularly to general development plans, the regional plan, and individual development plans.

"With regard to the Department of Public Health and the Environment, the titular Minister shall remain responsible for general policy and the management of his department; the Deputy Minister shall deal with those files appertaining to the Walloon region on behalf of the whole Department of Public Health and the Environment.

"As Minister for Walloon Affairs, he is a full Cabinet Minister and it goes without saying that he is not subordinate to any other Minister.

"The regional Ministers have not been instructed to exercise a sort of tutelary authority over other members of the Government, whether Ministers or Secretaries of State. The latter retain their specific competence and freedom of action. The regional Ministers are to encourage regionalization and to initiate ways of organizing the concerted approach which is essential as between colleagues having responsibilities in one and the same region with regard to matters that remain provisionally and temporarily national at the present time, pending their regionalization.

"The two Secretaries of States for Institutional Reform are not considered to be responsible for regionalized matters. They should rather be regarded as representatives of an ideology. In agreement with the Deputy Prime Minister in charge of coordinating institutional problems, they are to frame documents which are then to be submitted for discussion, first in the Ministerial Committee for Institutional Problems, and then in the Cabinet."

It should be underlined that this abandonment of a direct link between Ministers and Ministries can only be commended, for its result has been to permit, firstly, the appearance of Ministers in charge of urgent and important problems without, on the other hand, jeopardizing the stability of the administrative machinery. It is obvious, of course, that a complete reshuffle of departments every time a new Government comes into office could only destroy the efficiency of the administration. This tendency to operate a distinction as between Ministers and Ministries is beginning to show up particularly in the royal decrees defining the competence of the Secretaries of State. Whereas, initially, such royal decrees dealt with a particular Secretary of State and gave him authority in several Ministries depending on the powers vested in him, the present trend is to draw up such royal decrees on the basis of a particular Ministry and to specify the respective powers of the Ministers or Secretaries of State who have to deal with the Ministry concerned. As an example of this, a draft royal decree which, owing to circumstances, never saw the light of day, regulated the exercise of authority in the Ministry of Communications and of Posts, Telegraphs and Telephones by defining the powers vested in the Secretary of State for Ports and Harbours, those of the Secretary of State for Tourism, and those of the Secretary of State for Posts, Telegraphs and Telephones. By means of this new procedure the fundamental structure of the administration is preserved, and is no longer dependent on the political whims of the moment.

The administrative history of Belgium has also, on various occasions, witnessed other categories of Ministers without any corresponding government department. They are known as the "Ministers without Portfolio". They were Ministers under whose authority no administrative department had been placed, and in some cases they were not given any specific authority either. Generally they were vested with a broader degree of competence and their mission was more of a general one.

Their function therefore consisted in helping the Prime Minister in his onerous task of directing the overall policy of the Government, and to be, so to speak, the wise men of the Cabinet. They appeared on the political scene in the early days of independence; the institution was later abandoned.

It rose to the surface again on several occasions, particularly in difficult circumstances such as the period of currency devaluation in 1935.

More recently, it has been rare for Ministers without Portfolio to be appointed because, as we have seen, their work has been carried out more efficiently by the coordinating Ministers, by the Deputy Prime Ministers in charge of general affairs, or by the Secretaries of State placed in charge of special problems.

One last category of Ministers deprived of all powers of decision remains to be dealt with: that of the Ministers of State.

Ministers of State do not enjoy genuine Ministerial prerogatives such as those guaranteed by the Constitution. For instance, they have no authority to countersign any act of the King's; they are not members of the Government and therefore, in principle, they do not attend Cabinet meetings; as such, they do not have access to the Houses of Parliament, in respect of which they assume no political responsibility. Since 1921, nonetheless, the Constitution does refer to their existence since Article 56-B, Section 1, provides that they are eligible as Senators. Ministers of State are appointed—virtually for life—by the King under the countersignature of a Minister in office; being deprived of all political responsibility, they do not take the constitutional oath, and they receive no emoluments.

The following are generally awarded this honorific title: the Presidents (Speakers) of the Senate and the Lower House; former Prime Ministers; former Deputy Prime Ministers; the Presidents of the major political parties; Ministers who have distinguished themselves in the course of a long Government career owing to their important achievements, their wisdom, ponderation, or their eminent services to the nation.

The King takes care to preserve a certain degree of linguistic and political equality in the appointment of Ministers of State.

The honorific title of Minister of State, which dates back moreover to the first years of independence, entitles its holders in particular to the right of entry to the Crown Council, already mentioned earlier on. This Council is presided over by the Head of State and, apart from the Ministers of State, it comprises the Cabinet Ministers in office. Owing to its composition, the Crown Council is by no means representative of public opinion, and accordingly it is devoid of all political influence.

In actual fact, it is only convened on the initiative of the Head of State in quite exceptional circumstances. As a result, it meets very seldom. The Crown Council has met for the most part when there was a serious threat overhanging Belgium: in 1870 during the Franco-Prussian War; in 1914 and in 1940 owing to the outbreak of war; in 1919 for the purpose of ratification of the Treaty of Versailles; in 1950 during the crisis of the monarchy; and in 1960 to deal with the problems of decolonization and the accession of the Congo to independence.

From this lengthy review, it would appear that the major problem has been, for several decades now, that of how the Government should be structured so as to achieve maximum practical efficiency.

To create a dynamic Government able to respond to the essential needs of all citizens is a difficult task indeed.

It would also appear that no Government structure can ever be a permanent one, and that it remains conditioned not only by political and linguistic imperatives but also by the urgent nature of the new problems constantly arising in the life of the nation.

Some elements in that structure, chiefly born out of custom and tradition and in some cases recently sanctioned by the Constitution, may nevertheless be singled out as being of special interest: they are, on the one hand, the functions of Prime Minister and Deputy Prime Minister, and on the other, the Council of Ministers or Cabinet. This hub and axis of the Government structure itself rests to a growing extent on the reinforced stability of the great Ministries which are, so to speak, the very bones of the public administration.

The almost continuous process of adapting the Government structure in keeping with the necessities of the time affords indisputable proof of the vitality and the dynamic political character of the Belgian nation.

ARTICLE 87

"No member of the Royal Family may become a Minister."

This article dates from 1831 and has never been modified.

Its origins are historic ones. Indeed, this was the way in which the Constituent Assembly chose to react against an abuse of power perpetrated during the regime preceding independence, during which the King (of Holland) had appointed two of his sons as Ministers and was thus enabled to flout the Houses of Parliament by getting round the rules of countersignature and ministerial responsibility.

Theoretically, however, this provision is justified in two ways:

1) A member of the Royal Family could hardly assume ministerial responsibility for an act signed by the Head of the State by endorsing such an act with his own countersignature. If so, the King would either lose his constitutional inviolability, or at the very least it would be seriously called in question.

2) A possible heir to the throne must avoid accepting any posts which, of their very nature, are likely to attract criticism to their holders. Indeed, a constitutional monarch must in almost all cases conceive it as his duty to adopt a reserved attitude that will permit him to appear as the symbol of the entire nation in the eyes of all the people. Now, a Minister who assumes full responsibility for his political acts is called upon to take up a definite position in regard to national problems and to opt for one side or another in controversial questions.

Such an attitude would be quite at variance with the essential reserve attributed to royalty—a reserve which is also incumbent on any prince who may be called upon to reign in later years. It should be noted that in terms of article 91-B, this provision also applies to an appointment to the post of Secretary of State.

ARTICLE 88

"Ministers are only entitled to speak and vote in one or other of the Houses when they are a member of it.

"They are authorized to enter either House and must be heard whenever they so request.

"The Houses may request the presence of the Ministers."

This article dates from 1831 and has never been modified.

By means of this ruling, the Constituent Assembly wished to regulate the relationship between Cabinet Ministers and the two Houses of Parliament. This is a fundamental clause in the Constitution because it is at the very basis of the parliamentary system whereby the Houses must be able to exercise an effective control over the acts of the Executive.

Effectual co-operation between the Executive and the Legislative powers is thus organized along the lines of a dialogue between those two powers within the Houses themselves. The system is a perfectly balanced one :

— Ministers may speak to the elected representatives of the Nation at any time;

— conversely, those representatives may demand the presence of the Ministers so as to hear their views on problems for which they are responsible.

This article, which establishes the form of collaboration between the Government and Parliament, gives full political significance to the ministerial responsibility provided for in terms of Articles 63, 64 and 89.

It should be remembered that this article is equally valid in respect of the Cultural Councils in terms of Article 59-B reviewed above.

Finally, it should be pointed out that the presence of members of the government (Prime Minister, Cabinet Ministers and Secretaries of State) is not restricted to the public and plenary sittings of the House of Representatives, the Senate, and the cultural Councils: it is equally effective in the very frequent meetings of the parliamentary committees set up by the various institutions just enumerated.

The practical implementation of Article 88 has also been provided for in the House of Representatives and Senate Rules, and in the law of 21 July 1971 governing the competence and functioning of the Cultural

Councils for the French-language community and the Dutch-language community, as also in the law of 10 July 1973 relating to the German Cultural Community.

1. In so far as the Lower House is concerned, the rules provide for instance that the prescribed time limit on speeches does not apply to Ministers, and recalls in at least two instances that the Ministers have the right to be heard in committee by the House whenever they request it.

2. The Senate Rules in turn provide that seats are reserved for Cabinet Ministers on the floor of the Senate. They also recall that Ministers may attend sittings of committees and may be heard there whenever they so request.

3. The law of 21 July 1971 mentioned above has more or less recopied Article 88 of the Constitution in its own Article 13, adapting it to the two Cultural Councils with which it deals.

4. The law of 10 July 1973 on the Council of the German Cultural Community has done likewise in its Article 48.

ARTICLE 89

"In no case may any verbal or written order from the King exempt a Minister from his responsibility."

This article dates from 1831 and has never been modified.

The ministerial responsibility established by Articles 63 and 64 is one of the questions to which the Constituent Assembly quite rightly attached the greatest importance.

That is why the 1831 Constituent Assembly has given proof of great caution in laying down the terms of Article 89.

Today, the country's institutions are running so smoothly that Article 89 has become redundant. It was moreover merely a practical consequence of Articles 63 and 64.

It should be remembered that in terms of Article 91-B, Article 89 applies equally to Secretaries of State.

ARTICLE 90

"The House of Representatives has the right to impeach Ministers
and to bring them before the Court of Cassation, which alone has
the right to judge them in the presence of both Houses, except as
it shall be laid down by the law with regard to the exercise of
civil proceedings by the injured party and to the crimes and
misdemeanours that the Ministers may have committed outside
the exercise of their official functions.

"A law shall specify the cases of responsibility, the penalties to
be imposed on Ministers, and the procedure to be adopted in their
regard, either on the basis of the impeachment accepted by the
House of Representatives or on the legal action brought by the
injured parties. "

This article dates from 1831 and has never been modified.

Articles 63 and 64 established the political responsibility of Ministers.

The latter are, however, subject to other forms of responsibility, referred
to by Article 90 in particular.

a) *Penal responsibility*

In this regard, the Constitution has provided for a special status for
Ministers so that they may not be prevented from discharging their
specific duties. The protection thus afforded them is primarily concerned
with preserving the independence and dignity of the Executive, and is
therefore dictated by lofty considerations of the public interest. In a
ruling of 13 January 1848, the Court of Cassation deemed that Article 90
of the Constitution should be construed less as a favour for the benefit
of Ministers than as an arrangement of a public nature justified by the
necessities of Government. In this spirit also, the Penal Code contains
special measures designed to repress intrigues and violence towards
Ministers (Cfr. Art. 275 et seq. of the Penal Code).

Several rules are embodied in Article 90:

1. In the first place, the right to impeach Ministers is withheld from
the Public Prosecutor's department and attributed to the House of
Representatives. Indeed, it would be difficult to conceive that a public
prosecutor's department which is subject to the Minister of Justice
should be able to institute proceedings against the latter, or against one
of his colleagues in the Government.

2. Instead of the usual courts of law, the only judicial authority competent in such matters is the Court of Cassation, which is an independent tribunal and the highest jurisdiction in the country. Thus, judgment may not be rendered by the House of Representatives, for it would not be suitable for a Minister to be subjected to the judgment of his political friends or enemies.

3. An Act of Parliament may nevertheless submit to common law the trial of a lawsuit brought by the injured party, as also the crimes and misdemeanours committed by a Minister outside the exercise of his official functions. In actual fact, such a law has never been invoked for it has been considered that even an offence under common law might have political repercussions. Hence it is more desirable to abide by the exceptional provisions that offer better protection for the normal functioning of the country's institutions.

4. A law may also specify the cases of liability, the penalties to be imposed and the proper procedures to be adopted in respect of Ministers, either on the basis of an accusation accepted by the House of Representatives or on that of the legal action brought by the injured parties.

Here again, such a law has never been invoked. With regard to the responsibility and the penalty imposed, Article 134 of the Constitution has provided a provisional solution, which remains the only one now applicable. Article 134 has indeed given the Lower House discretionary powers, which constitute a very important derogation of the general principles bound up with the penal code of laws. Similarly, as penal procedures do not exist where the Court of Cassation is concerned, it would seem that the best procedure is that followed in a court of summary jurisdiction, since there is no trial by jury.

b) *Civil responsibility*

In view of the absence of any law in this sphere, civil lawsuits remain subject to the same rules as those governing penal cases.

c) *Responsibility for private acts*

The same rule applies, since no law has decreed that such matters should be referred back to common law.

*
**

In this way, the Constituent Assembly was much more concerned with the proper and uninterrupted functioning of national institutions and with preventing ill-judged actions from being brought by private persons, for the only result of such lawsuits would be to end by paralysing all Government activity.

It should also be mentioned that in terms of Article 91-B, the provisions of Article 90 are equally applicable to the Secretaries of State.

The complementary Government statement of 12 June 1974 announced that ministerial liability is to be defined and dealt with in implementation of Article 90 of the Constitution.

ARTICLE 91

"The King may not reprieve a Minister sentenced by the Court of Cassation save at the request of one of the two Houses."

This article dates from 1831 and has never been modified.

We know that Article 73 has acknowledged the right of reprieve as being vested in the King, but at the same time that article already foreshadowed the derogation embodied in Article 91.

It may happen that a Minister is prosecuted and sentenced for having assumed personal and political responsibility for an intentional act of the King's. It is therefore not surprising that the right of reprieve vested in the King may not be exercised without the consent of the nation's representatives.

Thus, the fullness of ministerial responsibility towards Parliament is preserved.

It should also be remembered that in terms of Article 91-B, the provisions of Article 91 are equally applicable to the Secretaries of State.

SECTION III — THE SECRETARIES OF STATE

ARTICLE 91-B

"The King appoints and dismisses the Secretaries of State.

"These are members of the Government. They do not form part of the Cabinet. They are attached to a Minister.

"The King determines their powers and the limits within which they may be given authority to sign.

"The constitutional provisions relating to Ministers apply to them with the exception of Articles 79 paragraph 3, 82 and 86-B."

This article was adopted during the Third Revision (1967-1971).

It deals with one of the structural problems confronting the Government —a problem that had become very thorny indeed with the passage of time. It is part and parcel of the Government's concern to maintain the efficiency and effectiveness of the Executive while sharing authority on a wider basis.

Article 86-B has already indicated that two important functions have become progressively apparent in the work of Government.

As time went by, the duties incumbent on the Government have grown and multiplied. This phenomenon is clearly noticeable in the increase in the number of Cabinet Ministers since 1830. From 5 in 1830, their number rose indeed to 12 in 1917, to 16 in 1939, to 19 in 1960, to 27 in 1965 (including two Minister-Secretaries of State and a Royal Commissioner), to 29 in 1968 (including two Minister-Secretaries of State), until it finally reached the unprecedented figure of 36 (including 14 Secretaries of State) in 1973.

This rapid growth rate, moreover, only reflects the increasingly complex nature of public affairs. It goes side by side with the continual rise in the number of public departments and State Corporations which, along with the traditional Ministries, are entrusted with important administrative duties in vital sectors such as: communications, social security, credits, public health, etc., with a corresponding increase in the number of officials working for the State.

There was therefore a clear risk of seeing the central authority crumble.

The first attempts to preserve the unity of power and to maintain the Government's role as a central coordinating authority date back to 1960, a year in which two new types of Minister came to the fore: the coordinating Ministers and the Under-Secretaries of State. At that time, the hierarchy of Government could therefore be set out as follows:

— the Prime Minister,

— the Deputy Prime Minister,

— the coordinating Ministers,

— the ordinary Ministers,

— the Minister-Under-Secretaries of State.

In 1960 there were three coordinating Ministers, one of whom was also in charge of a Ministry whereas the other two, as their title implied, coordinated the work of several of their colleagues.

Apart from these, there were four Minister-Under-Secretaries of State attached to Ministers who were effectively heads of their Departments and entrusted with specific Cabinet posts. This new category of Ministers was responsible in particular for cultural affairs, the Post Office (including Telephones and Telegraphs), the Budget, and Energy (Fuel and Power).

The experiment, however, did not last long owing to an early dissolution of Parliament.

Under the next Government, which lasted from 1961 to 1965, the coordinating Ministers and the Minister-Under-Secretaries of State disappeared. On the other hand, the new Government included three Deputy Ministers who, again as their title implies, while holding full Cabinet rank, were each attached to a Minister who was effectively head of his Department.

The following Government, from 1965 to 1966, attempted to set up a genuine ministerial hierarchy, for apart from the Prime Minister and the Deputy Prime Minister, it again included four coordinating Ministers, 14 ordinary Ministers, 7 Minister-Secretaries of State, and one Royal Commissioner. Thus the coordinating Ministers, along with the Prime Minister and the Deputy Prime Minister, formed a sort of super-government whose task was to lay down the broad outlines of Government policy. Once again the experiment lasted only a short time and was rather a disappointing one, probably due precisely to the determination of those concerned to rationalize and establish a definite hierarchy governing ministerial functions. The system—a very logical one in itself—was discovered to be very difficult to implement, precisely because the whole structure was too logical and rational.

This experiment in establishing a chain of command was therefore abandoned by the next Government which remained in office from 1966 to 1968, although the latter did retain the Secretaries of State.

The general principle of a better distribution of work and authority within the Government was, however, not abandoned. That is why it received special attention from the Commission set up to examine the reform of Government institutions.

Indeed, up to that time—and this was perhaps one of the biggest difficulties from the practical standpoint—the Secretaries of State, who had not been provided for in terms of the Constitution, had retained full Cabinet rank, so that there was a great temptation for them to escape from the tutelary authority of their respective Ministers, seeing that Article 91-B inserted in the Constitution was formally published on 24 December 1970.

The Commission for Institutional Reform therefore advocated that a clause regarding Secretaries of State should be inserted in the Constitution itself. According to the Commission, the Constitution—while establishing the status and responsibility of the Secretaries of State—must also frame the following rules in their regard:

— Secretaries of State would be genuine members of the Government, and would therefore have authority to sign in matters falling within their competence. But they would not form part of the Cabinet.

— They would have access to both Houses of Parliament in the same way as Ministers.

— Their responsibility would be identical to that of Ministers.

The Commission, however, foresaw that such constitutional rules should allow for a great deal of flexibility so as to prevent any inflationary trend in the Government. So these rules should also be framed in such a way as to permit:

— certain activities to be regrouped within a single Ministry;

— the coordination of activities proper to several Ministries;

— the reallocation of certain activities, bearing in mind both linguistic and regional particularities;

— the establishment of complex budgets, bearing in mind regional problems and in an attempt to harmonize the interests of both national communities;

— in case of need, a Secretary of State to be entrusted with a temporary task in connection with an important problem arising unexpectedly.

348

The Statement of Intent to Revise adopted by both Houses and by the King included the principle of creating the post of Secretary of State.

Article 91-B inserted in the Constitution was formally published on 24 December 1970.

In terms of this article, and as indicated in the preparatory work, the Secretaries of State are Ministers insofar as Parliament and the outside world are concerned, but within the Government they remain Deputy Ministers.

Like Cabinet Ministers, they are appointed and dismissed by the King; they have the right of entry to both Houses and may be questioned there; as occasion may arise, they are subjected to the same penal provisions as full Ministers.

Though they belong to the Government, they are not members of the Cabinet, and therefore they do not take part in Cabinet discussions. This rule applies to ordinary Cabinet meetings and even more so in cases where the Cabinet is called upon, in terms of the Constitution, to assume clearly defined duties (at the death of the King, in the event of his inability to reign, etc.). It also applies to the linguistic distribution of seats in the Government. On this latter point, it is important to emphasize that the number of French-speaking Secretaries of State and that of the Dutch-speaking Secretaries of State need not be equal, linguistic parity being a condition affecting full Cabinet Ministers alone.

It is, of course, possible for a Cabinet to summon a Secretary of State and to have him be present when the Cabinet is discussing a matter within the province of the Secretary of State concerned.

In terms of Article 91-B, it is the King who determines the powers of the Secretary of State and the limits within which he is given authority to sign. This system of arrangement by means of a Royal Decree was found preferable to the enactment of a law, so as to preserve the flexibility desirable in establishing the status of the Secretaries of State.

In implementation of this paragraph, a Royal Decree of 24 March 1972 defined and limited the powers of Secretaries of State.

In terms of this decree, the Secretary of State enjoys all the powers of a full Minister in those matters entrusted to his responsibility.

However, apart from his own signature, that of the Minister to whom he is attached is required for tabling bills in the Legislative Houses, or proposed decrees in the Cultural Councils, as also for the sanctioning and promulgation of laws and decrees, for statutory royal decrees, and finally for those royal decrees which create posts or appoint persons to high-ranking posts in Government departments or public organizations.

Furthermore, the Secretaries of State only exercise their statutory powers with the agreement of the Minister to whom they are attached, and their competence does not exclude that of the Minister, so that the latter remains free to bring up a matter or to subordinate any decision to his own agreement.

The royal decree of 24 March 1972 has, moreover, been more precisely defined by a circular issued by the Prime Minister's office dated 26 January 1973. This circular stipulates in particular that the royal decree of 24 March 1972 is, so to speak, only in the nature of a frame-work decree and that its provisions may be completed or defined in a royal decree relating directly to the Government department involved. So in this way special decrees have been issued in respect of the Civil Service, Co-operation in Development, Foreign Trade, Environment and Housing, Budget, Family Welfare, Brussels Affairs, and the Eastern Cantons.

The circular referred to also states that the practical terms and condi-tions governing the collaboration of the titular Minister and the Secre-taries of State are laid down by a protocol proper to the Government department concerned, signed by the Minister and the Secretary of State responsible.

Finally, the circular recalls the established rule that a royal decree covering special provisions made in respect of Secretaries of State is countersigned by the Prime Minister as well as by the Titular Minister.

Clearly defined though they seemed to be, those arrangements never-theless failed to satisfy members of Parliament, who wanted to know how the Legislative authority could remain in contact with the Executive and oversee its work. Parliament particularly wished to know whether it would not be possible to draw up a precise organic graph of ministerial responsibilities, similar to that illustrating the various managerial posts in large commercial enterprises.

To this question, the Prime Minister replied that the duties and respon-sibilities of all members of the Government are succinctly outlined in the Royal Decree of Appointment, and further defined where necessary in complementary royal decrees.

*
* *

The new system, henceforward enshrined in the Constitution, was put into practice for the first time when the 1971-1973 Government was formed. This administration numbered 19 Ministers and 10 Secretaries of State, the latter sharing between them the responsibility for Scientific Policy and Planning, Foreign Trade, Co-operation in Development, Housing and Environment, the Civil Service, the Middle Classes, the Budget, and Regional Economy.

Once again, due to the precarious nature of this Government which lasted only a year, it was virtually impossible to assess the effectiveness of the new system.

The Government which took office in 1973 was able for the first time to make a conclusive trial of the new system of Secretaries of State, for it comprised 22 Ministers and 14 Secretaries of State. The latter held almost the same posts as their predecessors, except that a Secretary of State was appointed for the Eastern Cantons and Tourism, another for Ports and Harbours, and two more were put in charge of Institutional and Administrative Reform.

However, a Government consisting of 36 people soon revealed itself as being overcrowded, to such an extent that a reshuffle became imperative in October 1973, as a result of which the number of Ministers remained at 22 while that of the Secretaries of State was brought down to 6.

In view of this reduction in number, it is obvious that ministerial portfolios had to be reorganized at the same time. And so the Government was seen to revert to methods already applied in previous years, even though the terms of reference had changed, by calling on Ministers —whether they were in charge of a Government department or not—to take over at the same time responsibility for other sectors of other ministries under the seal of the titular Ministers concerned. In this way there appeared a Minister for French Culture in charge of Environment and Housing in the French-speaking region; a Minister for Brussels Affairs in charge of Co-operation in Development; a Minister of Communications in charge of Ports and Harbours; a Minister of Scientific Policy in charge of the Eastern Cantons and Tourism; a Minister of the Middle Classes in charge of Institutional and Administrative Reforms and a Minister of Finance in charge of External Trade Relations.

This was just posing once again the problem that had been raised earlier, since certain Ministers once again found themselves with full Cabinet rank in the sector of which they were titular heads, but to a certain extent dependent on one or other of their colleagues for the secondary sphere in which they were called upon to assume responsibility.

Certain members of Parliament did not fail to question this arrangement; they wanted to know what subordinate links, if any, existed for instance between the Minister of Foreign Affairs and the Minister in charge of Co-operation in Development. They were particularly anxious to find out whether a new top-rank portfolio, independent of the Minister of Foreign Affairs, had thus been created.

When this question was referred to him, the Prime Minister did not fail to underline that there must be no confusion between the ministerial function, which implies responsibilities in a precisely defined and limited sphere, and the distribution among ministries of services placed at the disposal of members of the Government in order to assist them in the performance of their tasks. The Prime Minister nevertheless stressed the fact that a degree of coordination in the policy to be implemented and concerted discussions on the decisions to be made must of necessity take place between members of the Government whose attributions were akin or connected, and that the relationship between two Ministers who were theoretically on a footing of equality but one of whom was in fact subordinate to the other, must be regulated by means of protocols signed by the two Ministers concerned.

Such protocols were the more necessary seeing that, in practice, the Secretaries of State usually belonged to different political parties from those of their titular Ministers. In the absence of such a protocol, the allocation of authority on the basis of political criteria could have given rise to serious conflicts.

But again the existence of this Government was abruptly terminated by an early election, so that the efficiency of the new system has not yet been fully proven.

***

Generally speaking, therefore, it may be said that in theory at least the long-awaited machinery is now in place to increase the Government's efficiency. Article 91-B and the statutory regulations that have defined its conditions of implementation should be sufficient to ensure such efficiency.

In practice, however, this is not so and one might say that the institution of the Secretaries of State is still in the experimental stage. The first attempt in 1972 was too short to permit assessment of the system. The second attempt in 1973 ended in a superabundance of ministers and the inflation of the Executive's responsibilities which *ipso facto* detracted from the Government's efficiency, in sharp contrast to the hoped-for result.

Furthermore, the fact that titular Ministers and Secretaries of State belonged to different political parties did not always make for smooth co-operation between them, especially as there was sometimes friction when it came to drawing up the protocol defining their respective attributions.

Finally, despite the constitutional provision, some Secretaries of State had the impression that they were really only second-rank Ministers, while others—over-reacting to it—thought that in practice they could enjoy full ministerial prerogatives, and did not fail to claim them, especially the right to participate more often in Cabinet meetings.

In conclusion, therefore, one might say that the machinery has been brought in and assembled: it remains to see whether it actually works.

CHAPTER III

THE JUDICIARY

ARTICLE 92

"Contestations arising out of civil rights come under the exclusive jurisdiction of the law courts."

This article dates from 1831 and has never been modified.

The entire range of provisions laid down by this and the two subsequent articles have caused a great deal of ink to flow. The problems involved will be reviewed in detail with respect to Articles 93 and 94.

For the time being we shall merely state what is to be understood by civil rights. Even this simple concept has given rise to a great deal of discussion. Some have felt that a pragmatic system should be maintained, and that from the moment when the law courts appear as exclusively competent, then the case is one of civil rights. Others on the contrary believe that the term refers to relations between private persons and not to those between private persons and public authorities. This latter theory has however been set aside by the Court of Cassation in a ruling of 5 November 1920, which specified that civil rights include all the private rights embodied in and codified by the Civil Code and the laws which complement it, even if they are claimed in respect of the State itself. This ruling, however, is of itself too restrictive, seeing that civil rights are not merely those embodied in the Civil Code but also embrace most of the fundamental rights acknowledged in respect of all Belgians by Chapter II of the Constitution (Articles 7 to 24).

The best definition of civil rights would seem to be that supplied by the most recent doctrine. Civil rights are the natural or artificial rights acknowledged or instituted by law for the benefit of every human being, Belgian and foreigner alike, (apart from his status as a citizen) the immediate purpose of which is to safeguard the individual and personal welfare of the individual. There can therefore be no question, as some have wished, of assimilating purely and simply these civil rights with patrimonial rights. The Constituent Assembly has decreed that the law courts alone are competent to judge these rights. We shall examine its reasons for doing so in connection with Article 93.

The guarantee thus afforded to citizens is further strengthened by Article 106 of the Constitution which grants the Court of Cassation the sole right to rule in conflicts of authority. This supreme organ of the Judiciary is indeed above all suspicion of wishing to undermine the competence of that Authority.

ARTICLE 93

"Contestations arising out of political rights come under the jurisdiction of the law courts, except in such cases as are laid down by the law."

This article dates from 1831 and has never been modified.

This is the point at which it is necessary to examine the aims and objectives borne in mind by the Constituent Assembly.

The French Revolution had proclaimed the principle of the separation of powers in order to withhold from the competence of ordinary tribunals those contestations in which the administration was involved. However, this was tantamount to opening the door to arbitrary action on the part of the administration.

The regime which Belgium experienced between the years 1815 to 1830 did not correct this failing since the fundamental law remained silent regarding the rights born out of relations between the authorities and the citizens, and the law courts were refused the right to control the legality of acts performed by the administration. Instructed by these two previous experiments, the Constituent Assembly was determined to fight the arbitrary and irresponsible character of the administration, and that is why it was at pains to attribute the jurisdictional competence solely to the law courts established by Act of Parliament. The authority of the Judiciary is thus asserted in Articles 92 and 93 of the Constitution.

Their competence is an exclusive one in cases of contestations arising out of civil rights.

Where other rights are concerned, the competence vested in the Courts of Law is a matter of principle, though the Legislator may vest such competence in other jurisdictions to be established by law alone. Thus, the Constituent Assembly having asserted the principle of the authority of the Judiciary in order to avoid any recourse to arbitrary decisions, it authorizes no exception save under the control of Parliament alone.

It is however necessary to define what is meant by political rights, and this is where endless legal arguments have taken place.

Again, some felt that the Legislator alone should establish the distinction between civil and political rights. If the Legislator has intervened to attribute the settlement of contestations to some other form of jurisdiction, then the question is necessarily one of political and not civil rights. It might be feared that the Legislator could thus act arbitrarily but one must start from the principle that, to the judge, the law is always presumed to be in accordance with the Constitution and that this presumption may not be countered by any proof to the contrary.

The preparatory work in drafting these constitutional clauses is not very helpful in specifying what is meant by political rights, apart from the formal criterion of competence.

Thus, for instance, the Constituent Assembly cited as an instance of political rights the *jus tributi,* i.e. the right of each citizen not to be taxed save as the law prescribes. It is also traditional to consider as a political right the *jus militiae,* or the right not to be called up for military service save as the law prescribes.

Some people have always restricted the concept of political rights by considering that they were only the rights conferred on citizens for purposes of electing, nominating and appointing candidates to posts in the Government service, and/or conferring and exercising the authority vested in such posts.

Others have attempted to define political rights as being individual rights implying a contribution by the citizens to the establishment or exercise of public powers, and to the financial and military burdens essential to the maintenance and functioning of those powers.

This definition, which was in keeping with 19th century concepts, has however been revealed as too narrow in application.

*
**

Indeed, because of the evolution of economic and social affairs, other rights have progressively made their appearance which some people have tried to marshall into a special category to be known as administrative or social rights.

In defending this third separate and distinct category of rights, the partisans of this theory did not see that they were placing them outside the framework of the Constitution and that such rights could not, therefore, be guaranteed.

Now, Articles 92 and 93, completed by Article 94, were regarded by the Constituent Assembly as signifying that any contestation arising out of a subjective right must find a judge to settle it. Consequently, this article states a general principle which is valid for all rights of whatever kind.

The turning-point in the notion of political rights was signalled above all by a ruling of 21 December 1956 by the Court of Cassation, in which this supreme legal authority recognised that the right to unemployment benefits is part and parcel of the rights stipulated in Article 93 of the Constitution under the term of "political rights".

The result is that, by political rights, it is necessary to understand:

— not only the right of every citizen to participate actively in the exercise of power, as many authors had understood it,

— but also the rights arising out of the citizen's passive participation in the community, rights which have moreover grown unceasingly in parallel to the development of State activities.

This must be taken to include the services and advantages afforded by the public authorities, which rights are not rights of exercise but rights of enjoyment. And in this regard, all foreigners—which again is counter to a narrow conception of Article 93— may also benefit from the protection of the courts in so far as the law provides that they may share the advantages and facilities concerned.

Thus, the fundamental aims of the Constituent Assembly have been respected: nobody may judge his own case, not even the administration. Any exceptions that withhold or withdraw competence from the ordinary courts and tribunals must be specified by Act of Parliament.

ARTICLE 94

"No tribunal nor court of arbitration may be set up save under a law. No extraordinary commissions or courts may be set up under any denomination whatsoever."

This article dates from 1831 and has never been modified.

Taken together with Articles 92 and 93, it forms a whole. The Legislator is free to create new jurisdictions, but such tribunals or courts of arbitration may not be set up save in order to settle contestations arising out of rights other than civil rights.

The question arose primarily in 1956 concerning the courts of arbitration set up by the Executive. In point of fact, the evolution of social affairs had brought about the creation of numerous jurisdictional commissions, particularly in regard to matters such as unemployment benefits, social security, etc.

Article 94 is couched in unequivocal terms. Only the law may set up a court of arbitration.

Some have attempted to defend the idea that as the King could organize public service, he was thereby empowered to reserve to the administration alone the right to adjudicate in disputes. From that concept, we may deduce that the King might set up a court of arbitration merely by issuing a decree of implementation of a law passed by Parliament.

The legality of such a court instituted by the Executive was denied by a ruling of 21 December 1956 by the Court of Cassation, quite in conformity with the Constitution.

Others have tried to uphold the competence of the Executive by basing their argument on the budgetary law, since Parliament voted the appropriations for operating the administrative commissions.

This theory was also discounted, for a budgetary law does no more than open a credit by authorizing payment. The passing of such a law does not imply the assent of Parliament to the existence and functioning of the commissions concerned, especially as a jurisdictional commission is, in principle, a permanent one whereas the budget is an annual affair.

*
**

It should also be noted that Parliament, basing itself on Articles 93 and 94, has lawfully instituted a number of administrative jurisdictions with special powers, i.e. which are competent to hear and rule on contestations arising out of specific matters. In this connection let us mention the permanent deputations in the sphere of municipal elections, the various jurisdictions set up to deal with the militia, the commissions charged with hearing disputes arising out of legislation for the benefit of war victims, the numerous commissions charged with ruling on contestations arising out of the implementation of social security laws, etc. A reform of these jurisdictions would moreover be essential since they were generally instituted without the benefit of any overall plan, on a random basis as circumstances dictated. It should be pointed out here that the law of 10 October 1967 containing the Code of Justice is a first step towards rationalisation since it led to the setting up of the Labour Courts which are now part of the Judiciary; this law also abolished a number of administrative jurisdictions that had by then become redundant.

*
**

Before reverting to the administrative jurisdictions, let us refer back to the second sentence of Article 94, the implications of which are twofold. Firstly, this provision establishes judicial equality, meaning that all citizens who find themselves in an identical situation must be judged by the same courts of law. This provision therefore prohibits any special ruling, either more favourable or more severe, to be given in respect of certain citizens depending on what charge is brought against them.

Furthermore, such judicial equality—in implementation of Article 8 of the Constitution—entails a ban on the establishment either of temporary Commissions set up to rule on specific matters, or of extraordinary tribunals that are more permanent in character, and political jurisdictions in particular. Indeed, the Constituent Assembly rightly distrusted certain experiences undergone by Belgium in the course of previous regimes.

The prohibition is a peremptory one, meaning that it allows for no exception, either in favour of the Executive or even in favour of the Legislative power.

*
**

In connection with administrative jurisdictions, we must refer here to the most important of these, its importance deriving from its general competence: the Council of State.

Let us briefly recall the provisions of the previous articles:

— Article 92 provides that the courts of law alone are competent to rule on contestations arising out of civil rights;

— Article 93 stipulates that, in principle, the courts of law are competent to rule on contestations arising out of political rights, except in such cases as are laid down by a particular law.

We have already seen that on the basis of this latter provision, a great many administrative jurisdictions with special powers have been set up. But there is one which must be set apart from the others owing to the wider competence attributed to it.

*
**

The Council of State was created by a law of 23 December 1946. This law has moreover been modified on several occasions, usually in order to extend the powers of that supreme assembly. The latest amendment is dated 10 July 1973.

While it functions according to the standards governing the Judiciary, the Council of State comes under the Executive alone and, as such, it depends on the Minister of the Interior and not the Minister of Justice. Consequently, it is really and truly an administrative tribunal.

Briefly, let us point out that over and above the administrative personnel required to ensure the proper functioning of this body, the Council of State comprises:

— 18 members, including a supreme president, a president, four court presidents, and 12 State councillors;

— An auditory, comprising an Auditor General, a Deputy Auditor General, 8 leading auditors and 29 auditors and deputy auditors;

— A coordination office comprising two Chief Referendaries, four referendaries and deputy referendaries;

— A records office comprising a Chief Registrar, a Section Registrar, and five clerks.

The coordination office itself is bound up with the auditory. Its work consists in coordinating the laws, the organic Royal Decrees, and the various general regulations in force, and in maintaining and updating all documentation pertaining to the jurisprudence of the Council of State. Its work therefore, as its name indicates, is one of coordination which, as such, is not binding on the Judiciary, the parties concerned, or the Council of State itself.

It is unnecessary in this context to go into the conditions governing the appointment of members of this Council.

At the present time, the Council of State comprises three sections:
— a legislation section;
— an administration section, and
— a section dealing with conflicts of authority.

Let us take a brief look at the tasks and authority of the legislation section and the conflicts of authority section.

The *legislation section* is charged with giving a motivated recommendation on all drafts of bills, proposals and amendments laid before it by the president (Speaker) of one of the two Houses of Parliament.

Similarly, except in cases of emergency, Cabinet Ministers must submit for its motivated recommendation all draft bills or decrees of implementation, both organic and statutory. The sole exception admitted is the budget and bills pertaining thereto. Furthermore, Ministers may request the motivated recommendation of this section in regard to any bill or proposal and to any amendment to bills or proposals tabled in Parliament.

Also submitted for the motivated recommendation of this section are all the drafts of proposed decrees by the Cultural Councils, with the exception of budget proposals. The Ministers and the Presidents of the Cultural Councils may furthermore request the section to give its motivated recommendation on all proposed decrees or amendments to draft or proposed decrees.

The Presidents of the Cultural Councils are bound to request such a recommendation when at least one-third of the members of the Council concerned demand it.

The legislation section is equally competent to give a recommendation, at the request of the Minister of Labour, on the proposed Royal Decrees that render collective bargaining agreements compulsory.

Finally, the Prime Minister may instruct the section to draft the text of laws or regulations, the subject and purpose of which he specifies.

As for the *section dealing with conflicts of authority*, it is charged with reviewing conflicts arising between laws and decrees, or between a decree of the Cultural Council of the French-language community and a decree of the Cultural Council of the Dutch-language community. It is also competent to rule, on a pre-judicial basis, on questions pertaining to the contradiction between a law and a decree, or between decrees of the two Cultural Councils, when such questions are laid before it by the courts, tribunals, or any other jurisdiction.

It is, however, the *administration section* which must be examined primarily within the context of Article 94, for this section wields extremely important powers in the sphere of administrative contestations.

It should first be mentioned that apart from its jurisdictional task, the administration section may give motivated recommendations regarding difficulties or contestations which it is up to the Executive to solve or settle, as long as such matters submitted to it do not involve litigation. Thus, to some extent, it becomes the Government's legal adviser in the sphere of general administration. The same is true in the sphere of mining where, exceptionally, no concession, extension or maintenance of a mining concession may be granted against the advice of the Council of State.

The work of the administration section, however, usually takes the form of rulings.

The authority to issue rulings vested in the administration section is threefold:

— claims of rescission;
— claims of full jurisdiction;
— conflicts of authority.

1. *Claims of rescission*

a) If there is no other jurisdiction competent to rule, the administration section of the Council of State decides equitably on claims for indemnity relating to reparations for exceptional moral or material damage caused by an administrative authority.

The claim is, moreover, only allowable if the authority in question has rejected a prior claim for indemnity in whole or in part, or if it has for a period of 60 days omitted to deal with the matter.

b) But the hand of the administration section of the Council of State is particularly noticeable in the case of requests for rescission formulated in respect of acts or regulations by the administrative authorities, or in respect of contentious administrative decisions.

The section is empowered to rule by means of decree on such requests on condition that the person concerned has not already instituted similar proceedings in a court or tribunal set up by law as part of the Judiciary. Furthermore, rescission is only possible in cases of violation of form and substance or where these are proscribed on pain of invalidity, or in cases of abuse or alienation of authority.

The Council of State may therefore be incompetent to act for three reasons:

— if the applicant asks, not that the decision be rescinded, but only that it be altered, or if he merely asks the judge to advise or to censure the administration;

— if the claim does not refer to an act by an administrative authority. Thus, the Council of State is not competent to hear claims lodged in respect of the Legislative power, the Audit Office, the Judiciary and its ancillary authorities, etc.;

— if the claimant has any possibility of instituting judicial procedures capable of achieving the same result as an appeal to the Council of State.

In this case, the incompetence of the Council of State may be the result either of a formal legal provision which lays down those jurisdictions which are competent to rule on certain matters, or purely and simply of Article 92 of the Constitution which has reserved for the ordinary courts and tribunals alone the power to rule on litigations arising out of civil law.

Certain qualities are also demanded of the claimant if his appeal is to be allowable:

— first, he must be habilitated to take action with the administrative jurisdiction;

— furthermore, he must have a direct, actual and personal interest in the rescission of the act under dispute. The Council of State has, however, given a fairly broad interpretation to this latter concept by admitting that the interest may be of a corporate nature, i.e. that of associations endowed with a legal personality such as mutual societies, as well as a functional interest allowing those who exercise a function to appeal against a decision that is not injurious to them personally, but is injurious to the administrative body of which they are members (e.g., the members of a borough council).

iii) There are four grounds for rescission:

— violation of the substantial forms which, in general, have been laid down in order to protect the rights of all citizens or which are connected with public order. These are, for instance: the advice to be sought, the prior formalities to be observed, consultations with committees, etc.;

— violation of the law or of the rule of law. This is the most common case of abuse of authority when the administration makes a decision which runs counter to a formal text. It is also the case when an administrative authority wrongly interprets or wrongly applies a mandatory text;

— incompetence. This may arise out of usurpation of authority, or of incompetence *ratione materiae,* or of incompetence *ratione loci.* Such would be the case, for instance, when the King or a Minister intervenes in a matter reserved for the Legislative or the Judiciary;

— alienation of authority. This is one of the most delicate grounds for rescission, since it requires the Council of State to investigate the intentions of the authority whose decision is the subject of the claim. By alienation of authority is meant that an administrative body has acted in accordance with its competence and in obedience to the forms laid down by the law, and even in the letter of the law, but that it has exercised its authority for a purpose other than that for which such authority was conferred on it.

c) The rescission of an administrative decision by the Council of State has a twofold effect:

— firstly, the Council's ruling is retroactive to the date on which the act complained of was accomplished;

— secondly, the Council's ruling has the full authority of a judgment, either *erga omnes* in the case of a purely administrative act, or solely *inter partes* if the question is one of a purely jurisdictional decision.

2. *Claims of full jurisdiction*

The administration section is also competent to rule on claims of full jurisdiction, meaning that in the cases listed below the Council of State acts as a Judge of Appeal, rules on the content, and its decision overrides that previously made:

— claims under the law concerning municipal elections;

— claims for the revision of certain contracts entered into before or during the war;

— claims under the heading of public assistance.

3. *Claims arising out of conflicts of authority*

Finally, the administration section of the Council of State is also competent to settle, by means of an authoritative ruling, certain difficulties arising out of spheres of competence:

a) firstly, difficulties connected with the respective spheres of competence of the provincial and municipal authorities or of administrative organizations subordinated to the provinces or the boroughs;

b) again, difficulties connected with the respective spheres of competence of the King, the Ministers, and the Council of the German Cultural Community;

c) finally, claims intended to prevent or to settle conflicting decisions between the administrative jurisdictions coming within the competence of the administration section.

Special regulations have also defined the rules of procedure governing recourse to the administration section of the Council of State, the rules governing the use of languages, and the forms and time schedules governing appeals to the Court of Cassation against rulings by the Council of State.

Indeed, while it is a matter of principle that the rulings of the Council of State are always final and that they cannot therefore be appealed against nor be laid before the Court of Cassation, the fact is that some rulings may be laid before that Court, in particular when the administration section of the Council of State decides not to hear a claim on the grounds that such a hearing is a matter for the authorities coming under the Judiciary. If the Council of State and an ordinary court of law state either that they are both competent, or that they are both incompetent, to hear the same claim, then the question as to which of them is competent to proceed with the hearing is judged as a matter of urgency by the Court of Cassation.

It should also be added that, faced with the many difficulties in interpreting Articles 92 and 93 of the Constitution, the Committee for Institutional Reform had proposed, prior to the latest revision of the Constitution, to begin with the principle already enunciated that every legal dispute must find a judge. On this basis, the Committee put forward the following proposals:

a) disputes concerned with rights (or legal disputes) would be settled in the courts of law;

b) in terms of the law, it may be possible to refer some disputes of this kind to other jurisdictions, with the exception of criminal cases and of political and press misdemeanours;

c) the existence of the Council of State should be made official by the Constitution and be the subject of a Chapter III-B added to Chapter III of the Constitution.

The Houses had adopted the Government's projected revision except for Article 92, but the Constituent Assembly did not see its way to pursuing the Statement of Intent to Revise which had been adopted by both Houses and by the King.

As a result, these difficulties of interpretation persist and the Council of State has not yet acquired a constitutional character.

ARTICLE 95

" There is one Court of Cassation for the whole of Belgium.

"This court does not deal with the content of the affairs submitted to it, save in regard to the judgment of Ministers."

This article dates from 1831 and has never been modified.

In setting up a single Court of Cassation for the whole of Belgium, the paramount concern of the Constituent Assembly was to ensure uniformity of jurisprudence. It is blindingly obvious that such uniformity is absolutely essential in any state of law. The Court of Cassation is a supreme regulating jurisdiction which controls the strict implementation of the laws. It is not, therefore, merely one of the jurisdictional orders.

But at the same time, in terms of para. 2 of the same constitutional ruling, the Constituent Assembly was at pains to prevent any possible abuse of authority on the part of this Supreme Court. Indeed, had it been given the power to rule, not only in law but in fact, on all legal disputes, it might have overstepped its limitations and trespassed in the sphere reserved for the Legislative authority. It is for this reason that the Court of Cassation may not rule on the content of any case submitted to it, and accordingly it may not, after quashing a legal decision, pass sentence on the matter concerned. Only the court to which it has referred the case back is competent to reopen an investigation into the facts of the matter and then pass judgment in accordance with the law. The Court of Cassation does not, therefore, settle the litigation between the parties concerned; all it does is to examine whether the judicial decision which is being challenged is an exact implementation of the law, or whether it has exceeded its powers.

The importance of the task entrusted to the Court of Cassation is underlined by the provisions of the legal code quoted hereunder.

In principle, the Court of Cassation takes cognizance of decisions rendered without appeal, which have been referred to it either because it is claimed that they contravene the law or because they constitute a violation of the prescribed forms which must be observed on pain of rendering the decision null and void. The Legal Code has abolished the traditional concept of substantial forms in the matter of civil and criminal proceedings; on the other hand, in the matter of administrative litigation, the Council of State remains competent to appraise whether the substantial forms have been upheld by an administrative authority.

The Court of Cassation also rules on requests for annulment of:

1. decisions rendered by the courts and tribunals on all matters and without appeal;

2. rulings whereby the Administration Section of the Council of State decides that it cannot take cognizance of the request on the grounds that cognizance of such a matter comes within the competence of the Judiciary authority, and also rulings whereby the said section rejects a declinatory plea on the grounds that the request comes within the competence of that authority;

3. rulings by the Audit Office in respect of accountants;

4. judgments rendered without appeal by Belgian consuls abroad;

5. decisions made by the Permanent Deputations of the provincial councils in the matter of direct municipal and provincial taxes, with the exception of decisions in the matter of taxes analogous to the licences taken out by joint-stock companies and companies limited by shares;

6. decisions rendered by the permanent deputations of the provincial councils in the matter of taxes levied for the benefit of polders and land drainage works;

7. decisions by the Higher Militia Council and the Recruiting Boards (Art. 609 of the Code of Justice).

The Court of Cassation also takes cognizance of requests for annulment of regulations framed by the General Council of the Bar which are indicted as being in excess of their competence, contrary to the laws, or adopted by means of irregular procedures (Art. 611 of the Code of Justice).

So as to preserve unity of jurisprudence, the Court of Cassation takes cognizance of appeals lodged against final decisions that are contrary to the law or to proper procedure, especially when they reveal persisting differences of interpretation on a point of law (Art. 612 of the Code of Justice).

The Court of Cassation rules on requests for annulment of:

1. decisions pronounced by the appellate councils of the Bar;

2. decisions pronounced by the provincial councils or the appellate councils of the Order of Medical Practitioners;

3. decisions pronounced by the provincial councils or the appellate councils of the Order of Dispensing Chemists;

4. decisions pronounced by the joint appellate councils of the Order of Veterinary Surgeons;

5. decisions pronounced by the appellate committee of the Institute of Company Auditors;

6. decisions pronounced by the appellate councils of the Order of Architects;

7. decisions pronounced by the Appellate Council for Conscientious Objectors;

8. decisions of the Court of Maritime Enquiry.
(Art. 614 of the Code of Justice).

The Court of Cassation takes cognizance of requests for the annulment of acts whereby judges and officials of the Public Prosecutor's Department, together with the disciplinary authorities of ministerial officials and of the Bar, have transgressed their respective competences (Art. 610 of the Code of Justice).

In terms of Article 106 of the Constitution, the Court of Cassation rules on conflicts of authority: this is indeed one of its most important and vital tasks.

We have already pointed out in our commentary on Article 9 of the Constitution that the House of Representatives has the right to impeach Ministers and to arraign them before the Court of Cassation which alone is competent to judge them. This is the only instance when the Court of Cassation is called upon to judge the facts of the case.

The Constituent Assembly considered that, in order to prevent political reprisals and ensure the independence of Cabinet Ministers, it was necessary to submit their case to the highest jurisdiction in the Kingdom. In such cases, the Court of Cassation sits in full session. No distinction is made between infringements arising out of their ministerial function and other misdemeanours.

The indictment is a matter for the House of Representatives. If the Minister concerned is also a member of the Senate, his arrest and prosecution while Parliament is sitting are subject to the consent of that august assembly (Art. 45 of the Constitution).

The prosecution of Cabinet Ministers was formerly the subject of a law dated 19 June 1865 which was framed for the purpose of arranging for the trial of Baron Chazal, charged with fighting a duel. The law was placed on the statute-book only for one year dating from its promulgation; nevertheless it may be regarded as a precise embodiment of constitutional principles, and one may draw the conclusion, for instance, that Cabinet Ministers remain amenable to the ordinary courts of law where minor infractions of police regulations are concerned.

A vigilant guardian of legality, the Court of Cassation has rendered outstanding services to the Nation. It has also played a considerable part in interpreting certain fundamental provisions of the Constitution.

In giving all citizens an essential guarantee that they do in fact live in a state of law, the Supreme Court stands out like a strong buttress in defence of the liberty whose benefits are constantly appreciated by all Belgians.

ARTICLE 96

"Hearings in the courts and tribunals are public unless such publicity is prejudicial to good order or morals; in this case the court shall so declare in an official ruling.

"In matters connected with political or press misdemeanours, a session *in camera* can only be ordered on a unanimous basis."

This article dates from 1831 and has never been modified.

The public nature of hearings before the civil and criminal courts is a guarantee in favour of the persons on trial; the Nation may thus judge its judges.

One exception has however been provided for : cases when such publicity would be prejudicial to good order or morals. The decision to hold a trial *in camera* must be founded on a judgment. This single exception is further restricted, when political or press misdemeanours are concerned, by the need for unanimous agreement : in other words, each member of the court or tribunal has in such matters the genuine power to veto such a proposal.

ARTICLE 97

"Every judgment shall be motivated. It is pronounced in open court."

This article dates from 1831 and has never been modified.

The public nature of the judgments and sentences pronounced rounds off the requirement that hearings in the courts and tribunals shall be public (see Article 96). The twofold publicity thus given to the due process of law, coupled with the compulsory motivation of every judgment, are so many guarantees in favour of the persons on trial : justice is not only done, it is seen to be done.

It should however be pointed out that there are exceptions to the rule concerning public hearings, for a trial may be conducted *in camera.*

But there is absolutely no exception to the rule governing the public pronouncement of the judgment : to pass sentence *in camera* is constitutionally impossible.

The fact that every judgment must be motivated enables the condemned person to appreciate the legal nature of the penalty imposed on him, and provides him with a further guarantee that Article 9 of the Constitution is being effectively implemented.

The importance of the publicity surrounding trials is to be found in the presence of the general public in the courtrooms, and in the fact that newspaper reporters are often among them. Trial reporting occupies a major place in the Belgian press, and constitutes one of the most widely read features of newspapers.

ARTICLE 98

"A jury is empanelled for all criminal affairs and for political and press misdemeanours."

This article dates from 1831 and has never been modified.

In judging crimes that may be liable to the death penalty, hard labour, imprisonment or internment, and in judging political misdemeanours, meaning those that may injure political institutions, as well as misdemeanours connected with an abuse of the liberty of the press, the first Constituent Assembly provided an additional guarantee which consists of introducing trial by jury. The jury is composed of citizens who are not necessarily jurists themselves. This institution thus makes it possible to associate the nation as a whole with the repression of those crimes and misdemeanours which are liable to very heavy penalties or which are vitally important to society.

The composition of a jury is regulated by Clauses 217 to 253 of the law dated 10 October 1967 containing the Code of Justice. Every four years, a municipal list is established by means of the drawing of lots, the names being taken from the latest electoral roll. From the list, the Burgomaster eliminates the names of all people who have not reached the age of 30 years and all those who have reached the age of 60 years as of the first day of January of the current year. He also eliminates, after an enquiry, the names of all persons who are illiterate or who are unable to speak the procedural language of the district, as well as those who are liable to exclusion for any of the reasons listed in Clause 224 of the Code of Justice. When it has been compiled and checked in this way, the list is sent to the Permanent Deputation of the Provincial Council which draws up the provincial list and forwards it to the president of the Court of First Instance in the administrative capital of the province. The president of this Court instructs a judge to draw up the definitive list of persons liable for jury service. At least thirty days prior to the opening date of the session, the names on this list are used in a ballot to determine those jurymen and women who will be empanelled for each case to be tried. At least 40 hours prior to the hearing, the list of jurymen is notified to each defendant. First the defendant and then the Public Prosecutor may request the dismissal and replacement of an equal number of members of the jury.

It should be pointed out here that the jury is required to take cognizance of the criminal act or misdemeanour and to decide whether its perpetrator is liable to punishment.

The jury's verdict, either for or against the defendant, is reached on a majority basis on pain of being declared null and void. When the

372

defendant has been declared not guilty, the judge will pronounce his acquittal and rule that he be set free. A defendant who is acquitted may claim damages from the people who denounced him on the grounds of calumny. When the defendant is found guilty, the Public Prosecutor demands that the full force of the law be applied to him. The Court pronounces the acquittal of the defendant if the act in respect of which he has been found guilty is not prohibited by a penal law. If such an act is prohibited, then the Court and the jury decide on what penalty is applicable in terms of the penal law. Such decisions are made on the basis of an absolute majority vote (Code of Criminal Procedure, Clauses 347 to 364) and the Judge then pronounces sentence.

Finally, it should be emphasized that the requirement to empanel a jury for the trial of press misdemeanours is another guarantee surrounding the freedom of the press (see Article 18).

ARTICLE 99

"Justices of the peace and judges of the various courts are directly appointed by the King.

"Counsellors of the Courts of Appeal, the presidents and vice-presidents of the Courts of First Instance within their jurisdiction, are appointed by the King on the basis of two double lists, one submitted by the courts concerned and the other by the provincial councils.

"Counsellors of the Court of Cassation are appointed by the King on the basis of two double lists, one submitted by the Senate and the other by the Court of Cassation.

"In both cases, candidates named on one list may also be named on the other list.

"The names of all candidates are made public at least fifteen days before the appointment is made.

"The courts shall choose their own presidents and vice-presidents from among their magistrates. "

This article dates from 1831 and has never been modified.

The method of appointing judges is a combination of nomination, co-option, presentation, and election.

Nomination concerns the recruiting of magistrates (Justices of the peace and magistrates courts).

Presentation refers normally to promotions (to the offices of president and vice-president of the courts).

Co-option takes place in the case of secondary nominations (counsellors of the Courts of Appeal and of Cassation).

Election is the method used for the highest magistrates (for the offices of president and vice-president of the courts).

The presentation of candidates involves a double list coming from the Judiciary (Courts of Appeal and of Cassation) and the political bodies (provincial councils and the Senate).

The principle which requires the names of candidates to be made public before their appointment is an additional guarantee of the propriety of such procedures.

Finally, it should be emphasized that this article refers solely to the Bench, i.e. to the judges, justices and magistrates who pronounce judgments and rulings.

ARTICLE 100

"Judges are appointed for life.

"No judge may be deprived of his office or suspended except by a specific judgment.

"The transfer of a judge can only be made on the basis of a new appointment and with his consent."

This article dates from 1831 and has never been modified.

Judges—or, according to the term hallowed by popular usage, the Bench—are alone qualified to pass sentence. They pronounce judgment in implementation of the law.

The principle that judges enjoy fixity of tenure of office is an absolutely vital guarantee for the ordinary citizen; indeed the method of appointing magistrates is less important than their total independence. This vital quality is ensured by the rule that they may not be deprived of office nor suspended save in terms of a specific judgment, i.e. by an act of their peers and not by any decision made by the Executive.

The fixity of tenure of office conferred on the Bench does not, of course, prevent them from being retired owing to age or to their physical inability to perform their task. In such cases their retirement is essential to the proper administration of justice.

ARTICLE 101

"The King appoints and dismisses the officials of the Public Prosecutor's department in the courts and tribunals."

This article dates from 1831 and has never been modified.

The officials of the Public Prosecutor's department, who are the law officers of the State, have the task of prosecuting those who commit crimes, misdemeanours and minor offences; they must also guard the interests of the State and of the public authorities, as well as those of minor children and absent persons.

They are a branch of the Executive authority in the law courts and tribunals; they come under the authority of the Minister of Justice who may order them to institute proceedings. The Minister of Justice is answerable for their acts. It is therefore logical that they should be appointed by the Executive and that they should not benefit from the fixity of tenure of office laid down in respect of judges (see Article 100).

ARTICLE 102

"The salaries of members of the Judiciary are fixed by law."

This article dates from 1831 and has never been modified.

It goes without saying that their fixity of tenure of office is not sufficient to render judges completely independent of the Government: they must not depend financially on the Executive in any way. That is why the Constituent Assembly has entrusted the Legislative with the task of regulating the emoluments of the Bench.

This constitutional rule is an additional guarantee of the independence of the Judiciary as a whole in regard to the Executive.

ARTICLE 103

"No judge may accept a salaried post from the Government unless he exercises it without charge, and except for the cases of incompatibility laid down by the law."

This article dates from 1831 and has never been modified.

The administrative and pecuniary independence of the Bench in regard to the Government would indeed be illusory if judges were permitted to accept salaried posts from that same Government. Hence the insertion of this rule in the Belgian Constitution.

As for the cases of incompatibility laid down by the law, it should be pointed out that these exist between judicial functions and the exercise of public elective mandates or administrative posts.

On the other hand, plurality of office is permitted for magistrates in connection notably with employment in the sphere of university education or in that of selection committees and examining boards.

ARTICLE 104

"There are five Courts of Appeal in Belgium:

"1. that of Brussels, whose jurisdiction comprises the province of Brabant;

"2. that of Ghent, whose jurisdiction comprises the provinces of West Flanders and East Flanders;

"3. that of Antwerp, whose jurisdiction comprises the provinces of Antwerp and Limburg;

"4. that of Liège, whose jurisdiction comprises the provinces of Liège, Namur and Luxemburg;

"5. that of Mons, whose jurisdiction comprises the province of Hainaut."

TRANSITIONAL ARRANGEMENT

"A law shall determine the date of entry into force of Article 104 and shall regulate its implementation. The bill must be tabled in the Legislative Assemblies within two years following promulgation of the present article.

"The existing text shall apply until such time as the said law comes into force."

This article was drafted during the Third Revision and replaces the 1831 text which read as follows:

"There are three Courts of Appeal in Belgium.

"The law determines their jurisdiction and the places where they are set up."

This modification of Article 104 responded to a twofold aim: firstly, the wish for greater decentralization, and secondly the desire to render the jurisdictions of the Courts of Appeal homogenous from the linguistic standpoint. Indeed, in terms of the old Article 104, the capital and two major cities benefited from the existence of an appellate court, a fact which gave them certain definite moral and material advantages. By bringing the number of appellate courts up to five, the Constituent Assembly has broadened these advantages to embrace two other cities, and has thereby lightened the burden imposed on the capital.

The implementation of this constitutional clause has been regulated by the law of 26 June 1974.

The Brussels Court of Appeal was formerly set over the provinces of Antwerp, Brabant and Hainaut. Today its jurisdiction is restricted to a single province, that of Brabant—though in truth this is the most highly populated province of all. The Antwerp and Hainaut provinces now come under the respective jurisdictions of the new Courts of Appeal set up in Antwerp and in Mons.

The jurisdiction of the Ghent Court of Appeal, embracing the provinces of East and West Flanders, remains unchanged.

The Liège Court of Appeal has relinquished one province—Limburg—to the appellate court in Antwerp, and retains its jurisdiction over the provinces of Liège, Namur and Luxemburg.

In a word, the jurisdictions of the appellate courts in Brussels and Liège have been reduced for the benefit of those in Mons and Antwerp.

Formerly, one of the three Courts of Appeal (Ghent) was unilingual and the two others (Brussels and Liège) were bilingual. Today, however, only one of them (Brussels) is bilingual, whereas the four other appellate courts are unilingual. This new distribution will help to reduce tensions, simplify the organizational procedures, and furthermore it corresponds to the desire for territorial homogeneity of both Walloons and Flemings.

The increase in the number of appellate courts does not threaten to compromise the unity of jurisprudence since the latter is ensured by the Court of Cassation, which remains unique (see Article 95).

Moreover, such an increase is justifiable in terms of the growing population figure, which has more than doubled since 1831—a phenomenon which has brought about a considerable increase in the work load.

From another standpoint, it should be noted that the new wording of Article 104 is far stricter than that of the former version, which merely stated the number of appellate courts and left it up to the Legislative to decide upon their jurisdictions and the places where they were to be set up. As these jurisdictions are determined in reference to the provinces, their boundaries may, in terms of Article 3 of the Constitution, be modified if necessary by means of an ordinary law.

ARTICLE 105

"Special laws regulate the organisation of military tribunals, their powers, the rights and obligations of the members of such tribunals, and the duration of their term of office.

"There shall be commercial courts set up in places to be specified by the law which also regulates their organisation, their powers, the method of appointing their members, and the duration of the latters' term of office.

"The law also lays down the organisation of the labour courts, their powers, the procedure for appointing their members, and the duration of the latters' term of office. "

The first two paragraphs of this article date from 1831, at which time they formed the entire article.

The third paragraph is the work of the fourth Constituent Assembly (1967-1971).

The military jurisdictions (Councils of War and Courts-Martial) judge all infringements of the military penal code or common law perpetrated by those people who, at the time of the offence, were serving in the armed forces.

The Consular jurisdictions (commercial courts) handle litigation arising out of commercial matters.

As for the labour jurisdictions, they have existed since 1842 in the form of the "Conseils de Prud'homme" (Wise Men's Councils, or Conciliation Boards) both ordinary and appellate, but by means of a law dated 10 October 1967 (which went into effect in November 1970) the Legislative has converted them into Labour Courts and Tribunals, thus integrating them effectively with the Judiciary.

ARTICLE 106

"The Court of Cassation delivers its verdict on conflicts of jurisdiction in the manner laid down by the law."

This article dates from 1831 and has never been modified.

It entrusts the supreme organ of the Judiciary with settling all conflicts between a tribunal and an administrative body concerning matters of jurisdictional competence.

This constitutional arrangement protects the independence of the Judiciary against interference by the Executive, and guarantees the individual liberties of the citizen.

As for the other tasks which the Constituent Assembly has entrusted to the Court of Cassation, readers may refer to Articles 90 and 95.

ARTICLE 107

"The courts and tribunals shall not apply any general, provincial or local decrees and regulations save insofar as they are in accordance with the law."

This article dates from 1831 and has never been modified.

It embodies a dual principle :

a) the law is binding not only on all citizens, but also on those in authority.

b) the Judiciary verifies the legality of all acts by the Executive and by the provincial and municipal authorities.

It should be pointed out that the courts and tribunals are not called upon to judge the opportune character of any acts accomplished by the Executive or by provincial and municipal authorities : the only criterion here is whether they are in accordance with the laws of the country.

It should be added that while a jurisdiction is entitled to refuse to implement a decree or regulation which it deems to be illegal, it has no right either to modify or abrogate it.

Finally, it should be stressed that judges may not rule on the constitutionality of the laws passed. In doing so, they would infringe on the prerogative of the nation's elected representatives who alone have the right to rule on the authoritative interpretation of the supreme charter.

To make sure that the preceding articles and their commentaries are properly understood, it may be useful here to take a brief look at the organisation of the Belgian Judiciary, i.e. those jurisdictions which belong to that arm of the State concerned with law and order. Its organisation, with the sole exception of the Courts Martial and military tribunals which are the subject of special laws, is governed by the Code of Justice laid down in the law of 10 October 1967. This Code has replaced most of the laws pertaining to the organisation of the Judiciary which had been in force up to that time.

A. *The courts and tribunals*

There are :

1. in every judicial canton, a *justice of the peace* (conciliation court) dealing with all claims the amount of which does not exceed 25,000 francs; there may also be a *police court* which handles minor infringements and certain misdemeanours.

2. in every judicial district :

a) a *district court* presided by judges of the three courts mentioned hereunder, and which rules on questions of competence in the event that the authority of the judge chosen to hear the case is contested.

b) a *court of first instance* comprising one or several civil courts, one or several courts of summary jurisdiction, and one or several children's courts. As its name implies, it is the first to be apprised of all cases save only those which are referred directly to the Court of Appeal and to the Court of Cassation. In criminal cases, the courts of first instance, as courts of summary jurisdiction, try all misdemeanours the penalty for which is in excess of seven days' imprisonment and a fine of twenty-five francs.

c) a *labour court,* consisting of a president who is a judge of the labour court, and assessors who are councillors on social affairs. This court hears disputes pertaining to employment contracts, civil litigation arising out of infringements of the laws and decrees governing the statutory organisation of labour, claims for damages as a result of accidents on the job, disputes concerning the rights and obligations of employers and workers in the sphere of social security, etc.

d) a *commercial court* consisting of a president who is a judge of the commercial court, and consular judges. It is the first to hear cases of disputes between traders on matters deemed to be commercial ones by the law and which do not come within the sphere of competence of the justices of the peace, as well as litigation regarding bills of exchange. It is also competent, among other things, to try cases involving bankruptcies, compositions, and respites of payment, trade marks and brand names, inscriptions in the trade register, etc.

3. in Brussels, Ghent, Antwerp, Liège and Mons (see Article 104):

a) a *Court of Appeal* comprising civil courts, criminal courts and children's courts. It is composed of a presiding judge known as the first president, the court judges and assessors, and it is called upon in particular to try cases of appeal against decisions first rendered in the court of first instance and in the commercial court, appeals against decisions made on electoral matters by the Mayor and Corporation of boroughs and by the main electoral offices, and appeals against decisions made by the provincial and regional Tax Inspectors regarding income tax, etc.

b) an *Appellate Labour Court* consisting of a presiding judge, the court judges, assessors of the labour court and councillors on social affairs. It hears cases arising out of decisions first rendered in the labour courts.

4. in each province : an *Assize Court,* consisting of a judge and two assessors, aided by a jury comprising 12 members (see Article 98). This court tries criminal cases and those arising out of political and press misdemeanours.

5. in Brussels, for the entire Kingdom : a *Court of Cassation* (Supreme Court of Appeal) which comprises three courts and which consists of a presiding judge (known as the first president), a judge and some assessors. This court does not rule on the content of the cases laid before it, except with respect to the impeachment of Ministers (see Article 95).

B. *The Public Prosecutor's Department*

There are :

1. at the Court of Cassation : the Attorney-General, assisted by Advocates-General (directors of public prosecutions);

2. at each Court of Appeal : a Public Prosecutor, assisted by Advocates-General and Deputy Public Prosecutors;

3. at each Labour Court : a general auditory, comprising one or several Advocates-General and one or several Deputy Public Prosecutors, placed under the supervision and authority of the Public Prosecutor to the Court of Appeal;

4. at the chief town in each district : a Public Attorney assisted by one or several deputies. He performs his function in the district court, the court of first instance, the commercial court, and in the district police courts;

5. at each labour court: a Labour Advocate assisted by one or several deputy labour advocates.

CHAPTER IIIc

THE REGIONAL INSTITUTIONS (1)

ARTICLE 107-D (1)

"Belgium comprises three regions : the Walloon region, the Flemish region, and the Brussels region.

"The law confers on the regional bodies which it sets up, and which are composed of elected representatives, the power to rule on such matters as it shall determine, with the exception of those referred to in Articles 23 and 59-B, within such jurisdiction and in accordance with such procedure as it shall determine.

"Such a law must be passed with a majority vote within each linguistic group of both Houses, on condition that the majority of the members of each group are present and that the total votes in favour in the two linguistic groups attains two-thirds of the votes cast."

Over the last twenty years or so, Belgian politics have been profoundly affected by a current of reform that is both more recent and more widespread than the move towards cultural autonomy which found its material expression in Article 59-B.

Under a variety of names—which are not always in accordance with correct legal terminology—such as decentralisation, regionalisation, federalisation, etc., this general trend takes on various aspects. Broadly speaking, one might say that its common denominator and prime

---

(1) The foreign reader will undoubtedly be surprised to note that the text of the Constitution goes directly from Article 107 in Chapter III to Article107-D which, in fact, is the only article under the heading of Chapter III-C. Chapter III-B together with both articles 107-B and 107-C are lacking.

What happened was that the Government submitted a proposal to the Constituent Assemblies concerning the insertion, under Heading III, Chapter III of the Constitution, of an Article 107-B designed to settle the question of non-application of domestic law in the event that its provisions ran counter to those of international or community law issuing from supranational institutions. It also proposed to insert a Chapter III-B that would deal with administrative jurisdictions and the Council of State within the framework of a new Article 107-C.

However, the dissolution of Parliament in September 1971 prevented the Constituent Assembly from completing its work. This break in continuity and subject-matter will have to be made good during some future revision of the Constitution.

objective was the transfer of social, economic and administrative authority from the central Government to the outlying components of the Kingdom. Numerous working parties and official commissions were set up over the last two decades to look into the reforms which might be put in hand for this purpose. The following are some of the most important:

— the "Research Centre for a national solution of the social, political and juridical problems of the various regions", usually known as the "Harmel Centre" (law of 3 May 1948);

— the "Commission for Institutional Reform" set up by the Lefèvre Government in 1962;

— the "Permanent Committee for the Improvement of Relations between the Belgian linguistic communities", also known as the "Meyers-Vanderpoorten Committee" (law of 1 July 1966);

— the "Working Party on Community Problems" or the "Twenty-eight Group" (also referred to as the Eyskens Working Party) set up in 1969.

Attitudes and opinions contrasted greatly and continued to do so for a long time, particularly with regard to the composition of the representative bodies (provincial councillors, Deputies and Senators, separately or together, directly elected members, etc.), the nature of the executive bodies and that of the powers they should wield (advisory competence, the power to issue edicts with or without full force of law), relations with the central Government (supervision, autonomy, rival or co-operative powers) and, finally, territorial competence (provinces, regions), let alone the main stumbling-block : the problem of boundaries for the Brussels area.

Article 107-D is a reply in principle to all those questions, and it is an important point of departure since it constitutionally acknowledges the existence of three separate regions in Belgium. For the rest, it is up to the Legislative to give form and substance, by means of a law passed on the basis of a special qualified majority vote, to the regional bodies and their powers. From this angle, the Constitution is restricted to providing some general indications.

The geographical boundaries of the regions defined by Article 107-D do not coincide with those of the linguistic regions established in terms of Article 3-B.

The regional bodies may be granted all powers save only those referred to in Articles 23 and 59-B, namely: authority to handle linguistic and cultural matters.

One of the greatest problems which the Legislative will have to settle is that of the position which the edicts, or orders-in-council which is the term more generally used, issued by the regional institutions are to occupy in the list of legal enactments drawn up in order of importance—in a word, where is their place in the hierarchy of laws? The Constitution merely provides that the regional bodies will be competent "to settle matters". While this obviously confirms that the regional bodies will be more than purely advisory ones, it does not state whether their "orders-in-council" will have the full effect of statutory regulations or laws. The preparatory work on this article clearly indicates some degree of statutory authority. It may indeed be asserted that the granting of a measure of legislative competence requires a precise and unambiguous constitutional provision to that effect, as in the case of the cultural councils. Furthermore, the Constituent Assembly has not said that only members of Parliament could be members of the regional bodies which are to be set up: other elected representatives may therefore be designated by the Legislative. In those circumstances, the regional bodies could hardly be entrusted with the task of legislation. The fact remains, however, that certain political circles and opinions do not exclude the possibility that such "orders-in-council" might have a legal compass and significance far in excess than that of a mere statutory regulation and that they might even, subject to certain conditions, modify an existing law. The Government statement of 30 April 1974 provides in this connection that "The rulings of the regional councils shall take the form of orders-in-council which, in the hierarchy of authority, shall come between the law and the royal decree. The conditions under which an order-in-council may modify an existing law must be defined".

On the other hand, the fact that the regional bodies will not have fiscal authority is not open to question. The central Government may however make certain financial means available to them. The lack of fiscal authority derives logically from Articles 110 and 113 of the Constitution, which embody a restrictive list of the official bodies which are authorised to levy taxes, namely : the State, the provinces, the urban areas and federations of boroughs, and the boroughs themselves.

Since the promulgation of Article 107-D of the Constitution, a considerable number of regionalisation projects have been put in hand. None of them has managed to secure the majority vote stipulated by the Constitution, either because the various regions could come to no agreement among themselves, or because of differences of opinion as to the nature of the competence to be vested in the regional bodies to be set up, or again the composition of the latter.

In the Government statement of 30 April 1974 the Prime Minister, Mr. Leo Tindemans, explained the Government's intentions from the regional standpoint as follows :

388

"The key to the reform of the State is regionalisation.

"Since the adoption of Article 107-D of the Constitution, attempts have been made on several occasions to draw up a plan for this regionalisation. Up to now, none of these projects has secured the necessary constitutional majority, either because the three regions were unable to agree on the project, or because they started out with contradictory views. The concept of "regionalisation" may indeed take on a totally different significance, depending on the actual content which this term is required to embody.

"A good regionalisation scheme must in fact be considered within the overall context of our institutions. If the new structures were to complicate rather than simplify our institutions, if citizens were to be no better off under the new institutions, and if the latter did not lead to a definite improvement in the relations between Walloons, Flemings and the people of Brussels, then there can be no question of an acceptable regionalisation scheme.

"During the negotiations which led to the formation of this Government, one regionalisation proposal was worked out which, had it been possible to reach an agreement on the boundaries of Brussels, would have been a completely satisfactory one.

"Certainly the rules governing such negotiations are that no agreement exists as long as there is any disagreement on part of the package. But the Government nevertheless believes that the time has come to present the results achieved to date as being the broad outlines of the kind of regionalisation it intends to accomplish.

"In this connection, it should also be pointed out that this agreement should lead, on one side, to a degree of specialisation in the work of the Lower House and the Senate, and on the other, to a revision of the Constitution so as to take the reforms which have been announced to their logical conclusion.

"In this sense, both sides may call it a transitional settlement.

"In the event that, after further negotiations, an agreement is reached, then a bill governing the organisation of the regionalisation process would be tabled within a very short time, based on the following major options:

Competence and prerogatives

"Each of the three regions could rule on the following matters :
— town planning, land development and land policy;
— regional economic expansion and employment policies;
— certain aspects of industrial legislation and energy policy;

— the housing policy;

— policies connected with family planning and population growth;

— public health and hygiene;

— tourism and ancillary matters;

— fishing, hunting and forestry;

— water supplies;

— the re-allocation of rural holdings, urban renovation and the clearance of abandoned industrial sites.

"The dates on which competence and the administrative departments in charge of its exercise are to be effectively transferred, will be set by royal decree.

"It is understood that :

a) the cultural aspects of tourism, together with professional training and reclassification, will remain under the authority of the cultural councils; the law of 21 July 1971 will be modified accordingly.

b) each region may set up in another region such establishments, with the exception of cultural ones, as it sees fit, with the reservation that such establishments shall be set up in obedience to the laws, decrees and orders-in-council governing that region.

Regional Councils

"The Walloon Regional Council and the Flemish Regional Council should each be composed of Senators belonging to the French-speaking group and the Dutch-speaking group respectively, given that :

a) French-speaking senators elected in the Brussels district shall not be members of the Walloon Regional Council;

b) Dutch-speaking Senators elected in the Brussels district and who have their place of residence in the Brussels area shall not be members of the Flemish Regional Council.

"The Brussels Regional Council shall consist of :

1. half the members of the Urban Area Council, designated on the basis of proportional representation;

2. Senators having their place of residence in the Brussels area.

"With regard to the Brussels Urban Area Council, guarantees will have to be provided for in order to safeguard the interests of the Flemish community.

"The rulings of the Regional Councils should take the form of orders-in-council which, in the hierarchy of authority, would rank between an Act of Parliament and a royal decree. The conditions under which such an order-in-council might modify an existing law must be clearly defined.

Executive bodies

"The executive body in each region shall be set up within the Government.

a) For this purpose, the following shall be set up : a Ministerial Committee for Walloon Affairs, a Ministerial Committee for Flemish Affairs, and a Ministerial Committee for Brussels Affairs.

b) The Committee for Walloon Affairs and the Committee for Flemish Affairs will be headed by the corresponding Minister for Regional Affairs, and should include those Ministers and Secretaries of State whose competence includes regionalised matters.

c) The Ministerial Committee for Brussels Affairs would include basically the Minister in charge of Brussels Affairs, assisted by a Secretary of State belonging to the other language group. All orders-in-council and other enactments shall be signed at least by these two members of the Government.

d) The Secretaries of State would be attached to the Minister of Regional Affairs, it being understood that normative orders-in-council and other enactments are to be countersigned also by the Minister who is competent on the national plane.

e) Every Minister in charge of Regional Affairs may be questioned in his regional council solely on the basis of an individual fault or deficiency in his management of affairs, and such interpellation may extend to a concept of criticism that has no direct political influence.

Finances

"Each Council would receive an annual endowment made available to it by Parliament.

"The overall endowment to be appropriated by the Government in its general budget would be distributed among the three regions at the rate of one-third in proportion to the population figure, one-third in proportion to the territorial area, and one-third in proportion to the amount of income tax payable by private persons.

"For each budgetary year, the basis for calculation will be the figures for the penultimate year.

"The boundaries of the regions have yet to be defined.

"The Government is convinced that such a broadly-based proposal for agreement must become the foundation of the progressive implementation of the regionalisation scheme in the interests of the country at large. If a thorough discussion of these concepts could be undertaken once more, it might well be possible to secure a very wide range of agreement.

"The Government appeals urgently to all members of Parliament and the political parties who believe that satisfactory regionalisation could be accomplished by this method. It is convinced that on the basis of this formula, a policy can be put in hand that is better fitted to meet the needs and desires of the regions without the risk of dismantling essential national institutions.

"The Government is ready to embark at once on discussions as to how this regionalisation plan is to be achieved and to examine the way in which the majority constitutionally required for the implementation of Article 107-D of the Constitution may be secured."

On 12 June 1974, after enlarging his Government, Prime Minister Tindemans read a further Government statement on the subject. Faced with the impossibility of securing the majority stipulated by Article 107-D of the Constitution, chiefly because of the problems surrounding the boundary of the Brussels region, the Government felt that some invaluable enlightenment might perhaps be derived from a preparatory or experimental form of regionalisation, and it had therefore drawn up a detailed plan entitled "The Preparatory Phase of Regionalisation", which document was attached to the Government statement as Annexure II. (1)

The Government at once proceeded to submit its project to the legislative procedure. After requesting the opinion of the Council of State (and we shall refer back to this farther on), it tabled a bill in Parliament, which was passed by the Senate on 12 July 1974 and by the Lower House on 20 July 1974. This law was sanctioned and promulgated on 1 August 1974 and gazetted in the *Moniteur belge* of 22 August 1974.

The Government's theory was that the projected law, as indeed evidenced by its heading ("Law setting up regional institutions in preparation for the implementation of Article 107-D of the Constitution") should not be construed as an instrument in implementation of the Constitutional

---

(1) The annexure is not given as, textually, it is virtually identical to the law of 1 August 1974.

article itself. Its legal foundation, according to the Government, did not lie in Article 107-D of the Constitution : the new law merely set up regional councils on an advisory basis, without any power to "rule on matters" as provided for under Article 107-D; for the rest, this piece of legislation regulates relations between the Government and those advisory councils as well as the way in which projects involving regional matters are to be debated in the Cabinet. From the legal standpoint, the Government asserted, none of these organic arrangements requires the special majority stipulated in Article 107-D of the Constitution: Parliament retains the full scope of its legislative authority and no change has been made in the normative power, whereas Article 107-D is specifically aimed at a new distribution of those powers.

The Opposition parties in Parliament nevertheless considered that this law was effectively an instrument of implementation of Article 107-D because it defined the boundaries of the regions, set up regional bodies, and granted them certain powers *ratione materiae.*

The law of 1 August 1974 may be summarised under five headings: territorial competence (or regional boundaries); competence *ratione materiae* (or the definition of functions), the regional councils, the ministerial committees, and the financing system.

a) Territorial competence

Like Article 107-D of the Constitution, the law of 1 August 1974 divides the country into three regions : the Walloon region, the Flemish region, and the Brussels region. The boundaries of these regions are not definitively fixed and are only valid insofar as this law is concerned. The definitive tracing of the boundaries does in fact call for a special majority vote. The Brussels region comprises the territory of the administrative district of Brussels-Capital, or in other words the 19 boroughs forming the Brussels Urban Area.

b) Competence *ratione materiae*

The bodies set up in terms of this law are competent to deal with a range of matters which, save for a few modifications, can be found in some of the previous proposals (such as the land development policy and town planning proposals formulated by the Twenty-eight Group), namely :

1. The policy relating to land development and town planning, including the land ownership policy, the re-allocation of rural holdings, urban renovation, and the clearance of abandoned industrial sites;

2. regional economic expansion and employment policies;

3. the housing policy;

4. policy connected with family planning and population growth;

5. public health and hygiene;

6. tourism;

7. water supplies;

8. hunting, fishing and forestry;

9. industrial and energy policies;

10. borough organisation."

The matters included under these headings are not automatically and compulsorily submitted to the decision-making procedure laid down by the law; they form a framework within which the Government and the regional councils may chart a regional policy. The degree of intensity of regionalisation will therefore depend on the degree of political determination to go ahead in that direction. No clause in this law obliges either the regional councils or the ministerial committees to treat the above-mentioned matters as regional ones. But those councils and committees nevertheless hold the absolute and unrestricted power of initiative in this sphere. In this regard, Clause 4 is characteristic: it provides that "each of the regional councils may, by means of a reasoned motive, take the initiative of making a recommendation on the need to enact, modify or abrogate any legal or statutory provision the implementation of which is restricted to its own region, part of its region, or an institution set up in its region, and to do so in all matters where a differentiated regional policy is justified either in whole or in part." Within the context of their advisory competence, the regional councils are therefore free to decide what, in their opinion, deserves to be regionalised, and they have a free choice as to the legal, statutory or organic measures which they feel should be enacted for regionalisation purposes.

The same goes for the ministerial committees. Here we may start with Clause 10, para. 1 : each ministerial committee shall debate on any bill applicable only to its region, but the Government remains free to table such bills and to decide their purpose and content. Clauses 6 and 10 proceed from the same concept. Clause 11 (finance) deserves special attention in this connection : here again, it is up to the Government to decide what greater or lesser amount is to be appropriated every year in the State budget to cover expenses incurred in pursuing the regionalisation policy. The law is therefore a very flexible one. The breakdown of those matters which are to remain national and those which are to be regionalised could no longer, in the Government's opinion, be done on the basis of questions of principle and abstract theories: years

394

of argument had shown that this kind of approach was fruitless. On the contrary, the Government felt that it would be better, within a sufficiently broad context, to go ahead pragmatically and to rely on the dynamic forces in Parliament, the Government and the regional councils, whose members are nearly all partisans in principle of the regionalisation process.

c) Regional councils

Each region is to have a regional council. The Walloon and Flemish regional councils consist of Senators having their legal place of residence in the region concerned and who are members respectively of the French-speaking or Dutch-speaking group. In order to avoid placing the Flemings of Brussels on a minority footing, the law has arranged the composition of the Brussels regional council in such a way that it comprises firstly those Senators who have their place of residence in the Brussels area, and who belong to either of the two language groups, Dutch or French; and secondly, 42 members of the Brussels Urban Area Council, these 42 seats being allocated in ratio to the effective strength of each language group and, within each group, the seats are allocated by means of a ballot based on a list of candidates, in the same way as seats in the House of Representatives are shared out following a general election.

As we have said, the task of the regional councils is purely an advisory one. The regional council may take the initiative in making a recommendation on the legislative, statutory and organic measures to be enacted (Clause 4) and, more generally, on all aspects of regional policy classified under the ten regionalisable headings (Clause 6, para. 1). Furthermore, it is consulted by the Government on all bills to be tabled in Parliament (Clause 5) and all budget credits (Clause 6, para. 2) pertaining to regional policies and, *a posteriori*, on the decentralisation and devolution measures taken by the Government during the previous twelvemonth (Clause 7).

To sum up : while all laws, even those governing regional matters, continue as in the past to be voted by the National Parliament, the regional councils have nevertheless been granted an unlimited right of initiative enabling them to take an active part in the work of legislation. And it is here that we run into one of the two major objections formulated by the Council of State with respect to the original draft of the bill. This stated that the advice of the regional councils on all bills affecting the regions was to be mandatory. Now, failure to give such advice could have blocked the legislative procedure since, without it, the Government could not table the bill in Parliament. In this regard, the Council of State pointed out that "the Government's viewpoint would be acceptable on the constitutional plane if the projected bill were limited to the creation of regional councils vested with advisory competence. But the advisory regional councils under consideration here have been included in a decision-making process which must lead in the end to a set of regional laws; they thus form, provisionally at least, the corner-stone of a regionalisation phase which comprises the corresponding institution, within the Government itself, of mandatory concertation bodies that are regional in character. This might lead to an encroachment upon the sphere of application of Article 107-D of the Constitution."

The Government considered that it had good and sufficient reasons to dispute the opinion of the Council of State. The Minister for Institutional Reform told the Senate (Parl. Annals, Senate, 11 July 1974, p. 832) : "Firstly, the National Parliament retains its full powers; there is no dismemberment of authority;

"Secondly, the National Parliament may create advisory councils of all kinds with or without any mandatory prior consultation; this has been done on various occasions.

"Thirdly, the National Parliament may vote national laws of regional application; this too has happened on various occasions.

"Fourthly, as all the foregoing points are affirmative, no combination of them can be negative."

The disputed clause was, however, modified in such a way that the advice of the regional councils would be requested, though not actually stipulated or made mandatory: thus, both Parliament and the Government retain their full freedom to legislate.

d) The Ministerial Committees for Regional Affairs.

Clause 9 of the law provides that the three ministerial committees are to be set up by a royal decree debated in the Council of Ministers (Cabinet). This decree was enacted on 8 October 1974. Consequently, the Legislative itself has not specified the composition of these committees. It has indeed defined their task, made rules for the chairmanship and stated the debating method to be followed in them. This system was adopted as a result of the second major objection raised by the Council of State in connection with the original draft of the bill. This stated that the law itself should determine the composition of the ministerial committees and that it should do so in the following way. The following were to sit on the Flemish and Walloon committees : the Ministers in charge of Regional Affairs, those Secretaries of State whose sphere of competence included the matters enumerated in Clause 4, and finally, the Flemish or, as the case might be, French-speaking Ministers and Secretaries of State designated by a royal decree debated in the Cabinet. As for the Brussels Committee, this would consist of the Minister for

Brussels Affairs and two Secretaries of State designated by royal decree debated in the Cabinet, one of whom would belong to a different language group from that of the Minister. The Council of State queried whether these arrangements did not in fact disregard the King's constitutional right to regulate the way in which the Executive authority is organised: "It is true that in many cases, the Legislative lays down that a royal decree must be debated in the Cabinet. In doing so, it grants the latter a certain measure of competence. It is not, however, up to the Legislative to decide on the composition of the Cabinet : it is up to the King in terms of the Constitution (Article 86-B in particular, relative to the linguistic equality as between French-speaking and Dutch-speaking Ministers). As an example, we may cite Clause 3, Section 4 of the law of 16 March 1974 pertaining to the supervision of certain public utilities, which provides : "The Cabinet, or the Ministerial Committee appointed by the King, shall ensure that the bodies referred to in Clause 1 shall adjust their receipts and cut down their expenditure when the latter is such as to cause prejudice to the financial policy of the State." The question therefore arises as to whether the composition of the Ministerial Committees on Regional Affairs should not be reserved for the King."

The law of 1 August 1974 does in fact entrust the composition of the Ministerial Committees on Regional Affairs to the King. The Sovereign is, however, bound by two provisions of the law : firstly, the committees are to be headed by the Ministers in charge of regional affairs in their respective region, and secondly, the Brussels committee must include two Secretaries of State, one of whom must belong to a different language group from that of the Minister for Brussels Affairs. In the event that the present text should leave room for doubt regarding the number of members who are to sit on the Brussels Ministerial Committee, it should be underlined that the Government's intention is clearly reflected in the draft bill and in the additional Government statement of 12 June 1974 : "the Brussels Ministerial Committee shall consist of three members."

The Ministerial Committee for Walloon Affairs comprises :

— the Minister for Walloon Affairs, as its chairman;

— the Minister of National Education (French-speaking);

— the Minister for Institutional Reform (French-speaking);

— the Secretary of State for Forestry, Hunting and Fishing, attached to the Minister for Walloon Affairs;

— the Secretary of State for Regional Economy, attached to the Minister for Walloon Affairs;

— the Secretary of State for Social Affairs, attached to the Minister for Walloon Affairs.

The Ministerial Committee for Flemish Affairs comprises :

— the Minister for Flemish Affairs, as its chairman;
— the Minister of National Education (Dutch-speaking);
— the Minister for Institutional Reform (Dutch-speaking);
— the Secretary of State for Regional Economy, attached to the Minister for Flemish Affairs;
— the Secretary of State for Territorial Development and Housing, attached to the Minister for Flemish Affairs;
— the Secretary of State for Forestry, Hunting and Fishing, attached to the Minister of Flemish Affairs.

The Ministerial Committee for Brussels Affairs comprises :

— the Minister for Brussels Affairs, as its chairman;
— the Secretary of State for Housing, attached to the Minister for Brussels Affairs;
— the Secretary of State for Regional Economy, attached to the Minister for Brussels Affairs.

To provide for the implementation of Clause 9 of the law of 1 August 1974, and in particular the composition of the regional ministerial committees, Prime Minister Tindemans has widened his Government by appointing two new Secretaries of State.

In the same way as the regional councils, the ministerial committees, as constituted bodies, are deprived of powers of decision. They debate on projected laws that are regional in character, on motions and recommendations submitted by their regional council, and proposals for the creation, decentralisation and devolution of public offices; they make proposals regarding the allocation of budget credits and any recommendations they judge necessary in respect of regional policy. From the legal standpoint, there has been absolutely no change in the powers of decision and responsibility to Parliament of the Ministers and Secretaries of State. But, for the first time in the political history of Belgium, a ministerial body—most of whose members, if not all of them, have been granted exclusively regional powers,—is able to devote its entire attention to regional policy, with the support and advice of a representative regional council as it does so.

A safeguard against any ill-judged or partisan regional policy can be found in the principle of an indivisible collegiate body which has been written into the law. Its scope is clearly indicated by the last sentence of Clause 9, which says : "Failing an agreement (between the members of the regional ministerial committee) the matter is submitted to the Cabinet for its decision."

The rock-bottom problem of regionalisation is unquestionably that of relations between the two echelons which have been created. The above-mentioned clause guarantees that a wider discussion on the national plane must take place if disagreement is revealed at the regional ministerial level. Another organic bond between the national and the regional level is established by the clause providing that any Minister (national) or Secretary of State (national) may be called upon in an advisory capacity by a regional ministerial committee, and that he may ask to be heard by that committee.

e) *Finances*

As already stated, Article 107-D has not conferred on the regions the power to levy taxes. *A fortiori* it is forbidden to arrange for such direct fiscal financing by means of an ordinary law. The financial means required to implement the regional policy must therefore of necessity be supplied through the channel of the central machinery of the State.

The financing system worked out for the regions is defined in Clause 11 of the law. It comprises three phases. In the first phase, an overall sum destined to cover expenditures incurred by the regional policy in each of the three regions is appropriated in the State budget. This sum is then distributed among the three regions on the basis of the following criteria, each of which may be regarded as being advantageous for one of the regions: one-third to be distributed in ratio to the population figure of each region; one-third in ratio to the total territorial area of each region; and one-third in ratio to the fruit of the income-tax paid by private persons in the region. In the third phase, the credits thus allocated to each region are used, on the proposal of each regional ministerial committee, to cover certain expenses arising out of regional policy, and become the subject of separate budgets to be tabled in Parliament.

It is up to each ministerial committee to propose the specific purposes for which the credits allocated to each region are to be used. The way in which the overall amount was originally calculated implies no obligation, nor even any general directive, for the final use of the credits that have been allocated. An important factor of the experiment put under way by the Government, this system might subsequently be hailed as a revolutionary departure : the criteria adopted are selfcorrecting ones, and in sharing out the credits the economic and social development of each region is automatically reckoned with.

The process of regionalisation outlined above cannot be dissociated from *economic planning and decentralisation* as instituted by the law of 15 July 1970. It therefore seems useful at this juncture to examine what the Belgian Legislative has already done as a first step towards putting the principle of economic planning and decentralisation into practice.

One of the essential features of the law of 15 July 1970 governing the organisation of economic planning and decentralisation—a law which was the outcome of bill n° 125 tabled in the Lower House on 22 October 1968—is the replacement of an economic policy which was centralised both as to conception and implementation by a policy which, while preserving its national and overall character and still based on a single overall strategy, is intentionally and firmly regional.

This is reflected in the first place by closely associating the regions in the charting and implementation of the Plan. The question here is one of a Five-Year Economic Plan that embraces the public sector and private enterprise alike, and which covers all aspects : national, regional and sectorial. It is worked out by an Office specially set up for the purpose : the Planning Office, which comprises a general directorate, a sectorial directorate and a regional directorate. Once it has been adopted the Plan is mandatory where the public authorities are concerned (and this is reflected annually in the budgets), contractually binding on those industrial enterprises which benefit from State encouragement, and indicative for the rest. Framed with great flexibility, it permits— through the channel of the "economic budget"— an annual process of adaptation in step with fluctuations in the general economy and with unexpected developments. Democratically, the Plan is the fruit of consultations between social partners at a threefold level : the national level, within the National Committee for Economic Expansion, the Central Economic Council and the National Labour Council; at the industrial sector level, within the Trade and Industrial Councils; and at the regional level, in the Regional Economic Councils. It is also democratic in that the Plan must be formally approved by Parliament.

The Legislative's desire to see a frankly regional economic policy go into force is also reflected by the institutionalisation of certain economic bodies that had been set up on a pragmatic basis, but mainly by the creation of Regional Economic Councils and the setting up of Regional Development Corporations.

In Belgium, unlike the situation prevailing in most of the other countries of Western Europe, the concept of a policy of regional development in the strict sense of the term (i.e., a policy aimed at eliminating the discrepancies between the various regions) is a fairly recent one.

It may be stated that the starting signal for a specifically regional development policy was only given in 1959. It was the law of 18 July 1959 that instituted special measures designed to overcome the economic and social difficulties confronting certain regions. It is true that some action in this direction had already been taken, such as a study of the regional economic situation and the charting of action programmes.

These initiatives were generally put in hand either by the provincial and regional administrations or by private enterprise, and in many cases by both of them acting jointly.

The first economic development body to appear in Belgium was the "Walloon Economic Council" set up in 1945 on the initiative of private persons belonging to the borough councils and to workers' and employers' associations.

From 1950 on, the same line was followed in the Flemish part of the country, with the setting up of an "Economische Raad voor Vlaanderen" in 1952 and, on the provincial plane, the "Limburgse Economische Raad" (1951), the "West-Vlaamse Economische Raad" (1954), and the "Raad voor Antwerpen" (1956). In 1959 we witnessed the inception of the Economic Council for the Brussels District, and in 1960, that of a Provincial Committee for economic expansion in Brabant. Finally, in 1969, the "Economische Raad voor Vlaams Brabant" came into existence.

In the Walloon part of the country, the Walloon Economic Council had meanwhile been organising branch offices in Hainaut, the Liège province, the Luxemburg province, the Namur province, and Walloon Brabant.

The action initiated at the level of the boroughs was aimed essentially at attracting new capital investment to the territory of the borough concerned. Experience was however to demonstrate in short order that the borough context was far too narrow to allow of really effective progress, for instance in such spheres as electrification, water supplies, etc.

The law of 1 March 1922 had already made it possible for the boroughs to enter into associations for purposes of public utility, and these associations could be extended—providing that the influence of the boroughs remained paramount—to embrace the State, the provinces, and private persons. The above-mentioned law of 18 July 1959 was however to create a new kind of intermunicipal association, namely : the regional engineering corporations.

Some of the corporations thus created operated on a provincial basis. Most of them, however, were set up on a more restricted geographical basis. The work of the intermunicipal associations is largely directed both towards economic expansion and the development of the area in which it operates.

By recognising the provincial committees for economic expansion (Ministerial decrees of 13 July 1959 and 23 February 1960 (1) and by authorising the setting up of regional economic engineering corporations (law of 18 July 1958), the Government had already manifested its intention of encouraging the inception of regional structures.

The problem of economic decentralisation was thoroughly analysed for the first time by the Commission for Institutional Reform. This body reached the conclusion that economic decentralisation should respond to the threefold concern outlined as follows:

"1. It should promote the economic growth or redevelopment of the regions;

2. It should secure the participation of the local population in that achievement;

3. It should adapt and simplify the functioning of existing institutions."

On this basis, the Commission worked out a decentralisation plan, some features of which found their way into the law of 15 July 1970.

Government and Parliament alike considered that economic decentralisation was permissible within the existing context and that no revision of the Constitution was necessary in this sphere. Consequently, ordinary legislative procedures were followed in providing for the legal establishment of economic decentralisation, and in particular an affirmative vote in the Senate and the Lower House on 2 and 3 July 1970 on a bill providing for the organisation of economic programming and decentralisation, which became law on 15 July 1970.

As already stated, the important feature of this law insofar as the present subject is concerned was not only the creation of a Planning Office comprising, among others, a regional directorate, but also and above all the creation or the institutionalisation of Regional Economic Councils and the setting up of regional development corporations.

---

(1) The following have been recognised as provincial committees for economic expansion :

— the "Limburgse Economische Raad";
— the "West-Vlaamse Economische Raad";
— the "Economische Raad voor Oost-Vlaanderen";
— the "Economische Raad voor Antwerpen";
— the Hainaut Economic Expansion Committee;
— the Province of Liège Economic Expansion Committee;
— the Province of Namur Economic Expansion Committee.

I. THE REGIONAL ECONOMIC COUNCILS

By creating these Councils in the form of institutions endowed with a legal status, the legislators of 15 July 1970 fulfilled the wish often expressed by the unofficial representatives of the regions. The institutionalisation of the Walloon Economic Council and the Economische Raad voor Vlaanderen, which had hitherto been non-profitmaking associations, now permitted them to exercise permanent influence over the public authorities.

The law of 15 July 1970 thus created or institutionalised :

— the Regional Economic Council for Wallonia;
— the Regional Economic Council for Flanders;
— the Regional Economic Council for Brabant.

The Regional Economic Council for Wallonia and the Regional Economic Council for Flanders are each composed of :

a) 18 members of Parliament presented by the political parties;

b) 12 members of the provincial councils presented by those councils;

c) 15 members presented by the organisations representing industry, the middle classes, and agriculture;

d) 15 members presented by the organisations representing the workers.

These members are appointed by the King on the basis of double lists. The members thus appointed designate at least six and at most ten of their number, chosen for their specific economic qualifications.

The composition of the Regional Economic Council for Brabant is rather a special one because of the bilingual nature of the province and the fact that its territorial area contains the urban area of Greater Brussels. We shall refer back to this at the end of our commentary on this constitutional article.

The Regional Economic Councils are not vested with statutory authority nor with powers of decision. Their competence is purely an advisory one coupled with general powers of recommendation.

Their specific tasks are as follows :

1. to study economic problems;

2. to make prior recommendations on :

a) the appointment of members of the regional directorate of the Planning Office;

b) the geographical compass of the regional development corporations;

c) the allocation of the principal budget credits appropriated for regional economic expansion and the way in which they are used, such as those involving infrastructures and social engineering;

d) bills and proposals for laws or general regulations pertaining to regional development and to decisions as to the regions to be developed;

e) either on their own initiative or at the request of the Government, on any problem affecting economic development.

3. to amass all data and suggestions coming from the regional development corporations, coordinate them and, if necessary, reconcile possibly divergent interests;

4. to adopt projects under the regional plan;

5. to forward such projects to the Planning Office;

6. to amass all information or reports pertaining to the implementation of that part of the Plan involving their region.

By means of a decree debated in the Cabinet, the King may extend the advisory competence vested in the Regional Economic Councils and specify those cases in which it is mandatory for the Government to consult them.

In terms of Clause 8, para. 2 of the law of 15 July 1970, the Regional Economic Councils also participate in the management of the Industrial Promotion Office, a public utility endowed with legal status set up under the same law and whose essential task involves a systematic search for all viable production possibilities. The General Council of this Office (Royal decree of 12 June 1971) does in fact include among its members six representatives of the Regional Economic Councils (two for each Regional Council).

Thus, the Regional Economic Councils are called upon to become the valid interlocutors of central Government on the regional plane, and to act, so to speak, as the universal joint in the new structures which are rounded off by the regional development corporations.

2. THE REGIONAL DEVELOPMENT CORPORATIONS

These corporations have been set up under civil law and endowed with legal status. Their tasks and prerogatives are defined as follows in Clause 15, para. 2 of the law of 15 July 1970 :

"2. The regional development corporations :

a) deal with the general survey, charting and promotion of economic development within their compass;

b) draw up an inventory of requirements in their region, prepare a progress report on the work in hand, and forward to the Regional Economic Council concerned all pertinent data for use in charting the projected regional plan and in its implementation;

c) for the purpose of accomplishing the plan, are vested with a general competence to put forward suggestions, to promote and coordinate proposals both in respect of private circles and of the public authorities, in order to promote productive forms of activity, the development of the territory, social engineering and regional infrastructures; ;

d) may, on their own authority, expropriate, engineer, equip, lease, sell or convey any building, and undertake any material action likely to accelerate or amplify the private or public investment provided for in terms of the plan;

e) by delegation, and at State expense or possibly that of the province or the boroughs, perform or cause to be performed all expropriations, work and any other public tasks of a technical nature; ;

f) may directly proceed with industrial projects, particularly those suggested by the Industrial Promotion Office, with the technical and financial assistance of the National Investment Corporation or of any Regional Investment Corporation, in the event of non-co-operation on the part of the private sector. The powers necessary for these purposes are defined by Royal decree on the recommendation of the competent Regional Economic Council."

In terms of Clause 15, Section 1, para. 2 of the law, the initiative in setting up the regional development corporations is vested in the provincial councils and, where Brabant is concerned, in each section of the Provincial Council. The territorial compass of these corporations may cover one or several provinces or parts of them. It is determined on the basis of a motivated recommendation from the competent Regional Economic Council, by Royal decrees debated in the Cabinet.

A Royal Decree of 16 June 1972, regulating procedures with regard to the initiative of creating the regional development corporations, convened the provincial councils in extraordinary session on 22 June 1972 with a mandatory item on its agenda : "The initiative of creating regional development corporations."

The provincial councils of Antwerp, Limburg, East Flanders, West Flanders, and Luxemburg proposed that a regional development corporation should be set up whose territorial compass should coincide with the present administrative boundaries of each of those provinces.

In the provinces of Hainaut, Liège and Namur, the creation was proposed of a single regional development corporation whose territorial compass should include the whole of the Hainaut, Liège and Namur provinces plus the administrative district of Nivelles.

The sections of the Brabant Provincial Council suggested on 6 July 1972 the creation of :

1. one regional development corporation for the administrative district of Brussels-Capital;

2. one R.D.C. for the district of Hal-Vilvorde;

3. one R.D.C. for the Louvain district; and

4. the attachment of the Nivelles administrative district to a R.D.C. whose compass would be combined with that of the Walloon Regional Economic Council.

In terms of the Royal decree of 16 June 1972 (Clause 6), the Regional Economic Councils were required to frame, within thirty days of the receipt of proposals submitted by the provincial councils, a motivated recommendation concerning the territorial compass of the regional development corporations. The "Gewestelijke Economische Raad voor Vlaanderen" (G.E.R.V.) formulated a recommendation on 10 July 1972 advocating the creation of a single R.D.C. for the provinces of Antwerp, Limburg, East and West Flanders, and of another R.D.C. whose territorial compass should embrace the Flemish part of the province of Brabant.

The Regional Economic Council for Wallonia gave its opinion on 10 July 1972 that only one R.D.C. should be set up, whose territorial compass should coincide with that of the Council itself, namely : the provinces of Hainaut, Liège, Luxemburg, and Namur, plus the administrative district of Nivelles.

The Brabant Economic Council, for its part, recommended on 17 July 1972 that the territorial compass of the regional development corporations to be set up in Brabant should be drawn so as to coincide firstly with the territory of the administrative district of Brussels-Capital, and secondly with the overall territory of the administrative districts of Hal-Vilvorde and Louvain, while the territory of the Nivelles district would come within the compass of the R.D.C. whose overall territory coincided with that of the Regional Economic Council for Wallonia.

A Royal decree of 2 August 1972 finally specified as follows the respective territorial compass of the regional development corporations :

1. the province of Antwerp;

2. the province of Limburg;

3. the province of East Flanders;

4. the province of West Flanders;

5. the administrative districts of Hal-Vilvorde and Louvain;

6. the provinces of Hainaut, Liège, Luxemburg, and Namur, plus the administrative district of Nivelles;

7. the administrative district of Brussels-Capital.

This leads to the conclusion that five regional development corporations will be set up within the compass of the "Gewestelijke Economische Raad voor Vlaanderen" (which, in terms of the Royal Decree of 12 March 1971 defining the compass and terms of appointment of members of the Regional Economic Councils, comprises the provinces of Antwerp, Limburg, East and West Flanders, and the administrative districts of Louvain and Hal-Vilvorde).

Within the compass of the Regional Economic Council for Wallonia, there exists one regional development corporation whose statutes were approved by Royal Decree on 17 September 1973.

Within the compass of the Brabant Economic Council—which comprises the province of Brabant—three regional development corporations are operating, namely : the Brussels-Vilvorde-Louvain regional development corporation, the Brussels-Capital regional development corporation, and insofar as the Nivelles district is concerned, the regional development corporation for Wallonia.

The competence and prerogatives of the R.D.C.s. (Clause 15, para. 2-b) reveal that they act in very close liaison with their respective Regional Economic Council when it comes to charting and implementing the regional plan.

The Regional Economic Councils themselves, under Clause 13, para. 2, n° 3 of the law, are called upon to act as coordinators where the R.D.C.s. operating within their respective compass are concerned, and to ensure proper co-operation with all the offices or institutions involved.

Furthermore, in terms of Clause 15 (f) of that same law, the R.D.C. may, in the event of non-co-operation by the private sector, proceed at once with the implementation of industrial projects, particularly those suggested by the Industrial Promotion Office. The necessary powers for this purpose are defined by Royal decree on the basis of a recommendation from the competent Regional Economic Council.

It should also be noted that the framework law of 15 July 1970 provides explicitly that the tasks of the R.D.C. shall not be prejudicial to the competence vested in the intermunicipal associations governed by the law of 1 March 1922 and that of the regional economic engineering corporations provided for by the law of 18 July 1959 previously mentioned.

As for the territorial compass of the Brabant Regional Economic Council, it comprises the entire province of Brabant, namely : Brussels-Capital (all 19 boroughs) and the administrative districts of Hal-Vilvorde, Louvain, and Nivelles.

Apart from Brussels-Capital, the province of Brabant comes under the Brabant Regional Economic Council itself, or under the Gewestelijke Economische Raad voor Vlaanderen (Hal-Vilvorde) or under the Regional Economic Council for Wallonia (district of Nivelles).

The Brabant Regional Economic Council, which holds the same prerogatives as the Gewestelijke Economische Raad voor Vlaanderen and the Regional Economic Council for Wallonia (Clause 13 of the law of 15 July 1970) nevertheless differs somewhat in its composition, principally because it is characterised by a dual form of equality : firstly, the linguistic equality of its members, and secondly, equality as between Brussels-Capital and the other parts of the Brabant province. In point of fact, the Brabant Regional Economic Council comprises 24 members representing the Brussels Urban Area and 24 members representing the rest of the province, half of whom are sponsored by the Gewestelijke Economische Raad voor Vlaanderen and the other half by the Regional Economic Council for Wallonia.

A final comment is that, in accordance with the provisions of Clause 10 of the law of 15 July 1970, the Regional Economic Council for Wallonia has chosen the city of Namur as its headquarters; the Gewestelijke Economische Raad voor Vlaanderen has opted for Antwerp; and the Brabant Regional Economic Council is established in the city of Brussels.

CHAPTER IV

THE PROVINCIAL
AND MUNICIPAL INSTITUTIONS

ARTICLE 108

"Provincial and municipal institutions are regulated by the law.

"The law sanctions the application of the following principles :

" 1. The direct election of the members of provincial and borough councils;

" 2. The attribution to provincial and borough councils of all matters of provincial and borough interest, without prejudice to the approval of their acts in such cases and in accordance with such procedure as the law may determine;

" 3. The decentralisation of authority in favour of provincial and borough institutions;

"4. Public sittings by provincial and borough councils within the limits prescribed by law;

"5. Publication of budgets and accounts;

"6. The intervention of the tutelary authority or of the Legislative to prevent infringement of the law or injury to the general interest.

"Several provinces or several boroughs may come to an agreement or form an association under such conditions and according to such procedure as shall be determined by the law, for the purpose of settling and jointly pursuing objectives of provincial or of borough interest. This notwithstanding, it is not permissible that several provincial councils or several borough councils should hold meetings for deliberating together. "

In 1831, Article 108 was drawn up as follows :

"Provincial and municipal institutions are regulated by laws.

"These laws sanction the application of the following principles :

"1. Direct election, save any exceptions which the law may establish in regard to the heads of the municipal administrations and the government commissioners on the provincial councils;

"2. The attribution to provincial and borough councils of all matters of provincial and borough interest, without prejudice to the approval of their acts in such cases and in accordance with such procedure as the law may determine;

"3. Public sittings by provincial and borough councils within the limits prescribed by law;

"4. Publication of budgets and accounts;

"5. The intervention of the King or of the legislative authority to prevent the provincial and borough councils from overstepping the limits of their attributions and from injuring the general interest."

During the Second Revision (1919-1921), the following paragraph was added after Section 2:

"Several provinces or several boroughs may come to an understanding or form an association under the conditions and according to the procedure to be determined by law, for the purpose of settling and jointly pursuing objectives of provincial or of borough interest. However, it cannot be permitted that several provincial councils or several boroughs should deliberate together."

The present text was adopted during the Third Revision (1967-1971).

It differs in various ways from the former wording.

N° 1 is worded more accurately, and therefore more concisely and simply : the former version established the principle of direct election and provided for exceptions, whereas the new version establishes the principle of the direct election of all members of the borough and provincial councils.

It should be recalled that the borough councils elect their aldermen from among their own members, so that the latter are in fact elected at one remove. The provincial councils elect from among their members those who are to serve on the Permanent Deputation, which is also an indirect election. As for the Burgomasters (Mayors) of boroughs and the Governors of provinces, they are appointed by royal decree.

N° 2 has remained unchanged.

N° 3, an entirely new clause, is of capital importance : it enables the legislator to entrust certain attributions to the provincial and borough institutions. One of the targets of the Revision was to react against what was regarded as excessive centralisation. By means of this new clause, the fourth Constituent Assembly has opened up a constitutional road leading to decentralisation, the extent of which remains for the Legislative to decide. As everything which is of provincial or borough interest has already been entrusted to the provincial and borough councils in terms of clause 2, the law may now entrust certain tasks which are nationwide in character to those same subordinate authorities.

N° 4 is the same as the former N° 3.

N° 5 is the same as the former N° 4. The principle of public sessions of the provincial and borough councils corresponds to the rule governing public sittings of the Houses.

N° 6 (formerly N° 5) comprises two innovations :

— the intervention of the King has been replaced by the intervention of the tutelary authority, which allows the legislator to lighten the task of overseeing or to entrust it to other bodies closer to the municipal authorities. The purpose here is to render administrative supervision more effective, less cumbersome, but above all, faster. In fact, this clause opens up another possible form of decentralisation by making the systematic intervention of the central authorities no longer necessary.

— the second innovation consists of replacing the words "to prevent the provincial and borough councils from overstepping the limits of their attributions" by the words "to prevent infringement of the law", which is far more precise.

The original article 108 was the foundation of municipal and provincial autonomy and democracy; the new text adds a further concept, that of decentralisation.

ARTICLE 108-B

"Section 1. The law shall create urban areas and federations of boroughs. It shall determine their organisation and their powers, applying the principles laid down in Article 108.

"For each urban area and for each federation there shall be a council and an executive body.

"The Chairman of the executive body shall be elected by the council from amongst its members; his election shall be ratified by the King; the law shall determine his status.

"Articles 107 and 129 shall apply to decrees and regulations issued by the urban areas and federations of boroughs.

"The boundaries of urban areas and federations of boroughs may not be altered or amended other than by legislation.

"Section 2. The law shall set up the body within which each urban area and the nearest federations of boroughs shall act in concert, under such conditions and according to such procedure as it shall specify, to examine common problems of a technical nature coming within their respective fields of jurisdiction.

"Section 3. Several federations of boroughs may come to an understanding amongst themselves or enter into association under such conditions and according to such procedure as the law shall determine for the purpose of settling and jointly pursuing objectives coming within their jurisdiction. It is not permissible for their councils to hold joint meetings for deliberating together."

This article was adopted during the Third Revision (1967-1971).

It institutes the urban areas and federations of boroughs.

There is no difference, from the legal standpoint, between the federations of boroughs and the urban areas, either essentially or structurally, or in the composition of the bodies operating within them, or in the method whereby their members are elected. The sole difference between them is a factual one : the term "urban area" refers, as its name implies, to urban concentrations, whereas the federations comprise less populated entities.

The federations and urban areas are not voluntary associations; the decision to create them rests with the Legislative, depending or not on the wishes of the borough councils concerned.

The democratic management of the new entities is guaranteed by a council and an executive body.

The council of a federation or an urban area is elected by the population. Members of the executive body are elected by the council from among its own members. The chairman of the executive body is also elected on this basis, subject to ratification by the King. In a word, it is the same procedure as that governing the election of Burgomasters (Mayors) of ordinary boroughs.

As the councils of the federations and urban areas have no legislative authority, it is normal that their decrees and regulations (which only become compulsory when they have been made public by the proper procedure) may be censured by the law courts and tribunals.

Section 3 provides for the setting up of a body within which each urban area and the nearest federations of boroughs may act in concert; this applies also to the interfederations. Like the provincial and borough councils, those of the urban areas and federations of boroughs may not deliberate together in joint sessions.

The law referred to in Section 1 of Article 108-B was promulgated on 26 July 1971. It set up five urban areas : the Antwerp area, the Brussels area, the Charleroi area, the Ghent area, and the Liège area; as well as five peripheral federations : Hal, Asse, Vilvorde, Zaventem, and Tervuren. By "peripheral federation" should be understood a federation uniting those boroughs nearest to an urban area. Any borough in the Kingdom which is not part of an urban area may become part of a federation. During the period beginning on 1 January 1975 and ending on 31 December 1976, the King shall designate which federation every borough in the Kingdom belongs to which is not already part of one or another federation or urban area or which, even after a merger, does not constitute a sufficiently large entity.

Clause 4 of the law defines the competence of the urban areas and federations as follows :

"Section 1. The urban areas and federations shall promote coordination of action between the boroughs, particularly the technical coordination of the borough police departments.

Section 2. In the following matters, the competence of the boroughs shall be transferred to the urban area or federation :

1. The adoption of general development plans, after securing the recommendation of the boroughs, in the conditions laid down by the King;

2. recommendations on individual development plans;

3. recommendations on plans for each sector;

4. regulations governing building construction and land apportionment;

5. garbage collection and sewerage;

6. floodwater drainage and prevention in low-lying areas;

7. transportation of fare-paying passengers;

8. economic expansion, as regulated by the law of 30 December 1970;

9. the defence and protection of the environment, including green belts, the fight against noise and pollution, and the restoration of beauty-spots and historic buildings;

10. fire-fighting and fire prevention;

11. urgent medical assistance.

Section 3. With the agreement or at the request of at least half the boroughs which constitute it, and on condition that those boroughs represent at least two-thirds of the population, the urban area or federation may regulate :

1. the creation, taking over, management and lighting of all streets in the urban area or federation, further rules governing the traffic police and traffic regulations in those streets, the alignment plans pertaining thereto, and the granting of land apportionment permits involving the creation or alteration of the street system;

2. airports;

3. decisions as to the location of open-air markets of interest to the federation, urban area, or region;

4. slaughterhouses;

5. public parking areas for cars;

6. tourist promotion, reception and information;

7. camping, including caravaning;

8. crematoria and columbaria;

9. the organisation of services providing technical assistance to the boroughs of which it is composed.

Section 4. The urban area or the federation shall furthermore exercise :

1. the competence presently exercised by the State or the province and which has been transferred to it under the heading of decentralisation and devolution;

2. such competence as the urban area council or the federation council agrees to exercise at the request of one or several of the boroughs in its territory.

Section 5. In the matters referred to under Sections 2, 3 and 4, the urban area and the federation hold powers of decision which are exercised, in terms of the present law, through their competent bodies.

These bodies exercise the competence vested in them by means of statutory decrees.

In the matter of any other problems affecting the urban area or federation, the latter is empowered to make recommendations to the borough authorities.

Within the period stipulated in the recommendation, the authority to which it is addressed shall advise what action has been taken."

Clauses 6 to 42 of the law lay down the detailled regulations governing the composition, institution and competence of the bodies referred to in para. 2 of Section 1 of Article 108-B of the Constitution, namely : the urban area council or the federation council, and its executive committee.

The *urban area or federation council,* the number of whose members is fixed by the King in ratio to the population figure (with a minimum of 15 and a maximum of 83) is completely renewed every six years in a direct ballot of all the municipal electorate. When the municipal electorate is summoned to proceed with the ordinary re-election of the borough councils, it will at the same time proceed to re-elect the urban area or federation council. The law regulates details of the electoral procedure to which a certain number of clauses of the law governing municipal elections apply.

As for its competence and prerogatives, the urban area or federation council :

1) regulates everything coming within the competence of the urban area or federation in terms of the law;

2) debates on every matter submitted to it by the higher authorities;

3) frames the regulations governing the internal administration and policing of the urban area or federation;

4) may establish police penalties sanctioning infringements of its regulations and edicts.

The *executive committee* consists of a president and of members chosen from the council who are mandated for a six-year term. The number of members forming the committee is fixed by the King in ratio to the number of councillors (with a minimum of 3 and a maximum of 9). The president of the committee is elected by the members of the urban council by means of a secret ballot and on the basis of an outright majority vote. His election is ratified by the King. When the results of the ballot for the election of the council have been proclaimed, the urban area office (electoral office) sets the number of members of the committee, with the exception of its president, to be drawn from each list of candidates respectively. When the president has been elected, the councillors elected from each list of candidates shall forward to the president a list of members' names taken in order from the roll of elected councillors and who are to be members of the executive committee.

In terms of Clause 42 of the law, the committee is entrusted, within the context of the competence conferred on the urban area or federation:

1. with the implementation of the council's decisions;

2. with the implementation of the laws, decrees and edicts, whether of a general nature or provincial;

3. with framing the draft budget of receipts and expenditures;

4. with the management of income, the authorisation of payment for expenditures, and the supervision of accounts;

5. with the management of the common inheritance and existing establishments, and the preservation of the rights and entitlements of the urban area or federation;

6. with the management of the general services and facilities of the urban area or federation, including its public corporations;

7. with the supervision of work projects;

8. with the management and supervision of personnel;

9. with the granting of permits and authorisations;

10. with legal proceedings, either as plaintiff or as defendant.

However, the council's authorisation is required when legal proceedings are instituted as plaintiff, other than summary procedures of injunction, actions for possession, conservatory acts, or suits for the interruption of prescription or forfeitures."

The personnel of an urban area or federation comprises, among others: a secretary (and possibly an assistant secretary) and a receiver, appointed by the council. Members of the personnel of municipal institutions and offices affected by the transfer of competence to the urban area or federation are automatically taken over by the latter. The employees of State corporations and public utilities as specified by law, and of provincial departments specified by the Permanent Deputation of the provincial council may, at their own request, be transferred to the urban area or the federation.

On the financial plane, the urban area or federation may levy taxes, levy the additional centimes added to the provincial taxes, the additional centimes on the immovable property taxes, an additional levy on the taxes paid by private persons, all of these being subject to the King's approval. The urban area and the federation may also receive subsidies, donations and legacies, and they may contract or float loans, subject to the King's approval. Until such time as a Local Authorities Fund is set up for the benefit of the urban areas, federations and boroughs, a special credit is to be appropriated annually in the State budget. The urban area or federation council may ask the boroughs to contribute to expenses incurred by the urban area or federation in the exercise of their prerogatives in terms of Clause 4, Section 4, paragraph 2, of the law.

With the King's permission, the urban area and the federation may undertake expropriations for reasons of public utility.

Administrative supervision is exercised by the King alone in respect of the urban areas and the boroughs of which they consist, and by the Permanent Deputation in respect of the federations and the boroughs which are part of them.

Finally, the law has instituted for each urban area and its peripheral federations, a "concertation committee" which may submit to the urban area and federations concerned such opinions, recommendations and proposals for agreement as may relate to problems of a technical nature coming within the competence of the urban area and the federations concerned and which affect more than one of those institutions.

ARTICLE 108-C

"Section 1. Article 108-B applies to the urban area to which the capital of the Kingdom belongs, except as is hereinafter specified.

"Section 2. For those cases laid down in the Constitution and by legislation, the members of the urban area council are divided into a French language group and a Dutch language group in the manner prescribed by law.

"The executive body is composed of an uneven number of members. With the exception of the Chairman, there is the same number of members in the French language group as in the Dutch language group.

"Section 3. Except in the case of budgets, a reasoned motion signed by at least three-quarters of the members of a linguistic group in the urban area council and tabled before the final voting in public session may declare that such provisions as it specifies in a draft or proposed regulation or decree by the urban area council are likely to do grave harm to relations between the communities.

"In this case, the procedure in the urban area council is suspended and the motion referred back to the executive body which, within thirty days, pronounces its reasoned judgment on the matter and amends the draft or proposed instrument where necessary.

"The tutelary power in respect of the regulation or decree adopted after this procedure is exercised by the King on a motion by the Cabinet.

"This procedure may only be applied once by the members of a linguistic group in respect of one and the same draft or proposal.

"Section 4. In the urban area there is a French committee for culture and a Dutch committee for culture which are composed of an equal number of members elected respectively by the French language group and by the Dutch language group in the urban area council.

"Each has the same powers in respect of its cultural community as the other organising authorities:

"1. in pre-schooling, post educational and cultural matters;

"2. in education.

"Section 5. The French committee and the Dutch committee for culture together constitute joint committees. Decisions of the joint committees are only adopted if they obtain in each committee the majority of votes cast.

"The joint committees are competent in the matters laid down in Section 4 which are of common interest and which promote the national and international mission of the urban area.

"Section 6. The committees referred to in Sections 4 and 5 also fulfil the functions vested in them by the Legislative, the Cultural Councils or the Government.

"The law regulates the organisation and operating procedures of these committees."

Like the previous one, this article was adopted during the Third Revision (1967-1971).

Brussels, in view of its importance as the capital city, together with the neighbouring boroughs all forming an urban area, is now the subject of a special article written into the Constitution.

The new article organises such an urban area with special attention to its bilingual character: indeed, the Dutch-speaking minority living there benefits by a degree of protection similar to that afforded, on the national scale, to the French-speaking minority.

The council of the Brussels urban area is, like the national representative assemblies, divided into a French-language group and a Dutch-language group, each with the right to table a reasoned motion whereby either language group may state that this or that draft or proposed regulation or urban decree is likely to do grave harm to relations between the communities.

Within the urban area, French-speaking and Dutch-speaking residents enjoy a cultural autonomy which is exercised by two committees for culture.

Finally, the executive body, with the exception of a single member, is composed of an equal number of French-speaking and Dutch-speaking members.

It follows that the Constituent Assembly has created a system protecting the Dutch-speaking minority in the Brussels urban area which is similar to the guarantees introduced for the benefit of the French-speaking population on the national plane. Indeed, the French-speaking community is protected by the institution of cultural autonomy, the so-called "alarm-bell" system, and linguistic equality in the Cabinet; likewise, at the level of Brussels, the Dutch-speaking community benefits from what amounts to numerical parity in the executive body, the "alarm-bell" procedure, and the setting-up of the two committees for culture.

*
* *

Article 108-C was implemented by means of Clauses 61 to 83 of the law of 26 July 1971 which provided for the organisation of urban areas and federations of boroughs.

It will be recalled that the Brussels Urban Area includes the territories of the following boroughs : Anderlecht, Auderghem, Berchem-Sainte-Agathe, Brussels, Etterbeek, Evere, Forest, Ganshoren, Ixelles, Jette, Koekelberg, Molenbeek-Saint-Jean, Saint-Gilles, Saint-Josse-ten-Noode, Schaerbeek, Uccle, Watermael-Boitsfort, Woluwe-Saint-Lambert, and Woluwe-Saint-Pierre.

Clause 62 of the law of 26 July 1971 mentioned above defines the criteria according to which the decision is made as to which of the linguistic groups, French or Dutch, a candidate member of the Brussels Urban Area Council belongs.

In terms of Clause 65 of the same law, the executive committee of the Brussels Urban Area comprises a president, six members from the French language group and six members from the Dutch language group, all chosen from among the Council's members for a term of six years. Clause 72 of the same law stipulates that the French Culture Committee and the Dutch Culture Committee provided for in terms of Article 108-C of the Constitution have been given the following specific tasks within the context of the matters placed within their sphere of competence by that article :

"1. to frame and implement a programme covering the cultural, educational, pre- and post-school infrastructure;

"2. to set up the necessary institutions, assume the management of them, and to grant subsidies under the conditions laid down by the law of 29 May modifying the legislation pertaining to kindergarten, primary, intermediate, secondary, normalian, technical and artistic education;

"3. to submit recommendations to Parliament, the Cultural Councils, the Government, the provincial authorities, the urban area and the boroughs forming the urban area, and to give those authorities the benefit of its considered opinion, either on the initiative of the Committee itself or at the request of the said authorities;

"4. to take the initiative in cultural matters and to promote such initiatives;

"5. to accomplish any other tasks that might be laid on it by the Legislative, by a Cultural Council, or by the Government."

The joint committees shall exercise the prerogatives of each committee when the question is one of matters of common interest.

In matters coming within their sphere of competence, the committees may frame regulations and edicts which are to be submitted for the King's approval.

Each committee consists of eleven members, elected for a term of six years, either by the French language group in the Council (for the French culture committee) or by the Dutch language group in the Council (for the Dutch culture committee).

ARTICLE 109

"The establishing of birth, marriage and death certificates and the keeping of the registers come exclusively within the competence of the borough authorities."

This article dates from 1831 and has never been modified.

It entrusts a specific task to the municipal authorities.

In the old days, this work was done by the ministers of religion. But freedom of worship and opinion, which also includes the freedom not to belong to any religion, required that the civil registers be kept by a neutral authority acceptable to all citizens. Such an authority is furthermore in the best position to carry out this task since it is in close contact with the people concerned.

HEADING IV

FINANCES

ARTICLE 110

"No tax for the benefit of the State may be levied other than in pursuance of a law.

"No charge or levy may be imposed by a province, urban centre, federation of boroughs, or borough other than on a resolution by their respective councils.

"The law shall determine, in the case of the levies forming the subject of paragraph 2, such exceptions as shall be seen to be necessary."

This article was modified during the Third Revision (1967-1971) and replaces the former text of 1831 reading as follows:

"No tax for the benefit of the State may be levied other than in pursuance of a law.

"No provincial charge or levy may be imposed save with the consent of the provincial council.

"No municipal charge or levy may be imposed save with the consent of the borough council.

"The law shall determine the exceptions which experience has shown to be necessary, with respect to provincial and municipal taxation."

The 1970 Constituent Assembly, like that of 1831, considered that no tax should be levied without the consent of the actual representatives elected by the citizens concerned.

As the 1970 Constituent Assembly had brought new institutions into being: the urban areas and the federations of boroughs (see Article 108-B), the Assembly deemed it essential to extend the implementation of the principle laid down in Article 110 to embrace those new institutions.

The scope of the former Article 110 and that of the new version are identical: any taxation levied by a public body must receive the prior assent of the corresponding representative assemblies.

Institutions at five levels have the right to levy taxes: the borough, the federation of boroughs, the urban area, the province, and the State, even though it should be remembered that a federation of boroughs and an urban area are terms describing one and the same thing, so that each citizen will pay taxes to four institutions at the very most.

It should be added that a proposal had been made to give the regions and the cultural communities similar powers to levy taxes, but such proposals were set aside by the Constituent Assemblies (see Articles 107-D and 59-B).

ARTICLE 111

" Taxes for the benefit of the State are voted annually.

"The laws establishing them are effective during one year only, unless they are renewed."

This article is the work of the first Constituent Assembly.

The yearly vote on taxation is a powerful weapon in the hands of the Legislative Assemblies in so far as the Executive is concerned : indeed, a Government could remain in office without passing any new laws, but it cannot remain without the financial means provided by State revenue accruing from taxation.

The article is not exactly fiscal in character; rather it upholds yet again the pre-eminence of the nation's representatives, who are chosen directly by the electorate, over the authority of the Executive branch.

ARTICLE 112

"No privilege may be established where taxes are concerned. No exemption nor abatement of taxes may be established save through a law."

This article dates from 1831 and has never been modified.

The first sentence states the equality of all Belgians as taxpayers, and should be read in conjunction with Article 6 (the legal equality of all Belgians) and Article 75 (absence of any privilege granted to the nobility.)

As for the second sentence, it arises directly out of Article 110 which reserves for the Legislative alone the right to levy taxes for the benefit of the State. Nor may any exemptions or abatements of taxes be granted save by the representatives of the nation.

ARTICLE 113

"Apart from cases formally excepted by law, no payment may be required of citizens except by way of taxes for the benefit of the State, province, urban centre, federation of boroughs, or borough. No change is made in the system existing at present as regards polders and drainage work which is still subject to normal legislation."

This article was adopted during the Third Revision (1967-1971) and replaces the former article which read as follows :

"Apart from cases formally excepted by law, no payment may be required of citizens except by way of taxes for the benefit of the State, the province and the borough. No innovation is applied to the system existing at present as regards polders and drainage work which is still subject to normal legislation."

Apart from a purely formal modification (the words "No innovation is applied to" are replaced by "No change is made in"), the only difference in the new text is the addition of the words "urban centre, federation of boroughs". This addition is a logical part of the system set up in 1831 by the Constituent Assembly and, in actual fact, is no more than an adaptation of the article in keeping with the terms of the new Article 108-B.

Article 113, both in its original and its modernised wording, rounds off Article 110 which establishes the principle of the democratic assent that must be given to every tax levied.

ARTICLE 114

"No pension and no gratuity chargeable to the public treasury may be granted save in accordance with a law."

This clause is the work of the first Constituent Assembly of 1831.

Its purpose was to put an end, once for all, to the prodigal behaviour of former monarchs who, in absolute sovereignty, arbitrarily granted favours that in very many cases were quite undeserved.

Furthermore, since it is the Legislative Power that decides on what taxes are to be levied, it is logical that this power should also decide on what expenditures are to be made. Otherwise, some Government might incur expenses that would oblige the representatives of the nation to levy additional taxes in order to pay for them.

ARTICLE 115

"Each year the Houses pass the law on State accounting and vote on the budget.

"All the receipts and expenditures of the State must be included in the budget and in the accounting."

This article dates from 1831 and has never been modified.

Article 111 established the principle governing the annuality of taxation, which constitutes the State's main source of finance. This principle of yearly recurrence would be an empty word if it were not coupled with an annual budget covering the revenues and expenditures of the State.

By only authorising the levy of taxes and the liquidation of expenditure during a relatively short period of time, the Houses retain all their financial prerogatives intact.

The yearly nature of the budget laid down in the first paragraph of Article 115 is rounded off by the principle laid down in the second paragraph: that of the universal nature of the budget. By compelling the Government and its administration to make all their revenues and their expenditures public, this provision also ensures that they are available for inspection by the general public, for such publicity is the best means of exercising control.

ARTICLE 116

"The members of the Audit Office are appointed by the House of Representatives and for a term of office laid down by the law.

"This office is in charge of the examination and winding up of the accounts of the general administration and of all vouchers on the public treasury. It ensures that no article of expenditure in the budget is exceeded, and that no transfer takes place. It winds up the accounts of the various State administrative offices and is in charge of collecting, for this purpose, any information and accountable receipts that may be necessary. The general accounts of the State are submitted to the Houses along with the comments of the Audit Office.

"This office is organised by a law."

This article dates from 1831 and has never been modified.

The purpose which the Constituent Assembly had in mind is clear and goes without saying: the Audit Office being entrusted with verifying the accounts of the Executive, it was essential to place it outside the province of that Authority. Consequently, the law of 29 October 1846 which provided for the organisation of the Audit Office stipulates, in implementation of the Constitutional ruling, that the members of the Office are appointed for a term of six years by the House of Representatives which has the right at all times to dismiss any or all of them.

It may be wondered why the House of Representatives alone has been made responsible for the appointment of members of the Audit Office. The explanation is a purely historical one since, up to the Constitutional Reform of 15 October 1921, Article 27 of the Constitution laid down that "any law pertaining to State receipts or expenditures... must first be voted by the House of Representatives". As a result, Article 116 reflects to some extent the special competence which, in financial matters, was originally acknowledged in respect of the Lower House as opposed to the Senate. The fact remains, however, that the Audit Office is responsible to Parliament as a whole, as indeed is underlined by Article 116 itself when it lays down that "the general accounts of the State are submitted to the Houses". Similarly, Clause 14 of the law of 29 October 1846 pertaining to the organisation of the Audit Office provides that any communications from the Office are to be forwarded to both Houses.

The Office consists of two Chambers. Each of these comprises a president, four counsellors and a registrar. The law of 29 October 1846 is couched in rather laconic terms when it comes to defining the conditions and qualifications required of candidates for the post of counsellor or registrar. It simply states that both presidents and counsellors must be over 30 years of age, while registrars must be aged at least 25 years. This terse phrasing was intentional at the time so as to allow the House of Representatives complete freedom in appointing persons to fill these posts. Even so, certain degrees of incompatibility are provided for in terms of the law of 29 October 1846: the members of the Audit Office may not be members of Parliament, nor may they hold any other Government post; there must be no kinship or other connexion between them up to the fourth remove inclusively nor, at the time of their first appointment, must there be any kinship or other connexion between themselves and a Cabinet Minister or the head of a Government Department, up to and including the fourth remove; they may not examine any matters which are of interest to them personally or to their kinsmen or connexions up to and including the fourth remove; and finally they are forbidden to undertake any form of trade or commerce, or any other kind of activity in the industrial or commercial sector, either personally or through any other party, including their spouses.

The Office's rulings against accountants are executive ones: they may be referred by the latter to the Court of Cassation on the grounds of improper form or illegality, and if that Court should decide to nullify the ruling, the matter is referred back to an *ad hoc* committee set up by the House of Representatives whose decision is then final. In point of fact, there is in Belgium no section of the Audit Office qualified to rule on appeals, so that the law of 29 October 1846 was obliged to lay down, in Clause 13, an *ad hoc* procedure involving a committee set up within the House of Representatives. But the law governing the organisation of the Audit Office did not stipulate what procedure should be followed by such a committee. Up to now, such an exceptional procedure has only been resorted to on one occasion. Indeed, when a ruling by the Audit Office was quashed by the Court of Cassation for the first time in Belgium on 20 January 1946, the House of Representatives set up a committee from among its members, consisting of nine persons who elected one of themselves as chairman. This committee upheld the decision of the Court of Cassation in its final pronouncement made on 3 March 1948.

In a ruling given on 25 October 1934, the Court of Cassation stated that the Audit Office is a body issuing from, and responsible to, the House of Representatives; and that consequently it may not be regarded as an administrative jurisdiction. It follows that the decisions of the Audit Office may not be submitted for the censorship of the Council of State.

In terms of Article 116, two degrees of competence are vested in the Audit Office: an administrative competence and a jurisdictional function, for in this respect the Audit Office is a genuine tribunal set up by the Constituent Assembly.

On the administrative plane, the Audit Office is entrusted with the examination and winding up of the accounts of the general administration and of all vouchers on the public treasury. It ensures that no article of expenditure in the budget is exceeded and that no transfer takes place. It winds up the accounts of the various State administrative departments and is in charge of collecting, for this purpose, all relevant information and accountable receipts. The Office has the right to call for any statements, information and explanations regarding the receipt and expenditure of State and provincial funds. Furthermore, no voucher for payment is accepted by the Treasury until it has received the seal of approval of the Audit Office. This is known as the prior endorsement system. The principle of this system, however, has often been criticised because it causes delays in payment, which is sometimes very inconvenient, especially for suppliers and purveyors to the State. Exceptions to the system have, however, been provided for, particularly in regard to all fixed expenditures, i.e. those which are both regular and periodical (such as salaries, indemnities, etc.)

When the Audit Office feels itself obliged to withhold its endorsement, the reasons for its refusal are examined by the Cabinet. If the Ministers judge that payment should nevertheless be made under their responsibility, the Audit Office then endorses the voucher subject to its reservation, and immediately submits a report on its reasons for doing so to the Houses of Parliament. Generally speaking, the Audit Office reports all infringements of the budget laws to Parliament without delay. In its jurisdictional function, the Audit Office:

1) settles and winds up the accounts of the State and the provincial authorities, and establishes by means of final rulings whether the accounts balance or whether they show an excess on the credit or the debit side;

2) decides on what sums are to be collected by the persons delegated by the Minister to pass accounts;

3) pronounces in respect of accountants who are in arrears, and who have been duly called upon to explain the reasons therefor, a fine which may not exceed half their salary.

From the foregoing, it will be realised that the Audit Office holds very real jurisdictional powers; the formula of implementation is, moreover, exactly the same as that used in framing rulings or judgments.

The Audit Office is certainly one of the great offices of the State. There can be nothing but praise for the wisdom of the Constituent Assembly which endowed the Belgian State with such a first-class instrument of financial control, which is totally independent of the Executive Authority since it is answerable solely to the House of Representatives. The Audit Office quite rightly enjoys a very considerable measure of prestige in Belgium.

ARTICLE 117

"The salaries and pensions of ministers of religion are chargeable to the State; the sums necessary for this purpose are included in the annual budget."

This article dates from 1831 and has never been modified.

The principle of freedom of worship embodied in Article 14 of the Constitution has not been regarded as an obstacle to the recognition of certain forms of worship, with the result that ministers of these religions have been enabled to obtain their salaries and pensions which are paid out of the national Treasury.

At the present time, the Belgian State officially recognises five forms of worship :

— the Roman Catholic religion;

— the Protestant religion;

— the Anglican religion;

— the Jewish religion.

— the Islamic religion.

The municipal and provincial authorities are also required to bear certain expenses in connection with the practice of these religions (the maintenance of churches and the housing of priests and ministers).

HEADING V

THE ARMED FORCES

ARTICLE 118

"The method of recruiting for the armed forces is laid down by law. It also regulates the promotion, rights and obligations of the military."

This article dates from 1831 and has never been modified.

The fact that the Head of State is, in terms of Article 68 of the Constitution, the Commander-in-Chief of the armed forces, places no obstacle in the way of making the Legislative responsible for deciding upon the method of recruiting, promotion, the rights and obligations of those serving in them, and this provides an invaluable guarantee for those concerned.

As we shall see from our perusal of Articles 119 and 120, the Constituent Assembly did not wish to provide the Executive with complete control over such a dangerous weapon as the armed forces.

The status of career and reserve officers, and that of warrant officers on active service with the Army, Navy and Air Force, is currently regulated by the law of 1 March 1958 and the law of 27 December 1961.

ARTICLE 119

"The armed forces contingent is voted annually. The law which establishes it is only effective for one year unless it is renewed."

This article dates from 1831 and has never been modified.

It should first be pointed out that this clause is the natural complement of Article 118 : in both cases, the Constituent Assembly has given the Legislative Power complete authority over the armed forces.

Furthermore, the military service arising out of the voting of the contingent is a duty payable in kind. Now, the intention of the Constituent Assembly was that the sacrifices imposed on the nation, whether in the form of taxation or personal service, should have the full consent of the representatives of the people.

It is interesting to stress the parallel nature of this article and Article 111 which requires an annual vote on the amount of taxes to be paid to the State.

Compulsory military service is regulated by the coordinated laws of 30 April 1962.

A set of rules governing conscientious objectors was framed by means of a law dated 3 June 1964.

ARTICLE 120

"The organisation and attributions of the gendarmerie are the subject of a law."

This article dates from 1831 and has never been modified.

It is logical that if the organisation of the armed forces has been placed within the competence of the legislative power, that of the gendarmerie — which is also an armed force — should also be incumbent on the Houses.

The law referred to in this article of the Constitution was voted very late: in fact, it did not go into the Statute Book until 2 December 1957. Until that time, as provided for by Article 138 of the Constitution, an ancient body of legislation dating back to the French regime (1794-1814) and the Netherlands period (1814-1830) had remained in force. In terms of the new law, the gendarmerie is made responsible for maintaining law and order and for seeing that the laws are obeyed.

From the standpoint of organisation and general administration (organisation of the units, personnel training and administration, discipline, etc.) the gendarmerie is placed under the authority of the Minister of National Defence.

In performing its task, however, the gendarmerie comes under :

— the Minister of the Interior, for all matters pertaining to the functions of the administrative police, the implementation of general police laws and decrees, and for everything connected with the maintenance of law and order;

— the Minister of Justice, through the channel of the Public Prosecutors of the Courts of Appeal and the Auditor-General of the Courts-Martial, for all matters pertaining to the functions of the criminal investigation department; it comes directly under him for everything connected with the police surveillance of foreigners and State security;

— the Minister of National Defence in all matters pertaining to the supervision exercised over armed forces personnel who are absent from their units, and to the operations involved in preparing for the mobilisation of troops.

ARTICLE 121

"No foreign troops may be admitted to the service of the State, nor may they occupy or pass through the territory, save in terms of a law."

This article dates from 1831 and has never been modified.

The hiring of foreign troops was a frequent occurrence under the old regime, and this explains why the 1831 Constituent Assembly devoted special attention to the subject. It made it the Legislative's responsibility to call on foreign troops even though such a measure would seem more likely to come within the scope of the Executive. This article is therefore an expression of mistrust of any such appeal, and it demonstrates the nationalist spirit of the young State. This clause remains an important one even today, for Belgium is part of a vast military alliance : the North Atlantic Treaty Organisation (N.A.T.O.).

ARTICLE 122

"The organisation of a civic guard, if necessary, is regulated by law."

This text is the work of the Third Constituent Assembly and dates back to the Second Revision (1919-1921). It replaces the 1831 wording which was as follows :

"There is a civic guard; its organisation is regulated by law.

"Officers of all ranks, up to and including that of captain, are nominated by the guards, except for special cases deemed necessary for the accountants."

Whereas the First Constituent Assembly had set up a permanent civic guard, the Third restricted itself merely to providing for its existence in case of need.

The civic or municipal guard of olden times had the task of maintaining law and order within the country when the army, upon the outbreak of war, was sent to the frontiers. The democratic way in which it was organised deserves to be emphasized. It should be added that the civic guard or citizens' militia could also be used for the defence of the country.

The civic guard was in existence up to 1914.

ARTICLE 123

Abrogated.

The text of this article, which was abrogated during the 1920-1921 Revision, was as follows:

"The civic guard may not be mobilised save in terms of a law."

The civic guard provided for under the old Article 122 was essentially a sedentary body. Also destined to serve, if necessary, as a counterweight to the power of the Executive, it could only be mobilised as a result of a decision taken to that effect by the representatives of the nation.

ARTICLE 124

"The military may not be deprived of their rank, honours and decorations, or pensions, save in the manner laid down by the law."

This article dates from 1831 and has never been modified.

It should be read in conjunction with Article 118, which also reserves to the Legislative the right to fix the legal status of members of the armed forces.

This provision seems to have been inspired by some distrust of the Executive, and once again it sets the seal on the pre-eminent nature of the elected power, i.e. the Houses of Parliament, or the Legislative.

Article 124 constitutes an effective guarantee of the rights of men serving their country in the armed forces.

HEADING VI

GENERAL CLAUSES

ARTICLE 125

"The Belgian nation has adopted the colours red, yellow and black, and for its coat of arms, the Lion Belgium with the device : 'Unity is Strength'."

This article is the work of the first Constituent Assembly and has never been modified.

The colours referred to in this clause were already to be found in the ancient banner of Brabant. The lion is to be found in the armorial bearings of nearly all the Belgian provinces.

The colours are arranged in vertical stripes and from right to left in the order laid down by this constitutional ruling.

ARTICLE 126

"The city of Brussels is the capital of Belgium and the seat of the Government."

This article dates from 1831 and has never been modified.

It must be read in conjunction with article 3-B which provides notably that Brussels-Capital constitutes a bilingual region, and with Article 108-C which concerns the urban area of Brussels.

ARTICLE 127

"No oath may be imposed save in accordance with the law, which lays down the wording thereof."

This article dates from 1831 and has never been modified.

Only the representatives of the people (i.e., Parliament) have the right to impose an oath and to determine the wording to be used for that purpose. Taking the oath is compulsory in law courts and tribunals. Furthermore, Cabinet Ministers and civil servants are sworn in when they take office. Members of Parliament are also sworn in.

The wording used differs, of course, according to the purpose for which the oath is imposed or the functions attributed to the person being sworn in.

ARTICLE 128

"Any foreigner who is on Belgian territory enjoys the same protection granted to persons and property, save in exceptional cases to be established by law."

This article dates from 1831 and has never been modified.

The personal liberties acknowledged by Articles 4 to 24 have been grouped together under the title "Concerning Belgians and their rights", from which one might infer that the Constituent Assembly reserved such rights for Belgian nationals alone. By means of Article 128, the first Constituent Assembly extended them to embrace all foreigners who find themselves on Belgian soil. It goes without saying that political rights are withheld from foreigners who, on the other hand, must obey the laws of Belgium.

Article 128 constitutes no obstacle to the expulsion of foreigners whose presence is dangerous or prejudicial to the peace, order or security of the country. For the purpose of safeguarding the legitimate interests of foreigners, the proper procedure has been laid down by law.

ARTICLE 129

"No law, decree, or administrative regulation of a general, provincial or municipal character is compulsory until it has been published in the manner laid down by the law."

This article is the work of the first Constituent Assembly and has never been modified.

It is obvious that a citizen can only obey those judicial rulings which have been duly brought to his attention. In this respect, Article 129 rounds off the provisions contained in Articles 7 and 9 of the Constitution.

The publication of laws, decrees and royal edicts in the *Moniteur belge* (official gazette), that of provincial regulations in the *Mémorial administratif* (administrative bulletin) and that of municipal regulations by means of posters or proclamations, give full significance to the saying "nobody is deemed to be in ignorance of the law."

446

ARTICLE 130

"The Constitution may not be suspended, either in whole or in part."

This article dates from 1831 and has never been modified.

It sets the seal on the inviolability of the Constitution and the maintenance of public rights and liberties.

Neither the Executive nor the Legislative may suspend the Constitution, no matter what pretext or special reason may be invoked (such as a state of war, serious disturbances, etc.).

No exceptions can exist under Belgian law.

HEADING VII

REVISION OF THE CONSTITUTION

ARTICLE 131

"The legislative power has the right to state that it is necessary to revise such constitutional clause as it shall designate.

"Following this statement, both Houses are automatically dissolved.

"Two new Houses will be convened in accordance with Article 71.

"These Houses, in agreement with the King, shall pronounce judgment on the points submitted for revision.

"In the case, the Houses may not debate unless at least two-thirds of the members of each of them are present, and no alteration shall be adopted unless it secures at least two-thirds of the total votes cast."

This article dates from 1831 and has never been modified.

It quite naturally attributes constituent powers to the representatives of the people in the national assemblies which already exercise the legislative power.

Such statements by the Legislative entail the complete and automatic dissolution of both Houses. The dissolution is recorded in the preamble to the Royal Decree which convenes the electorate within forty days, in accordance with the provisions of Article 71 of the Constitution.

The convening of the new Houses is the subject of a Royal Decree and takes place within two months of the date of dissolution (Article 71).

The new Houses elected as a result of the decision to dissolve the previous Parliament are known as Constituent Assemblies. The duration of their powers coincides with that of the legislature.

What are their powers?

Firstly, the Constituent Assemblies may reject any revision. In this case, the unrevised article or articles remain in force. A rejection of the proposal to revise is not subject to the two-thirds quorum of votes laid down in Article 131 of the Constitution.

While the Constituent Power may only revise those articles specifically designated in the Statement of Intent to Revise, it does on the other hand hold full powers as to how they are to be revised. It may either reject them in principle, or it may abrogate articles, modify them in whole or in part, or alter their individual clauses. Transitional arrangements may also be introduced.

The only obligation placed on the Constituent Assemblies is therefore to pronounce on the principle and the terms of revision.

Resolutions involving a revision of constitutional articles are, when they have been adopted by both Houses, submitted for the sanction of the Head of the State. No precedent exists whereby the King has refused to sanction resolutions passed by the Houses of Parliament on this subject. Once sanctioned and promulgated, the revised articles are published in the *Moniteur belge* (official gazette).

A note should be made of special procedures designed to prevent any revisions of the national charter from being undertaken by a very small or weak parliamentary majority :

— any revision shall be a partial one;

— any revision shall be accomplished in two stages;

— any revision presupposes a general election called for this specific purpose, which is therefore tantamount to a national referendum;

— the quorum of members present shall be at least two-thirds of the total members of each of the two Houses;

— the majority in the ballot shall be at least two-thirds of the votes cast.

The Constitution's ruling is therefore a strict one and rigidly enforced. In all, there have been three revisions : that of 1893, that of 1919-1921, and that of 1967-1971. All of them involved a limited number of articles, so that most of the articles drawn up for the original Constitution of 1831 have remained unchanged.

The State of Belgium has therefore remained a model of constitutional stability, even though Belgian society itself has undergone profound and widespread transformations during the intervening period.

It should also be stressed that there are two Constituent Powers : the original Constituent Power wielded in 1830-1831 by the National Congress, and the derivative Constituent Power founded on Article 131 and exercised jointly by Parliament and by the King during the three aforementioned periods (1893; 1919-1921; and 1967-1971).

It will be seen that the first Constituent Assembly did its work within a unicameral framework (the National Congress), whereas the other Constituent Assemblies accomplished their revisions within a bicameral framework (the House of Representatives and the Senate). This perhaps explains why the original Constitution was so quickly framed, and why later revisions have been attended by so many delays and hesitations. Finally, it should be recalled that in terms of Articles 84 of the Constitution, no constitutional revision may be undertaken during a Regency.

*
* *

In connection with the Statement of Intent to Revise the Constitution, a college of eminent jurists was called in to give legal advice to the statesman designated by the King in January 1974 to form a government. This statesman had raised the following questions :

"Starting from the hypothesis that a government, because of internal stresses, has offered its resignation and that this resignation has been accepted by the King, is it in conformity with constitutional doctrine that :

1) without the Government intervening in the debate, Parliament should continue to deliberate on the various pending proposals stemming from parliamentary initiative which are designed to lead to a Statement of Intent to Revise the Constitution ?

2) if such a statement is made, the King should sign it alongside the countersignature of one or several Ministers of the outgoing Cabinet ?

3) the outgoing Government should still be able to table in Parliament a Statement of Intent to Revise the Constitution and, for this purpose, should call for a vote prior to the dissolution of Parliament, if necessary appealing to the discipline of its parliamentary majority ?"

The reply of the college of jurists was as follows :

1) "A Government which has offered its resignation that has not yet been accepted by Royal Decree, may not table a proposed Statement of Intent to Revise the Constitution before Parliament. To embark on a procedure tending to modify the fundamental law goes beyond the sphere of day-to-day business that an outgoing or "caretaker" Government may still handle; it is a very serious political act."

2) "In the absence of any Government capable of exercising its full powers, members of Parliament may not validly table a Statement of Intent to Revise, nor debate such a statement or proposal : such a statement is in fact an act performed by the "Legislative Power" in its entirety, in which all three branches of the Legislative must collaborate." (Constitution, Art. 131, para. 1, & Art. 26).

3) "An outgoing Government is not entitled to countersign the King's statement."

4) "No precedent to the contrary can be found in the events of February 1968. The situation was quite different then. Of course, the Vanden Boeynants Government had resigned. But the Houses were Constituent Assemblies. The proposed Statement, which was identical to that of 1968 save for the two articles already promulgated, was regarded as merely extending the period during which the Legislative could examine the utility of a revision and, eventually, decide upon it." (Sess. 1967-1968, H.R. Report Doc. N° 561; Senate Report Doc. N° 168; Sitting of 29 February 1968).

5) "To submit to the King a proposed Statement of Intent to Revise, or to countersign the royal statement, it would be necessary today to have a new Government. This could be the present Government, all or some of whose members having withdrawn their resignation with the assent of the King, and the linguistic parity laid down by Article 86-B being respected."

6) "An outgoing Government may propose the dissolution of Parliament to the King. Such dissolutions took place in 1939 and in 1950; in the second of these instances, the Regent at first refused to accept the resignation of the Government."

7) "Furthermore, at whatever time during its period of office, there is nothing to prevent a Government—even an outgoing Government — from appealing to the discipline of its parliamentary majority, indicating if necessary the possibility that Parliament may be dissolved."

ARTICLE 131-B

"No revision of the Constitution may be entered upon, nor pursued, in time of war or when the Houses are prevented from meeting freely on the national territory."

This is a new article inserted during the Third Revision (1967-1971); it is designed to strengthen yet further the strict provisions of the fundamental charter concerning the political organisation of the country, since it prohibits any activity of a constituent, or even a pre-constituent, nature during periods which may be lengthy ones indeed.

Its inclusion is justified by the fact that the Fourth Constituent Assembly (1967-1971) considered that even a nation steeped in the democratic tradition might, under pressures arising out of war or enemy occupation, take steps to alter its Constitution in ways capable of overturning its very foundations. Indeed, such changes might very well run counter to the free will of the nation, or disregard permanent necessities and lasting concepts.

The term "in time of war" covers the period beginning on the day specified by royal decree for the general mobilisation of the armed forces, and ending on the day when, also by royal decree, the armed forces are restored to their peacetime footing. The question here is one of a concept of internal law which is foreign to that of a state of war as used in international civil law.

It should also be added that this prohibition relates not only to wartime but also to the period during which the Houses are prevented from meeting freely on the national territory. While in most cases the latter period would normally be covered by the former, exceptions may occur, which is why the Constituent Assemblies have specifically mentioned both eventualities.

HEADING VIII

TRANSITIONAL ARRANGEMENTS

ARTICLE 132

"Until such time as the Catholic University of Louvain, including its ancillary branches of intermediate and technical education, is transferred outside the Dutch language region, the cultural council for the French cultural community shall, notwithstanding Article 59-B, Section 4, paragraph 1, have jurisdiction over this institution.

"The linguistic system at present in force, both as regards education and administrative matters, will continue to apply until such appointed time."

This article was inserted during the Third Revision of the Constitution (1967-1971) and replaces the 1831 text reading as follows, the purpose of which was entirely different:

"For the initial choice of the Head of State, a derogation of the first clause of Article 80 may be made." Article 80 referred to sets the legal coming-of-age of the King at his eighteenth birthday.

At the time when the original article was being drafted, the National Congress — the first Belgian Constituent Assembly — was thinking of electing the Duke of Nemours, son of Louis-Philippe, King of the French, as King. However, the election of the Duke of Nemours who was then aged sixteen, would have required the appointment of a Regent. That would have been an unfortunate beginning for a new State and a new dynasty. Consequently, in order to avoid a possible two-year regency period, the Congress provided for a derogation of the date constitutionally set for the coming-of-age of Belgian Heads of State.

However, matters unfolded in quite another way. The Duke of Nemours was effectively chosen but his father, under pressure from Great Britain which feared that this might be a disguised form of annexing Belgium to France, was obliged to renounce the throne on behalf of his son. A Regent was therefore elected: this was Erasmus Surlet de Chokier, aged 61 years. He did not, however, remain Regent for more than a few months, for Leopold of Saxe-Coburg, aged 40, was elected King of the Belgians on 4 June 1831.

To sum up: this transitional arrangement was by now not only redundant, it had indeed never been implemented. Its abrogation during the

Third Revision was therefore a logical move, and one can only wonder why it had not been abrogated long before during the two previous revisions.

It was replaced by the present text during that same Third Revision which saw the institution of the Cultural Councils. The new text is founded upon the following considerations.

The "Catholic University of Louvain" (that is, the French-language university) is established in Louvain within the Dutch-language linguistic region (Article 3-B of the Constitution).

In terms of Article 59-B, Section 4, para. 1, the Cultural Council for the Dutch cultural community is competent to vote decrees having the force of law throughout the Dutch-language region.

The Constituent Assembly wished therefore to remove the French-language university from the jurisdiction of the Dutch-language Cultural Council and place it under that of the French-language Cultural council; it therefore prohibited any change of the linguistic regime in force as long as the university remained in Louvain.

This transitional clause will become redundant as soon as the university concerned has been transferred to the French-language region. Construction work on "New Louvain" is proceeding in the area of Ottignies in Walloon Brabant, while the Faculty of Medicine is being progressively instituted at Woluwe-Saint-Lambert, a borough of the Brussels Urban Area.

ARTICLE 133

"Foreigners who were established in Belgium prior to January 1, 1814 and who have continued to reside there, are regarded as Belgians by birth on condition that they declare their intention of enjoying the privileges provided for under the present clause.

"This declaration must be made within six months dating from the day on which the present Constitution becomes compulsory, if the persons concerned are of age, or during the year following their coming-of-age if they are still minors.

"The declaration shall be made in the presence of the provincial authority whose jurisdiction includes their place of residence.

"It shall be made in person or by proxy, the latter to be in possession of special and authentic powers of attorney."

This was a transitional clause inserted by the first Constituent Assembly, a clause which has never been either modified or abrogated.

It goes without saying that there is now nobody to whom this article could possibly apply.

ARTICLE 134

"Until a law has been passed in this regard, the House of Representatives shall exercise discretionary powers in impeaching a Minister, and the Court of Cassation shall exercise similar powers in judging him, the misdemeanour being specified and the penalty being determined.

"Nevertheless, the penalty may not exceed that of penal internment, without prejudice to cases expressly provided for under the penal laws."

This is a transitional arrangement established in 1831 by the first Constituent Assembly, but which has remained in force owing to the fact that the law mentioned in the article has never been passed.

It should be noted that internment is a penalty of imprisonment for a term of five to ten years.

This article also applies to the Secretaries of State.

ARTICLE 135

Abrogated

Article 135 was the work of the first Constituent Assembly and read as follows :

"The personnel of the law courts and tribunals is maintained as it now exists until this matter has been regulated by law.

"This law must be passed during the first legislative session."

By means of this transitional clause, the 1831 Constituent Assembly provided for the continuity of the judicial system. The Legislative accomplished the task laid on it by the Constituent Assembly when it voted the law of 4 August 1832 (which has since been replaced by a later law.)

Since that date, the article had been redundant and its abrogation during the Third Revision (1967-1971) therefore presented no difficulty.

ARTICLE 136

Abrogated

This transitional clause was the work of the first Constituent Assembly and it read as follows :

"A law to be voted during the same session shall determine the method to be adopted for the first appointment of members of the Court of Cassation."

The words "the same session" refer of course to the first session of the Belgian Parliament.

In the event, this was not a question of ensuring continuity, but of the effective setting-up of the Court of Cassation which the Constituent Assembly had just brought into being, as soon as possible.

The Legislative accomplished the task thus laid on it by voting the law of 4 August 1832.

As it had become redundant, this transitional clause was abrogated during the Third Revision (1967-1971) without any particular problem being encountered.

ARTICLE 137

"The fundamental law of August 24, 1815 is abolished, as also the provincial and local statutes. However, the provincial and local authorities shall retain their powers until such time as other arrangements have been made by law."

This transitional clause was drafted by the first Constituent Assembly in 1831 and has never been modified.

Its purpose was to ensure the continuity of provincial and local services.

The passing of the laws dated 30 March 1836 and 30 April 1836, which respectively regulated the status of the municipal and provincial authorities, made Article 137 redundant.

ARTICLE 138

"Dating from the day on which the Constitution comes into force, all laws, decrees, ordinances, regulations and other acts which are contrary to it shall be abolished."

This article was drafted by the first Constituent Assembly in 1831 and has never been modified.

Although it is a transitional clause, it is still applicable : any legal provisions dating from the period before the Constitution of 7 February 1831 came into force, and which were not abrogated by the Belgian Legislative at a later date, remain in force on condition that they do not run counter to the national charter.

COMPLEMENTARY CLAUSES

ARTICLE 139

Abrogated

This was a provision laid down in 1831 whereby the National Congress — the first Belgian Constituent Assembly — had entrusted the Legislative with a number of tasks. The original article was worded as follows:

"The National Congress states that it is necessary to make provision, by means of separate laws and within the shortest possible period of time, for the following objectives:

1. the press;

2. the organisation of the jury system;

3. finances;

4. provincial and municipal organisation;

5. the responsibility of Ministers and other agents of authority;

6. the organisation of the judiciary;

7. a revision of the pension list;

8. measures designed to prevent abusive plurality of office;

9. a revision of the legislation governing bankruptcies and stays of execution;

10. the organisation of the army, the rights of promotion and retirement, and the military penal code;

11. revision of the penal and civil codes."

The first point concerning the press was the subject of a decree of 20 July 1831. Later, in 1867, the penal code repressed certain abuses arising out of the freedom of the press. Finally, a law of 30 December 1963 instituted measures protecting the title of professional journalist.

The organisation of the jury system (in the assize courts) was first regulated by means of a decree of 19 July 1831 and by a law of 1 March 1832, and later by the law of 15 May 1838 subsequently modified by the Judiciary Organisation Act of 18 June 1869.

Public finances are governed by the law (subsequently modified) of 15 May 1846 on State accounting.

Provincial and municipal organisation was the subject of the provincial law of 30 April 1836 and the municipal law of 30 March 1836.

The responsibility of government ministers and secretaries of State is the subject of various other constitutional clauses (Articles 63, 64, 89, 90, 91, 91-B and 134). The responsibility of officials and civil servants was defined, in time of war, by a law of 5 March 1935 and, in time of peace, by the Statutes of the Civil Service (royal decree of 2 October 1937, modified since on numerous occasions).

The organisation of the Judiciary was regulated in particular by the laws of 4 August 1832, 18 June 1869 and 10 October 1967.

The State pension system was first the subject of a law of 21 July 1844 and thereafter of a great number of other laws.

The problem of abuses of plurality of office was dealt with by several laws, especially that of 25 May 1848 on parliamentary incompatibility, subsequently modified on various occasions and in fact now replaced by the law of 6 August 1931 and by that of 18 June 1869 concerning members of the magistrature.

Legislation on bankruptcies and stays of execution found its place in the Commercial Code (law of 18 April 1851).

The organisation of the armed forces has been the subject of numerous pieces of legislation, and in particular the Military Penal Code of 27 May 1870 and the law of 15 June 1899 governing military penal procedures.

As for the Codes, the Legislative has undertaken the revision of several (the Penal Code, the Code of Justice, the Code of Criminal Procedure, the Commercial Code).

It may be stated that the Legislative has accomplished to a very great extent the multifarious tasks made incumbent on it by the first Constituent Assembly.

It was therefore decided, during the Third Revision of the Constitution, to abrogate the supplementary provisions contained in Article 139. This abrogation has moreover entailed no curtailment of the competence vested in the Legislative which may at any time legislate on all the matters enumerated in Article 139, both in terms of other constitutional clauses and by virtue of its residual powers.

ARTICLE 140

"The text of the Constitution is drawn up in French and in Dutch."

This is an entirely new clause dating from 1967. The Belgian Constitution of 7 February 1831 had been drafted solely in French : indeed, on 16 November 1830 the Provisional Government had chosen French as the only official language of the new State.

However, as the country became progressively more democratic with the broadening of the franchise, an important body of legislation was enacted on the use of languages. The following is a brief summary of the various stages in the slow process of evolution that led to the full and complete acknowledgement of the equality of the Dutch and French languages in Belgian public affairs.

— 17 August 1873 : law concerning the use of the Flemish language for legal purposes.

— 22 May 1878 : law concerning the use of the Flemish language for administrative purposes.

— 15 June 1883 : law governing the use of the Flemish language for secondary education in the Flemish part of the country.

— 30 July 1894 : law concerning the taking of oaths in one of the languages used in the country.

— 18 April 1898 : law concerning the use of the Flemish language in official publications, the so-called equality law (making the two languages officially equal in all legal documents).

— 22 February 1908 : law concerning the use of the Flemish language for judicial purposes in the Brussels district.

— 2 July 1913 : law governing the use of languages in the armed forces.

— 19 May 1914 : law making school attendance compulsory (in primary schools, the children's mother-tongue is the language used.)

— 31 July 1921 : law concerning the use of languages for administrative purposes.

— 7 November 1928 : law concerning the use of languages in the armed forces.

— 28 June 1932 : law concerning the use of languages for administrative purposes.

— 14 July 1932 : law concerning the languages to be used in primary and secondary schools.

— 15 June 1935 : law concerning the use of languages in law courts and tribunals.

— 30 July 1938 : law concerning the use of languages in the armed forces.

— 30 July 1963 : law concerning the languages to be used in educational establishments.

— 2 August 1963 : law concerning the use of languages for administrative purposes.

It should be noted that the above laws, which met the legitimate desires of the Flemish-speaking population, were voted in both Houses with a large majority in each case, consisting of both Walloon and Flemish votes.

As soon as the question arose in 1952-1953 of adapting the text of the national charter in keeping with contemporary realities, it was proposed that Belgium should be given an authentic Dutch text of her Constitution. For this purpose, it was considered necessary both to have the entire text translated into Dutch and to round off the Constitution by adding an Article 140 stating that the Constitution has now been drawn up in French and in Dutch and that both versions are equally valid.

The effective implementation of this proposal took several years. Indeed, the question was not one of merely translating the text, but of drafting an equivalent version that would be as authoritative and compulsory as that drafted in the other language.

The draft was prepared by the "Committee appointed to draw up the Dutch text of the Constitution, the Codes and the principal laws and decrees". It was revised and approved by the "Central Committee on Dutch legal and administrative language in Belgium".

Finally, the *Moniteur Belge* (official gazette) of 3 May 1967 published both the new Dutch text of the Constitution and the new final Article 140 which naturally complements it.

ALPHABETICAL INDEX (1)

---

(1) Figures in heavy type refer to the Articles, those in light type to the page numbers.

Association, right of/freedom of 20, 50.
Associations of Boroughs, 107-D, 401; 31, 98.
Associations — intermunicipal, 31, 97.
Audit Office, 116, 430-433.
— endorsement of 116, 432.
Author (press), 18, 47.
Authoritative interpretation (laws), 25, 68; 28, 88.
Authoritative interpretation (treaties) 68, 249.
Authoritative rulings (Council of State), 59-B, 199-201; 94, 362.
Authority, alienation of 94, 364.
Authority, conflicts of 59-B, 199-201; 94, 364-365.
Autonomy, cultural, 59-B, 160-162.
Autonomy, municipal, 31, 94, 36.
Autonomy, provincial, 31, 94-95.

Balances struck in government. 86-B, 315-316.
Ballot, secret, 39, 116.
Banknotes, 74, 271-272.
Belgian :
    — by birth/marriage/naturalisation/preferential option, 5, 19.
    — citizenship, 4, 18.
Belgian National Bank, 74, 271-272.
Belgian national colours/device, 125, 442.
Belgian Socialist Party, 26, 85.
Bench, independence of 30, 93; 100, 375.
Bench, (magistrature), 99, 374; 100, 375.
Benediction, nuptial, 16, 38.
Bilingual region of Brussels-Capital, 3-B, 14, 15; 23, 54-55.
Bills, parliamentary — definition, 27, 87.
Bills, parliamentary — passing, 41, 119; 46, 125-127.
Birth certificates, 109, 422.
Boroughs, 31, 96-98; 108, 409-411.
Boroughs — merging of 31, 98.
Boroughs — on the linguistic frontier, 23, 57.
Boroughs — peripheral, 3-B, 16-B (map); 23, 58.
Brabant, Vice-Governor of 3-B, 15.
Brussels, 3-B, 16-B (map); 126, 443.
Brussels — Capital, bilingual region, 3-B, 14, 16; 23, 54, 58.
Brussels — Free University, 23, 60.

Duke of Nemours, 132, 453.

Dutch Cultural Committee (Brussels area), 108-C, 420-421.

Dutch Cultural Council, 59-B, 160, 167-186.

Dutch language region, 3-B, 15; 23, 53, 57.

Dutch text of Constitution, 140, 463-464.

Dynasty, choice of 85, 291.

Eastern Cantons, 59-C, 213-215.

Economic planning and decentralisation, 107-D, 386-408.

Economic Research and Coordination Dept. (Prime Min.), 86-B, 300.

Editor (press), 18, 47.

Education, 17, 39-46.
  — freedom of 39.
  — operating expenses, 41.
  — statuts of teachers, 43.

Electoral bodies, 48, 131.

Electoral districts, 131-132.

Electoral divisor, 132.

Electoral figure, 133.

Electoral quotient, 134.

Electoral system (general survey), 48, 131-135.

Electorate, parliamentary, 47, 130.

Eligibility — to Lower House, 50, 137.
           — to Senate, 56, 145, 56-B, 147-149.

Employees, State (statute), 66, 239-240.

Endorsement of Audit Office, 116, 432.

Endowment (Prince of Liège), 77, 277.

Equality, principle of 6, 20.

Equality under law, 94, 359.

European Coal and Steel Community, 25-B, 73.

European Economic Community, 25-B, 73-74.

Executive body (urban area or federation), 108-B, 415.

Executive body (Brussels area), 108-C, 419.

Executive Power, The 25, 71-72; 29, 89-90; 67, 242-246.

Executive — de facto primacy of 26, 83; 85, 292.

Exemption or abatement of taxes, 112, 426.

Expenses, operating (education), 17, 41.

Explanation, requests for (Cultural Councils), 59-B, 173.

Expropriations, 11, 29-32.

Expulsion of foreigners, 128, 445.

Protection of Dutch-spkg. minority in Brussels area, **107-D**, 395.
— French-spkg. minority in Brussels area, **107-D**, 397.
Provinces, **1, 10**.
— division into, **1, 7**.
Provinces, towns and boroughs, **31**, 94-95.
Provincial autonomy, **31**, 94-95.
Provincial committee for economic expansion, **107-D**, 402.
Provincial council, **31**, 94-95; **108**, 409-411.
Provincial councillors, **31**, 94; **108**, 409-410.
Provincial governor, **31**, 95.
Provincial and municipal education, **17**, 39-46.
Provincial and municipal institutions, **108 to 109**, 409-422.
Provincial Senators, **53**, 142; **56-C**, 150.
Public acts of the King, **64**, 225.
Public education, **17**, 39-46.
Public Prosecutors, **101**, 376.
Public Prosecutor's Department, **101**, 376; **107**, 385.
Public hearing in law courts, **96**, 370.
Public nature of Parliamentary sittings, **33**, 103.
Public rendering of Court judgments, **97**, 371.
Public gatherings, **19**, 49.
Public utilities (status), **66**, 240.
Publication of laws, decrees and regulations, **129**, 446.

Questions, written and oral (Parliament), **46**, 129.
Quorum (House and Senate) **1, 9**; **38**, 112-113.
Quotient, electoral, **48**, 134.

Rank in armed forces (conferral), **66**, 238.
Rapporteur (Parliament), **32**, 100; **46**, 125.
Rassemblement wallon (political party), **26**, 85.
Reading (of a bill), **46**, 126.
Receipts and expenditures, State, **115**, 429.
Referendum, **25**, 67; **82**, 286-287.
Regency, **80**, 283; **81**, 284; **82**, 286; **83**, 288-289; **84**, 290; **85**, 291.
Regional Councils, **107-D**, 390, 395.
Regional development corporations, **107-D**, 404-408.
Regional economic councils, **107-D**, 403-404.
Regional engineering corporations, **107-D**, 401.
Regionalisable matters, **107-D**, 389-390, 393-394.

Subsidies — education, 17, 39-46.
Succession to the Throne, 60, 219-220.
— disqualification from 60, 220.
Suffrage, universal, 47, 130.
Surlet de Chokier, Baron (Regent), 83, 288; 132, 453.
Suspension of the Constitution, 130, 447.
Suspension or exemption from implementing laws, 67, 242.

Taxation 110 to 113, 423-427.
Taxes — exemption or abatement of 112, 426.
— yearly nature of 111, 425.
Ten-year census, 49, 135.
Territory, 1, 7-8.
Territorial waters, 1, 10.
Territories, overseas, 1, 7, 8.
Text of Constitution, Dutch, 140, 463-464.
Throne — disqualification from 60, 220.
— succession to 60, 219-220.
— vacancy of 61, 221; 83, 288, 85, 291.
Time of War, 131-B, 452.
Titles of Nobility, 75, 273.
Traditional parties, 26, 85.
Transitional clauses of the Constitution, 132 to 138, 453-460.
Treasury notes, 74, 272.
Treaties — authoritative interpretation of 68, 249.
— international, 25-B, 73-74, 77; 68, 247-253.
— validity of 68, 247.
Tribunals — commercial, 105, 381; 107, 384.
— district, 107, 384.
— extraordinary (prohibition), 94, 358-359.
— first instance, 107, 384.
— labour, 107, 384.
— military, 105, 381.
— police, 107, 383.
Troops, foreign, 121, 438.
Truce, Schools, 17, 39-42.

Unionism, 65, 229.
Unity of jurisprudence, 95, 367.
Universal suffrage, 47, 130.
Universality of budget, 115, 429.
Universities of Brussels, Ghent and Liège, 23, 60.

486

Universities, free, 23, 60.

University of Louvain, Catholic, 23, 60; 132, 454.

Urban areas and federations, 108-B, 412-417.

Urban council, 108-B, 413, 415-416.

Vacancy of Throne, 61, 221; 83, 288; 85, 291.

Validity of treaties, 68, 247.

Verification — of accounts, 116, 430-433.
　　　　　　— of constitutionality, 25, 68; 107, 383.
　　　　　　— of powers (Parl.), 34, 104.

Vice-Governor of Brabant, 3-B, 15.

Violation of substantial forms, 94, 363.

Volksunie (political party), 26, 85.

Vote — property assessment and capability system, 47, 130.
　　　— plural, 47, 130.
　　　— right to 47, 130.

Voting (in Parliament), 39, 116.
　　　　— article by article, 41, 119.
　　　　— on bill as a whole, 41, 119; 46, 126.
　　　　— by proxy or correspondence, 47, 130.
　　　　— push-button, 39, 116.
　　　　— roll-call, 39, 116; 41, 119.
　　　　— sitting and standing, 39, 116.

Walloon Economic Council, 107-D, 401.

War, time of 131-B, 452.

Warrant for arrest, 7, 24.

Warrant officers (status), 118, 435.

Waters, territorial, 1, 10.

Women in government, 86, 293-294.

Worship — freedom of 14, 35-36.
　　　　　— recognised forms of 14, 36; 117, 434.

Written questions (Parliament), 46, 129.

Yearly nature — of budget, 115, 429.
　　　　　　　— of taxes, 111, 425.

TABLE OF CONTENTS

ANNEXURE — Table showing the evolution of the wording during the framing of Article 59-B.